3rd Edition

# Ventures

## Basic

## TEACHER'S EDITION

**Gretchen Bitterlin** ▪ **Dennis Johnson** ▪ **Donna Price** ▪ **Sylvia Ramirez**

**K. Lynn Savage (Series Editor)**

**CAMBRIDGE**
UNIVERSITY PRESS

Shaftesbury Road, Cambridge CB2 8EA, United Kingdom

One Liberty Plaza, 20th Floor, New York, NY 10006, USA

477 Williamstown Road, Port Melbourne, VIC 3207, Australia

314–321, 3rd Floor, Plot 3, Splendor Forum, Jasola District Centre, New Delhi – 110025, India

103 Penang Road, #05–06/07, Visioncrest Commercial, Singapore 238467

Cambridge University Press & Assessment is a department of the University of Cambridge.

We share the University's mission to contribute to society through the pursuit of education, learning and research at the highest international levels of excellence.

www.cambridge.org
Information on this title: www.cambridge.org/9781108573214

First published 2008
Second edition 2014

20  19  18  17  16  15  14  13  12  11  10  9  8  7

Printed in Mexico by Litográfica Ingramex, S.A. de C.V.

*A catalogue record for this publication is available from the British Library*

ISBN  978-1-108-44953-3  Student's Book
ISBN  978-1-108-44998-4  Workbook
ISBN  978-1-108-44966-3  Literacy Workbook
ISBN  978-1-108-44932-8  Online Workbook
ISBN  978-1-108-44919-9  Class Audio CDs
ISBN  978-1-108-45027-0  Presentation Plus

Additional resources for this publication at www.cambridge.org/ventures

Cambridge University Press & Assessment has no responsibility for the persistence or accuracy of URLs for external or third-party internet websites referred to in this publication, and does not guarantee that any content on such websites is, or will remain, accurate or appropriate. Information regarding prices, travel timetables, and other factual information given in this work is correct at the time of first printing but Cambridge University Press & Assessment does not guarantee the accuracy of such information thereafter.

# CONTENTS

# TO THE TEACHER

## What is *Ventures*?

*Ventures* is a six-level, four-skills, standards-based, integrated-skills series that empowers students to achieve their academic and career goals.

- Aligned to the new NRS descriptors while covering key English Language Proficiency Standards and WIOA requirements.
- A wealth of resources provide instructors with the tools for any teaching situation, making *Ventures* the most complete program.
- Promotes 21st century learning complemented by a suite of technology tools.

## How Does the Third Edition Meet Today's Adult Education Needs?

- The third edition is aligned to the NRS' interpretive, productive, and interactive outcomes at each level.
- To help students develop the skills they need to succeed in college and the workplace, *Ventures* 3rd Edition offers a dedicated College and Career Readiness Section (CCRS) with 10 worksheets at each level, from Level 1 to Transitions (pages 136–155).
- Audio tracks and grammar presentations linked to QR codes can be accessed using smartphones (see page x), promoting mobile learning.
- Problem-solving activities added to each unit cover critical thinking and soft skills key to workplace readiness.
- A QR code that connects learners to an animated grammar presentation has been added, providing an additional modality especially helpful for Basic level learners.

## What are the *Ventures* components?

### Student's Book

Each of the core **Student's Books** contains ten topic-focused units, with five review units. The main units feature six skill-focused lessons.

- **Self-contained lessons** are perfectly paced for one-hour classes. For classes longer than 1 hour, additional resources are available via the Workbook and Online Teacher's Resources.
- **Review units** recycle and reinforce the listening, vocabulary, and grammar skills developed in the two prior units and include a pronunciation activity.

### Teacher's Edition

The interleaved **Teacher's Edition** includes easy-to-follow lesson plans for every unit.

- Teaching tips address common problem areas for students and additional suggestions for expansion activities and building community.
- Additional practice material across all *Ventures* components is clearly organized in the *More Ventures* chart at the end of each lesson.
- Multiple opportunities for assessment such as unit, mid-term, and final tests are available in the Teacher's Edition. Customizable tests and test audio are available online (www.cambridge.org/ventures/resources/).

### Online Teacher's Resources
**www.cambridge.org/ventures/resources/**

*Ventures* Online Teacher's Resources offer hundreds of additional worksheets and classroom materials including:

- *A placement test* that helps accurately identify the appropriate level of *Ventures* for each student.
- *Collaborative Worksheets* for each lesson develop cooperative learning and community building within the classroom.
- *Writing Worksheets* that help literacy-level students recognize shapes and write letters and numbers, while alphabet and number cards promote partner and group work.
- *Picture dictionary cards and Worksheets* that reinforce vocabulary learned in Levels Basic, 1, and 2.
- *Self-assessments* give students an opportunity to reflect on their learning. They support learner persistence and help determine whether students are ready for the unit test.

### Workbook

The **Workbook** provides two pages of activities for each lesson in the Student's Book.

- If used in class, the Workbook can extend classroom instructional time by 30 minutes per lesson.
- The exercises are designed so learners can complete them in class or independently. Students can check their answers with the answer key in the back of the Workbook. Workbook exercises can be assigned in class, for homework, or as student support when a class is missed.
- Grammar charts at the back of the Workbook allow students to use the Workbook for self-study.

### Literacy Workbook

The Literacy Workbook develops reading and writing readiness skills by focusing on letter formation, the conventions of writing in English, and the connection between written and spoken language. For each lesson in the Basic Student's Book, the Literacy Workbook has two pages of activities focusing on key words and sentences.

- The left-hand page is for students who are pre-, non-, or semiliterate in their own languages. Capital letters are introduced before lower case letters, and letters are sequenced based on strokes to form them; for example, straight lines such as *t* before curved lines such as *s*. Letters are presented in the context of words practiced in the lesson of the Student's Book that the workbook lesson supports.

- The right-hand page is for students who are literate in their first languages, but unfamiliar with the Roman alphabet used in English. When appropriate, students who complete the left-hand page with confidence can move to the right-hand page.
- Students who begin with the right-hand page, but require remediation, can move to the left-hand page.

## Online Workbooks

The self-grading **Online Workbooks** offer programs the flexibility of introducing blended learning.

- In addition to the same high-quality practice opportunities in the print workbooks, the online workbooks provide students instant feedback.
- Teachers and programs can track student progress and time on task.

### Presentation Plus
**www.esource.cambridge.org**

Presentation Plus allows teachers to project the contents of the Student's Book in front of the class for a livelier, interactive classroom. It is a complete solution for teachers because it includes the Class audio, answer keys, and the *Ventures* Arcade. Contact your Cambridge ESL Specialist (www.cambridge.org/cambridgeenglish/contact) to find out how to access it.

### Ventures Arcade
**www.cambridge.org/venturesarcade/**

The Arcade is a free website where students can find additional practice for the listening, vocabulary, grammar, and reading found in the Student's Books. There is also a Citizenship section that includes questions on civics, history, government, and the N-400 application.

## Unit organization

*LESSON A Listening* focuses students on the unit topic. The initial exercise, **Before you listen**, creates student interest with visuals that help the teacher assess what learners already know and serves as a prompt for the unit's key vocabulary. Next is **Listen**, which is based on conversations. Students relate vocabulary to meaning and relate the spoken and written forms of new theme-related vocabulary. **After you listen** concludes the lesson by practicing language related to the theme in a communicative activity, either orally with a partner or individually in a writing activity.

*LESSON B* focuses on vocabulary in the Basic Student's Book. It introduces vocabulary through illustrations and listening, followed by practice exercises that check understanding, relate spoken to written form, and provide conversation practice. The lesson ends with an interaction activity.

*LESSON C* focuses on grammar. The lessons move from a **Grammar focus** that presents the grammar point in chart form; to **Practice** exercises that check comprehension of the grammar point and provide guided practice; and, finally, to **Communicate** exercises that guide learners as they generate original answers and conversations. These lessons often include a *Culture note*, which provides information directly related to the conversation practice (such as the use of titles with last names) or a *Useful language* note, which introduces useful expressions.

*LESSON D Reading* develops reading skills and expands vocabulary. The lesson opens with a **Before you read** exercise, designed to activate prior knowledge and encourage learners to make predictions. The **Read** section includes audio, which provides additional practice in connecting sound with print, a skill especially important for Basic level learners. The reading section of the lesson concludes with **After you read** exercises that check comprehension. In Levels Basic, 1, and 2, the vocabulary expansion portion of the lesson is a **Picture dictionary**. It includes a *word bank*, pictures to identify, and a conversation for practicing the new words. The words expand vocabulary related to the unit topic. In Books 3 and 4, the vocabulary expansion portion of the lesson uses new vocabulary from the reading to build skills such as recognizing word families, selecting definitions based on the context of the reading, and using clues in the reading to guess meaning.

*LESSON E Writing* focuses on basic writing skills. In preparation for the writing, students fill in missing letters in words or missing words in sentences. Next, they fill in missing words in a paragraph, which serves as a model for them to write their information or ideas. The lesson ends with students sharing their writing with a partner.

*LESSON F Another view* brings the unit together with opportunities to review lesson content. **Life-skills reading** develops the scanning and skimming skills used with documents such as forms, charts, schedules, announcements, and ads. Multiple-choice questions (modeled on CASAS[1] and BEST[2]) develop test-taking skills. **Solve the problem** focuses on critical thinking, soft-skills, and workplace development. **Fun with vocabulary** provides interactive activities that review and expand the vocabulary of the unit.

---

[1] The Comprehensive Adult Student Assessment System. For more information, see www.casas.org.
[2] The Basic English Skills Test. For more information, see www.cal.org/BEST.

# SCOPE AND SEQUENCE

| UNIT TITLE TOPIC | FUNCTIONS | LISTENING AND SPEAKING | VOCABULARY | GRAMMAR FOCUS |
|---|---|---|---|---|
| **Welcome**<br>pages 2–5 | ■ Identifying the letters of the alphabet<br>■ Spelling names<br>■ Identifying classroom directions<br>■ Identifying numbers | ■ Saying classroom directions<br>■ Saying the alphabet<br>■ Saying numbers | ■ Classroom directions<br>■ The alphabet with capital and lowercase letters<br>■ Numbers | |
| **Unit 1**<br>**Personal information**<br>pages 6–17<br><br>Topic:<br>**Describing people** | ■ Identifying names<br>■ Identifying area codes and phone numbers<br>■ Identifying countries of origin<br>■ Exchanging personal information | ■ Asking and answering questions about personal information | ■ Personal information<br>■ Countries<br>■ Months of the year | ■ Possessive adjectives (*my, your, his, her*) |
| **Unit 2**<br>**At school**<br>pages 18–29<br><br>Topic:<br>**The classroom** | ■ Identifying classroom objects<br>■ Describing location<br>■ Finding out location | ■ Asking what someone needs<br>■ Asking about and giving the location of things | ■ Classroom furniture<br>■ Classroom objects<br>■ Days of the week | ■ Prepositions of location (*in, on, under*) |
| Review: Units 1 and 2<br>pages 30–31 | | ■ Understanding conversations | | |
| **Unit 3**<br>**Friends and family**<br>pages 32–43<br><br>Topic:<br>**Family** | ■ Identifying family relationships<br>■ Describing a family picture | ■ Asking and answering questions about family relationships | ■ Family relationships<br>■ Family members<br>■ People | ■ Yes / No questions with *have* |
| **Unit 4**<br>**Health**<br>pages 44–55<br><br>Topic:<br>**Health problems** | ■ Describing health problems | ■ Asking and answering questions about health problems | ■ The doctor's office<br>■ Body parts<br>■ Health problems | ■ Singular and plural nouns |
| Review: Units 3 and 4<br>pages 56–57 | | ■ Understanding conversations | | |
| **Unit 5**<br>**Around town**<br>pages 58–69<br><br>Topic:<br>**Places and locations** | ■ Identifying buildings and places<br>■ Describing location | ■ Asking and answering questions about where someone is<br>■ Asking and answering questions about the location of buildings and places<br>■ Describing your neighborhood | ■ Buildings and places<br>■ Transportation | ■ Prepositions of location (*on, next to, across from, between*)<br>■ *Where* questions |

| READING | WRITING | LIFE SKILLS | PRONUNCIATION |
|---|---|---|---|
| ▪ Reading classroom directions<br>▪ Reading the alphabet<br>▪ Reading numbers | ▪ Writing the alphabet<br>▪ Writing numbers | ▪ Understanding classroom directions | ▪ Pronouncing the alphabet<br>▪ Pronouncing numbers |
| ▪ Reading a paragraph about a new student | ▪ Completing sentences giving personal information<br>▪ Completing an ID card | ▪ Reading an ID card | ▪ Pronouncing key vocabulary<br>▪ Pronouncing area codes and phone numbers |
| ▪ Reading a note about school supplies<br>▪ Reading a memo about class information | ▪ Completing sentences about class information | ▪ Reading a class schedule | ▪ Pronouncing key vocabulary |
|  |  |  | ▪ Pronouncing *a* as in *name* and *o* as in *phone* |
| ▪ Reading a paragraph about a family | ▪ Completing sentences about a family<br>▪ Completing sentences about your family | ▪ Reading a housing application | ▪ Pronouncing key vocabulary |
| ▪ Reading a paragraph about a visit to the doctor's office | ▪ Completing a sign-in sheet at the doctor's office | ▪ Reading a label on a box of medicine | ▪ Pronouncing key vocabulary |
|  |  |  | ▪ Pronouncing *e* as in *read, i* as in *five*, and *u* as in *June* |
| ▪ Reading a notice about a library opening<br>▪ Reading a description of someone's street | ▪ Completing sentences describing your street | ▪ Reading a map | ▪ Pronouncing key vocabulary |

| UNIT TITLE TOPIC | FUNCTIONS | LISTENING AND SPEAKING | VOCABULARY | GRAMMAR FOCUS |
|---|---|---|---|---|
| **Unit 6** **Time** pages 70–81 Topic: **Daily activities and time** | ▪ Asking the time ▪ Asking for and giving information about the days and times of events | ▪ Asking and answering questions about the time ▪ Asking and answering questions about events | ▪ Clock time ▪ Activities and events ▪ Times of the day | ▪ *Yes / No* questions with *be* |
| Review: Units 5 and 6 pages 82–83 | | ▪ Understanding conversations | | |
| **Unit 7** **Shopping** pages 84–95 Topic: **Clothes and prices** | ▪ Identifying clothing items ▪ Reading prices ▪ Identifying colors | ▪ Asking and answering questions about prices ▪ Identifying the colors of clothing | ▪ Clothing ▪ Prices ▪ Colors | ▪ *How much is? / How much are?* |
| **Unit 8** **Work** pages 96–107 Topic: **Jobs and skills** | ▪ Identifying jobs ▪ Identifying job duties | ▪ Asking and answering questions about jobs ▪ Asking and answering questions about job duties | ▪ Names of jobs ▪ Job duties | ▪ *Yes / No* questions with simple present ▪ Short answers with *does* and *doesn't* |
| Review: Units 7 and 8 pages 108–109 | | ▪ Understanding conversations | | |
| **Unit 9** **Daily living** pages 110–121 Topic: **Home responsibilities** | ▪ Identifying family chores | ▪ Asking and answering questions about family chores ▪ Asking and answering questions about people's activities | ▪ Chores ▪ Rooms of a house | ▪ *What* questions with the present continuous |
| **Unit 10** **Free time** pages 122–133 Topic: **Free time** | ▪ Identifying free-time activities ▪ Describing what people like to do | ▪ Asking and answering questions about free-time activities | ▪ Free-time activities | ▪ *like to* + verb ▪ *What* questions with *like to* + verb |
| Review: Units 9 and 10 pages 134–135 | | ▪ Understanding conversations | | |

| READING | WRITING | LIFE SKILLS | PRONUNCIATION |
|---|---|---|---|
| ■ Reading a paragraph about a person's schedule <br>■ Reading someone's daily schedule | ■ Completing a schedule <br>■ Completing sentences about a schedule | ■ Reading an invitation | ■ Pronouncing key vocabulary <br>■ Pronouncing times |
| | | | ■ Pronouncing *a* as in *at* and *o* as in *on* |
| ■ Reading an email about a shopping trip | ■ Completing a shopping list | ■ Reading a store receipt | ■ Pronouncing key vocabulary <br>■ Pronouncing prices |
| ■ Reading an article about the employee of the month <br>■ Reading a letter about people's jobs | ■ Completing sentences about people's jobs | ■ Reading help-wanted ads | ■ Pronouncing key vocabulary |
| | | | ■ Pronouncing *e* as in *red*, *i* as in *six*, and *u* as in *bus* |
| ■ Reading an email about problems with family chores <br>■ Reading a chart of family chores | ■ Completing a chart about family chores <br>■ Completing sentences about family chores | ■ Reading a work order | ■ Pronouncing key vocabulary |
| ■ Reading an email to a friend | ■ Completing sentences about free-time activities | ■ Reading a course description | ■ Pronouncing key vocabulary |
| | | | ■ Reviewing pronunciation of *a*, *e*, *i*, *o*, and *u* in key vocabulary |

# CORRELATIONS

| UNIT | CASAS Competencies | Florida Adult ESOL Low Beginning | LAUSD ESL Beginning Low Competencies |
|---|---|---|---|
| **Welcome Unit** Pages 2–5 | | | |
| **Unit 1 Personal information** Pages 6–17 | 0.1.2, 0.1.4, 0.1.5, 0.2.1, 2.3.2, 4.8.1, 6.0.1, 7.4.1, 7.4.2, 7.4.3, 7.5.1 | 1.01.01, 1.01.02, 1.01.03, 1.01.04, 1.01.05, 1.01.06, 1.01.10, 1.03.12, 1.04.01 | I. 1a, 1b, 1c, 2, 3, 4 II. 5m III. 8, 9 |
| **Unit 2 At school** Pages 18–29 | 0.1.2, 0.1.5, 1.4.1, 2.3.2, 4.5.1, 4.8.1, 7.4.1, 7.4.2, 7.4.3, 7.5.1 | 1.01.02, 1.01.04, 1.01.05, 1.03.10, 1.03.12, 1.03.16, 1.04.09 | I. 3 II. 6b III. 8, 9, 11 |
| **Unit 3 Friends and family** Pages 32–43 | 0.1.2, 0.1.4, 0.1.5, 0.2.1, 4.8.1, 7.4.1, 7.4.2, 7.4.3, 7.5.1, 8.3.1 | 1.01.03, 1.02.07, 1.03.12, 1.04.04, 1.05.01 | I. 1d, 3 III. 9 |
| **Unit 4 Health** Pages 44–55 | 0.1.2, 0.1.4, 0.1.5, 0.2.1, 3.1.1, 3.1.3, 3.3.1, 3.3.2, 3.4.1, 4.8.1, 7.4.1, 7.4.2, 7.4.3, 7.5.1, 8.3.2 | 1.01.04, 1.02.07, 1.03.12, 1.03.16, 1.05.01, 1.05.02, 1.05.03, 1.05.04, 1.07.03 | I. 3 II. 7 III. 9 |
| **Unit 5 Around town** Pages 58–69 | 0.1.2, 0.1.4, 0.1.5, 0.2.1, 1.1.3, 2.2.1, 2.2.3, 2.2.5, 2.5.4, 4.8.1, 7.1.1, 7.4.1, 7.4.2, 7.4.3, 7.4.8, 7.5.1, 7.5.6 | 1.01.03, 1.02.01, 1.02.02, 1.02.10, 1.03.12, 1.04.09, 1.06.01, 1.06.02, 1.06.03 | I. 3 II. 5k III. 10 |

For more details and correlations to other state standards, go to: www.cambridge.org/ventures/correlations

**Interpretive**
- Identify key words and phrases relating to personal information.
- Recognize vocabulary relating to personal information and to countries and months of the year.
- Scan for key information in a reading about a new student.
- Scan for key information in an ID card.

**Productive**
- Use *possessive adjectives*.
- Ask and answer questions about personal information.
- Complete an ID card by giving personal information.

**Interactive**
- Participate in a short conversation and written exchanges about personal information.
- Project: Participate in a research project about contact information for your classmates.

**Interpretive**
- Identify key words and phrases relating to the classroom.
- Recognize vocabulary relating to classroom furniture, classroom objects, and days of the week.
- Scan for key information in a reading about class information and school supplies.
- Scan for key information in a class schedule.

**Productive**
- Use *prepositions of location*.
- Ask what someone needs and about the location of things.
- Complete sentences about class information.

**Interactive**
- Participate in a short conversation and written exchanges about the classroom.
- Project: Participate in a research project about shopping for school supplies.

**Interpretive**
- Identify key words and phrases relating to friends and family.
- Recognize vocabulary relating to family relationships, family members, and people.
- Scan for key information in a reading about family.
- Scan for key information in a housing application.

**Productive**
- Use *Yes/No* questions with *have*.
- Ask and answer questions about family relationships.
- Complete sentences about your family.

**Interactive**
- Participate in a short conversation and written exchanges about friends and family.
- Project: Participate in a research project about making a family chart.

**Interpretive**
- Identify key words and phrases relating to health.
- Recognize vocabulary relating to the doctor's office, health problems, and body parts.
- Scan for key information in a reading about a visit to the doctor's office.
- Scan for key information in a label on a box of medicine.

**Productive**
- Use *singular* and *plural nouns*.
- Ask and answer questions about health problems.
- Complete a sign-in sheet at the doctor's office.

**Interactive**
- Participate in a short conversation and written exchanges about health.
- Project: Participate in a research project about finding a health clinic near your home.

**Interpretive**
- Identify key words and phrases relating to places and locations.
- Recognize vocabulary relating to buildings, places, and transportation.
- Scan for key information in readings about a notice for a library opening and a description of someone's street.
- Scan for key information in a map.

**Productive**
- Use *prepositions of location* and *where* questions.
- Ask and answer questions about the location of buildings and places.
- Complete sentences describing your street.

**Interactive**
- Participate in a short conversation and written exchanges about places and locations.
- Project: Participate in a research project about creating a map of your community.

| UNIT | CASAS Competencies | Florida Adult ESOL Low Beginning | LAUSD ESL Beginning Low Competencies |
|---|---|---|---|
| Unit 6 Time Pages 70–81 | 0.1.2, 0.1.4, 0.1.5, 0.2.1, 2.3.1, 2.3.2, 4.5.3, 4.8.1, 6.0.1, 7.1.1, 7.1.4, 7.4.1, 7.4.2, 7.4.3, 7.5.1 | 1.01.03, 1.01.05, 1.02.02, 1.03.09, 1.03.12, 1.03.16, 1.04.01 | I. 3 II. 6a, 6c |
| Unit 7 Shopping Pages 84–95 | 0.1.2, 0.1.4, 0.1.5, 0.2.1, 1.1.6, 1.2.1, 1.2.2, 1.3.9, 1.6.3, 4.8.1, 6.0.1, 7.1.1, 7.4.1, 7.4.2, 7.4.3, 7.5.1, 8.1.4 | 1.01.03, 1.03.12, 1.03.16, 1.04.01, 1.04.02, 1.04.06 | I. 3 III. 13, 14 |
| Unit 8 Work Pages 96–107 | 0.1.2, 0.1.4, 0.1.5, 0.2.1, 1.1.6, 2.3.2, 4.1.3, 4.1.6, 4.1.8, 4.8.1, 4.8.2, 6.0.1, 7.1.1, 7.1.4, 7.4.1, 7.4.2, 7.5.1 | 1.01.03, 1.03.01, 1.03.02, 1.03.12, 1.03.14 | I. 3 III. 8, 13 |
| Unit 9 Daily living Pages 110–121 | 0.1.2, 0.1.5, 0.2.1, 0.2.4, 1.4.1, 1.7.4, 4.1.8, 4.7.3, 4.7.4, 4.8.1, 7.1.1, 7.4.1, 7.4.2, 7.4.3, 7.5.6, 8.1.4, 8.2.1, 8.2.2, 8.2.3, 8.2.4, 8.2.5 | 1.01.03, 1.01.04, 1.03.12 | I. 3 II. 7 III. 8 |
| Unit 10 Free time Pages 122–133 | 0.1.1, 0.1.2, 0.1.4, 0.1.5, 0.2.1, 0.2.4, 2.3.1, 2.3.2, 4.8.1, 7.1.1, 7.4.1, 7.4.2, 7.4.3, 7.5.1, 7.5.6 | 1.01.02, 1.01.03, 1.01.04, 1.03.12 | I. 3 II. 5 |

For more details and correlations to other state standards, go to: www.cambridge.org/ventures/correlations

## NRS Educational Functioning Level Descriptors

**Interpretive**
- Identify key words and phrases relating to daily activities and time.
- Recognize vocabulary relating to clock time, activities, and events and times of the day.
- Scan for key information in someone's schedule.
- Scan for key information in an invitation.

**Productive**
- Use *Yes/No* questions with *be*.
- Ask and answer questions about the time and about events.
- Complete a schedule.

**Interactive**
- Participate in a short conversation and written exchanges about daily activities and time.
- Project: Participate in a research project using the Internet to find library hours.

**Interpretive**
- Identify key words and phrases relating to clothes and prices.
- Recognize vocabulary relating to clothing, prices, and colors.
- Scan for key information in an e-mail about a shopping trip.
- Scan for key information in a store receipt.

**Productive**
- Use *how much is* and *how much are* questions.
- Ask and answer questions about prices and identify colors of clothing.
- Complete a shopping list.

**Interactive**
- Participate in a short conversation and written exchanges about clothes and prices.
- Project: Participate in a research project using the Internet to find a shopping center near your home.

**Interpretive**
- Identify key words and phrases relating to jobs and skills.
- Recognize vocabulary relating to names of jobs and job duties.
- Scan for key information in a reading about people's jobs and the employee of the month.
- Scan for key information in help-wanted ads.

**Productive**
- Use *Yes/No* questions with *simple present* and short answers with *does/doesn't*.
- Ask and answer questions about jobs and job duties.
- Complete sentences about people's jobs.

**Interactive**
- Participate in a short conversation and written exchanges about jobs and skills.
- Project: Participate in a research project about finding a job.

**Interpretive**
- Identify key words and phrases relating to home responsibilities.
- Recognize vocabulary relating to chores and rooms of a house.
- Scan for key information in an e-mail and a chart about family chores.
- Scan for key information in a work order

**Productive**
- Use *what* questions with the *present continuous*.
- Ask and answer questions about family chores and people's activities.
- Complete a chart about family chores.

**Interactive**
- Participate in a short conversation and written exchanges about home responsibilities.
- Project: Participate in a research project about creating and giving a class survey.

**Interpretive**
- Identify key words and phrases relating to free-time activities.
- Recognize vocabulary relating to free-time activities.
- Scan for key information in an e-mail to a friend.
- Scan for key information in a course description.

**Productive**
- Use *like to + verb* and *what* questions with *like to + verb*.
- Ask and answer questions about free-time activities.
- Complete sentences about free-time activities.

**Interactive**
- Participate in a short conversation and written exchanges about free-time activities.
- Project: Participate in a research project about a movie theater near your home.

# FEATURES OF THE STUDENT'S BOOK

## The Most Complete Course for Student Success

■ Helps students develop the skills needed to be college and career ready and function successfully in their community

■ Covers key NRS and WIOA requirements

■ Aligned with the English Language Proficiency (ELP) Standards

### *The Big Picture*

· Introduces the unit topic and creates an opportunity for classroom discussion.
· Activates students' prior knowledge and previews the unit vocabulary.

### *Unit Goals*

Introduces the competencies students will learn.

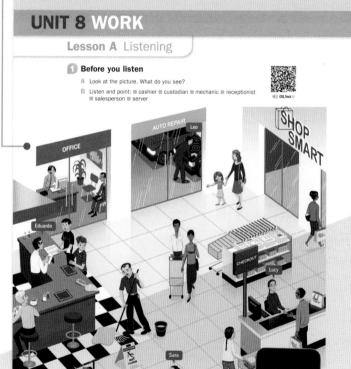

### *How to use a QR code*

· Open the camera on your smartphone.
· Point it at the QR code.
· The camera will automatically scan the code. If not, press the button to take a picture.
\* Not all cameras automatically scan QR codes. You may need to download a QR code reader. Search "QR free" and download an app.

### *3 Easy Ways to Access Audio*

· Scan QR codes
· Download from *Ventures* Online Resources: www.cambridge.org/ventures/audio/
· Play from Class audio CDs

## Vocabulary Practice

Explicit vocabulary practice with accompanying audio equips students with the tools necessary to succeed outside the classroom.

## Additional Grammar Activities

Ensures students have the chance to practice more grammar to meet the rigor of CCRS.

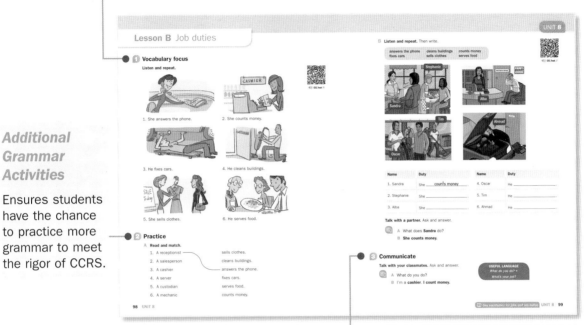

## Natural Progression

Moves from controlled to communicative activities for students to ask and answer questions about familiar text, topics, and experiences.

## Real-life Practice

Engages students and provides meaningful application of the grammar.

## Grammar Chart

· Presents and practices the grammar point.
· Extra grammar charts online can be used for reference and give additional support.

## Grammar Presentation

Animated grammar presentations to watch on mobile devices using QR codes allow for self-directed learning and develop digital literacy.

## Reading

- Uses a 3-step reading approach to highlight the skills and strategies students need to succeed.
- Combines reading with writing and listening practice for an integrated approach to ensure better comprehension.
- Brings text complexity into the classroom to help students read independently and proficiently.

## Picture dictionary

Expands unit vocabulary and practices pronunciation for deeper understanding of the topic.

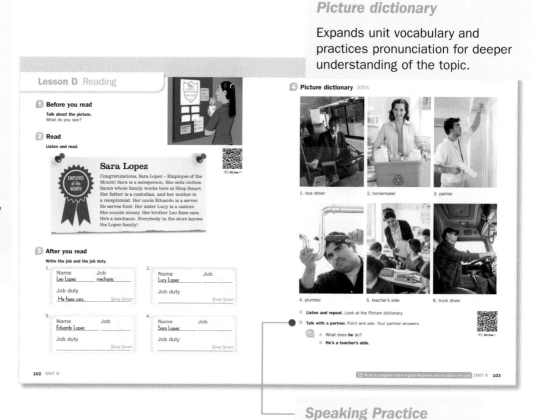

## Speaking Practice

Helps students internalize the vocabulary and relate it to their lives.

## Writing

- Helps students develop a robust process-writing approach.
- Supports students to meet the challenges of work and the classroom through academic and purposeful writing practice.

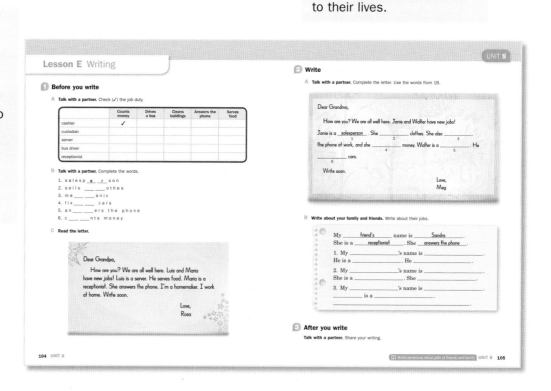

## Document Literacy

Builds real-life skills through explicit practice using authentic document types.

## Fun with Vocabulary

Provides interactive activities that review and expand the vocabulary of the unit.

## Test-taking Skills

Prepares students for standarized tests like the BEST by familiarizing them with bubble answer format.

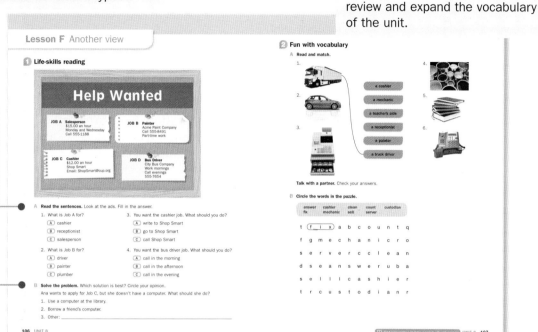

## Problem-solving Activity

Covers critical thinking and soft skills – crucial for workplace readiness – and helps students meet WIOA requirements.

## Review Pages

Provides review and confirms retention of vocabulary and grammar after every two units.

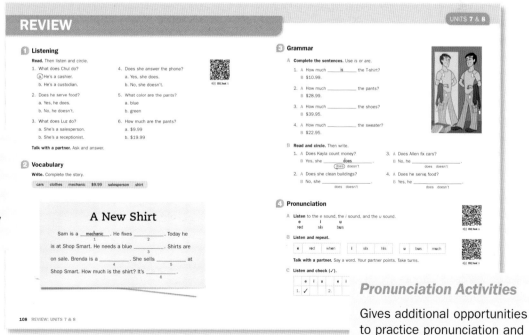

## Pronunciation Activities

Gives additional opportunities to practice pronunciation and promotes spoken fluency.

# FEATURES OF THE TEACHER'S EDITION

## Introduction

The *Ventures* Teacher's Edition includes step-by-step teaching notes for each lesson. The teaching notes divide the lesson into six stages. Each lesson begins with a warm-up and review followed by a presentation stage. The practice, comprehension, application, and evaluation stages do not follow a strict sequence in the Teacher's Edition. They vary depending on the content of the lesson being presented.

## Stages of a lesson

**Warm-up and review** Each lesson begins with a review of previous material and connects that material to the current lesson. Quick review activities prompt students' memories. Warm-up activities at the beginning of class introduce the new lesson. These activities may take many forms, but they are quick, focused, and connected to the new material to be introduced. A warm-up also helps teachers ascertain what students already know about the topic and what they are able to say.

**Presentation** During this stage of the lesson, the teacher presents new information, but it should not be a one-way delivery. Rather, it is a dynamic process of student input and interaction – a give-and-take between the teacher and students as well as among students. The teacher may give examples rather than rules, model rather than tell, and relate the material to students' experiences.

**Practice** It is important that students have enough time to practice. A comfortable classroom environment needs to be created so that students are not afraid to take risks. The practice needs to be varied and interesting. There should be a progression from guided to independent practice. In the *Ventures* grammar lessons, for example, practice begins with mechanical aspects such as form, moves to a focus on meaning, and ends with communicative interactions.

**Comprehension check** Asking, "Do you understand?" is not enough to ascertain whether students are following the lesson. The teacher must ask concrete questions and have students demonstrate that they understand. In this stage, students are asked to repeat information in their own words. Students are also invited to come to the board or to interact with other students in some way.

**Application** A teacher must provide opportunities for students to practice newly-acquired language in realistic situations. These situations could be in class or outside of class. The important point is that students use what they have learned in new ways. In the grammar lessons, for example, the Communicate section asks students to role-play, interview, share information, or ask questions.

**Evaluation** An ongoing part of the lesson is to determine whether students are meeting the lesson objectives. This can be done formally at the end of a unit by having students complete the Self-assessment and then giving the unit test, but it can also be done informally toward the end of the lesson. Each lesson in the Teacher's Edition ends with a review and verification of understanding of the lesson objectives. Any in-class assignment or task can serve as an evaluation tool as long as it assesses the objectives. Having students complete Workbook pages can also serve as an informal evaluation to gauge where students may be having difficulty.

The following chart presents the most common order of lesson stages and suggests how long each stage could take within a one-hour class period.

| Stages of the lesson | Approximate time range |
| --- | --- |
| Warm-up and review | 5–10 minutes |
| Presentation | 10–20 minutes |
| Practice | 15–20 minutes |
| Comprehension check | 5–10 minutes |
| Application | 15–20 minutes |
| Evaluation | 10–15 minutes |

## The Teacher's Edition includes:

- Interleaved Student's Book pages with answers
- Lesson objectives and step-by-step teaching instructions
- Expansion activities, extra teaching tips, and culture notes
- Activities to encourage learner persistence and community building
- Tests and games
- Ideas for multilevel classroom management
- Class audio listening scripts

---

## LESSON A Listening

### PRESENTATION

- Before class. Bring to class full-page clip-art images to illustrate each of the key vocabulary terms. Save the images to use later in other parts of the unit.
- Direct Ss' attention to Exercise 2A and read the instructions aloud. As you say each word or phrase, hold up the appropriate picture and ask Ss to repeat after you.

### PRACTICE

- **CD1, Track 38** Play or read the audio (see audio script, page T-146). Ss listen and repeat the vocabulary as you hold up the clip-art images. Repeat the audio as needed.
- Listen carefully to Ss' pronunciation and make corrections as needed.

*Learner persistence* (individual work)
- **CD1, Track 38** Ss can listen to the audio for Exercise 2A at home for reinforcement and review. They can also listen to the audio for self-directed learning when class attendance is not possible.

#### Literacy Tip
Use the clip-art images you found to make smaller flash cards for your literacy Ss.

- Direct Ss' attention to Exercise 2B and read the instructions aloud.
- **CD1, Track 39** Model the task. Hold up the Student's Book and say: *Number one.* Play or read the audio for number 1 (see audio script, page T-146). Point to the two answer choices in number 1 and ask Ss: *What did you hear – a or b?* Elicit: *b.* Point to the letter *b* next to the second picture and tell Ss: *Circle the letter "b."*
- **CD1, Track 39** Play or read the complete audio. Ss listen and circle the correct answers. Repeat the audio as needed.
- **CD1, Track 39** Read aloud the second part of the instructions for Exercise 2B. Play or read the audio again so Ss can listen and check their answers.

*Learner persistence* (individual work)
- **CD1, Track 39** Ss can listen to the audio for Exercise 2B at home for reinforcement and review. They can also listen to the audio for self-directed learning when class attendance is not possible.

### COMPREHENSION CHECK

- Write the numbers 1–4 on the board. Ask a few Ss to come to the board and write the correct answers to Exercise 2B next to each number.

- **CD1, Track 39** Play or read the audio again. Pause the audio after each conversation. Point to the answer on the board and ask: *Is this correct?* Ask another S to make any necessary corrections.

#### Teaching Tip
Use the same spatial arrangement as the textbook when replicating exercises on the board. This makes the process of checking answers less demanding for Ss and allows them to concentrate on the language.

### APPLICATION

- Direct Ss' attention to Exercise 3 and read the instructions aloud.
- Model the task. Hold up the Student's Book and point to the pictures in Exercise 2B. Say to one S: *Point to a picture.* Say to the first S's partner: *Say the word.*
- Ss complete the exercise in pairs. Walk around and help as needed.

*Expansion activity* (student pairs)
- Have Ss practice the conversations from Exercise 2B in pairs. Ask Ss to turn to the audio script on page 146 in the Student's Book.
- Ask Ss to choose Role A or B and read aloud the conversations. Then have Ss switch roles and read the conversations again. Walk around and help as needed.

### EVALUATION

- Direct Ss' attention to the lesson focus on the board. Arrange the large clip-art images that you used in Exercise 2A on the board or on a table so Ss can see all of them. Say the key vocabulary in random order and call on individual Ss to select the corresponding image and hold it up for everyone to see. Have Ss replace the image each time so that every S can choose from all five.
- Check off the lesson focus as Ss demonstrate an understanding of what they have learned in the lesson.

| More Ventures, Unit 4, Lesson A | |
|---|---|
| Literacy Workbook, 15–30 min. | |
| Basic Workbook, 15–30 min. | |
| Writing Worksheets, 15–30 min. | www.cambridge.org/ventures/resources/ |
| Collaborative Worksheets, 30–45 min. | |
| Student Arcade, time varies | www.cambridge.org/venturesarcade/ |

T-45 Unit 4

---

UNIT GOALS
Identify health problems · Interpret a medicine label
Identify reasons for a visit to a doctor

### 2 Listen

**A** Listen and repeat.

  1. doctor    2. doctor's office    3. medicine    4. nurse    5. patient    ◀)) CD1, Track 38

**B** Listen and circle.

◀)) CD1, Track 39

1. a. / (b.)

2. (a.) / b.

3. (a.) / b.

4. (a.) / b.

**Listen again.** Check your answers.

### 3 After you listen

**Talk with a partner.** Point to a picture. Your partner says the word.

Listen for and identify a patient's request   UNIT 4   **45**

*FEATURES OF THE TEACHER'S EDITION* **xix**

# END-OF-UNIT ACTIVITIES

*Ventures* provides several resources to help wrap up a unit:

The **Self-assessments** are available via the Online Teacher's Resources (www.cambridge.org/ventures/resources/). They can be used in several ways:

■ To identify any needs for additional practice before the unit test.

■ For portfolio assessment. Print out copies for each student and keep completed Self-assessments in a folder.

■ For pre- and post-assessment. Print out two Self-assessments for each student. Have students complete one before beginning and another after finishing the unit.

The **Projects** are another useful tool and a fun way to wrap up a unit. They are available via the Online Teacher's Resources.

The **Unit Tests** are a third end-of-unit activity. They are available at the back of this book. Customizable tests and test audio are available via a secure download site. Contact your Cambridge ESL Specialist (www.cambridge.org/cambridgeenglish/contact) for more information.

## Class time guidelines

*Ventures* is designed to be flexible enough for use with one-, two-, and three-hour classes.

| Component | One-hour class | Two-hour class | Three-hour class |
|---|---|---|---|
| **Teacher's Edition** | Follow lesson plan in Teacher's Edition | | |
| **Workbook** | Assign as homework | | Use in class |
| **Student Arcade** | Assign for lab or homework | | |
| **Online Teacher's Resources** | | | Use Collaborative Worksheets in class |

(Top row) Dennis Johnson, K. Lynn Savage; (bottom row) Gretchen Bitterlin, Donna Price, and Sylvia G. Ramirez. Together, the *Ventures* author team has more than 200 years teaching ESL as well as other roles that support adult immigrants and refugees, from teacher's aide to dean.

**Gretchen Bitterlin** has taught Citizenship, ESL, and family literacy through the San Diego Community College District and served as coordinator of the non-credit Continuing Education ESL program. She was an item writer for CASAS tests and chaired the task force that developed the TESOL Adult Education Program Standards. She is recipient of The President's Distinguished Leadership Award from her district and co-author of *English for Adult Competency*. Gretchen holds an MA in TESOL from the University of Arizona.

**Dennis Johnson** had his first language-teaching experience as a Peace Corps volunteer in South Korea. Following that teaching experience, he became an in-country ESL trainer. After returning to the United States, he began teaching credit and non-credit ESL at City College of San Francisco. As ESL site coordinator, he has provided guidance to faculty in selecting textbooks. He is the author of *Get Up and Go* and co-author of *The Immigrant Experience*. Dennis is the demonstration teacher on the *Ventures Professional Development DVD*. Dennis holds an MA in music from Stanford University.

**Donna Price** began her ESL career teaching EFL in Madagascar. She is currently associate professor of ESL and vocational ESL / technology resource instructor for the Continuing Education Program, San Diego Community College District. She has served as an author and a trainer for CALPRO, the California Adult Literacy Professional Development Project, co-authoring training modules on contextualizing and integrating workforce skills into the ESL classroom. She is a recipient of the TESOL Newbury House Award for Excellence in Teaching, and she is author of *Skills for Success*. Donna holds an MA in linguistics from San Diego State University.

**Sylvia G. Ramirez** is a Professor Emeritus at MiraCosta College, a teacher educator, writer, consultant, and a recipient of the California Hayward award for excellence in education, honoring her teaching and professional activities. She is an online instructor for the TESOL Core Certificate. Her MA is in education / counseling from Point Loma University, and she has certificates in ESOL and in online teaching.

**K. Lynn Savage** first taught English in Japan. She began teaching ESL at City College of San Francisco in 1974, where she has taught all levels of non-credit ESL and has served as Vocational ESL Resource Teacher. She has trained teachers for adult education programs around the country as well as abroad. She chaired the committee that developed *ESL Model Standards for Adult Education Programs* (California, 1992) and is the author, co-author, and editor of many ESL materials including *Crossroads Café*, *Teacher Training through Video*, *Parenting for Academic Success*, *Building Life Skills*, *Picture Stories*, *May I Help You?*, and *English That Works*. Lynn holds an MA in TESOL from Teachers College, Columbia University.

# WELCOME

## 1 Meet your classmates

Look at the picture. What do you see?

Teaching objectives
● Provide practice with school vocabulary
● Provide practice with the alphabet

# WARM-UP

● Before class. Write today's lesson focus on the board.
*Welcome unit:*
*School vocabulary*
*The alphabet (Aa, Bb, Cc . . .)*

● Before class. Prepare a name card for each S. Fold pieces of card stock lengthwise so that they can "stand" like a tent on a desk or table. Use your class roster to write Ss' first and last names in capital letters on both sides of the cards so that the names are easily visible to anyone in the classroom.

### Teaching Tip

Collect the name cards at the end of class and use them again in later classes to help you and the Ss learn everyone's name.

● Begin class. Books closed. Say: *Welcome to English class!*

● Write your name on the board. Point to it. Say: *My name is _____.* Ask a S: *What's your name?* If the S doesn't answer, ask different Ss until someone can answer you.

● As Ss tell you their names, place the name cards you prepared earlier on Ss' desks or tables. Use any remaining cards to find out the names of Ss who haven't spoken yet.

● Go around the room and ask all the Ss to say their names. After each S speaks, say: *Nice to meet you, _____.*

### Teaching Tip

Don't expect every S to understand you or be able to respond at this point. Friendly facial expressions and a little extra help from you will reassure the true beginners in your class and allow them to follow along with class activities.

# PRESENTATION

● Books open. Set the scene. Hold up the Student's Book. Show Ss the picture on page 2. Ask: *What do you see?* Point to your eyes and then to the picture to illustrate the meaning of *see.* Elicit and write on the board any vocabulary that Ss know, such as: *classroom, cafeteria, computer lab, hallway, students, books,* etc.

● If Ss don't know any English words for what they see in the picture, say to the class: *I see a school. In the school are classrooms. Some classrooms have a number. How many classrooms do you see?* Repeat the process with *woman, books, hallway, computer lab, students, backpack,* and with other words for items in the picture.

● Point to each of the words on the board and say it aloud. After you say each word, indicate that Ss should repeat after you.

● Hold up the Student's Book. Point to the items in the picture that correspond to the words you and the Ss just said. For example, point to the students. Ask the class: *Are they students?* Nod your head and encourage Ss to say *yes.*

● Repeat the process with each of the words you wrote on the board.

## Expansion activity *(whole group)*

● If you have some of the items from the picture in your classroom, walk around and ask the class about the items. For example, pick up a book and ask: *Is this a book?* Nod your head and encourage Ss to say *yes.* Some Ss may be able to name the items.

● Point to the sign that says "101" in the picture. Ask the class: *Do you see the numbers?* Say the word *numbers* and indicate that Ss should repeat the word after you.

● Write the numbers *1–10* across the board. Say each number and indicate that Ss should repeat after you.

● If this exercise is easy for your class, have Ss say the numbers without your help, or continue with the numbers *11–20.*

### Literacy Tip

If you have literacy Ss in the class, encourage them to participate actively in this first page of the Welcome unit which is primarily communicative in nature.

# WELCOME UNIT

## PRESENTATION

- Direct Ss' attention to the lesson focus on the board (School vocabulary). Read the second part of the lesson focus aloud (the alphabet) and indicate that Ss should repeat after you. Point to the letters *Aa, Bb, Cc . . .* and say them aloud.

- Write the alphabet on the board using large capital letters. Ask Ss: *What is this?* Elicit: *the alphabet.*

- Circle one letter on the board. Tell the class: *This is a letter.* Write the word *letter* on the board. Say the word and ask Ss to repeat after you.

- Circle another letter. Ask Ss: *What is this?* Elicit: *a letter.* Gesture toward all the letters and say to the class: *These are the letters of the English alphabet.*

- To introduce the idea of capital and lowercase letters, write the following on the board: *A = a, B = b, C = c.* Tell the class: *There are two ways to write letters.* Point to and read aloud the pairs of letters.

- Direct Ss' attention to the chart in Exercise 2A. Point to the capital and lowercase letters on the board. Read the first pair aloud. Then point to *Aa* in the Student's Book chart and repeat the letters to help Ss see that each letter is written two ways.

### Teaching Tip

When you write on the board, be aware that some Ss may recognize only capital letters. You might use only capital letters at first, or else write two versions of a word, one in capitals and one in lowercase.

## PRACTICE

- ▶ *CD1, Track 2* Read the instructions for Exercise 2A aloud. Then play or read the audio (see audio script, page T-144). Ss listen and point to the letters. Repeat the audio as needed.

- ▶ *CD1, Track 2* Read aloud the second part of the instructions for Exercise 2A. Play or read the audio again. Ss listen and repeat the letters of the alphabet.

### *Learner persistence* (individual work)

- ▶ *CD1, Track 2* Ss can listen to the audio for Exercise 2A at home for reinforcement and review. They can also listen to the audio for self-directed learning when class attendance is not possible.

### Literacy Tip

Literacy Ss should be able to perform the "Listen and point" exercise in Exercises 2A and 4A. In the other exercises, while the rest of the class is writing, assign pages 2–5 in the *Literacy Workbook.*

## COMPREHENSION CHECK

- Direct Ss' attention to Exercise 2B and read the instructions aloud.

- ▶ *CD1, Track 3* Model the exercise. Hold up the Student's Book and point to number 1. Play or read aloud the first part of the audio (see audio script, page T-144). Point to the blank in number 1 and ask Ss: *What letter?* Elicit: *A.* Make sure Ss understand the task.

- ▶ *CD1, Track 3* Play or read the complete audio. Ss listen and write the first letter of each name. Repeat the audio as needed.

- Check answers with the class. Write the numbers *1–8* on the board. Call on individual Ss to write the names from Exercise 2B on the board. Point to each answer and ask Ss: *Is this correct?* Make corrections on the board.

### *Learner persistence* (individual work)

- ▶ *CD1, Track 3* Ss can listen to the audio for Exercise 2B at home for reinforcement and review. They can also listen to the audio for self-directed learning when class attendance is not possible.

## APPLICATION

- Direct Ss' attention to the first part of Exercise 2C and read the instructions aloud. Have Ss write their first names.

- Read aloud the instructions for the second part of Exercise 2C. Point to the picture and read aloud the example sentence. Make sure Ss understand the task.

- Ss complete the exercise in groups of four. Walk around and help as needed.

## EVALUATION

- Turn Ss' attention to the first line of the lesson focus on the board. Elicit some of the school vocabulary from page 2. Write the words on the board and call on individual Ss to say the words and point to them in the big picture on page 2.

- Focus Ss' attention on the second part of the lesson focus (the alphabet). Ask Ss to say the alphabet aloud as you point to the letters on the board.

- Erase the letters from the board. Invite a S to come to the board. Hand the S a marker. Say: *Write the letter "C."* Continue with different Ss writing the remaining letters *A–Z.*

- Check off the lesson focus as Ss demonstrate an understanding of what they have learned in the lesson.

## 2 The alphabet

**A** **Listen and point.** Look at the alphabet.

CD1, Track 02

| Aa | Bb | Cc | Dd | Ee | Ff | Gg | Hh | Ii |
|----|----|----|----|----|----|----|----|----|
| Jj | Kk | Ll | Mm | Nn | Oo | Pp | Qq | Rr |
| Ss | Tt | Uu | Vv | Ww | Xx | Yy | Zz | |

Listen again and repeat.

**B** **Listen and write.**

1. _A_ nita
2. _D_ aniel
3. _P_ eizhi
4. _Y_ uri
5. _F_ ranco
6. _L_ ee
7. _H_ akim
8. _K_ arla

CD1, Track 03

**C** **Write your name.**

_Answers will vary._

**Talk with 3 classmates.** Say your name. Spell your name.

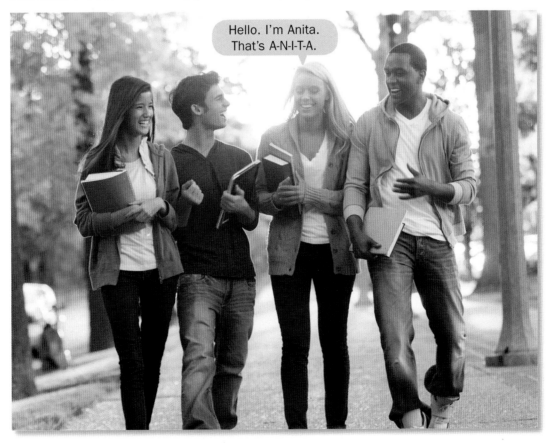

Hello. I'm Anita. That's A-N-I-T-A.

## 3 Classroom directions

**A Listen and point.** Look at the pictures.

CD1, Track 04

1. Look.

2. Listen.

3. Point.

4. Repeat.

5. Talk.

6. Write.

7. Read.

8. Circle.

9. Match.

**Listen again and repeat.**

**B Talk with a partner.** Say a word. Your partner points to the picture.

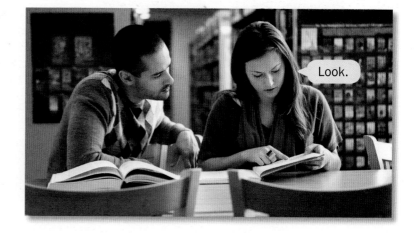

Look.

**Teaching objectives**
- Provide practice with classroom directions
- Provide practice with the numbers *1–20*

## WARM-UP AND REVIEW

- Before class. Write today's lesson focus on the board.
  *Welcome unit:*
  *Classroom directions*
- Begin class. Books open. Review vocabulary words from the last lesson. Gesture around you. Ask: *What is this room?* (A classroom.) Point to other classroom objects and ask: *What's this?* (book, backpack, student, etc.)

## PRESENTATION

- Direct Ss' attention to the lesson focus on the board. Read the lesson focus aloud.
- Direct Ss' attention to the pictures in Exercise 3A. Tell Ss: *These are classroom directions.* Point to the corresponding picture as you read each word aloud. Indicate that Ss should repeat each word after you.
- As you go through the classroom directions, use gestures and items in your classroom to further illustrate meaning.

## PRACTICE

- Read aloud the instructions for Exercise 3A. As you say *Listen and point,* cup your hand behind your ear and then point to the pictures in the book.
- ▶ **CD1, Track 4** Model the exercise. Play or read aloud the first word on the audio (see audio script, page T-144). Hold up the Student's Book and point to the first picture. Make sure Ss understand the task.
- ▶ **CD1, Track 4** Play or read the complete audio. Ss listen and point to the pictures in the Student's Book. Repeat the audio as needed.
- Read aloud the second part of the instructions for Exercise 3A.
- ▶ **CD1, Track 4** Model the exercise. Play or read aloud the first word on the audio. Then repeat the word. Make sure Ss understand the task.
- ▶ **CD1, Track 4** Play or read the complete audio. Ss listen and repeat the words.

### Learner persistence *(individual work)*
- ▶ **CD1, Track 4** Ss can listen to the audio for Exercise 3A at home for reinforcement and review. They can also listen to the audio for self-directed learning when class attendance is not possible.

- Direct Ss' attention to Exercise 3B and read the instructions aloud.
- Model the exercise. Point to the pictures in Exercise 3A. Say to a S: *Please say a word.* Indicate the complete exercise to show that the S can choose any word.
- After the first S says a word from the Student's Book page, say to his or her partner: *Point to the picture.* If the S doesn't understand you, point to the appropriate picture yourself to demonstrate.
- Model the formation of pairs with two Ss who are sitting near each other. Say to one S, for example: *Marlene, Yoko is your partner.* Say to the other S: *Yoko, Marlene is your partner.* Use the Ss' names to help everyone in the class find a partner.
- Ss practice saying the words from the Student's Book page and pointing to the corresponding pictures in pairs. Walk around and help with pronunciation as needed.
- When Ss are finished, have them switch roles so that both Ss have a chance to say the words.

### Expansion activity *(whole group)*
- Before class. Write the words from Exercise 3A on cards large enough to be seen easily.
- Arrange the cards in random order along the chalk tray or tape them to the board or wall.
- Review the vocabulary by eliciting the words from Ss. For example, start writing on the board. Point to the word cards and ask the class: *What word?* Elicit or say: *Write.* Point to or hold up the appropriate word card.
- Continue with the remaining words. For example, circle one of the words in the sentence you wrote on the board. Ask: *What word?* Elicit: *Circle.* Use gestures to elicit the words *look, listen, write,* and *read;* say the same word twice using two different voices to elicit *Repeat.* Write a simple matching exercise on the board and draw a line between two items to elicit *Match.*
- Finally, gather the cards and show the class one of them. Say the word and call on a S to perform the action. For the words *Write, Match,* and *Circle,* invite the S to the board to perform the action.

### Community building *(whole group)*
- To review Ss' names, write on the board: *My name is _____.* Point to each word as you read it aloud. Then point to and say each word again and have Ss repeat after you.
- Say to the class: *My name is _____.* Have Ss say their names using the model sentence.

# PRESENTATION

- Point to the second part of the lesson focus on the board. Say the word *numbers*.
- Direct Ss' attention to the chart in Exercise 4A. Tell the class: *These are numbers.*

# PRACTICE

- Read the instructions in Exercise 4A aloud.
- ▶ **CD1, Track 5** Play or read the audio (see audio script, page T-144). Ss listen and point to the numbers in their books. Repeat the audio as needed.
- Read aloud the second part of the instructions in Exercise 4A.
- ▶ **CD1, Track 5** Play or read the audio again. Ss listen and repeat the numbers.

### Learner persistence *(individual work)*
▶ **CD1, Track 5** Ss can listen to the audio for Exercise 4A at home for reinforcement and review. They can also listen to the audio for self-directed learning when class attendance is not possible.

> **Teaching Tip**
>
> Some Ss may have trouble pronouncing the "teen" numbers. You can help by modeling the numbers with two distinct syllables with equal stress and a clearly pronounced /t/ sound. For example: in *seventeen*, stress the first and third syllables.

# COMPREHENSION CHECK

- Direct Ss' attention to Exercise 4B and read the instructions aloud.
- ▶ **CD1, Track 6** Model the exercise. Play or read aloud the first number on the audio (see audio script, page T-144). Hold up the Student's Book and point to where 6 has been written for number 1. Make sure Ss understand the task.
- ▶ **CD1, Track 6** Play or read the complete audio. Ss listen and write the numbers they hear. Repeat the audio as needed.
- Read aloud the second part of the instructions in Exercise 4B. Ss check their answers in pairs.

- Check answers with the class. Write the numbers 1–8 on the board. Call on individual Ss to write their answers on the board. Point to each answer and ask Ss: *Is this correct?* Make any necessary corrections on the board.

### Learner persistence *(individual work)*
▶ **CD1, Track 6** Ss can listen to the audio for Exercise 4B at home for reinforcement and review. They can also listen to the audio for self-directed learning when class attendance is not possible.

### Expansion activity *(whole group)*
- You can expand on your presentation of numbers by including numbers over 20, a list of which can be found on page T-141 of the Student's Book.

### Expansion activity *(whole group)*
- Make sequentially numbered word cards and give one to each S, trying to keep the numbers more or less in order.
- Ask Ss to "count off," starting with *one*. If you have more than 20 Ss in the class, be prepared to assist Ss who receive the higher numbers. Alternatively, you can divide the class into two or more groups.

  **Option 1** Make the activity easier by writing the numeral on one side of the card and the corresponding word on the other side.

  **Option 2** Make the activity more challenging by distributing the numbers randomly around the room.
- Collect the numbers and keep them for Ss to use as flashcards.

# EVALUATION

- Direct Ss' attention to the lesson focus on the board.
- Write some of the classroom directions from Exercise 3A on the board. Call on individual Ss to say the words and perform the actions.
- Write the numbers 1–20 on the board one at a time and call on Ss to say the numbers.
- Erase the numbers from the board. Invite a S to come to the board. Say, for example: *Write the number "4."* Continue with different Ss writing the remaining numbers 1–20.
- Check off each part of the lesson focus as Ss demonstrate an understanding of what they have learned in the lesson.

# 4 Numbers

### A Listen and point. Look at the numbers.

CD1, Track 05

| | | | | |
|---|---|---|---|---|
| **1** one | **2** two | **3** three | **4** four | **5** five |
| **6** six | **7** seven | **8** eight | **9** nine | **10** ten |
| **11** eleven | **12** twelve | **13** thirteen | **14** fourteen | **15** fifteen |
| **16** sixteen | **17** seventeen | **18** eighteen | **19** nineteen | **20** twenty |

Listen again and repeat.

### B Listen and write the number.

CD 1, Track 06

1. _____6_____    2. _____18_____    3. _____5_____    4. _____3_____
5. _____12_____    6. _____11_____    7. _____15_____    8. _____9_____

**Talk with a partner.** Check your answers.

## 1 Before you listen

**A** Look at the picture. What do you see?

**B** Listen and point: ■ area code ■ country ■ first name ■ ID card
■ last name ■ phone number

CD1, Track 07

# UNIT 1

## Teaching objectives
- Introduce Ss to the topic
- Find out what Ss know about the topic
- Preview the unit by talking about the picture
- Provide practice of key vocabulary
- Provide practice that develops listening skills

## WARM-UP AND REVIEW

- Before class. Write today's lesson focus on the board.
  *Lesson A:*
  *Personal information*
- Begin class. Books closed. Review vocabulary for classroom directions from the Welcome unit. Write the following words on the board: *Look, Listen, Point, Repeat, Talk, Write, Read, Circle, Match.*
- Point to each word as you say it aloud. After each word, say to Ss: *Please repeat.*
- Use gestures, classroom items, and the board to review the meanings of the words. For example, gesture with your hand from your eyes to something or someone you are looking at. Say: *Look.* Ask Ss to repeat after you, using the same gestures.
- Continue in this manner with all the words for classroom directions.
- Point to the words *Personal information* on the board. Say each word aloud. After each word, say to Ss: *Please repeat.* Point to yourself when you say *personal.*
- Say to Ss: *Personal information is about you – for example, your name and your telephone number.*

### Literacy Tip

If you have literacy Ss in your class, it might be helpful to spend time at the beginning of any activity with art or photos talking about the pictures before focusing Ss' attention on the printed words in the exercise. Have Ss work in pairs. Tell them to ask each other: *What do you see?* Encourage Ss to describe the pictures to each other. Consider pairing literacy Ss with Ss who can help them read the text in the exercise. This will help preview the exercise for literacy Ss and make them more confident as the exercise continues.

## PRESENTATION

- Books open. Set the scene. Hold up the Student's Book. Show Ss the picture on page 6. Ask: *What do you see?* Elicit and write on the board any vocabulary that Ss know, such as: *classroom, student, backpack, clock, ID card, cell phone.* Point to similar items in the classroom as you go over each vocabulary word.

## PRACTICE

- Direct Ss' attention to the key vocabulary in Exercise **1B**. Read aloud each word or phrase while pointing to the corresponding part of the picture. Ask Ss to repeat and point.
- ▶ *CD1, Track 7* Play or read the audio (see audio script, page T-144). Tell Ss: *Listen and point to the picture.* As Ss hear the key vocabulary, check to see that they are pointing to the correct part of the picture. Repeat the audio as needed.

## COMPREHENSION CHECK

- Ask Ss *Yes / No* questions about the picture. Cup your hand behind your ear and tell the class: *Listen. Say "yes" or "no."* Nod or shake your head to illustrate the meanings of *yes* and *no.*
  Point to the picture. Ask: *Is this a classroom?* (Yes.)
  Point to Mexico on the map. Ask: *Is this a country?* (Yes.)
  Point to the ID card. Ask: *Is this an ID card?* (Yes.)
  Point to the name *Ernesto* on the ID card. Ask: *Is this a last name?* (No.)
  Point to the phone number on the ID card. Ask: *Is this a phone number?* (Yes.)
  Point to the area code. Ask: *Is this a last name?* (No.)

### Teaching Tip

Do not expect Ss to answer with more than *yes* and *no.* The purpose of these questions is to show whether or not Ss understand what you are asking them.

### *Expansion activity* (whole group)

- Hold up the Student's Book and point to the *I ♥ Mexico* T-shirt in the picture on page 6. Write on the board: *I love Mexico.* Say the sentence again and have Ss repeat it.
- Circle the word *Mexico.*
- If you have a map in the classroom, point to Mexico and say the name aloud. Point to where you are from on the map and say the name of the country. Ask volunteers to stand up and say the names of their countries. Point to the countries on the map as they say them.

### Literacy Tip

For an alternative activity, refer literacy Ss to pages 6–7 in the *Literacy Workbook* at any time during the lesson.

# LESSON A Listening

## PRESENTATION

- Draw on the board a simple version of the ID card on page 6. Point to and say each piece of information and the corresponding key vocabulary term.
- Direct Ss' attention to Exercise 2A. Tell Ss: *This is personal information.*
- Point to the lesson focus on the board. Say *personal information* and ask Ss to repeat after you.
- Read the instructions for Exercise 2A aloud.

## PRACTICE

- ▶ **CD1, Track 8** Play or read the audio (see audio script, page T-144). Repeat the vocabulary with Ss. Repeat the audio and correct Ss' pronunciation as needed.
- Draw a picture of an ID card on the board using your information. Point to your first name. Ask: *First name?* Elicit: *Yes.* Continue with last name, phone number, and area code.

### Learner persistence *(individual work)*
- ▶ **CD1, Track 8** Ss can listen to the audio for Exercise 2A at home for reinforcement and review. They can also listen to the audio for self-directed learning when class attendance is not possible.

### Expansion activity *(whole group)*
- Write the vocabulary from Exercise 2A on the board in random order in a numbered column. To the right, make a lettered column with examples of each term in random order.
- Point to the two columns and say: *Please match the number with the letter.* Write on the board: *Match.* Point to the word as you say it aloud and have Ss repeat.
- Model the task. Draw a line from a word in the left-hand column to the correct item on the right.
- Ask for volunteers to match the remaining items.

## COMPREHENSION CHECK

- Erase the lines drawn between the columns. Ask a volunteer to come to the board. Gesture to the left-hand column and say: *Listen and point.*
- ▶ **CD1, Track 8** Play or read the audio again. Pause the audio after each word or phrase. Have the S point to the word and ask the class: *Yes? Is this correct?*
- Direct Ss' attention to Exercise 2B and read the instructions aloud.
- ▶ **CD1, Track 9** Model the task. Hold up the Student's Book and say: *Number one.* Play or read the audio for number 1 (see audio script, page T-144). Elicit: *a.* Point to the *a* next to the first picture and tell Ss: *Circle the letter "a."*

- ▶ **CD1, Track 9** Play or read the complete audio. Ss listen and circle the answers. Repeat the audio as needed.
- ▶ **CD1, Track 9** Read aloud the second part of the instructions for Exercise 2B. Play or read the audio again so that Ss can check their answers.

### Learner persistence *(individual work)*
- ▶ **CD1, Track 9** Ss can listen to the audio for Exercise 2B at home for reinforcement and review. They can also listen to the audio for self-directed learning when class attendance is not possible.

### Useful Language
Read aloud the information in the tip box. Write the number *201* on the board. Say each number aloud and ask Ss to repeat. Write on the board phone numbers with zero and read them with the class.

## COMPREHENSION CHECK

- Write the numbers *1–4* on the board. Ask a few Ss to come to the board and write the correct answers to Exercise 2B next to each number.
- ▶ **CD1, Track 9** Play or read the audio again. Pause after each conversation. Point to the answer on the board and ask: *Is this correct?* Ask another S to make any necessary corrections.

## APPLICATION

- Direct Ss' attention to Exercise 3 and read the instructions aloud.
- Model the task. Hold up the Student's Book and point to the pictures in Exercise 2B. Say to one S: *Point to a picture.* Say to S1's partner: *Say the word.*
- Ss complete the exercise in pairs. Help as needed.

## EVALUATION

- Direct Ss' attention to the lesson focus on the board. Check Ss' understanding of the key vocabulary. Ask them to point to items in the picture on page 6 or on the ID card you drew on the board.
- Check off the lesson focus as Ss demonstrate an understanding of what they have learned in the lesson.

| *More Ventures, Unit 1, Lesson A* | |
|---|---|
| Literacy Workbook, 15–30 min. | |
| Basic Workbook, 15–30 min. | |
| Writing Worksheets, 15–30 min. | www.cambridge.org/ventures/ resources/ |
| Collaborative Worksheets, 30–45 min. | |
| Student Arcade, time varies | www.cambridge.org/venturesarcade/ |

UNIT GOALS
**Recognize** names and vocabulary for personal identification
**Identify** countries of origin   **Complete** an ID card

## 2 Listen

### A Listen and repeat.

1. area code
2. country
3. first name
4. ID card
5. last name
6. phone number

🔊 CD1, Track 08

🔊 CD1, Track 09

### B Listen and circle.

1. (a.)

b.

Address Book
Main | Home | Work
Name   **Barbara Simek**
Area Code   **415**
Phone Number   **555-5983**

2. (a.)

Address Book
Main | Home | Work
Name   **Barbara Simek**
Area Code   **415**
Phone Number   **555-5983**

b.

> **USEFUL LANGUAGE**
> Say *oh* for *zero.*
>
> 2    0    1
> *two   oh   one*

3. (a.)

b.

Class Sign Up
First name | Last name
Pilar | Mendez

4. a.

Class Sign Up
First name | Last name
Pilar | Mendez

(b.)

**Listen again.** Check your answers.

## 3 After you listen

**Talk with a partner.** Point to a picture.
Your partner says the words.

# Lesson B Countries

## 1 Vocabulary focus

**Listen and repeat.**

1. the United States
2. Mexico
3. Haiti
4. Brazil
5. Russia
6. Somalia
7. Vietnam
8. China

CD1, Track 10

## 2 Practice

**A Read and match.**

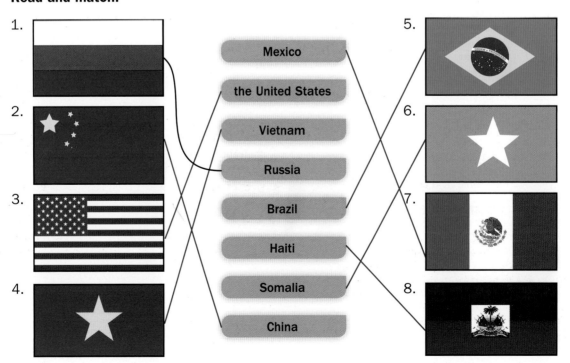

Mexico

the United States

Vietnam

Russia

Brazil

Haiti

Somalia

China

## Teaching objectives
- Introduce vocabulary for countries of origin
- Provide practice exchanging personal information
- Introduce questions with *Where*

## WARM-UP AND REVIEW

- Before class. Write today's lesson focus on the board.
  *Lesson B:*
  *Countries*
- Begin class. Books open. Direct Ss' attention to the picture on page 6. Review key vocabulary from the unit by asking Ss to point to the following in their books: *area code*, *country*, *first name*, *ID card*, *last name*, *phone number*.
- Walk around and check to see that Ss are pointing to the correct items in the picture.
- Write on the board: *Mexico*. Ask Ss: *What is Mexico?* When a S responds correctly, write on the board: *country*. Say the word aloud and ask Ss to repeat after you. Tell Ss: *Mexico is a country.* If you have a map in the classroom, show where Mexico is located.

## PRESENTATION

- Point to the word *Countries* at the top of page 8 in the Student's Book. Say the word aloud and ask Ss to repeat after you. Hold up one finger and say: *One country.* Hold up two fingers and say: *Two countries.*
- Direct Ss' attention to the map in Exercise 1. Read the instructions aloud.

## PRACTICE

- ▶ **CD1, Track 10** Play or read the audio (see audio script, page T-144). Listen and repeat along with Ss. Repeat the audio as needed.
- Listen carefully to Ss' pronunciation and correct as needed.
- Have pairs of Ss practice saying the names of the countries to each other and pointing to the appropriate word and flag in the exercise.
- Model the task. Stand near a S and say, for example: *Somalia.* Indicate the S's own book and say to the S: *Please point to Somalia.* Then ask the same S to say the name of a country. Point to that country in your book for the rest of the class to see.

> **Teaching Tip**
>
> There are many ways to divide the class into pairs, but the most transparent way to do this at the beginning level is to say two Ss' names, for example: *Michael and Jorge, you are partners.* At the same time, indicate with gestures that the two Ss should work together. With a very large class, using hand gestures alone to identify two Ss as you say the word *partners* can work quickly and almost as well.

## PRACTICE

- Direct Ss' attention to Exercise 2A. As you read aloud the instructions, hold up the Student's Book and indicate that Ss should look at the pictures and draw a line between the pictures and the corresponding words.
- Model the task. Hold up the Student's Book. Point to the first picture. Ask: *What country is this?* (Russia.) Say: *Match the picture with the word.*
- Ss complete the exercise individually. Help as needed.

## COMPREHENSION CHECK

- Write the numbers *1–8* on the board. Ask a few Ss to come to the board and write the answers to Exercise 2A on the board.
- Ask different Ss to read the answers on the board. After each answer is read, ask: *Is this correct?* Ask another S to make any necessary corrections on the board.

> **Teaching Tip**
>
> At the beginning of the course, avoid asking Ss who have difficulty writing to write answers on the board. Instead, ask for volunteers to do the writing so that Ss will not be embarrassed in front of the class.

> **Teaching Tip**
>
> To make all your Ss feel involved in the class, add the countries your Ss are from to the examples used in Lesson B. A reference list of countries and nationalities can be found on page T-142 of the Student's Book.

### *Expansion activity* (whole group)

- Before class, draw or print from the Internet color pictures of the flags from your Ss' countries.
- Tape the pictures across the board, leaving room for Ss to write the names of the countries.
- Point to each flag. Ask for a volunteer from that country to come to the board and write the name of the country under the flag. If you think your Ss will have difficulty with this, write the names of the countries yourself.
- Practice saying the names of the countries with the class.

> **Literacy Tip**
>
> For an alternative activity, refer literacy Ss to pages 8–9 in the *Literacy Workbook* at any time during the lesson.

# LESSON B Countries

## PRESENTATION

- Direct Ss' attention to the picture in Exercise 2B. Read aloud the names and the countries and ask Ss to repeat after you.
- Divide the board into two columns with *Name* and *Country* as headings.
- Point to the word *Name* on the board. Say the word aloud and have Ss repeat after you.
- Hold up the Student's Book and point to each person in the picture in turn. Ask the class: *What's his / her name?* List the names in the left-hand column of the chart.

### Teaching Tip

Don't expect Ss to produce questions or sentences by themselves at this point. However, they are likely to understand the word *name* and to understand from the context that they should respond with a person's name.

- Point to the word *Country* on the board. Say the word aloud and have Ss repeat after you.
- Point to each person in the picture in turn and ask: *What country?* List the countries in the right-hand column.
- Point to each name in the chart and ask, for example: *Where is Ivan from?* Point to that person's country and have the class say the name of the country as a group, for example: *Russia.*

## PRACTICE

- Read aloud the first part of the instructions for Exercise 2B.
- ▶ **CD1, Track 11** Model the task. Say: *Listen and repeat.* Play or read the audio for number 1 (see audio script, page T-144) and point to Ivan in the picture as you repeat. Say: *Then write.* Point to the word *Russia* written in the chart. Make sure Ss understand the task.
- ▶ **CD1, Track 11** Play or read the complete audio. Ss listen and repeat. Encourage Ss to point to the people in the picture as they repeat.
- Ss complete the chart individually. Repeat the audio as needed.
- Check answers with the class. Write the numbers *1–6* on the board and ask for volunteers to write their answers on the board. Point to each answer and ask the class: *Yes? Is this correct?* Make corrections on the board as needed.
- Read aloud the second part of the instructions for Exercise 2B. Point to and model the example conversation.
- Call on a pair of volunteers to read the example conversation aloud for the class.

- Point to another person in the picture on page 9. Ask a S: *Where is (name) from?* Elicit the answer. Repeat with different people in the picture. Indicate that Ss should ask and answer questions about all the people.
- Ss complete the exercise in pairs. Walk around and help as needed.

## APPLICATION

- Direct Ss' attention to Exercise 3 and read the instructions aloud.
- Model the task. Read each line of the example conversation and ask Ss to repeat after you. Point to where the information has been written in the chart.
- Ss complete the exercise in small groups. Depending on class size, you may want to prepare and distribute larger charts for Ss to fill in or else have Ss write the information in their notebooks.

### Teaching Tip

Remind Ss to look at the reference list of countries and nationalities on page T-142 of the Student's Book.

- When Ss are finished, walk around the room and ask about each person in the class. For example, gesture toward a S and ask his or her group: *Where is _____ from?* Elicit correct responses that the whole class can hear.

## EVALUATION

- Direct Ss' attention to the lesson focus on the board.
- Write across the board the names of the people in Exercise 2B. Point to each person's name and ask: *Where is he / she from?* As Ss respond correctly, invite them to the board to write the country under each name. Alternatively, write the names of the countries yourself.
- Check off the lesson focus as Ss demonstrate an understanding of what they have learned in the lesson.

| *More Ventures, Unit 1, Lesson B* | |
|---|---|
| **Literacy Workbook,** 15–30 min. | |
| **Basic Workbook,** 15–30 min. | |
| **Writing Worksheets,** 15–30 min. **Collaborative Worksheets,** 30–45 min. | www.cambridge.org/ventures/ resources/ |
| **Student Arcade,** time varies | www.cambridge.org/venturesarcade/ |

**B** **Listen and repeat.** Then write.

◀)) CD1, Track 11

| Name | Country | Name | Country |
|---|---|---|---|
| 1. Ivan | Russia | 4. Elsa | the United States |
| 2. Asad | Somalia | 5. Luisa | Brazil |
| 3. Eduardo | Mexico | 6. Jun-Ming | China |

**Talk with a partner.** Ask and answer.

  A  Where is **Ivan** from?

  B  **Russia.**

**3** **Communicate**

**Talk in a group.** Ask and answer. Complete the chart.

  A  What's your name?

  B  **Binh.**

  A  Where are you from?

  B  **Vietnam.**

| Name | Country |
|---|---|
| Binh | Vietnam |
| Answers will vary. | |

### 1 Grammar focus: *my, your, his, her*

| QUESTIONS | | | ANSWERS | | |
|---|---|---|---|---|---|
| | your | | My | | Angela. |
| What's | his | name? | His | name is | Kevin. |
| | her | | Her | | Julia. |

What's = What is

Watch

### 2 Practice

A **Read and circle.** Then write.

1.  **A** What's your name?
    **B** _____My_____ name is Nancy.
    (My) Your

2.  **A** What's his name?
    **B** _____His_____ name is Chin.
    (His) Her

3.  **A** What's her name?
    **B** _____Her_____ name is Alima.
    His (Her)

4.  **A** What's your name?
    **B** _____My_____ name is Vincent.
    (My) Your

**Listen and repeat.** Then practice with a partner.

CD1, Track 12

- Introduce possessive adjectives (*my, your, his, her*)
- Provide practice asking and answering questions about personal information

## WARM-UP AND REVIEW

- Before class. Write today's lesson focus on the board.
  *Lesson C:*
  *my, your, his, her*
  *What's _____ name?*
- Begin class. Books closed. Review *What's your name?* and *Where are you from?* Ask several Ss the first question. Then call on individual Ss to ask a classmate the question. Ask the second question and list Ss' countries on the board.
- Point to the word *your* on the board. Ask a S: *What's your name?* Point to the S to emphasize the meaning.
- Point to the word *his* on the board. Ask about several individual male Ss: *What's his name?*
- Point to the word *her* on the board. Ask about several individual female Ss: *What's her name?*

## PRESENTATION

- Use the animated grammar presentation in one or more of the following ways:
  - Preview it before class
  - Show it in class
  - Encourage Ss to watch it outside of class.
- Books open. Direct Ss' attention to the grammar chart in Exercise 1.
- Have Ss ask and answer the questions in the grammar chart in pairs.
- Write the names *Angela, Kevin,* and *Julia* on the board. Say them aloud and ask Ss to repeat after you. Point to *Angela.* Ask: *What's her name?* Elicit: *Her name is Angela.* Continue with *Kevin* and *Julia.* Emphasize the difference between *his* and *her.*

## COMPREHENSION CHECK

- Ask Ss the questions in the grammar chart about people in the class. Ss should answer appropriately.

## PRACTICE

- Direct Ss' attention to the first picture in Exercise 2A.

- Ask two Ss to read the example conversation aloud. After Speaker B's line is read, show Ss the two answer choices under the blank and ask: *My or Your?* Elicit: *My.*
- Read aloud the instructions for Exercise 2A.
- Model the task. Hold up the Student's Book and point to number 1. Say: *Read* as you point to and pretend to read the two speakers' words. Say: *Circle* as you pretend to circle the word *My* under the blank. Say: *Write* as you pretend to write the word *My* in the blank.
- Ss complete the exercise individually. Walk around and help as needed.

## COMPREHENSION CHECK

- Read aloud the second part of the instructions for Exercise 2A.
- ▶ **CD1, Track 12** Play or read the audio (see audio script, page T-144). Ss listen and repeat as they check their answers.
- Write the numbers *1–4* on the board. Ask volunteers to come to the board and write the words they circled. Make any necessary corrections on the board.
- Ss in pairs. Ask Ss to choose Role A or B and practice the questions and answers in Exercise 2A. Then have Ss switch roles and practice again. Walk around and help as needed.
- Ask several pairs to say the questions and answers for the rest of the class.

### *Expansion activity* (small groups)

- Divide the class into small groups, making sure to include at least one male S and one female S in each group.
- Have Ss take turns asking one of the questions from the grammar chart about the people in their group.
- To model the activity, sit down with one group and ask a question, for example: *What's her name?* Elicit the name from Ss in the group. If they don't know that S's name yet, ask her: *What's your name?*
- Gesture toward the S next to you and the questions in the chart to indicate that the S should ask the next question.
- If necessary, repeat the procedure with all the small groups so that Ss are sure what to do.

### Literacy Tip

For an alternative activity, refer literacy Ss to pages 10–11 in the *Literacy Workbook* at any time during the lesson.

# LESSON C What's your name?

## PRESENTATION

- Direct Ss' attention to one of the ID cards in Exercise 2B. Ask Ss: *What is this?* Elicit: *ID card.*

- Write on the board the key vocabulary terms as they appear on the ID card.

- Ask a S to write his / her information on the board. Tell the S he / she can invent the phone number if they prefer. Point to the first name on the board. Ask: *What's his / her first name? What's his / her last name?* etc.

### Learner persistence *(whole group)*

- Fill out the "ID card" on the board with your office telephone number if you have one. Tell Ss they can call you at your office to talk about the class.

## PRACTICE

- Read aloud the first part of the instructions for Exercise 2B.

- ▶ **CD1, Track 13** Model the task. Say: *Listen and repeat.* Play or read the audio for number 1 (see audio script, page T-144) and point to Jack's first name on his ID card as you repeat. Say: *Then write.* Point to the word *name* written in the chart. Make sure Ss understand the task.

- ▶ **CD1, Track 13** Play or read the complete audio. Ss listen and repeat. Encourage Ss to point to the items on the ID cards as they repeat.

- Ss complete the chart individually. Repeat the audio as needed.

- Check answers with the class. Write the numbers 1–8 on the board and ask for volunteers to write their answers on the board. Point to each answer and ask the class: *Yes? Is this correct?* Make any necessary corrections.

- Read aloud the second part of the instructions for Exercise 2B. Point to and model the example conversation.

- Call on a pair of volunteers to read the example conversation aloud for the class.

- Point to another item on one of the ID cards. Ask a S: *What's (her last name)?* Elicit the answer. Repeat with different items on the ID cards. Indicate that Ss should ask and answer questions about all the items.

- Ss complete the exercise in pairs. Walk around and help as needed.

## APPLICATION

- Direct Ss' attention to Exercise 3 and read the instructions and the example conversation aloud. Have Ss repeat each line after you. Point to where *Yuri* has been written in the chart.

- Point to each column of the chart. Read the headings aloud and ask Ss to repeat after you.

- Model the task. Draw on the board a simple ID card similar to the ID cards in Exercise 2B. Use the example first name *Yuri* and invent the other information.

- Ask a volunteer to come to the board. Point to the ID card on the board and tell the class: *I am Yuri.* Point to the example conversation in the Student's Book and say: *Talk to me.* Elicit the question from the example conversation: *What's your first name?* Respond with the example answer.

- Encourage the S to ask you the question from the *Useful language* box and then to write *Yuri* on the board.

- Write the four questions necessary to complete the chart on the board. Read each question aloud and ask Ss to repeat after you.

- Ask Ss to stand up, move around the classroom, and interview four classmates. Ss complete the chart.

- Walk around and listen to Ss' interviews. Help with pronunciation, grammar, and spelling as needed.

## EVALUATION

- Direct Ss' attention to the lesson focus on the board. Gesture toward different Ss in the class and call on individual Ss to answer questions, such as: *What's her first name? What's my last name? What's your area code? What's his last name?*

- Check off the lesson focus as Ss demonstrate an understanding of what they have learned in the lesson.

| *More Ventures, Unit 1, Lesson C* | |
|---|---|
| **Literacy Workbook**, 15–30 min. | |
| **Basic Workbook**, 15–30 min. | |
| **Writing Worksheets,** 15–30 min. | www.cambridge.org/ventures/ resources/ |
| **Collaborative Worksheets,** 30–45 min. | |
| **Student Arcade,** time varies | www.cambridge.org/venturesarcade/ |

**B** **Listen and repeat.** Then write.

**TOPS ADULT SCHOOL**

First name: Jack
Last name: Lee
Area code: 203
Phone number: 555-9687

**TOPS ADULT SCHOOL**

First name: Sara
Last name: Garza
Area code: 415
Phone number: 555-3702

◀)) CD1, Track 13

| What's his . . . ? | | | What's her . . . ? | | |
|---|---|---|---|---|---|
| 1. first _name_ | Jack | | 5. _area_ code | 415 | |
| 2. last _name_ | Lee | | 6. _phone_ number | 555-3702 | |
| 3. area _code_ | 203 | | 7. _last_ name | Garza | |
| 4. phone _number_ | 555-9687 | | 8. _first_ name | Sara | |

**Talk with a partner.** Ask and answer.

A What's **his first name**?

B **Jack.**

## ③ Communicate

**Talk with your classmates.** Complete the chart.

A What's your **first name**?

B My **first name** is **Yuri**.

**USEFUL LANGUAGE**
*How do you spell Yuri?*
Y-U-R-I

| First name | Last name | Area code | Phone number |
|---|---|---|---|
| Yuri | Answers will vary. | | |
| | | | |
| | | | |

# Lesson D Reading

METRO ADULT SCHOOL

## 1 Before you read

**Talk about the picture.**
What do you see?

## 2 Read

**Listen and read.**

CD1, Track 14

> # Welcome!
>
> Meet our new student.
>
> His first name is Ernesto.
>
> His last name is Delgado.
>
> He is from Mexico.
>
> Welcome, Ernesto Delgado!

## 3 After you read

**Read the sentences.** Circle *Yes* or *No*.

1. His name is Ernesto Mexico.          Yes     (No)
2. His first name is Ernesto.          (Yes)     No
3. His last name is Delgado.          (Yes)     No
4. He is from Ecuador.          Yes     (No)

Teaching objectives
● Introduce a welcome notice
● Introduce the months of the year
● Provide practice using new topic-related words

## WARM-UP AND REVIEW

● Before class. Write today's lesson focus on the board.
*Lesson D:*
*Read "Welcome!"*
*The months of the year*

● Begin class. Books closed. Write on the board:
*What's _____ first name?*
*What's _____ last _____?*
*Where _____ _____ from?*

● Read the questions aloud. Point to the blanks. Fill in the first one as an example. Write *your* in the blank. Ask Ss to fill in the correct words. Write the missing words in the blanks as Ss say them.

## PRESENTATION

● Books open. Direct Ss' attention to the picture in Exercise 1 and read the instructions aloud. Ask: *What do you see?* Elicit and write on the board any vocabulary that Ss know, such as: *school, student, backpack, bus.*

● Point to Ernesto in the picture and tell Ss: *His name is Ernesto. He is a new student.*

● Direct Ss' attention to the picture on page 6 of Lesson A. Ask Ss: *Do you see Ernesto?* Have Ss point to the appropriate person.

● Hold up the Student's Book as you point to the word *Welcome* in the picture on page 6. Say the word aloud and ask Ss to repeat after you.

## PRACTICE

● Direct Ss' attention to Exercise 2. Point to the title of the reading and ask Ss: *What word is this?* Elicit or provide: *Welcome.*

▶ *CD1, Track 14* Read aloud the instructions for Exercise 2. Play or read the audio and ask Ss to follow along (see audio script, page T-144). Repeat the audio as needed.

● Read aloud each sentence of the reading and ask Ss to repeat after you. Answer any questions Ss have about the reading.

● Ask Ss questions about the reading, For example: *What's his last name?*

### Learner persistence *(individual work)*

▶ *CD1, Track 14* Ss can listen to the audio for Exercise 2 at home for reinforcement and review. They can also listen to the audio for self-directed learning when class attendance is not possible.

### Literacy Tip

Literacy Ss should be able to participate in most parts of this lesson. For Exercise 3, have literacy Ss work with a higher-level partner who can read the questions and answer choices aloud.

## COMPREHENSION CHECK

● Read aloud the instructions for Exercise 3.

● Model the task. Point to and read aloud the first sentence. Then point to the answer choices and ask: *Yes or no?* Elicit: *No.* Tell Ss: *That's right. His name is not Ernesto Mexico.* Point to where *No* has been circled for number 1.

● Ss complete the exercise individually. Walk around and help as needed.

● Go over the answers with the class. Read each sentence aloud and call on Ss to give their answers. For the two false sentences, write on the board the beginning of each sentence and encourage Ss to supply the correct ending. For example: *His name is Ernesto . . . Delgado. That's right! His name is Ernesto Delgado.*

### Expansion activity *(whole group)*

● Write on the board *Ernesto, Delgado,* and *Mexico.*

● Point to each word on the board and ask: *What's the question?* If Ss don't understand you, point to and read the three questions you wrote on the board at the beginning of the class. Elicit the questions necessary to elicit the information in the reading: *What's his first name? / What's his last name? / Where is he from?*

### Literacy Tip

For an alternative activity, refer literacy Ss to pages 12–13 in the *Literacy Workbook* at any time during the lesson.

# LESSON D Reading

## PRESENTATION

- Direct Ss' attention to the Picture dictionary in Exercise 4. Point to the words *Months of the year*. Read the words aloud and ask Ss to repeat after you.

- If you have a wall calendar in the classroom, show examples of the months as you go through the list. Say, for example: *September. September is a month. October. October is a month.*

- Direct Ss' attention to Exercise 4A and read the instructions aloud.

- ▶ *CD1, Track 15* Play or read the audio (see audio script, page T-144). Listen to Ss' pronunciation as they repeat the names of the months. Correct pronunciation as needed.

### Teaching Tip

To help Ss with the pronunciation of the months, it is a good idea to emphasize stressed syllables clearly when saying the names of the months. You may also want to clap your hands when saying the strongest syllable.

### *Expansion activity* (individual work)

- Before class, create handouts with 12 numbered lines. On each line, make blanks for the letters of one of the months of the year with the first blank filled in, starting with January. For example, the first line would be:

  J _ _ _ _ _ _ .

- Give each S a handout and ask them to write the names of the months. Ss may use the Picture dictionary to help with spelling.

- Practice saying the months in order with the class or have pairs of Ss take turns saying the months to each other.

### *Learner persistence* (individual work)

- ▶ *CD1, Track 15* Ss can listen to the audio for Exercise 4A at home for reinforcement and review. They can also listen to the audio for self-directed learning when class attendance is not possible.

## PRACTICE

- Direct Ss to Exercise 4B and read the instructions aloud.

- Ask two Ss to read the example conversation aloud. Point to the information written in the chart.

- Model the task. Ask one or two Ss the questions in the exercise and pretend to write their answers in the chart in your book. Make sure Ss understand the task.

- Ss stand up, walk around the classroom, and talk to at least three classmates. Walk around and help as needed.

- Ask volunteers to perform the conversation for the rest of the class. As Ss answer, list on the board the months of the year in which they were born. Afterward, point to and say each month aloud and ask Ss to repeat after you.

## EVALUATION

- Direct Ss' attention to the lesson focus on the board. Hold up the Student's Book and point to the picture of Ernesto in Exercise 1. Ask: *What's his first name? What's his last name? Where is he from?* Elicit complete sentences, for example: *His first name is Ernesto.*

- Make a table with 12 numbered squares on the board. Fill in some of the squares with their corresponding months and leave some squares empty. Point to and say the names of the months you have written and ask Ss to repeat after you. Point to each empty square and call on Ss to supply the missing months.

- Ask several Ss: *When is your birthday?* After each S answers, ask a different S about the first S's answer: *When is his/her birthday?*

- Check off each part of the lesson focus as Ss demonstrate understanding of what they have learned in the lesson.

| *More Ventures, Unit 1, Lesson D* | |
|---|---|
| Literacy Workbook, 15–30 min. | |
| Basic Workbook, 15-30 min. | |
| Picture Dictionary activities, 30–45 min. | |
| Writing Worksheets, 15–30 min. | www.cambridge.org/ventures/resources/ |
| Collaborative Worksheets, 30–45 min. | |
| Student Arcade, time varies | www.cambridge.org/venturesarcade/ |

## 4 Picture dictionary Months of the year

| | | 1 | 2 | 3 | 4 | 5 | 6 |
1. **January**

| 1 | 2 | 3 | 4 | 5 | 6 |
| 7 | 8 | 9 | 10 | 11 | 12 | 13 |
| 14 | 15 | 16 | 17 | 18 | 19 | 20 |
| 21 | 22 | 23 | 24 | 25 | 26 | 27 |
| 28 | 29 | 30 | 31 | | | |

2. **February**

| | | | | 1 | 2 | 3 |
| 4 | 5 | 6 | 7 | 8 | 9 | 10 |
| 11 | 12 | 13 | 14 | 15 | 16 | 17 |
| 18 | 19 | 20 | 21 | 22 | 23 | 24 |
| 25 | 26 | 27 | 28 | | | |

3. **March**

| | | | | 1 | 2 | 3 |
| 4 | 5 | 6 | 7 | 8 | 9 | 10 |
| 11 | 12 | 13 | 14 | 15 | 16 | 17 |
| 18 | 19 | 20 | 21 | 22 | 23 | 24 |
| 25 | 26 | 27 | 28 | 29 | 30 | 31 |

4. **April**

| 1 | 2 | 3 | 4 | 5 | 6 | 7 |
| 8 | 9 | 10 | 11 | 12 | 13 | 14 |
| 15 | 16 | 17 | 18 | 19 | 20 | 21 |
| 22 | 23 | 24 | 25 | 26 | 27 | 28 |
| 29 | 30 | | | | | |

5. **May**

| | | 1 | 2 | 3 | 4 | 5 |
| 6 | 7 | 8 | 9 | 10 | 11 | 12 |
| 13 | 14 | 15 | 16 | 17 | 18 | 19 |
| 20 | 21 | 22 | 23 | 24 | 25 | 26 |
| 27 | 28 | 29 | 30 | 31 | | |

6. **June**

| | | | | | 1 | 2 |
| 3 | 4 | 5 | 6 | 7 | 8 | 9 |
| 10 | 11 | 12 | 13 | 14 | 15 | 16 |
| 17 | 18 | 19 | 20 | 21 | 22 | 23 |
| 24 | 25 | 26 | 27 | 28 | 29 | 30 |

7. **July**

| 1 | 2 | 3 | 4 | 5 | 6 | 7 |
| 8 | 9 | 10 | 11 | 12 | 13 | 14 |
| 15 | 16 | 17 | 18 | 19 | 20 | 21 |
| 22 | 23 | 24 | 25 | 26 | 27 | 28 |
| 29 | 30 | 31 | | | | |

8. **August**

| | | | 1 | 2 | 3 | 4 |
| 5 | 6 | 7 | 8 | 9 | 10 | 11 |
| 12 | 13 | 14 | 15 | 16 | 17 | 18 |
| 19 | 20 | 21 | 22 | 23 | 24 | 25 |
| 26 | 27 | 28 | 29 | 30 | 31 | |

9. **September**

| | | | | | | 1 |
| 2 | 3 | 4 | 5 | 6 | 7 | 8 |
| 9 | 10 | 11 | 12 | 13 | 14 | 15 |
| 16 | 17 | 18 | 19 | 20 | 21 | 22 |
| 23 30 | 24 | 25 | 26 | 27 | 28 | 29 |

10. **October**

| | 1 | 2 | 3 | 4 | 5 | 6 |
| 7 | 8 | 9 | 10 | 11 | 12 | 13 |
| 14 | 15 | 16 | 17 | 18 | 19 | 20 |
| 21 | 22 | 23 | 24 | 25 | 26 | 27 |
| 28 | 29 | 30 | 31 | | | |

11. **November**

| | | | | 1 | 2 | 3 |
| 4 | 5 | 6 | 7 | 8 | 9 | 10 |
| 11 | 12 | 13 | 14 | 15 | 16 | 17 |
| 18 | 19 | 20 | 21 | 22 | 23 | 24 |
| 25 | 26 | 27 | 28 | 29 | 30 | |

12. **December**

| | | | | | | 1 |
| 2 | 3 | 4 | 5 | 6 | 7 | 8 |
| 9 | 10 | 11 | 12 | 13 | 14 | 15 |
| 16 | 17 | 18 | 19 | 20 | 21 | 22 |
| 23 30 | 24 31 | 25 | 26 | 27 | 28 | 29 |

**A Listen and repeat.** Look at the Picture dictionary.

**B Talk with your classmates.** Complete the chart.

A What's your name?

B **Eva.**

A When's your birthday?

B **In April.**

◀)) CD1, Track 15

| Name | Month |
| --- | --- |
| Eva | April |
| *Answers will vary.* | |

# Lesson E Writing

## 1 Before you write

**A** **Talk with a partner.** Complete the words.

1. _f_ i r s t
2. _l_ a s t
3. _n_ a m e
4. a r e a   _c_ o d e
5. p h o n e   _n_ u m b e r

**B** **Read the ID card.** Complete the sentences.

**CULTURE NOTE**
Your signature is how
you write your name.

1. Her _____first_____ _____name_____ is Linda.
2. Her _____last_____ _____name_____ is Wong.
3. Her _____area_____ _____code_____ is 916.
4. Her _____phone_____ _____number_____ is 555-7834.
5. She is from _____China_____ .

# WARM-UP AND REVIEW

- Before class. Write today's lesson focus on the board.
  *Lesson E:*
  *Complete sentences with personal information*
  *Complete an ID card*
- Begin class. Books closed. Review vocabulary and grammar from the unit. Ask as many Ss as possible questions about the names and birth months of people in the class. For example, ask S1: *What's your name?* Elicit answer. Ask S2, indicating S1 or a different S: *What's his/her name?* Elicit answer. Ask S3: *When's your birthday?* Elicit answer. Ask S4, indicating S3: *When's his/her birthday?*

# PRESENTATION

- Books open. Direct Ss' attention to Exercise 1A and read the instructions aloud.
- Write the first item on the board, leaving a blank for the first letter. Point to the blank and ask: *What letter?* Ss should notice the example in the book and answer: *f.* Write the letter *f* in the blank. Then point to the word on the board and ask: *What's the word?* Elicit: *first.*

# PRACTICE

- Ss work in pairs to complete the words.
- When Ss are finished, call on different pairs to write their answers on the board. Go over the answers and have Ss make any necessary corrections on the board.

### Literacy Tip

If your literacy Ss are not able to do the writing in Lesson E, have them practice letter tracing and word recognition on pages 14–15 of the *Literacy Workbook* or have them practice forming the key vocabulary words using letter cards.

- Direct Ss' attention to the ID card in Exercise 1B.
- Ask Ss questions about the person pictured on the card, using vocabulary from the unit, for example: *What's her first name? What's her last name?*
- When you get to the word *signature* in Exercise 1B, ask: *What is a signature?* Ss will probably recognize from the example that a signature is a handwritten name. Write your signature on the board as another example.

- Ask volunteers to write their signatures on the board as examples.
- Print and write your name on the board. Point to your written name and ask: *Is this a signature?* (Yes.) Point to your printed name and ask: *Is this a signature?* (No.)

### Culture Note

Read the tip box aloud. Have Ss practice signing their names.

- Read the instructions for Exercise 1B aloud.
- Ss complete the sentences individually using information from the ID card. Walk around and help as needed.
- Check answers as a class. Write the numbers *1–5* on the board and ask for volunteers to write their answers on the board. Point to and say each answer and ask the class: *Yes? Is this correct?* Make any necessary corrections on the board.

# COMPREHENSION CHECK

- Ask Ss questions that can be answered using the sentences in Exercise 1B. For example: *What's her last name?* (Her last name is Wong.) *Where is she from?* (She is from China.)

### *Expansion activity* (whole group)

- On the board, draw a large ID card similar to the one in Exercise 1B. Draw a simple "photo" that is clearly male. Ask Ss: *What is this?* Elicit: *ID card.*
- Fill in the information on the card with the class. Point to different parts of the card and ask Ss, for example: *What goes here? What word?* If Ss don't seem to understand, fill in *last name* yourself. Elicit: *last name, first name, area code, phone number, country, signature.* Invite volunteers to write the words on the board.
- As a class, invent personal information for the ID card. Ask volunteers to give the man a first and last name, area code and phone number, and country. Have a volunteer write the man's signature.
- Ask Ss to take out a piece of paper and write five sentences about the man that are similar to the sentences in Exercise 1B but beginning with *His . . . .*
- If time allows, repeat this activity about a celebrity. Ask different Ss to come to the board and invent the celebrity's phone number and signature.

# LESSON E Writing

## PRESENTATION

- Direct Ss' attention to Exercise 2A and read the instructions aloud. Point to the blank ID card and ask the class: *What is this?* (ID card.) Point to the "photo" on the card and ask: *Who is this?* Elicit *Me* or tell Ss *You*. Say: *This is your ID card.*
- Ask Ss: *What will you write? Will you write your first name?* (Yes.) Elicit and list on the board the other pieces of personal information Ss will include on the ID card: *last name, area code, phone number, country, signature.*

### Teaching Tip

Remind Ss that they do not need to use their real phone numbers in the exercises.

## PRACTICE

- Ss complete the ID card individually. Encourage Ss to use the ID card in Exercise 1B as a model.
- Read aloud the instructions for Exercise 2B. Ss complete the sentences individually. Walk around and help as needed.

## COMPREHENSION CHECK

- Direct Ss' attention to Exercise 3 and read the instructions aloud.
- Model the task. Show your "ID card" to Ss and say the sentences in Exercise 2B using your own information.
- Ss share their sentences in pairs. Walk around and spot-check Ss' writing.

### Teaching Tip

While Ss are reading their sentences to each other, listen carefully to their pronunciation. When Ss are finished, list on the board any words Ss had difficulty pronouncing and practice saying them with the class.

### Expansion activity *(student pairs)*

- Have Ss exchange books and then stand up and tell the class about their partners using *His* or *Her*, for example: *His first name is Felix. His last name is Medina.*

### Community building *(pairs)*

- If Ss don't mind sharing their personal information with a classmate, have pairs of Ss copy their "ID cards" from Exercise 2A onto paper and exchange them with a classmate. Tell Ss: *You can call your classmate.* Pretend to make a telephone call and show that Ss can call each other to ask about homework or other issues; for example: *Hi, Sam. This is Steven. What's the homework for English class?*

## EVALUATION

- Direct Ss' attention to the lesson focus on the board. Write in various places around the board examples of personal information of the type found in the ID cards. Have Ss label the pieces of information with the key vocabulary: *first name, last name,* etc. (You may want to use celebrity names that Ss will easily recognize.)
- Ask volunteers to come to the board and write sentences. Dictate the beginnings of the sentences from Exercise 2B and have Ss complete the sentences with their own or invented information.
- Check off each part of the lesson focus as Ss demonstrate an understanding of what they have learned in the lesson.

| *More Ventures, Unit 1, Lesson E* | |
|---|---|
| Literacy Workbook, 15–30 min. | |
| Basic Workbook, 15–30 min. | |
| Writing Worksheets, 15–30 min. | |
| Real-life Document, 15–30 min. | www.cambridge.org/ventures/ resources/ |
| Collaborative Worksheets, 30-45 min. | |

## **2** Write

A **Complete the ID card.** Write about yourself.

Central Adult School Library

*Answers will vary.* _____
Last name           First name

_____    _____
Area code          Phone number

_____
Country

_____
Signature

B **Complete the sentences.** Write about yourself.

1. My first name is *Answers will vary* .
2. My last name is _____ .
3. My area code is _____ .
4. My phone number is _____ .
5. My birthday is in _____ .

## **3** After you write

**Talk with a partner.** Share your writing.

## 1 Life-skills reading

**A Read the sentences.** Look at the ID card. Fill in the answer.

1. His first name is _____.
   - (A) Ahmed
   - (B) Woodrow
   - ● Samir

2. His area code is _____.
   - (A) 33612
   - (B) 813
   - (C) 555

3. His birthday is in _____.
   - (A) January
   - ● February
   - (C) August

4. His last name is _____.
   - ● Ahmed
   - (B) Woodrow
   - (C) Tampa

**B Solve the problem.** Which solution is best? Circle your opinion.

Samir's ID card is wrong. His address is 1342 Woodrow Street. What should he do?

1. Write 1342 on the ID card.
2. Tell the teacher.
3. Other: _Answers will vary._

Teaching objectives
- Introduce reading an ID card
- Provide practice that develops test-taking skills
- Review vocabulary from the unit

## WARM-UP AND REVIEW

- Before class. Write today's lesson focus on the board.
  *Lesson F:*
  *Read an ID card*
- Before class. Write in random places on the board examples of the key vocabulary. For example, you might write: *Jennifer, 555-7924, Brazil, Clifton, (239),* or draw a picture of an ID card.
- Begin class. Books closed. Review key vocabulary from the unit by calling on Ss to circle the items on the board. For example: *Please circle the country. Country.* (S circles *Brazil* on the board.)
- Ask volunteers to go to the board. Say: *Write a country / phone number / area code / birthday / last name / first name.* Make sure that Ss write correct examples on the board.

## PRESENTATION

- Books open. Direct Ss' attention to the ID card in Exercise **1A**. Ask: *What is this?* (ID card.) Tell Ss: *That's right. This is an ID card from Midtown Adult School.* Point to and repeat the name of the school on the card.
- Ask: *What's the first name on the ID card?* (Samir.) Ask: *What is Samir's last name?* (Ahmed.)
- Read aloud the words in the left-hand column of the ID card and ask Ss to repeat after you.
- When you get to the word *address* on the ID card, ask: *What is an address?* Ss will probably recognize from the example that an address shows where a building is. (In this case, the address shows where Samir lives.)
- Write the street address of your school on the board as another example.

## PRACTICE

- Read aloud the instructions for Exercise **1A**. This task helps prepare Ss for standardized-type tests they may have to take.
- Write on the board the letters *A*, *B*, and *C*, each in a circle. Fill in one circle. Ask: *Is this fill in?* (Yes.) Circle another circle. Ask: *Is this fill in?* (No.) Put a check by another circle. Ask: *Is this fill in?* (No.)
- Write the first item on the board along with the three answer choices labeled *A*, *B*, and *C*
- Read the item and the answer choices aloud and then point to the student ID. Ask: *What is his first name?* Show Ss where to look for the information. Elicit: *Samir.*
- Point to the three answer choices on the board. Ask Ss: *A, B, or C?* (C) Fill in the letter *C* and tell Ss: *Fill in the answer.* Make sure Ss understand the task.
- Have Ss individually scan for and fill in the answers.

## COMPREHENSION CHECK

- Go over the answers to Exercise **1A** together. Make sure that Ss followed the instructions and filled in their answers. As Ss give their answers, have them point to the part of the ID card where they found the information.

## PRACTICE

- Books open. Direct Ss' attention to Exercise **1B**. Read aloud the problem described.
- Ask: *What is the address on the ID card?* (1432)
- Ask: *What is Samir's address?*
- Tell Ss: *Look at the solutions and choose one.*
- Go over Ss' choices together.
- Ask: *Who chose the first choice, "Write on the ID card"? Raise your hand.*
- Ask: *Who chose the second choice, "Tell the teacher"? Raise your hand.*
- Ask: *Who chose "Other?" Raise your hand.* Elicit reasons for their choices. Accept all plausible answers.

### *Expansion activity* (whole group)

- Teach Ss how to write an address on an envelope.
- On the board, draw a rectangle with a "stamp" in the upper right corner and write Samir's information as you would on an envelope:
  *Samir Ahmed*
  *1432 Woodrow Street*
  *Tampa, FL 33612*
- Bring in some envelopes that were addressed to the school. Point out how the name and address are written on the envelopes.
- Point out that the name is on one line, the street number and name on another line, and the city, state, and zip code on another line. (Explain that every part of the country has a different zip code.)
- Point out the capital letters and the comma between the city and the state.
- Give each S an envelope or ask Ss to take out a piece of paper and write their own name and address. Walk around and help Ss individually. If possible, provide information about the zip codes in the areas where your Ss live. If Ss prefer, they can write the name of the school on their envelopes.

### Literacy Tip

For an alternative activity, refer literacy Ss to pages 16–17 in the *Literacy Workbook* at any time during the lesson.

# LESSON F Another view

## PRESENTATION

- Books closed. Write the following list on the board:
  *November*
  *Ernesto* (or the name of a S in your class)
  *March*
  *January*
- Read aloud each item in the list and ask Ss to repeat. After each item, ask Ss: *What is this?* (month, first name, etc.)
- Point to each word and say to the class: *Month, first name, month, month.* Circle *Ernesto* and say: *Ernesto is a first name. It's not a month. It's different.*
- Write on the board and say the word *different.* Ask Ss to repeat after you.
- Write another similar example on the board and repeat the procedure, but this time, ask for a volunteer to circle the word that is different and, if possible, to explain his or her choice.

## PRACTICE

- Books open. Direct Ss' attention to Exercise 2A and read the instructions aloud. Read aloud the list in number 1 and ask Ss to repeat after you. Ask Ss: *What word is different?* (November.) Point to where *November* has been circled as an example. Make sure Ss understand the task.
- Ss complete the exercise individually.
- Read aloud the second part of the instructions for Exercise 2A. Have Ss compare their answers in pairs.
- Check answers as a class. Ask volunteer pairs to write the circled words on the board.

### Expansion activity *(whole group)*

- Ask Ss to work individually or in pairs to create a new list similar to the lists in Exercise 2A.
- Have each S or pair of Ss write their list on the board. Ask a volunteer from the class to go to the board and circle the word that is different.

## PRESENTATION

- Books closed. Demonstrate the process of writing something in order. Draw a large circle on the board and write the numbers *1–12* in a random arrangement inside the circle.
- On a different part of the board, begin to write the sequence *1–2–3.* Ask a volunteer to come to the board. Say: *Please finish. Write the numbers in order. In order.* The S should continue by writing *4–5–6* and so on through *12.*

## PRACTICE

- Books open. Direct Ss' attention to Exercise 2B and read the instructions aloud.

- Have Ss work in pairs to write the months in order in the calendar.
- Check answers as a class. Draw a large calendar similar to the one in Exercise 2B on the board. Call on individual Ss to come to the board and write one of the months. Then go over the calendar and ask the class: *Yes? Is this correct?* Make any necessary corrections on the board. If you have a wall calendar in the room, show each month in turn as you check the correct order.

### Expansion activity *(whole group)*

- Practice saying the months of the year starting at different points in the year. First, do this chorally by saying a month, for example: *March.* Ask Ss to repeat the month after you. Then continue with the rest of the months through February. Do this a few times using different months as starting points.
- Next, say a month and call on a S to repeat it and say the remaining months. Give as many Ss as possible an opportunity to say the months. Help with pronunciation as needed.

## EVALUATION

- Do a quick review of the unit. Have Ss turn to Lesson A. Ask the class to talk about what they remember about this lesson. Prompt Ss, if necessary, with questions, for example: *What words are on this page? What do you see in the picture?* Continue in this manner to review each lesson quickly.

### Expansion activity

- Before class. Print, for each student, one copy of the Self-assessment for this unit.
- Have Ss complete the Self-assessment either in class or outside of class.
- Provide feedback to Ss such as through a whole-class discussion, partners comparing their worksheets, or T reviewing each S's worksheet.
- If Ss are ready, administer the unit test on page T-154 of this Teacher's Edition. The audio script for the test is available on page T-192.

| More Ventures, Unit 1, Lesson F | |
|---|---|
| Literacy Workbook, 15–30 min. | |
| Basic Workbook, 15–30 min. | |
| Writing Worksheets, 15–30 min.<br>Collaborative Worksheets, 30–45 min.<br>Self-assessment, 10 min.<br>CASAS Test Prep Worksheet, 5–10 min. | www.cambridge.org/ventures/resources/ |

## 2 Fun with vocabulary

**A  What word is different?** Circle the word.

1. **Countries**

   Mexico          China          (November)          Somalia

2. **Months**

   April          September          May          (Russia)

3. **Phone numbers**

   555-4861          555-6978          (415)          555-7934

4. **Area codes**

   (555-6948)          813          212          915

5. **First names**

   Linda          Alima          Nasser          (Mexico)

6. **Last names**

   Cruz          (February)          Delgado          Lee

**Talk with a partner.** Check your answers.

**B  Work with a partner.** Write the months in order.

| April | August | December | February | January | July |
| June | March | May | November | October | September |

| 1 | 2 | 3 | 4 |
|---|---|---|---|
| January | February | March | April |

| 5 | 6 | 7 | 8 |
|---|---|---|---|
| May | June | July | August |

| 9 | 10 | 11 | 12 |
|---|---|---|---|
| September | October | November | December |

# UNIT 2 AT SCHOOL

## Lesson A Listening

### 1 Before you listen

A  Look at the picture. What do you see?

B  Listen and point: ▇ a book ▇ a chair ▇ a computer ▇ a desk
▇ a notebook ▇ a pencil

CD1, Track 16

# UNIT 2

## Teaching objectives
- Introduce Ss to the topic
- Find out what Ss know about the topic
- Preview the unit by talking about the picture
- Provide practice of key vocabulary
- Provide practice that develops listening skills

## WARM-UP AND REVIEW

- Before class. Write today's lesson focus on the board.
  *Lesson A:*
  *At school*
- Begin class. Books closed. Review the alphabet and the months of the year.
- Draw a calendar on the board with two rows and six columns. Write the word *January* in the first square. In each of the other squares, write only the first letter of the corresponding month.
- Point to the word *January*. Circle the letter *J* and ask: *What letter is this?* Elicit: *J*. Point to the word and ask: *What month is this?* Elicit: *January.*
- Circle the letter *F* in the next square and ask Ss: *What letter is this?* Elicit: *F*. Ask: *What month is this?* Elicit: *February*. Call on a higher-level S to complete the word *February* on the board.
- Continue in this manner until Ss have named the first letter of each month and filled in the calendar with the months of the year.
- Ask Ss a few questions about the months, for example: *What month is it now? When is your birthday?*
- Point to the lesson focus on the board. Read the words aloud and ask Ss to repeat after you. Say: *Today, we will talk about things at school. At school.*

### Literacy Tip
If you have literacy Ss in your class, it might be helpful to spend time at the beginning of any activity with art or photos talking about the pictures before focusing Ss' attention on the printed words in the exercise. Have Ss work in pairs. Tell them to ask each other: *What do you see?* Encourage Ss to describe the pictures to each other. Consider pairing literacy Ss with Ss who can help them read the text in the exercise. This will help preview the exercise for literacy Ss and make them more confident as the exercise continues.

## PRESENTATION

- Books open. Set the scene. Hold up the Student's Book. Show Ss the picture on page 18. Ask: *What do you see?* Elicit and write on the board any vocabulary that Ss know, such as: *classroom, students, desk, computer, clock.*

### Teaching Tip
If Ss don't know any vocabulary for things they see in the picture, say *OK* and go on to Exercise 1B.

## PRACTICE

- Direct Ss' attention to the key vocabulary in Exercise 1B. Read aloud each word or phrase while pointing to the corresponding part of the picture. Ask Ss to repeat and point.
- Point to the woman labeled *Sue* and ask: *What's her name?* Elicit or provide the name *Sue*.
- ▶ **CD1, Track 16** Play or read the audio (see audio script, page T-145). Tell Ss: *Listen and point to the picture.* As Ss hear the key vocabulary, check to see that they are pointing to the correct part of the picture. Repeat the audio as needed.

## COMPREHENSION CHECK

- Ask Ss *Yes / No* questions about the picture. Tell Ss: *Listen. Say "yes" or "no."*
  Point to the picture. Ask: *Is this a classroom?* (Yes.)
  Point to the desk. Ask: *Is this a chair?* (No.)
  Point to the teacher. Ask: *Is she a teacher?* (Yes.)
  Point to the computer. Ask: *Is this a book?* (No.)
  Point to the computer. Ask: *Is this a computer?* (Yes.)
  Point to the chair. Ask: *Is this a chair?* (Yes.)
  Point to the desk. Ask: *Is this a desk?* (Yes.)
  Point to the notebook. Ask: *Is this a pencil?* (No.)

### *Expansion activity* (whole group)
- Teach vocabulary for additional classroom objects in the picture. Write on the board: *clock, map, filing cabinet, white board*. Say the words aloud and ask Ss to repeat them after you.
- Ask Ss to point to each object in the picture. Hold up the Student's Book and point to each object for Ss who have not heard the words before.
- Ask follow-up questions about the objects. Ask Ss what time it is in the picture. Draw a large clock on the board to review the numbers *1–12* and assess Ss' knowledge of basic time-telling. Point to the map in the picture and ask: *What country is this?* (The United States.) Elicit and list on the board the names of other countries Ss know. If you have a filing cabinet in your classroom, open a drawer and ask Ss: *What is in a filing cabinet?* (Papers, files.) Show Ss examples of papers and files.
- Ask Ss: *What is in our classroom?* Point to objects in the classroom. Elicit the names of items listed in Exercise 1B as well as the names of the additional items written on the board for this expansion activity.

# LESSON A Listening

## PRESENTATION

- Direct Ss' attention to Exercise 2A. Tell Ss: *These are things at school.*
- Hold up or point to real classroom objects as you read each word aloud. Ask Ss to repeat after you. If you don't have one of the objects in your classroom, draw a quick sketch and label it on the board.
- Read aloud the instructions for Exercise 2A.

## PRACTICE

- ▶ **CD1, Track 17** Play or read the audio (see audio script, page T-145). Listen and repeat the vocabulary along with Ss. Repeat the audio as needed.
- Listen carefully to Ss' pronunciation and make corrections as needed.

### *Learner persistence* (individual work)
- ▶ **CD1, Track 17** Ss can listen to the audio for Exercise 2A at home for reinforcement and review. They can also listen to the audio for self-directed learning when class attendance is not possible.

### *Expansion activity* (whole group)
- Books closed. Write the six key vocabulary words on the board in any order: *a book, a chair, a computer, a desk, a notebook, a pencil.*
- Ask a S to come to the board. Say the vocabulary words randomly and have the volunteer point to each word.
- Repeat the procedure with other Ss. If you have all the objects available in your classroom, you could also have Ss point to the objects instead of to the words on the board.

> **Literacy Tip**
>
> For an alternative activity, refer literacy Ss to pages 18–19 in the *Literacy Workbook* at any time during the lesson.

## PRACTICE

- Direct Ss' attention to Exercise 2B and read the instructions aloud.
- ▶ **CD1, Track 18** Model the task. Hold up the Student's Book and say: *Number one.* Play or read the audio for number 1 (see audio script, page T-145). Point to the two answer choices in number 1 and ask Ss: *What did you hear – a or b?* Elicit: *b.* Point to the letter *b* next to the second picture and tell Ss: *Circle the letter "b."*
- ▶ **CD1, Track 18** Play or read the complete audio. Ss listen and circle the correct answers. Repeat the audio as needed.

- ▶ **CD1, Track 18** Read aloud the second part of the instructions for Exercise 2B. Play or read the audio again so Ss can listen and check their answers.

### *Learner persistence* (individual work)
- ▶ **CD1, Track 18** Ss can listen to the audio for Exercise 2B at home for reinforcement and review. They can also listen to the audio for self-directed learning when class attendance is not possible.

## COMPREHENSION CHECK

- Write the numbers *1–4* on the board. Ask a few Ss to come to the board and write the correct answers to Exercise 2B next to each number.
- ▶ **CD1, Track 18** Play or read the audio again. Pause the audio after each conversation. Point to the answer on the board and ask: *Is this correct?* Ask another S to make any necessary corrections.

## APPLICATION

- Direct Ss' attention to Exercise 3 and read the instructions aloud.
- Model the task. Hold up the Student's Book and point to the pictures in Exercise 2B. Say to one S: *Point to a picture.* Say to the first S's partner: *Say the word.* Indicate that the second S should say the word that the first S pointed to.
- Ss complete the exercise in pairs. Walk around and help as needed.

## EVALUATION

- Direct Ss' attention to the lesson focus on the board. Check Ss' understanding of the key vocabulary by asking them to point to the items in the picture on page 18 or to real items in your classroom: *a book, a chair, a computer, a desk, a notebook, a pencil.* Check that Ss are pointing to the correct items.
- Check off the lesson focus as Ss demonstrate an understanding of what they have learned in the lesson.

| *More Ventures, Unit 2, Lesson A* | |
|---|---|
| **Literacy Workbook**, 15–30 min. | |
| **Basic Workbook**, 15–30 min. | |
| **Writing Worksheets**, 15–30 min. | www.cambridge.org/ventures/resources/ |
| **Collaborative Worksheets**, 30–45 min. | |
| **Student Arcade**, time varies | www.cambridge.org/venturesarcade/ |

**UNIT GOALS**
**Identify** classroom objects   **Name** location of classroom objects
**Complete** school information form

## 2 Listen

### A   Listen and repeat.

1. a book          2. a chair          3. a computer

4. a desk          5. a notebook      6. a pencil

CD1, Track 17

### B   Listen and circle.

CD1, Track 18

1. a.           b.

2. a.           b.

3. a.           b.

4. a.           b.

**Listen again.** Check your answers.

## 3 After you listen

**Talk with a partner.** Point to a picture.
Your partner says the words.

# Lesson B Classroom objects

## 1 Vocabulary focus

**Listen and repeat.**

CD1, Track 19

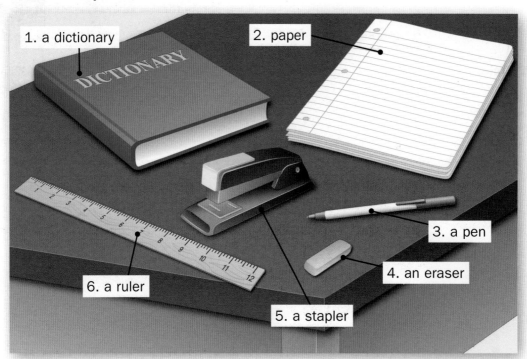

1. a dictionary
2. paper
3. a pen
4. an eraser
5. a stapler
6. a ruler

## 2 Practice

**A** **Read and match.**

1.

2.

3.

4.

5.

6.

paper

an eraser

a dictionary

a stapler

a ruler

a pen

Teaching objectives
• Introduce additional vocabulary for classroom objects
• Provide practice asking what someone needs

# WARM-UP AND REVIEW

- Before class. Write today's lesson focus on the board.
  *Lesson B:*
  *Classroom objects*
  *What do you need?*
- Before class. Write the key vocabulary from Lesson A on the board: *a book, a chair, a computer, a desk, a notebook, a pencil.*
- Point to each word on the board in turn and say: *Point to a book*, etc. Look around and make sure that Ss understand the meanings of the words.
- Begin class. Books open. Point to and say the key vocabulary words from Lesson A. Ask Ss to repeat.

> **Teaching Tip**
>
> If you have literacy Ss in the class, you can practice word recognition by calling on Ss to come to the board and point to the key vocabulary words as you say them, either in the order they are written or in random order.

- Direct Ss' attention to the picture on page 18. Say the key vocabulary words again and ask Ss to point to the corresponding parts of the picture. Walk around and check to see that Ss are pointing to the correct items in the picture.

# PRESENTATION

- Point to the words *Classroom objects* at the top of page 20 in the Student's Book. Say the words aloud. Tell the class: *Classroom objects are things in the classroom.* Gesture to indicate your own classroom or hold up the picture on page 18 to help clarify the meaning of the word *classroom.*
- Direct Ss' attention to Exercise 1. Read the instructions aloud.

# PRACTICE

- ▶ **CD1, Track 19** Play or read the audio (see audio script, page T-145). Listen and repeat along with Ss. Repeat the audio as needed.
- Listen carefully to Ss' pronunciation and correct as needed.

## *Expansion activity* (student pairs)

- Have pairs of Ss practice saying the words for classroom objects to each other and pointing to the appropriate part of the picture in the exercise.
- Model the task. Tell one S: *Say a word.* Point to the first vocabulary word in the Student's Book, indicating that he or she should say *a dictionary.* Then, say to his or her partner: *Please point to a dictionary in the picture.*

- Have Ss take turns saying the words and pointing to the picture. Alternatively, pair higher-level Ss with lower-level Ss and ask the higher-level Ss to say the words while the lower-level Ss point to the picture.

# PRACTICE

- Direct Ss' attention to Exercise 2A. As you read aloud the instructions, hold up the Student's Book and indicate that Ss should read the words and then draw a line between the pictures and the corresponding words.
- Model the task. Hold up the Student's Book. Point to the first picture. Ask: *What is this?* (A ruler.) Say: *Match the picture with the word.* Write the word *match* on the board. Point to it and say the word aloud.
- Ss complete the exercise individually. Help as needed.

# COMPREHENSION CHECK

- Write the numbers *1–6* on the board. Ask a few Ss to come to the board and write the answers to Exercise 2A.
- Ask different Ss to read the answers on the board. After each answer is read, ask: *Is this correct?* If it isn't correct, ask a volunteer to make corrections.

> **Literacy Tip**
>
> For an alternative activity, refer literacy Ss to pages 20–21 in the *Literacy Workbook* at any time during the lesson.

## *Expansion activity* (small groups)

- Give each group a set of 12 index cards with one vocabulary word from Lessons A and B on each card. Shuffle the cards and place them in a stack facedown.
- Give each group at least 12 pieces of blank scrap paper to draw pictures on.
- Model the activity. Take the top card from one group's stack and read the word but don't say the word aloud or show it to the Ss. Draw a picture of the classroom object and show it to the Ss, who try to guess what you drew. When Ss guess correctly, say: *Correct!* and show them the word on your card.
- Have Ss take turns choosing and drawing words until all the words are chosen.

> **Multilevel Tip**
>
> Match higher-level Ss with literacy Ss to work together in the expansion activity.

# LESSON B Classroom objects

## PRESENTATION

- Direct Ss' attention to the word bank in Exercise 2B. Read the words aloud and ask Ss to repeat after you.

- Point to the picture in Exercise 2B. Ask: *What do you see?* Elicit and write on the board any pictured vocabulary that Ss know, including the unit vocabulary for classroom objects.

- Point to each S in the picture and ask: *What's his / her name?* Write the names on the board and practice saying them with the class.

- To help Ss understand the situation, point to Carla's desk in the picture, desk number 1. Ask: *Does Carla have a ruler? A ruler?* (Yes.) Write *a ruler* on the board. Continue in this manner until all the classroom objects on Carla's desk have been listed on the board.

- Then ask Ss: *Does Carla have a dictionary? A dictionary?* (No.) Tell Ss: *Correct. Carla does not have a dictionary.* Write on the board: *Carla needs a dictionary.* Point to where *a dictionary* has been written for number 1.

- Point to several Ss' desks in the classroom in turns. Ask: *Does (name of S) have a dictionary? Does (name of S) have a ruler?* etc. Elicit *Yes / No* responses.

## PRACTICE

- Read aloud the first part of the instructions for Exercise 2B.

- ▶ **CD1, Track 20** Model the task. Say: *Listen and repeat.* Play or read the audio for number 1 (see audio script, page T-145) and point to the teacher and then Carla in the picture as you repeat. Say: *Then write.* Point to the words *a dictionary* written on the list. Make sure Ss understand the task.

- ▶ **CD1, Track 20** Play or read the complete audio. Ss listen and repeat. Encourage Ss to point to the people in the picture as they repeat.

- Ss complete the list individually. Repeat the audio as needed.

- Check answers with the class. Write the numbers *1–6* on the board and ask for volunteers to write their answers on the board. Point to each answer and ask the class: *Yes? Is this correct?* Make any necessary corrections on the board.

- Read aloud the second part of the instructions for Exercise 2B. Point to and model the example conversation.

- Call on a pair of volunteers to read the example conversation aloud for the class.

- Point to another person in the picture on page 21. Ask: *What do you need, (name)?* Elicit the answer from a volunteer. Repeat with different people in the picture. Indicate that Ss should ask and answer questions about all the people in the picture.

- Ss complete the exercise in pairs. Walk around and help as needed.

- Ask volunteers to say their questions and answers to the rest of the class.

## APPLICATION

- Direct Ss' attention to Exercise 3 and read the instructions aloud.

- Model the task. Read the example question and answer aloud and ask Ss to repeat after you. Point to the information that has been written in the chart.

### Teaching Tip

Look through old magazines and cut out pictures of the items in Exercise 2A on page 20. Alternatively, write the names of the items on slips of paper. Give each S one of the pictures to represent the item he or she needs in Exercise 3. As you hand out the pictures, tell Ss, for example: *Kara, you need a pen.*

- Ss complete the activity in small groups. Depending on class size, you may want to prepare and distribute larger charts for Ss to complete or have Ss write the information in their notebooks.

- Continue by asking individual Ss what they need. Then check to see that the Ss' group members have written that information in their charts.

## EVALUATION

- Direct Ss' attention to the lesson focus on the board.

- Hold up real examples of each classroom item from the lesson or point to the items in the pictures on page 20 and ask: *What is this?* As Ss respond correctly, invite them to the board to write the words.

- Collect the pictures you distributed earlier. Give one picture to a S and ask, for example: *Daisuke, what do you need?* After the S responds with the word for the classroom item in the picture, pretend to offer the item as you say: *Here you are.* Repeat the procedure with as many Ss as possible.

- Check off each part of the lesson focus as Ss demonstrate an understanding of what they have learned in the lesson.

| More Ventures, Unit 2, Lesson B | |
|---|---|
| Literacy Workbook, 15–30 min. | |
| Basic Workbook, 15–30 min. | |
| Writing Worksheets, 15–30 min. <br> Collaborative Worksheets, 30–45 min. | www.cambridge.org/ventures/resources/ |
| Student Arcade, time varies | www.cambridge.org/venturesarcade/ |

B **Listen and repeat.** Then write.

| a dictionary | an eraser | paper |
| a pen | a ruler | a stapler |

🔊 **CD1, Track** 20

1. a dictionary

2. an eraser

3. a ruler

4. paper

5. a pen

6. a stapler

**Talk with a partner.** Act it out.

A What do you need, **Carla**?

B **A dictionary.**

A Here you are.

3 **Communicate**

**Talk with your classmates.** Complete the chart.

A What do you need, **Mahmoud**?

B **An eraser.**

| Name | Classroom object |
|------|-------------------|
| Mahmoud | an eraser |
| Answers will vary. | |

1. Carla

2. Daw

Stefan  Felicia

3.  4.

Kim  Pablo

5.  6.

## Lesson C Where's my pencil?

### 1 Grammar focus: *in*, *on*, and *under*

in the desk

on the desk

under the desk

👁 Watch

### 2 Practice

A **Read and circle.** Then write.

1. A Where's my pencil?

   B _____**In**_____ the desk.

   (In) On Under

2. A Where's my notebook?

   B _____*On*_____ the desk.

   In (On) Under

3. A Where's my pen?

   B _____*On*_____ the floor.

   In (On) Under

4. A Where's my dictionary?

   B _____*Under*_____ the table.

   In On (Under)

5. A Where's my ruler?

   B _____*On*_____ the table.

   In (On) Under

6. A Where's my paper?

   B _____*Under*_____ the desk.

   In On (Under)

**Listen and repeat.** Then practice with a partner.

🔊 CD1, Track 21

**Teaching objectives**
- Introduce prepositions of location (*in*, *on*, and *under*)
- Provide practice asking about and giving the location of things

## WARM-UP AND REVIEW

- Before class. Write today's lesson focus on the board.
  *Lesson C:*
  *in, on, under*
  *Where's my _____?*
- Before class. List the following on the board: *a book, a chair, a computer, a desk, a dictionary, an eraser, a notebook, paper, a pen, a pencil, a ruler, a stapler.*
- Begin class. Books closed. Review vocabulary for classroom objects. Point to and say each vocabulary word on the board and ask Ss to repeat after you.
- Hold up or point to as many real examples of the classroom objects as possible and ask Ss: *What is this?* As Ss respond correctly, circle the vocabulary words on the board.

## PRESENTATION

- Use the animated grammar presentation in one or more of the following ways:
  - Preview it before class
  - Show it in class
  - Encourage Ss to watch it outside of class.
- Before class. Bring to class a small cardboard box or other object to place things in, on, and under.
- Point to the first part of the lesson focus on the board. Tell the class: *Today, we will learn about "in," "on," and "under."*
- Show Ss an eraser or other classroom object and ask: *What is this?* (An eraser.) Teach Ss *box* or the words for other objects you brought to class.
- Place the eraser inside the box and tell Ss: *The eraser is in the box. In.* Point to the word *in* on the board. Ask Ss to repeat it after you.
- Close the box (or turn it on its side) and place the eraser on top. Tell Ss: *The eraser is on the box. On.* Point to the word *on* written on the board. Ask Ss to repeat it after you. Put the eraser under the box. Tell Ss: *The eraser is under the box. Under.* Point to the word *under* on the board. Ask Ss to repeat it after you. Continue to put the eraser in, on, or under the box as you say the prepositions as many times as necessary. Then place the eraser in, on, or under the box and ask: *In, on, or under?* (Ss respond appropriately.)
- Books open. Direct Ss' attention to the pictures in Exercise 1. Read each phrase aloud as you point to the corresponding picture. Ask Ss to repeat the phrases after you.
- Point to each of the pictures in Exercise 1 and ask: *Where's the pencil?* Elicit: *in, on,* or *under the desk* as appropriate. Repeat with as many Ss as possible.

## PRACTICE

- Direct Ss' attention to the picture in Exercise 2A. Ask two Ss to read the example conversation aloud. When Speaker B's line is read, show Ss the three answer choices under the blank and ask: *In, on, or under?* Elicit: *In.*
- Read aloud the instructions for Exercise 2A. Point to where *In* has been circled and written for number 1.
- Ss complete the exercise individually. Walk around and help as needed.

> **Literacy Tip**
>
> Literacy Ss should be able to do Warm-up and review and Presentation in Lesson C, and in Exercise 2A, they can work with a higher-level partner who reads aloud the question and answer choices. The second page of this lesson, however, involves a large amount of reading and writing, so you may want to assign pages 22–23 of the *Literacy Workbook* as an alternative activity.

## COMPREHENSION CHECK

- Read aloud the second part of the instructions for Exercise 2A.
- ▶ **CD1, Track 21** Play or read the audio (see audio script, page T-145). Ss listen and repeat as they check their answers.
- Write the numbers *1–6* on the board. Ask volunteers to come to the board and write the words they circled. Make any necessary corrections on the board.
- Ss in pairs. Ask Ss to choose Role A or B and practice the questions and answers in Exercise 2A. Then have Ss switch roles and practice again. Walk around and help as needed.
- Ask volunteers to say the questions and answers for the rest of the class.

### *Expansion activity* (whole group)

- Write on the board: *the floor, the filing cabinet, the table, a chair.* Point to and say each word and ask Ss to repeat after you.
- Use your own classroom or the picture on page 18 to practice this vocabulary. Place various items on the floor and on the table (if you have one) and in or on the filing cabinet. Also place some items under the table or a chair. Ask Ss where the items are and elicit prepositional phrases.
- Ask Ss questions about the picture on page 18 if you don't have a filing cabinet or table in your classroom.

# LESSON C Where's my pencil?

## PRACTICE

- Direct Ss' attention to Exercise 2B and read the instructions aloud.
- Model the task. Point to number 1 and read aloud: *my book*. Point to the picture and ask: *Where is her book?* Elicit: *In the desk*. Point to the line that has been drawn as an example. Make sure Ss understand the task.
- Ss complete the task individually. Walk around and help as needed.
- Check answers with the class. Duplicate the four columns from the exercise on the board and ask volunteers to match the classroom objects to their locations. For each match, ask the class: *Is this correct?* Make any necessary corrections on the board.
- Read aloud the second part of the instructions for Exercise 2B.
- If you have a desk with a drawer, place a book in the drawer so Ss can see it. Point to and model the example conversation, pretending to be the woman in the picture when reading Speaker A's part.
- Read each line of the example conversation aloud and ask Ss to repeat after you.
- Point to the words *my stapler* in number 2 on the board. Call on two higher-level Ss to model the conversation and act it out, putting a stapler on a book. Indicate that Ss should act out conversations for all the items in Exercise 2B. Make sure Ss understand the task.
- Have Ss practice the conversations in pairs. When Ss are finished, call on several pairs to perform one of the conversations for the class.

## APPLICATION

- Direct Ss' attention to Exercise 3 and read the instructions aloud. Place a pencil on your desk and read the example conversation aloud. Point to the word *pencil* in the first column of the chart and to the phrase *on the desk* in the second column.
- Ask Ss to take out a pencil, a book, a piece of paper, a pen, a dictionary, and a notebook. Ask Ss to put the objects in, on, and under various objects around them, for example: on the desk, in a notebook, under a chair, or on the floor.
- Model the task. Stand near a S, point to his or her piece of paper, and say: *Ask the question "Where's my paper?"* (S1 asks the question.)

- Gesture toward S1's partner to indicate that he or she should answer. Elicit the appropriate prepositional phrase, for example: *on the floor*. Point to S1's chart and say: *Write "on the floor."*
- Have Ss work in pairs to complete their charts. Tell Ss: *Talk about your classroom objects.* Write the words. Walk around and help as needed.

### Teaching Tip

If you think your Ss need additional help with Exercise 3, write on the board the necessary questions to complete the chart. Read aloud each question and ask Ss to repeat after you.

### Useful Language

- Read aloud the sentence in the tip box and ask Ss to repeat after you. Illustrate the meaning of *I don't know* by shrugging your shoulders and shaking your head.
- Ask Ss about the location of a classroom object they cannot see as you pretend to look for it, for example: *Where's my ruler?* Indicate that Ss should answer: *I don't know*.
- Encourage Ss to use the useful language if applicable as they interview classmates in Exercise 3.

## EVALUATION

- Direct Ss' attention to the lesson focus on the board. Place real classroom objects in various places and ask, for example: *Where's my dictionary?* Elicit correct responses with *on*, *in*, and *under*, for example: *It's in the filing cabinet*.
- Call on Ss to ask their classmates questions about their own classroom objects.
- Check off each part of the lesson focus as Ss demonstrate an understanding of what they have learned in the lesson.

| More Ventures, Unit 2, Lesson C | |
| --- | --- |
| Literacy Workbook, 15–30 min. | |
| Basic Workbook, 15–30 min. | |
| Writing Worksheets, 15–30 min. Collaborative Worksheets, 30–45 min. | www.cambridge.org/ventures/resources/ |
| Student Arcade, time varies | www.cambridge.org/venturesarcade/ |

B **Look at the picture.** Match the words.

1. my book — in the desk
2. my stapler — on the book
3. my notebook — under the chair
4. my ruler — on the desk

5. my paper — on the paper
6. my pen — on the chair
7. my pencil — in the notebook
8. my dictionary — under the desk

**Talk with a partner.** Act it out.

A  Where's my **book**?

B  **In the desk.**

A  Thanks.

## 3 Communicate

**Talk with a partner.** Complete the chart.

A  Where's my **pencil**?

B  **On the desk.**

> USEFUL LANGUAGE
> *I don't know.*

| | |
|---|---|
| my pencil | on the desk |
| my book | *Answers will vary.* |
| my paper | |
| my pen | |
| my dictionary | |
| my notebook | |

# Lesson D Reading

## 1 Before you read

**Talk about the picture.**
What do you see?

## 2 Read

**Listen and read.**

CD1, Track 22

Sue,

It's Monday, your first day of English class! You need a pencil, eraser, notebook, and dictionary. The pencil is in the desk. The eraser is on the desk. The notebook is on my computer. And the dictionary is under the chair.

Have fun at school!

Mom

## 3 After you read

**Read and match.**

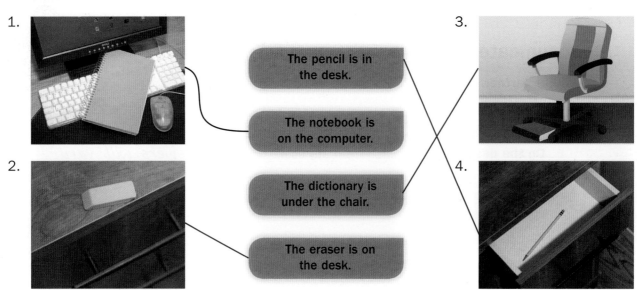

1.

The pencil is in the desk.

3.

The notebook is on the computer.

The dictionary is under the chair.

2.

4.

The eraser is on the desk.

● Introduce a note about school supplies
● Introduce the days of the week
● Provide practice using new topic-related words

# WARM-UP AND REVIEW

- Before class. Write today's lesson focus on the board.
  *Lesson D:*
  *Read a note*
  *Days of the week*
- Begin class. Books closed. Write on the board:
  *What do you need?*
  *Where's my notebook?*
- Read each question aloud and ask Ss to repeat after you.
- Review vocabulary from the unit. Hold up or arrange on a table several classroom objects, for example: a pen, a pencil, a ruler, a dictionary, paper, and a stapler. Ask as many Ss as possible: *What do you need?* As Ss respond with the vocabulary words, hand them the objects and say: *Here you are.*
- Collect the classroom objects you handed out and place them in various places. Ask as many Ss as possible: *Where's my _____ ?* As Ss respond with prepositional phrases, for example, *on the desk,* say: *Thanks!*

# PRESENTATION

- Books open. Direct Ss' attention to the picture in Exercise 1 and read the instructions aloud. Ask: *Who is this? What's her name?* Ss should recognize Sue from the picture on page 18.
- Ask: *What do you see?* Elicit and write on the board any vocabulary about the picture that Ss know, such as: *kitchen, refrigerator, juice.*
- Point to the note on the refrigerator. Write the word *note* on the board. Say the word and ask Ss to repeat after you. Tell Ss: *Sue is reading a note.*

# PRACTICE

- Direct Ss' attention to Exercise 2. Tell Ss: *This is the note.*
- ▶ *CD1, Track 22* Read aloud the instructions for Exercise 2. Play or read the audio and ask Ss to follow along (see audio script, page T-145). Repeat the audio as needed.
- Read aloud each sentence of the reading and ask Ss to repeat after you. Answer any questions Ss have about the reading.

## Teaching Tip

You can vary the presentation of the reading by asking Ss to read the note silently before they listen to the audio or to close their books and just listen before they read.

## Literacy Tip

If you have literacy Ss in your class, prepare a list of the key vocabulary words from the reading and one or two additional vocabulary words. Use large lowercase letters. While the rest of the class is reading the note, ask the literacy Ss to circle only those words on the list that they also see in the reading.

***Learner persistence*** *(individual work)*
▶ ***CD1, Track 22*** Ss can listen to the audio for Exercise 2 at home for reinforcement and review. They can also listen to the audio for self-directed learning when class attendance is not possible.

# COMPREHENSION CHECK

- Read aloud the instructions for Exercise 3.
- Model the task. Point to the first picture. Then point to the sentences and ask: *Which sentence?* Elicit: *The notebook is on the computer.* Point to the line drawn between the first picture and the second sentence. Say: *Match the picture with the sentence.*
- Ss complete the exercise individually. Walk around and help as needed.
- Go over the answers with the class. Write the sentences from Exercise 3 on the board, surrounded by numbered boxes to represent the pictures in the exercise. Read each sentence aloud, ask Ss to repeat after you, and call on Ss to match each sentence to the numbered pictures on the board. For each match, ask the class: *Is this correct?* Make any necessary corrections on the board.

## Literacy Tip

For an alternative activity, refer literacy Ss to pages 24–25 in the *Literacy Workbook* at any time during the lesson.

# LESSON D Reading

## PRESENTATION

- Direct Ss' attention to the Picture dictionary in Exercise 4. Point to the words *Days of the week*. Read the words aloud and ask Ss to repeat after you.
- Tell the class, for example: *Today is Monday. Monday.* Ask Ss to repeat the day. Tell Ss: *Monday is a day of the week.*
- Read aloud the instructions for Exercise 4A.
- ▶ **CD1, Track 23** Play or read the audio (see audio script, page T-145). Listen to Ss' pronunciation as they repeat the days of the week. Correct pronunciation as needed.

### Expansion activity *(individual work)*

- Before class. Create handouts with seven numbered lines. On each line, make blanks for the letters of one of the days of the week with the first blank filled in, starting with Monday. For example: __M__ ____ ____ ____ ____ ____. Alternatively, write the words with blanks on the board and ask Ss to copy them down and fill in the blanks.
- Give each S a handout and ask them to write the days of the week. Ss may use the Picture dictionary to help with spelling.
- Practice saying the days of the week with the class or have pairs of Ss take turns saying the days to each other.

### Learner persistence *(individual work)*

- ▶ **CD1, Track 23** Ss can listen to the audio for Exercise 4A at home for reinforcement and review. They can also listen to the audio for self-directed learning when class attendance is not possible.

## PRACTICE

- Direct Ss' attention to Exercise 4B and read the instructions aloud. Hold up your Student's Book and point to the iPad. Ask: *What's this?* (It's an iPad.) Point to the calendar on the iPad. Ask: *What's this?* (It's a calendar.) Point to *Monday* in the Picture dictionary. Ask two Ss to read the example conversation aloud.
- Model the task. Hold up your Student's Book and point to a different day of the week. Ask a S: *What day is it?* Elicit the day you are pointing to.

- Ss complete the activity in pairs. Say to one S: *Point to a day.* Say to his or her partner: *Say the day of the week.* Walk around and help as needed.
- When Ss are finished, write the days of the week in order across the board. Ask volunteers to come to the board, point to one of the days, and ask a classmate: *What day is it?*

## EVALUATION

- Direct Ss' attention to the lesson focus on the board. Hold up the Student's Book and point to the reading in Exercise 2. Ask: *What does Sue need for school?* List the needed items on the board and for each one, ask: *Where's the _____?* Elicit the locations given in the reading.
- Draw seven long blanks across the board. Point to each blank and ask for volunteers to fill in the blanks with the days of the week.

### Teaching Tip

If you have enough Ss in your class, it might be fun to have seven Ss at the board at the same time, working out which day each one will write in which blank.

- Ask Ss a few simple questions about days of the week, for example: *Is today Sunday? What day is today? What days do we have English class?*
- Check off each part of the lesson focus as Ss demonstrate an understanding of what they have learned in the lesson.

### More Ventures, Unit 2, Lesson D

| Literacy Workbook, 15–30 min. | |
| --- | --- |
| Basic Workbook, 15–30 min. | |
| Picture Dictionary activities, 30–45 min. Writing Worksheets, 15–30 min. Real-life Document, 15–30 min. Collaborative Worksheets, 30–45 min. | www.cambridge.org/ventures/ resources/ |
| Student Arcade, time varies | www.cambridge.org/venturesarcade/ |

## 4 Picture dictionary Days of the week

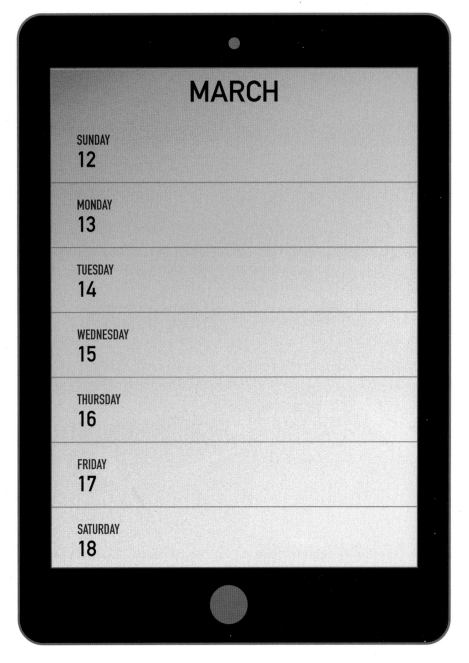

**MARCH**

| | |
|---|---|
| SUNDAY | 12 |
| MONDAY | 13 |
| TUESDAY | 14 |
| WEDNESDAY | 15 |
| THURSDAY | 16 |
| FRIDAY | 17 |
| SATURDAY | 18 |

A **Listen and repeat.** Look at the Picture dictionary.

B **Talk with a partner.** Point and ask. Your partner answers.

A What day is it?

B **Monday.**

CD1, Track 23

# Lesson E Writing

## 1 Before you write

**A** **Talk with a partner.** Complete the words.

1. e r a s e __r__
2. d i c t i o n a r __y__
3. p e __n__
4. p e n c i __l__
5. n o t e b o o __k__

**B** **Talk with a partner.** Look at the picture. Write the words.

1. dictionary
2. __notebook__
3. __pencil__
4. __pen__
5. __eraser__

- Prepare Ss for writing sentences about classroom objects
- Provide practice writing key vocabulary words

## WARM-UP AND REVIEW

- Before class. Write today's lesson focus on the board.
  *Lesson E:*
  *Write words for classroom objects*
  *Complete sentences about school*

- Begin class. Books closed. Review the meaning of the word *need*. Place a few classroom objects on a desk or table, for example, a ruler, a pen, and some paper. Hold up the ruler and ask Ss: *What's this?* (A ruler.) Tell Ss: *I have a ruler.*

- Look over the objects on the table and say:
  *Hmm . . . I have a ruler but no dictionary. I need a dictionary.*
  Write on the board: *I need a dictionary.* Look around the room hopefully and repeat: *I need a dictionary* until a S offers you a dictionary. Accept the dictionary and say: *Thanks.*

- Repeat the procedure with the other objects, telling Ss that you have a pen and paper, but you need, for example, a pencil and an eraser. Make sure Ss understand the meaning of *need*.

## PRESENTATION

- Books open. Direct Ss' attention to Exercise 1A and read the instructions aloud. Point to the first item and say to Ss: *Number 1. What's the word?* (Eraser.) Say to Ss: *e-r-a-s-e . . . What letter do we need?* (r) Point to where the letter *r* has been written for number 1.

## PRACTICE

- Ss work in pairs to complete the words.

- When Ss are finished, call on different pairs to write their completed words on the board. Review the alphabet by asking Ss who write answers on the board to say the letters aloud. Have Ss make any necessary corrections on the board.

### Expansion activity (small groups)

- Before class. Type out the words *dictionary*, *notebook*, *pencil*, *pen*, and *eraser*, using large letters. Make five copies and cut them into strips so that each strip has one word on it. If you have a larger class, make copies in multiples of five.

- Put the sets of words into five envelopes. Arrange the words so that each envelope is missing one of the five words and has two of the same word.

- Distribute the envelopes to five small groups of Ss. Write the five words on the board and tell Ss: *You do not have all the classroom objects. You need one classroom object. What do you need?*

- Give each group time to look at the words in their envelopes and determine which word is missing. Say: *Talk to your classmates. Ask them what they need.* Write on the board: *What do you need?* and *Here you are.*

- Model the task. Have a volunteer ask you the question you wrote on the board. Tell that S's group, for example: *I need a notebook. Do you have two notebooks?* If the group has only one, ask the other groups: *Do you have two notebooks?* Have the group with two notebooks give you one and say: *Here you are.*

- Have Ss talk to the other groups to get the word they need. Walk around and help as needed.

## PRACTICE

- Direct Ss' attention to the picture in Exercise 1B.

- Read the instructions for Exercise 1B aloud.

- Ss work in pairs to write the words for the classroom objects in the picture.

- Check answers with the class. Write the numbers *1–5* on the board and ask for volunteers to write their answers on the board. Point to and say each answer and ask the class: *Is this correct?* Make any necessary corrections on the board.

### Teaching Tip

Encourage Ss who did not write on the board in Exercise 1A to do the writing for Exercise 1B.

## COMPREHENSION CHECK

- Ask Ss to take out a piece of paper. Tell Ss: *Write the words.* Show the class real examples of the classroom objects on page 26. For example, hold up a pen and say: *Write the word.*

- Collect the papers to check Ss' writing or have Ss compare their writing in pairs.

### Literary Tip

For an alternative activity, refer literacy Ss to pages 26–27 in the *Literacy Workbook* at any time during the lesson.

# LESSON E Writing

## PRESENTATION

- Ask Ss' to turn to page 24 in the Student's Book. Direct their attention to the picture of Sue in Exercise 1. Remind Ss of the note from Sue's mother about things Sue needs for school. Ask questions such as: *Who is this?* (Sue.) *What is Sue reading?* Point to the note. *What is this?* (A note.) *What does Sue need for school?* (A pencil, a notebook, a dictionary, and an eraser.)

- Direct Ss' attention to Exercise 2A on page 27 and read the instructions aloud. Explain that *memo* is another word for *note*. Say *memo* aloud and ask Ss to repeat.

- Give Ss time to read the memo silently. Then read each line of the memo aloud and ask Ss to repeat. Answer any questions Ss have about the memo.

### Teaching Tip

To help Ss understand the meaning of *first*, write the numbers *1–3* on the board and read them aloud. Ask: *What number is first?* Elicit or point to *1*. Say: *Number one is first*. If you have a calendar, point to the date the class was first held and tell Ss, for example: *The first day of school*.

## PRACTICE

- Direct Ss' attention to Exercise 2B and read the instructions aloud.

- Read aloud the first prompt: *The first day of school is . . .* Ask: *What day?* Remind Ss by pointing to the day school started. If Ss still don't understand, tell them, for example: *The first day of school was Tuesday. Tuesday.*

- Ss complete the sentences individually. Walk around and help as needed.

## COMPREHENSION CHECK

- Direct Ss' attention to Exercise 3 and read the instructions aloud.

- Model the task. Show your memo to a S and say the sentences in Exercise 2B, using your own information. Ask that S to read and show you his or her sentences.

- Ss share their sentences in pairs. Walk around and spot-check Ss' writing.

## Expansion activity *(individual groups)*

- Ask Ss to write their completed sentences on a piece of paper and hand them in.

### Literacy Tip

If any of the writing exercises are too difficult for your literacy Ss, provide alternative tasks for them to work on at their desks or in self-access centers in the classroom. Appropriate tasks include copying or tracing letters, using letter cards to form words, or matching pairs of vocabulary flashcards.

### Community building

- If you have any extra school supplies, for example, pencils, pens, or paper, offer them to Ss. Say, for example: *Do you need a pencil?*

- Ask Ss if they need anything else for the class. If someone needs a notebook, for example, or an eraser, ask if anyone in the class has two of those things. Don't put any pressure on Ss to give away their school supplies, but if they want to help each other in this way, encourage them to do so.

## EVALUATION

- Direct Ss' attention to the first part of the lesson focus on the board. Read the phrase aloud and ask Ss to repeat. Show Ss real examples of classroom objects and call on individual Ss to write the corresponding words on the board.

- Direct Ss' attention to the second part of the lesson focus on the board. Read it aloud and ask Ss to repeat. Write sentence prompts on the board similar to the ones in Exercise 2B. Call on individual Ss to complete the sentences on the board.

- Check off each part of the lesson focus as Ss demonstrate an understanding of what they have learned in the lesson.

| More Ventures, Unit 2, Lesson E | |
|---|---|
| Literacy Workbook, 15–30 min. | |
| Basic Workbook, 15–30 min. | |
| Writing Worksheets, 15–30 min. | www.cambridge.org/ventures/ resources/ |
| Collaborative Worksheets, 30–45 min. | |

## 2 Write

**A  Read the memo.**

### Welcome to Miami Adult School!

The first day of school is Monday.

Your teacher is Ms. Moreno.

Your class is in Room 101.

For class, you need:

a dictionary

a notebook

a pencil

a pen

an eraser

**B  Complete the memo.** Write about yourself.

The first day of school is *Answers will vary*.

My teacher is _____.

My class is in Room _____.

For class, I need _____.

I need _____.

I need _____.

I need _____.

I need _____.

## 3 After you write

**Talk with a partner.** Share your writing.

# Lesson F Another view

## 1 Life-skills reading

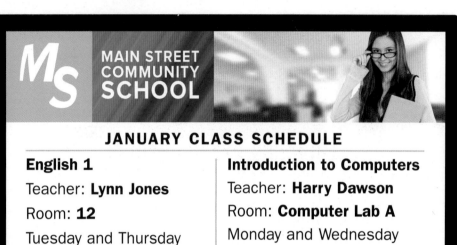

**MAIN STREET COMMUNITY SCHOOL**

### JANUARY CLASS SCHEDULE

**English 1**
Teacher: **Lynn Jones**
Room: **12**
Tuesday and Thursday
10:00 a.m.–12:00 noon

**Introduction to Computers**
Teacher: **Harry Dawson**
Room: **Computer Lab A**
Monday and Wednesday
1:00 p.m.–3:00 p.m.

**A  Read the sentences.** Look at the class schedule. Fill in the answer.

1. The English class is on _____.

   (A) Monday and Wednesday

   **(B)** Tuesday and Thursday

   (C) Tuesday and Wednesday

2. The computer class is on _____.

   **(A)** Monday and Wednesday

   (B) Tuesday and Thursday

   (C) Monday and Tuesday

3. The English class is in _____.

   (A) Room 1

   **(B)** Room 12

   (C) Lab A

4. The computer class is in _____.

   **(A)** Lab A

   (B) Lab B

   (C) Room 1

**B  Solve the problem.** Which solution is best? Circle your opinion.

Marcos needs English. Main Street Community School has English classes on Tuesday and Thursday. Marcos works on Tuesday and Thursday. What should he do?

1. Take the computer class.

2. Look for another English class on Mondays and Wednesdays.

3. Other: *Answers will vary.*

Teaching objectives
● Introduce reading a class schedule
● Provide practice that develops test-taking skills
● Review vocabulary from the unit

# WARM-UP AND REVIEW

● Before class. Write today's lesson focus on the board.
*Lesson F:*
*Read a class schedule*

● Before class. Write on the board:
*What class?*
*What teacher?*
*What room?*
*What days?*
*What time?*

● Begin class. Books closed. Review the days of the week by drawing seven long blanks on the board. Ask: *What day is today?* Write the day in the appropriate blank. Point to the next blank and ask Ss: *What day?* Elicit and write the remaining days of the week. Practice saying the days in order chorally.

# PRESENTATION

● Books open. Direct Ss' attention to the class schedule in Exercise 1. Tell Ss: *This is a class schedule.* Point to the words *Class Schedule.* Ask Ss to repeat after you.

● Tell Ss: *A class schedule tells us about classes at a school.* Ask: *What is the name of the school?* Point to and say: *Main Street Community School.* Ask Ss to repeat after you.

● Point to the schedule and ask: *What classes do you see? What classes?* (English 1 and Introduction to Computers.) Write the class titles on the board as the headings for two columns to the right of the questions on the board.

● To help Ss preview the class schedule, point to the questions on the board. Read each question aloud and elicit the answers. Write on the board in two columns the information about the two classes. Alternatively, ask a S volunteer to write the answers that other Ss say aloud.

# PRACTICE

● Read aloud the instructions for Exercise 1A. This task helps prepare Ss for standardized-type tests they may have to take.

● Write the first item on the board along with the three answer choices labeled *A*, *B*, and *C*.

● Read the item and the answer choices aloud and then point to the first class schedule in the exercise. Ask: *Is English class on Monday and Wednesday, Tuesday and Thursday, or Tuesday and Wednesday?* Continue to gesture toward the schedule to show Ss where to look for the information. Elicit: *Tuesday and Thursday.*

● Point to the three answer choices on the board. Ask Ss: *A, B, or C?* (B) Fill in the letter *B* and tell Ss: *Fill in the answer.* Make sure Ss understand the task.

● Have Ss individually scan for and fill in the answers.

# COMPREHENSION CHECK

● Go over the answers to Exercise 1A together. Make sure that Ss followed instructions and filled in their answers. As Ss give their answers, ask them to point to the information in the class schedule.

# APPLICATION

● Read the instructions for Exercise 1B aloud. Ask what they think Marcos should do. Accept all plausible answers.

● Have Ss talk to partners about what Marcos should do.

● Ss complete the task in pairs. Walk around and help as needed.

● When Ss are finished, ask them to find new partners to talk to about what Marcos should do.

## *Expansion activity* (small group)

● Before class. Bring in a large sheet of poster paper and markers for each group of Ss. Tell Ss: *Please make a class schedule for this class.*

● Walk around and help as needed. Make sure Ss include the class title at the top of the schedule as well as the teacher, the room, the days, and the time.

● When Ss are finished, have them tape their posters to the classroom walls and read the posters aloud for the rest of the class.

### Literacy Tip

For an alternative activity, refer literacy Ss to pages 28–29 in the *Literacy Workbook* at any time during the lesson.

# LESSON F Another view

## PRESENTATION

- Books closed. Write on the board three classroom objects or pieces of classroom furniture that you have in your classroom and one that you don't. For example, if you have all of these except a computer in your classroom, write:
  *a desk*
  *a stapler*
  *a computer*
  *a dictionary*
- Read aloud each item in the list and ask Ss to repeat. After each item, gesture around the classroom and ask Ss: *Do we have a _____?* Elicit short answers: *yes* or *no.* Check off each item that you have. In the example above, you would not check off *a computer.*

## PRACTICE

- Books open. Direct Ss' attention to Exercise 2A and read the instructions aloud.
- Model the task. Read aloud the first item, *a book.* Look around the classroom and ask Ss: *Do we have a book?* If the answer is *yes*, indicate that Ss should check the box next to *a book.*
- Ss complete the task in pairs.
- Follow up by asking different pairs about the items in the exercise. For every item Ss checked, ask them to show the rest of the class that item.

### Literacy Tip

The exercises on this page might be a challenge for literacy Ss, but if they work with a higher-level partner in Exercise 2A and if there is no pressure on them to finish Exercise 2B, they should be able to participate.

### Expansion activity *(whole group)*

- Using the words in the list in Exercise 2A, play a picture-drawing game with the class.
- Model the activity. Look at the words in the list. Then begin to draw the object on the board. As you draw, say to the class: *What classroom object? What is it?* Encourage Ss to guess what you are drawing.
- When a S guesses correctly, invite him or her to the board to draw a different classroom object.

## PRACTICE

- Direct Ss' attention to the word puzzle in Exercise 2B. Ask the class: *What is this? What do you see?* Ss may say that they see letters.

- Read aloud the instructions for Exercise 2B. Point to and say the first word in the word box: *book.* Point to the puzzle and ask Ss: *Do you see "book" here?* Ss should point to the circled example.
- Ss work individually or in pairs to find the words. When most of the Ss have finished, ask Ss if there are words they can't find in the puzzle. Have other Ss in the class show them where the words are.

## EVALUATION

- Do a quick review of the unit. Have Ss turn to Lesson A. Ask the class to talk about what they remember about this lesson. Prompt Ss, if necessary, with questions, for example: *What words are on this page? What do you see in the picture?* Continue in this manner to review each lesson quickly.

### Expansion activity

- Before class. Print, for each student, one copy of the Self-assessment for this unit.
- Have Ss complete the Self-assessment either in class or outside of class.
- Provide feedback to Ss such as through a whole-class discussion, partners comparing their worksheets, or T reviewing each S's worksheet.
- If Ss are ready, administer the unit test on page T-157 of this Teacher's Edition. The audio script for the test is available on page T-192.

| More Ventures, Unit 2, Lesson F | |
| --- | --- |
| **Literacy Workbook,** 15–30 min. | |
| **Basic Workbook,** 15–30 min. | |
| **Writing Worksheets,** 15–30 min. | |
| **Real-life Document,** 15–30 min. | www.cambridge.org/ ventures/resources/ |
| **Collaborative Worksheets,** 30–45 min. | |
| **Self-assessment,** 10 min. | |
| **CASAS Test Prep Worksheet,** 5–10 min. | |

## 2 Fun with vocabulary

**A** **Talk with a partner.** What's in your classroom? Check (✓). *Answers will vary.*

☐ a book  ☐ a chair  ☐ a computer

☐ a desk  ☐ a dictionary  ☐ an eraser

☐ a notebook  ☐ paper  ☐ a pen

☐ a pencil  ☐ a ruler  ☐ a stapler

**B** **Circle the words in the puzzle.**

| book | chair | computer | desk | dictionary | eraser |
|---|---|---|---|---|---|
| notebook | paper | pen | pencil | ruler | stapler |

```
h  s  h  f  e  b  o  o  k  t  z  a
q  u  p  e  n  c  i  l  a  f  r  s
l  i  g  o  w  n  e  r  a  s  e  r
v  y  b  d  e  s  k  a  f  l  k  o
d  i  c  t  i  o  n  a  r  y  o  j
f  e  t  h  s  t  a  p  l  e  r  e
w  r  n  n  o  t  e  b  o  o  k  r
p  e  n  k  v  l  z  o  j  s  y  n
o  t  c  o  m  p  u  t  e  r  m  q
t  r  u  l  e  r  g  a  r  x  z  a
h  o  m  t  c  z  e  c  h  a  i  r
p  a  p  e  r  n  y  i  d  e  m  t
```

# REVIEW

## 1 Listening

**Read.** Then listen and circle.

🔊 CD1, Track 24

1. What's his first name?
   a. Ali
   **b. Hassan**

2. What's his last name?
   **a. Ali**
   b. Garcia

3. Where is he from?
   a. Mexico
   **b. Somalia**

4. When is his birthday?
   **a. in August**
   b. in October

5. Where's the notebook?
   **a. on the desk**
   b. on the chair

6. Where's the paper?
   **a. in the notebook**
   b. on the chair

**Talk with a partner.** Ask and answer.

## 2 Vocabulary

**Write.** Complete the story.

> book   Brazil   card   February   name   Tuesday

# Welcome, Luisa Pinto!

Luisa is a new student. She is from ____Brazil____. Her
                                         1

last ___name___ is Pinto. Her birthday is in ___February___.
        2                                           3

In fact, her birthday is on ___Tuesday___. Happy birthday!
                                  4

Luisa needs a ___book___ and an ID ___card___.
                   5                      6

Welcome, Luisa!

Teaching objectives
- Review vocabulary from Units 1 and 2
- Introduce the pronunciation of *a* as in *name* and *o* as in *phone*

# WARM-UP AND REVIEW

- Before class. Write today's lesson focus on the board.
  *Review unit:*
  *Review vocabulary and grammar from Units 1 and 2*
  *Pronounce "a" as in "name" and "o" as in "phone"*

- Begin class. Books closed. Direct Ss' attention to the first two items in the lesson focus on the board. Help Ss understand the idea of review by showing them pages from Units 1 and 2.

- Review vocabulary from Units 1 and 2. Ask individual Ss, for example:
  *What's your first name? What's his first name?*
  *What's your last name? What's her last name?*
  *Where are you from? (What country?) Where are they from?*
  *When is your birthday? (What month?)*
  *Where's the computer? Where's my notebook?*

# PRACTICE

- Books open. Direct Ss' attention to Exercise 1 and read the instructions aloud. Read the question and answer choices in number 1 aloud.

- ▶ **CD1, Track 24** Model the task. Play or read only the first conversation from the audio (see audio script, page T-145). Point to the two answer choices in number 1 and ask: *Maria or Hassan?* (Hassan.) Point to where the letter *b* has been circled.

- Read aloud the remaining questions and answer choices. Say: *Now, listen and circle the correct answers.*

- ▶ **CD1, Track 24** Play or read the complete audio. Ss listen and circle the correct answers. Repeat the audio as needed.

- Check answers with the class. Read each question aloud and call on different Ss to answer.

### Teaching Tip

You may need to play the audio several times to give Ss a chance to extract the information they need. Then, to check comprehension and to help Ss who may be struggling, play the audio again and ask Ss to repeat the parts of the conversation that contain the answers to the questions.

- Read aloud the second part of the instructions for Exercise 1. Ss practice asking and answering the questions in pairs. Walk around and help as needed.

- Ask volunteers to ask and answer the questions for the rest of the class.

### Expansion activity *(small groups)*

- Divide the class into an even number of small groups and have each group create an oral quiz using questions similar to the ones in Exercise 1.

- Ask each group to choose a secretary to write down six questions about the people and classroom objects in their group. Unlike the questions in Exercise 1, these questions can be about different Ss. For example, one group might ask *What's her first name?* about one S and *What's his last name?* about another. Ss should also ask about the location of classroom objects, for example: *Where's the dictionary?*

- Ask half of the groups to join another group for the quiz. After the questions are asked and answered, have the groups switch roles.

# PRACTICE

- Direct Ss' attention to Exercise 2. Write the word *title* on the board. Say it aloud and ask Ss to repeat it after you. Point to the title of the story and ask: *What is the title of this story?* (Welcome, Luisa Pinto!) Read the title aloud for them.

- Have Ss read the story silently to get the main idea. When Ss are finished reading, ask: *Who is the story about?* (Luisa Pinto, a new student.)

- Read the instructions for Exercise 2 aloud. Read aloud the first and second sentences and ask Ss to repeat after you. Point to *Brazil* in the word bank so that Ss know where to find the answers.

- Ss read the story and fill in the blanks individually. Walk around and help as needed.

- Write the numbers *1–6* on the board. Ask volunteers to come to the board and write the answers.

- Read the story aloud using Ss' answers. If there is an error, say to Ss: *This is not correct. What is the correct answer?* Make any necessary corrections on the board.

### Expansion activity *(student pairs)*

- Tell Ss: *Today, you are a new student. Welcome!* Ask Ss to ask their partners questions so they can write a story about their partner like the one in Exercise 2. Brainstorm the questions they can ask and write them on the board. *(Where are you from? When's your birthday? What do you need?)* Tell Ss to write their stories about their partners in their notebooks.

# REVIEW

## WARM-UP AND REVIEW

- Write on the board: *in*, *on*, *under*.
- Point to the words. Place a classroom object *in* something in the room and ask Ss, for example: *Where's the ruler?* (In the desk, etc.) Place the object *on* something and ask Ss the same question. Elicit: *on the floor*, *on the chair*, *under the desk*, etc.
- Write on the board: *his*, *her*, *my*, *your*.
- Point to the words *his / her / my / your*. Ask Ss about their classmates' names. Gesture toward appropriate people in the class and ask their names.

## PRACTICE

- If students have difficulty with the grammar, you may want to show the animated grammar presentation for Unit 1 before or after they do Exercise **3A** and for Unit 2 before or after they do Exercise **3B**.
- Direct Ss to Exercise **3A**. Read the instructions aloud.
- Point to the picture in Exercise **3A** and ask Ss: *Where's the pen?* (Under the notebook.)
- Model the task. Read the beginning of the sentence in number 1: *The pen is . . . in*, *on*, *or under*? Point to where *under* has been written for number 1 and read aloud the complete sentence.
- Ss write their answers individually. Check answers by calling on Ss to read the sentences aloud. As Ss read the sentences, point to either *in*, *on*, or *under* on the board to make the answer clear.
- Direct Ss to Exercise **3B**. Read aloud the instructions.
- Point to Alberto in the picture in Exercise **3B** and ask: *What's his name?* (Alberto.)
- Read the sentence in number 1 without the first word: \_\_\_\_\_ *name is Alberto.* Point to the answer choices and ask Ss: *His or Her?* Point to where *His* has been circled and written for number 1. Read the complete sentence aloud.
- Ss write their answers individually. Check answers by calling on Ss to read the sentences aloud. As Ss read the sentences, point to the appropriate possessive adjective written on the board to help make the answer clear.

## PRESENTATION

- Direct Ss' attention to the second part of the lesson focus on the board.
- Write on the board: *name*, *day*, *say*. Point to and say each word and ask Ss to repeat.
- Underline the *a* in each of the words. Say a long *a* (/ei/) sound before repeating each word, for example: /ei/, *name*. Ask Ss to repeat after you.

- Write on the board: *phone*, *code*, *note*. Repeat the procedure, underlining the *o* in the words and pronouncing a long *o* (/ou/) sound.

## PRACTICE

- ▶ **CD1, Track 25** Direct Ss' attention to Exercise **4A** and read the instructions aloud. Play or read the audio (see audio script, page T-145). Ss listen to examples of the two vowel sounds.
- ▶ **CD1, Track 26** Direct Ss' attention to Exercise **4B** and read the instructions aloud. Play or read the audio (see audio script, page T-145). Ss listen and repeat what they hear.
- Read aloud the second part of the instructions for Exercise **4B**. Model the task. Point to the two charts and tell one S: *Say a word.* After that S says any word in the charts, tell his or her partner: *Point to the word.*
- Ss complete the task in pairs. Walk around and help as needed.
- ▶ **CD1, Track 27** Direct Ss' attention to Exercise **4C** and read the instructions aloud. Model the task. Play or read the first word from the audio (see audio script, page T-145). Ask: *Which letter is it? "a" or "o"?* Point to where the letter has been checked.
- ▶ **CD1, Track 27** Play or read the complete audio. Ss listen and make a checkmark under the letter they hear.
- ▶ **CD1, Track 27** Reproduce the chart from Exercise **4C** on the board and play or read the audio again. Pause after each word and ask a S to check the appropriate letter in the chart on the board.

### *Community building* (whole group)

- To help Ss be more comfortable when talking about local places, make a list of names of well-known places and streets in your community that contain the long *a* and *o* sounds. Conduct a class discussion of those places and practice pronouncing the names (e.g., *Blain's Market. Who shops at Blain's Market? Raise your hands. Good. Now, repeat:* /ei/, *Blain's*).

## EVALUATION

- Direct Ss' attention to the lesson focus on the board.
- Ask individual Ss questions similar to the ones in Exercise **1**. Be sure to use different possessive adjectives and the prepositions *in*, *on*, and *under* in your questions.
- Write on the board: *name*, *phone*. Call on individual Ss as you point to one of the words and ask the S to say it. Listen to pronunciation and correct as needed.
- Check off each part of the lesson focus as Ss demonstrate an understanding of what they have learned in the lesson.

## 3 Grammar

**A** **Complete the sentences.**

Use *in*, *on*, or *under*.

1. The pen is _____under_____ the notebook.

2. The dictionary is _____on_____ the desk.

3. The book is _____on_____ the chair.

4. The stapler is _____in_____ the desk.

**B** **Read and circle.** Then write.

1. _____His_____ name is Alberto.
   (His) Her

2. _____Her_____ name is Layla.
   His (Her)

3. A  What is _____your_____ name?
   his (your)

   B _____My_____ name is Kim.
   (My) Your

## 4 Pronunciation

**A** **Listen** to the *a* sound and the *o* sound.

    **a**        **o**
n**a**me   ph**o**ne

CD1, Track 25

**B** **Listen and repeat.**

| a | name | day | say |
|---|------|-----|-----|

| o | phone | code | note |
|---|-------|------|------|

CD1, Track 26

**Talk with a partner.** Say a word. Your partner points. Take turns.

**C** **Listen and check (✓).**

|    | a | o |    | a | o |    | a | o |    | a | o |    | a | o |
|----|---|---|----|---|---|----|---|---|----|---|---|----|---|---|
| 1. | ✓ |   | 2. |   | ✓ | 3. | ✓ |   | 4. |   | ✓ | 5. | ✓ |   |

CD1, Track 27

## Lesson A Listening

### 1 Before you listen

**A** Look at the picture. What do you see?

**B** Listen and point: ■ daughter ■ father ■ grandfather ■ grandmother ■ mother ■ son

◀)) CD1, Track 28

# UNIT 3

## Teaching objectives
- Introduce Ss to the topic
- Find out what Ss know about the topic
- Preview the unit by talking about the picture
- Provide practice of key vocabulary
- Provide practice that develops listening skills

## WARM-UP AND REVIEW

- Before class. Write today's lesson focus on the board.
  *Lesson A:*
  *Family*

- Begin class. Books closed. Review the months of the year from Unit 2. Write the word *January* on the board and 11 long blanks after it for the other months. Point to and say the word. Ask Ss to repeat after you.

- Point to the first blank and ask Ss: *What month is next?* (February.) Continue in this manner until all the months of the year are on the board. Practice saying the months with the class.

- Ask several different Ss: *When's your birthday?* As Ss answer, check their birth months on the board.

## PRESENTATION

- Books open. Set the scene. Hold up the Student's Book. Show Ss the picture on page 32. Tell Ss: *This is a birthday party. Happy birthday!*

- Direct Ss' attention to the lesson focus on the board. Say the word *family* and ask Ss to repeat after you. Show the class the people in the picture and say: *They are a family. Family.*

- Ask Ss about the picture: *What do you see?* Elicit and write on the board any vocabulary that Ss know, such as: *sofa, table, children, cake.*

## PRACTICE

- Direct Ss' attention to the key vocabulary in Exercise **1B**. Read aloud each word or phrase while pointing to the corresponding part of the picture. Ask Ss to repeat and point.

- ▶ **CD1, Track 28** Play or read the audio (see audio script, page T-145). Tell Ss: *Listen and point to the picture.* As Ss hear the key vocabulary, check to see that Ss are pointing to the correct part of the picture. Repeat the audio as needed.

## COMPREHENSION CHECK

- Ask Ss *Yes / No* questions about the picture. Tell Ss: *Listen. Say "yes" or "no."*
  Point to the picture. Ask: *Is this a family?* (Yes.)
  Point to the picture. Ask: *Is this a birthday party?* (Yes.)
  Point to the father. Ask: *Is he a mother?* (No.)
  Point to the mother. Ask: *Is she a mother?* (Yes.)
  Point to the daughter. Ask: *Is she a daughter?* (Yes.)
  Point to the son. Ask: *Is he a daughter?* (No.)
  Point to the son. Ask: *Is he a father?* (No.)
  Point to the grandmother. Ask: *Is she a grandmother?* (Yes.)
  Point to the grandfather. Ask: *Is he a grandmother?* (No.)

- Ask Ss questions about the names of people in the picture. For example, point to Gloria. Ask: *What's her name?* (Gloria.)

### *Expansion activity* (whole group)

- Teach vocabulary for birthdays and celebrations. Write on the board: *cake, candles, balloons, presents / gifts.* Point to and say each word aloud and ask Ss to repeat it. For each word, point to the corresponding parts of the picture or draw a simple picture of each item on the board.

- Provide Ss with "sticky notes," preferably cut in half to make narrow strips. Have Ss write the new vocabulary on the notes and then label the festive items in the picture on page 32 of the Student's Book.

# LESSON A Listening

## PRESENTATION

- Direct Ss' attention to Exercise 2A. Tell Ss: *These are words for people in a family.*
- Point to the family members in the picture on page 32 or in the family tree you drew on the board as you read each word aloud. Ask Ss to repeat the words after you.
- Read aloud the instructions for Exercise 2A.

## PRACTICE

- **CD1, Track 29** Play or read the audio (see audio script, page T-145). Listen and repeat the vocabulary along with Ss. Repeat the audio as needed.
- Listen carefully to Ss' pronunciation and make corrections as needed.

### Learner persistence (individual work)
- **CD1, Track 29** Ss can listen to the audio for Exercise 2A at home for reinforcement and review. They can also listen to the audio for self-directed learning when class attendance is not possible.

### Expansion activity (whole group)
- Books closed. Write the six key vocabulary words on the board in any order: *daughter, father, grandfather, grandmother, mother, son.*
- Ask for a volunteer to come to the board. Say each vocabulary word randomly and have the volunteer point to the word you say. Repeat the procedure with other Ss.

> **Literacy Tip**
>
> For an alternative activity, refer literacy Ss to pages 30–31 in the *Literacy Workbook* at any time during the lesson.

## PRACTICE

- Direct Ss' attention to Exercise 2B and read the instructions aloud.
- **CD1, Track 30** Model the task. Hold up the Student's Book and say: *Number one.* Play or read the audio for number 1 (see audio script, page T-146). Point to the two answer choices in number 1 and ask Ss: *What did you hear – a or b?* Elicit: *a.* Point to the letter *a* next to the first picture and tell Ss: *Circle the letter "a."*
- **CD1, Track 30** Play or read the complete audio. Ss listen and circle the correct answers. Repeat the audio as needed.

- **CD1, Track 30** Read aloud the second part of the instructions for Exercise 2B. Play or read the audio again so Ss can listen and check their answers.

### Learner persistence (individual work)
- **CD1, Track 30** Ss can listen to the audio for Exercise 2B at home for reinforcement and review. They can also listen to the audio for self-directed learning when class attendance is not possible.

## COMPREHENSION CHECK

- Write the numbers *1–4* on the board. Ask a few Ss to come to the board and write the correct answers to Exercise 2B next to each number.
- **CD1, Track 30** Play or read the audio again. Pause the audio after each conversation. Point to the answer on the board and ask: *Is this correct?* Ask another S to make any necessary corrections.

## APPLICATION

- Direct Ss' attention to Exercise 3 and read the instructions aloud.
- Model the task. Hold up the Student's Book and point to the pictures in Exercise 2B. Say to one S: *Point to a picture.* Say to the first S's partner: *Say the word.*
- Ss complete the exercise in pairs. Walk around and help as needed.

## EVALUATION

- Direct Ss' attention to the lesson focus on the board. Check Ss' understanding of the key vocabulary by asking them to point to the family members in the picture on page 32 or in the family tree on the board. Check to see that Ss are pointing to the correct items.
- Check off the lesson focus as Ss demonstrate an understanding of what they have learned in the lesson.

| More Ventures, Unit 3, Lesson A | |
|---|---|
| Literacy Workbook, 15–30 min. | |
| Basic Workbook, 15–30 min. | |
| Writing Worksheets, 15–30 min. | www.cambridge.org/ventures/resources/ |
| Collaborative Worksheets, 30–45 min. | |
| Student Arcade, time varies | www.cambridge.org/venturesarcade/ |

UNIT GOALS
**Identify** family members **Describe** a family picture
**Interpret** a housing application

## 2 Listen

### A Listen and repeat.

1. daughter
2. father
3. grandfather
4. grandmother
5. mother
6. son

🔊 CD1, Track 29

### B Listen and circle.

🔊 CD1, Track 30

1. (a.)    b.

2. a.    (b.)

3. a.    (b.)

4. a.    (b.)

**Listen again.** Check your answers.

## 3 After you listen

**Talk with a partner.** Point to a picture and ask.
Your partner says the words.

Who's that?

The grandmother.

📖 Listen for and identify family members   UNIT 3   **33**

# Lesson B Family members

## 1 Vocabulary focus

**Listen and repeat.**

◀)) CD1, Track 31

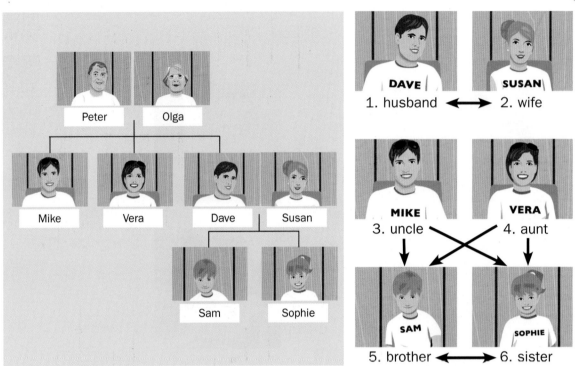

Peter  Olga

Mike  Vera  Dave  Susan

Sam  Sophie

DAVE  SUSAN
1. husband ⟷ 2. wife

MIKE  VERA
3. uncle  4. aunt

SAM  SOPHIE
5. brother ⟷ 6. sister

## 2 Practice

**A  Read and match.**

1. SUSAN

2. SOPHIE

3. MIKE

Sophie's uncle

Dave's wife

Sam's sister

Sophie's brother

Sam's aunt

Susan's husband

4. DAVE

5. SAM

6. VERA

Teaching objectives
• Introduce additional vocabulary for family relationships
• Provide practice asking and answering questions about family relationships

# WARM-UP AND REVIEW

• Before class. Write today's lesson focus on the board.
*Lesson B:*
*Family members*
*Who is Susan? Dave's wife.*

• Before class. Write the key vocabulary from Lesson A on the board: *daughter, father, grandfather, grandmother, mother, son.*

• Begin class. Books open. Ask volunteers to identify the family members in the picture on page 32. Tell Ss, for example: *Point to the grandmother.*

• Draw on the board a simple, unlabeled family tree that illustrates all the vocabulary words. Make sure that the people are clearly male or female. Ask for volunteers to come to the board and write, for example, the word *grandmother* next to the appropriate picture.

# PRESENTATION

• Point to the words *Family members* at the top of page 34 in the Student's Book. Say the words aloud. Tell the class: *Family members are people in a family.*

• Point to the key vocabulary on the board and tell Ss: *These people are family members. Today, you will learn more words for family members.*

• Direct Ss' attention to the family tree in Exercise 1. Ask: *Who are these people? Are they a family?* (Yes.)

• Go over the family members' names. Point to the man at the top of the family tree and say, for example: *His name is Peter. Peter. What's his name?* (Peter.)

# PRACTICE

• Read aloud the instructions for Exercise 1. Point to the vocabulary words under the smaller pictures in the exercise.

▶ **CD1, Track 31** Play or read the audio (see audio script, page T-146). Listen and repeat the vocabulary along with Ss. Repeat the audio as needed.

• Listen carefully to Ss' pronunciation and correct as needed.

### Expansion activity *(student pairs)*

• Before class. Create a table with two columns and four rows. In the top left cell, draw a simplified male figure. In the top right cell, draw a simplified female figure. To distinguish male from female, you might put trousers on the male and a skirt on the female. Make enough copies of this table for each pair of Ss.

• Make another copy of the table, and in the remaining cells, type or write the six vocabulary words from Exercise 1, using large letters.

• Make a copy of this table for each pair of Ss. Cut out the cells as "vocabulary cards."

• Give each pair of Ss a copy of the original document to use as a table along with a set of the words. Ask Ss to arrange the words in the appropriate columns, identifying the family members as male or female.

**Option** When Ss are finished, give them a new set of cards based on the key vocabulary from Lesson A and ask them to arrange those words according to gender.

# PRACTICE

• Direct Ss' attention to Exercise 2A. As you read aloud the instructions, hold up the Student's Book and indicate that Ss should read the words and then draw a line between the pictures and the corresponding words.

• Model the task. Hold up the Student's Book. Point to the first picture. Ask: *Who is this?* (Dave's wife.) Say: *Match the pictures with the words.*

• Ss complete the exercise individually. Help as needed.

# COMPREHENSION CHECK

• Write the numbers *1–6* on the board. Ask a few Ss to come to the board and write the answers to Exercise 2A on the board.

• Ask different Ss to read the answers on the board. After each answer is read, ask: *Is this correct?* If not, ask a student volunteer to make corrections on the board.

### Teaching Tip

Since this is the first time the 's possessive form is used, you may want to clarify its meaning using the already familiar *my* possessive adjective. For example, you could show the class your notebook (*My notebook is on my desk.*), then a S's notebook (*Linda's notebook is on her desk.*), and write both sentences on the board for Ss to read and repeat. You could also compare your own family relationships (*My wife is Julieta.*) with the family in these exercises (*Dave's wife is Susan.*).

### Literacy Tip

For an alternative activity, refer literacy Ss to pages 32–33 in the *Literacy Workbook* at any time during the lesson.

# LESSON B Family members

## PRESENTATION

- Direct Ss' attention to the picture in Exercise 2B. Tell the class: *This is a family picnic.* Write on the board and say the word *picnic.* Ask Ss to repeat after you.

- Point to the picture and ask: *Who do you see? Who is at the picnic?* Elicit and write on the board the names of the family members in the picture.

- Direct Ss' attention to the word bank. Read the words aloud and ask Ss to repeat after you.

## PRACTICE

- Read aloud the first part of the instructions for Exercise 2B.

- ▶ *CD1, Track 32* Model the task. Say: *Listen and repeat.* Play or read the audio for number 1 (see audio script, page T-146) and point to Vera in the picture as you repeat. Say: *Then write.* Point to the word *aunt* written in the chart. Make sure Ss understand the task.

- ▶ *CD1, Track 32* Play or read the complete audio. Ss listen and repeat. Encourage Ss to point to the people in the picture as they repeat.

- Ss complete the chart individually. Repeat the audio as needed.

- Check answers with the class. Write the numbers *1–6* on the board and ask for volunteers to write their answers on the board. Point to each answer and ask the class: *Yes? Is this correct?* Make corrections on the board.

- Read aloud the second part of the instructions for Exercise 2B. Point to and model the example conversation.

- Call on a pair of volunteers to read the example conversation aloud for the class.

- Point to another person in the picture on page 35. Ask a S: *Who is (name)?* Elicit the answer. Repeat with different people in the picture. Indicate that Ss should ask and answer questions about all the people.

- Ss complete the exercise in pairs. Walk around and help as needed.

## APPLICATION

- Direct Ss' attention to Exercise 3 and read the instructions aloud.

- Point to and read aloud the chart headings and the information written in the chart. Read the example question and answer aloud and ask Ss to repeat after you. Point to where Habib and his brother have been written in the chart as examples.

- Model the task. Duplicate the chart on the board and talk to the class as you complete it for your own family, for example: *Name: John. Family member: father.*

- Choose a S to act as your partner. Point to the example question in his or her book and say: *Please ask me this question.* Point to your chart and say: *Ask me about my family.* When the S asks, *Who is John?*, say: *My father.*

- Ss complete the chart individually and then ask and answer questions about their charts in pairs.

### Community building *(individual work)*

- Have Ss make their own family trees. Model the task by showing Ss your own family tree drawn on a large piece of poster paper. Talk about your family relationships using unit vocabulary, for example: *This is Rita. She is my aunt. She is also my mother's sister.*

- Give each S a large piece of poster paper and markers to draw their own family trees. When Ss are finished, help them tape their family trees to the classroom walls. Ask volunteers to talk to the class about their families.

### Teaching Tip

When making your own family tree, include only living family members in order to avoid the use of the past tense. When Ss are making their family trees, be aware that some Ss may have lost family members in ways they don't want to talk about in class or they may have family situations that differ from the family shown in the unit. Encourage Ss to reveal only as much personal information as they are comfortable with. Some Ss may even prefer to draw the family tree of a fictional family.

## EVALUATION

- Direct Ss' attention to the lesson focus on the board and to the large picture in Exercise 1 on page 34. Ask Ss questions about the family relationships between people in the picture, for example: *Who is Olga's husband?* (Peter.) *Who is Sam's mother?* (Susan.)

- Call on Ss to ask their classmates questions similar to the ones in Exercise 2B on page 35, for example: *Who is Olga?* (Sophie's grandmother, Peter's wife.)

- Check off each part of the lesson focus as Ss demonstrate an understanding of what they have learned in the lesson.

### More Ventures, Unit 3, Lesson B

| | |
|---|---|
| Literacy Workbook, 15–30 min. | |
| Basic Workbook, 15–30 min. | |
| Writing Worksheets, 15–30 min. | www.cambridge.org/venture/ resources/ |
| Collaborative Worksheets, 30–45 min. | |
| Student Arcade, time varies | www.cambridge.org/venturesarcade/ |

**B** **Listen and repeat.** Then write.

| aunt | brother | husband | sister | uncle | wife |

◁)) CD1, Track 32

| Who is . . . ? | | Who is . . . ? | |
|---|---|---|---|
| 1. Vera | Sam's ____aunt____ | 4. Susan | Dave's ____wife____ |
| 2. Mike | Sam's ____uncle____ | 5. Sam | Sophie's ____brother____ |
| 3. Sophie | Sam's ____sister____ | 6. Dave | Susan's ____husband____ |

**Talk with a partner.** Ask and answer.

  **A** Who is **Vera**?

  **B** **Sam's aunt.**

## 3 Communicate

**Complete the chart about your family.** Then talk with a partner.

| Name | Family member |
|---|---|
| Habib | brother |
| Answers will vary. | |
| | |
| | |

  **A** Who is **Habib**?

  **B** My **brother**.

## 1 Grammar focus: *Do you have . . . ?*

| QUESTIONS | ANSWERS | | | | | |
|---|---|---|---|---|---|---|
| Do you have a sister? | Yes, | I / we | do. | No, | I / we | don't. |

don't = do not

Watch

## 2 Practice

A **Read and circle.** Then write.

1. A Do you have a brother?
   B ___Yes, I do.___
   ( Yes, I do. ) No, I don't.

2. A Do you have a sister?
   B ___No, we don't.___
   Yes, we do. ( No, we don't. )

3. A Do you have a son?
   B ___Yes, I do.___
   ( Yes, I do. ) No, I don't.

4. A Do you have a daughter?
   B ___Yes, we do.___
   ( Yes, we do. ) No, we don't.

5. A Do you have a wife?
   B ___No, I don't.___
   Yes, I do. ( No, I don't. )

**Listen and repeat.** Then practice with a partner.

CD1, Track 33

- Introduce *Yes / No* questions with *have*
- Introduce short answers: *Yes, I do. / No, I don't.*
- Provide practice asking and answering questions about family relationships

## WARM-UP AND REVIEW

- Before class. Write today's lesson focus on the board:
  *Lesson C:*
  *Do you have a _____?*
  *Yes, I do. / No, I don't.*
- Before class. Write all the vocabulary for family members on the board: *a grandmother, a grandfather, a mother, a father, an aunt, an uncle, a husband, a wife, a sister, a brother, a son, a daughter.*
- Begin class. Books closed. Point to and say each vocabulary word on the board and ask Ss to repeat.
- Books open. Direct Ss' attention to the large picture in Exercise 1 on page 34. Ask Ss questions about the family, for example: *This is a family. Does the family have a grandmother?* (Yes.) *Who is the grandmother? What's her name?* (Olga.) *Does Olga have a daughter?* (Yes.) *Who is Olga's daughter?* (Vera.) *Does Vera have a brother?* (Yes. Two brothers.)
- Continue in this manner, asking questions to help Ss recall the vocabulary.

### Teaching Tip

This warm-up activity gives Ss the opportunity to retrieve the meaning of previously learned vocabulary without putting pressure on them to do much speaking.

## PRESENTATION

- Use the animated grammar presentation in one or more of the following ways:
  - Preview it before class
  - Show it in class
  - Encourage Ss to watch it outside of class.
- Direct Ss' attention to the grammar chart in Exercise 1 on page 36. Read each question and short answer aloud and ask Ss to repeat after you.
- Point to the small box above the grammar chart. Hold up one finger and tell Ss: *One word: "don't."* Hold up two fingers and say: *Two words: "do not."* They are the same.
- Draw three simple faces on the board and label them: *Mike, Vera, Dave.*
- Tell the class: *Let's talk to Mike.* Look at the picture of Mike on the board and ask: *Mike, do you have a sister?* Draw a speech bubble coming from Mike's mouth and indicate that Ss should say Mike's answer. Elicit and write in the speech bubble: *Yes, I do.*
- Erase Mike's speech bubble. Tell the class: *Let's talk to Mike and Dave.* Look at the pictures and ask the question from the grammar chart: *Mike and Dave, do you have a sister?* Draw speech bubbles coming from both men. Elicit and write in the bubbles: *Yes, we do.*

- Erase the speech bubbles and repeat the whole procedure verbally to convey to Ss that the word *you* can be singular or plural and to practice the short answers.

### Expansion activity *(whole group)*

- Write on the board:
  *Yes, I do. I have one sister / two sisters / three sisters.*
  *No, I don't.*
- Point to and say the answer choices and have Ss repeat. Then ask several different Ss: *Do you have a sister?* When Ss answer, *Yes, I do*, ask them: *What's her name?* or *What are their names?* Write the names of your Ss' sisters on the board. Ask Ss how to spell the names.
- Repeat the procedure with the question: *Do you have a brother?*

## PRACTICE

- Direct Ss' attention to the first picture in Exercise 2A. Read aloud the example conversation using different voices for Speaker A and Speaker B. When you read Speaker B's line, show Ss the two choices under the blank and ask: *Yes, I do* or *No, I don't?* Elicit: *Yes, I do.*
- Read aloud the instructions for Exercise 2A. Point to where *Yes, I do* has been circled and written for number 1.
- Ss complete the exercise individually. Walk around and help as needed.

### Literacy Tip

Literacy Ss will need to work with higher-level Ss to complete Exercise 2A, pointing to or saying the answers after the higher-level S reads the question and answer choices aloud. For an alternative activity, refer literacy Ss to pages 34–35 in the *Literacy Workbook* at any time during the lesson.

## COMPREHENSION CHECK

- Read aloud the second part of the instructions for Exercise 2A.
- ▶ **CD1, Track 33** Play or read the audio (see audio script, page T-146). Ss listen and repeat as they check their answers.
- Write the numbers *1–5* on the board. Ask volunteers to come to the board and write the answers they circled. Make any necessary corrections on the board.
- Ss in pairs. Ask Ss to choose Role A or B and practice the questions and answers in Exercise 2A. Then have Ss switch roles and practice again. Walk around and help as needed.
- Ask several pairs to say the questions and answers for the rest of the class.

# LESSON C Do you have a sister?

## PRESENTATION

- Direct Ss' attention to the pictures in Exercise 2B. Point to and read aloud the labels for the pictures. Write the names of the woman's family members on the board and ask Ss to repeat after you.
- Write the following matching task on the board:

  Ken            grandmother
  Rose           son
  Diana          sister
  Danny          husband

- Ask Ss about each person; for example: *Who is Ken?* Ss should be able to guess from the illustration who the people are. Elicit: *The woman's husband* or *Her husband* or *Ana's husband*. Draw lines on the board to show the family relationships or ask volunteers to come to the board and draw the lines.

## PRACTICE

- Read aloud the first part of the instructions for Exercise 2B.
- ▶ **CD1, Track 34** Model the task. Say: *Listen and repeat.* Play or read the audio for number 1 (see audio script, page T-146) and point to the woman's sister Diana as you repeat. Say: *Then write.* Point to the word *yes* written in the chart. Make sure Ss understand the task.
- ▶ **CD1, Track 34** Play or read the complete audio. Ss listen and repeat. Encourage Ss to point to the people in the pictures as they repeat.
- Ss complete the chart individually. Repeat the audio as needed.
- Check answers with the class. Write the numbers *1–6* on the board and ask for volunteers to write their answers on the board. Point to each answer and ask the class: *Yes? Is this correct?* Make any necessary corrections on the board.
- Read aloud the second part of the instructions for Exercise 2B. Point to and model the example conversation.
- Call on a pair of volunteers to read the example conversation aloud for the class. Then ask the same two Ss to model a different conversation about the family in the pictures on page 37 using, for example, *brother* or *son*.
- Indicate that Ss should ask and answer questions about all the family members in the chart. Make sure Ss understand the task.
- Ss complete the exercise in pairs. Walk around and help as needed.

## APPLICATION

- Direct Ss' attention to Exercise 3 and read the instructions aloud. Point to and read aloud the questions in the first column of the chart and ask Ss to repeat after you.
- Point to the name *Dinh* in the top of the chart and say the name aloud. Tell Ss: *"Dinh" is a first name.* Draw a stick figure on the board and label it *Dinh*.
- Say to the class: *Let's ask Dinh the questions.* Look at "Dinh" and ask: *Do you have a son?* Point to the check marks in the first column. Draw a speech bubble coming from Dinh's mouth. Elicit and write in the bubble: *No, I don't.*
- Tell Ss: *Write two classmates' names. Ask your classmates the questions.* Make sure Ss understand the task.
- Ss stand up, walk around, and talk with two classmates. Ss could also complete the exercise in groups of four. Walk around and help as needed.

### *Expansion activity* (individual work)

- Write on the board:
  *I have a sister. / You have a sister.*
  *He has a sister. / She has a sister.*
- Read the sentences aloud and ask Ss to repeat after you. Explain that *have* changes to *has* in sentences with *he* and *she*.
- Ask volunteers to report to the rest of the class information from the charts they completed in Exercise 3.
- Model the task. Say to one S, for example: *Tell me about Rafael.* Write on the board: *Rafael has a _____.* Elicit sentences such as: *Rafael has a son. Rafael has a sister.*
- Have each S give information about a classmate.

## EVALUATION

- Direct Ss' attention to the lesson focus on the board. Ask Ss questions about their own families, for example: *Do you have a brother? Do you have a wife?* Elicit short answers: *Yes, I do. / No, I don't.*
- Call on Ss to ask you questions about your family using *Do you have a _____?*
- Check off the lesson focus as Ss demonstrate an understanding of what they have learned in the lesson.

| More Ventures, Unit 3, Lesson C | |
| --- | --- |
| Literacy Workbook, 15–30 min. | |
| Basic Workbook, 15–30 min. | |
| Writing Worksheets, 15–30 min. <br> Collaborative Worksheets, 30–45 min. | www.cambridge.org/ventures/ resources/ |
| Student Arcade, time varies | www.cambridge.org/venturesarcade/ |

**B** **Listen and repeat.** Then write.

CD1, Track 34

| Do you have a . . . ? | |
|---|---|
| 1. sister | yes |
| 2. brother | no |
| 3. husband | yes |

| Do you have a . . . ? | |
|---|---|
| 4. son | yes |
| 5. daughter | no |
| 6. grandmother | yes |

**Talk with a partner.** You are Ana. Ask and answer.

A   Do you have **a sister**?

B   **Yes, I do.**

A   What's **her** name?

B   **Diana.**

A   Do you have a **brother**?

B   **No, I don't.**

## 3 Communicate

**Talk with your classmates.** Complete the chart.

| Do you have a . . . ? | Dinh | | | | | |
|---|---|---|---|---|---|---|
| | Yes | No | Yes | No | Yes | No |
| son | | ✓ | Answers will vary. | | | |
| daughter | ✓ | | | | | |
| sister | ✓ | | | | | |
| brother | ✓ | | | | | |

# Lesson D Reading

## 1 Before you read

**Talk about the picture.** What do you see?

## 2 Read

**Listen and read.**

www.myfamilypage.com

CD1, Track 35

### My Family

My name is Gloria. This is my family. This is my mother. Her name is Natalia. It is her birthday. This is my father. His name is Enrico. This is my husband, Luis. This is our daughter, Lisa. This is our son, Tony. I love my family!

## 3 After you read

**Read and circle.** Then write.

1. Luis is Gloria's _____ husband _____ .
   father (husband)

2. Natalia is Gloria's _____ mother _____ .
   daughter (mother)

3. Tony is Gloria's _____ son _____ .
   brother (son)

4. Enrico is Gloria's _____ father _____ .
   (father) mother

5. Lisa is Gloria's _____ daughter _____ .
   sister (daughter)

- Introduce a paragraph about a family
- Introduce vocabulary for talking about people
- Provide practice using new topic-related words

## WARM-UP AND REVIEW

- Before class. Write today's lesson focus on the board.
  *Lesson D:*
  *Read "My Family"*
  *Words for people*
- Begin class. Books open. Direct Ss' attention to the family picture in Exercise 2. Ask the class: *Who are these people?* Ss should recognize the family from the picture on page 32.
- Ask Ss to turn to page 32. Review the key vocabulary by pointing to and asking about each family member in the picture. For example, point to the grandmother and ask: *Who is she?* (The grandmother.) Point to the younger man and ask: *Who is he?* (The father.) Continue in this manner.

### Expansion activity *(whole group)*

- If Ss have a good grasp of the family names they have learned so far, teach them the words *granddaughter* and *grandson*. Write the words on the board, say them aloud, and ask Ss to repeat them. Point to the picture on page 32 and ask: *Who is the granddaughter? Who is the grandson?* Ss may be able to guess that the words refer to the young girl and boy in the picture.

## PRESENTATION

- Direct Ss' attention to the picture in Exercise 2 on page 38 and read the instructions aloud. Ask Ss: *What do you see?* Ss should recognize the family from the picture on page 32. Elicit and write on the board any vocabulary about the picture that Ss know, such as: *family, grandmother, son, daughter.*

## PRACTICE

- Direct Ss' attention to Exercise 2. Point to the title of the paragraph and ask: *What is the title?* (My Family.) or *What is the reading about?* (Gloria's family.)
- **CD1, Track 35** Play or read the audio and ask Ss to follow along (see audio script, page T-146). Repeat the audio as needed.
- Read aloud each sentence of the reading and ask Ss to repeat after you.
- Point to the family picture in Exercise 2 and ask the class: *Who is Gloria?* (Ss should indicate the mother of the children in the picture.)
- Answer any questions Ss have about the reading.

### Learner persistence *(individual work)*

- **CD1, Track 35** Ss can listen to the audio for Exercise 2 at home for reinforcement and review. They can also listen to the audio for self-directed learning when class attendance is not possible.

### Expansion activity *(whole group)*

- Ask Ss to turn to page 32. Read the paragraph on page 38 aloud and ask Ss to point to each person as they hear their name.
- Walk around and check to see that Ss are pointing to the correct person. Continue until all the people in the picture have been identified by name.

### Literacy Tip

Literacy Ss should be able to talk about the picture and listen to and repeat the lines of the reading passage. They may also be able to assist in Exercise 3 by saying or pointing to the answers while a higher-level S writes the words.

## COMPREHENSION CHECK

- Read aloud the instructions in Exercise 3.
- Model the task. Point to and read aloud the first item. Then point to the answer choices and ask Ss: *Father or husband?* Elicit: *husband.* Point to where *husband* has been circled and written for number 1.
- Ss circle and write their answers individually. Walk around and help as needed.
- Go over answers with the class. Write the sentence prompts from Exercise 3 on the board with blanks after them. Call on Ss to write their answers on the board.
- Point to and read aloud each completed sentence on the board and ask the class: *Is this correct?* Ask volunteers to read aloud or point to that part of the reading. Ask, for example: *Where is the answer in the reading?*

### Literacy Tip

For an alternative activity, refer literacy Ss to pages 36–37 in the *Literacy Workbook* at any time during the lesson.

# LESSON D Reading

## PRESENTATION

- Direct Ss' attention to the Picture dictionary in Exercise 4. Point to and say the word *People*. Tell Ss: *Today, we will learn more words to talk about people.*
- Read aloud the instructions for Exercise 4A.
- ▶ **CD1, Track 36** Play or read the audio (see audio script, page T-146). Listen to Ss' pronunciation as they repeat the words. Correct pronunciation as needed.

### Expansion activity *(student pairs)*

- Copy and cut out one set of the Unit 3 Picture dictionary cards from the *Online Teacher's Resource Room* for each S.
- Have Ss play "Match the Pictures" in pairs. Ss hold their picture cards like playing cards. S1 places a card face up on the desk or table and says the corresponding word. S2 finds the same picture card in his or her set and places it next to the matching card.
- Ss take turns putting down a card and finding the matching card.

> **Teaching Tip**
>
> Ask Ss to write the vocabulary words on the backs of their picture cards and take them home to use as flash cards.

### Learner persistence *(individual work)*

- ▶ **CD1, Track 36** Ss can listen to the audio for Exercise 4A at home for reinforcement and review. They can also listen to the audio for self-directed learning when class attendance is not possible.

## PRACTICE

- Direct Ss to Exercise 4B and read the instructions aloud. Ask two Ss to read the example conversation aloud.
- Model the task. Hold out your Student's Book and say to a S: *Show me the baby.* As the S points to the picture of the baby, he or she says: *Here's the baby.* Reverse the procedure so that the S asks you to show him or her one of the pictures.
- Ss complete the activity in pairs. Walk around and help as needed.

### Expansion activity *(whole group)*

- Make four columns on the board with the headings *Girl, Boy, Man, Woman.*
- Have Ss turn back to the pictures of the families on pages 34 and 38 and decide which column to write each person's name in. For example, *Enrico*, the name of the grandfather from page 38, would be written under the heading *Man*.

## EVALUATION

- Direct Ss' attention to the lesson focus on the board. Ask Ss to turn back to the reading on page 38. Call on individual Ss to answer questions about Gloria's family; for example: *Who is Natalia?* (Gloria's mother.) *Does Gloria have a son?* (Yes, Tony.)
- Play "Name That Picture." Hold up a picture card and name it incorrectly. For example, hold up the picture card of the baby and say: *This is a man.* Ss correct the statement.
- Check off each part of the lesson focus as Ss demonstrate understanding of what they have learned in the lesson.

| More Ventures, Unit 3, Lesson D | |
|---|---|
| Literacy Workbook, 15–30 min. | |
| Basic Workbook, 15–30 min. | |
| Picture Dictionary activities, 30–45 min. Writing Worksheets, 15–30 min. Collaborative Worksheets, 30–45 min. | www.cambridge.org/ventures/ resources/ |
| Student Arcade, time varies | www.cambridge.org/venturesarcade/ |

## 4 **Picture dictionary** People

1. baby

2. girl

3. boy

4. teenager

5. woman

6. man

**A** **Listen and repeat.** Look at the picture dictionary.

**B** **Talk with a partner.** Say a word. Your partner points to the picture.

A  Show me the **man**.

B  Here's the **man**.

◀)) CD1, Track 36

# Lesson E Writing

## 1 Before you write

**A** **Talk with a partner.** Complete the words.

**Frank's Family**

Frank

1. **d** a u g h t e r

2. **w** i f e

3. **s** i s t e r

4. **b** a b y

5. **s** o n

6. **b** r o t h e r

**B** **Talk with a partner.** Look at the picture. Complete the story.

## My Wonderful Family

My name is Frank. This is my family. This is my _____wife_____,
                                                    1

Marie. This is our _____son_____. His name is Patrick. This is our
                      2

_____daughter_____. Her name is Annie. This is our new _____baby_____,
        3                                                    4

Jason. He is a boy. Patrick is his _____brother_____. Annie is his
                                        5

_____sister_____. I have a wonderful family!
      6

Teaching objectives
• Prepare Ss for completing sentences about their families
• Provide practice writing key vocabulary words

# WARM-UP AND REVIEW

• Before class. Write today's lesson focus on the board.
*Lesson E:*
*Write words for family members*
*Complete sentences about families*

• Before class. Write the following on the board:

*My mother's mother is my _____.*
*My mother's father is my _____.*
*My father's sister is my _____.*
*My father's brother is my _____.*
*My son's sister is my _____.*

• Begin class. Books open. Review vocabulary for family members by asking Ss to solve the "riddles" on the board. Elicit: *grandmother, grandfather, aunt, uncle, daughter.*

# PRESENTATION

• Direct Ss' attention to the picture in Exercise 1A. Point to the title above the picture and ask Ss: *Is this my family?* (No.) Tell Ss: *You're right. It's Frank's family.*

• Read the instructions for Exercise 1A aloud. Tell Ss: *These are words for Frank's family members.*

• Point to the first item and say: *Number 1. Blank a-u-g-h-t-e-r . . . What's the word?* (Daughter.) *What letter do we need?* (d) Point to where the letter *d* has been written for number 1.

# PRACTICE

• Ss work in pairs to complete the words.

• When Ss are finished, call on different pairs to write their completed words on the board. Review the alphabet by asking Ss who write answers on the board to say the letters aloud. Have Ss make any necessary corrections on the board.

### Literacy Tip

For an alternative activity, refer literacy Ss to pages 38–39 in the *Literacy Workbook* at any time during the lesson.

• Read the instructions for Exercise 1B aloud. Write the title of the story on the board and tell Ss that *wonderful* means "very good."

• Model the task. Begin to read the story aloud but stop when you get to the first blank. Ask Ss: *What word do we need?* (Wife.) Point to the word *wife* in the picture and then to where *wife* has been written as an example. Make sure Ss understand that they are to fill in the blanks with the words from the picture.

• Ss work in pairs to fill in the blanks in the story.

• Check answers as a class. Write the numbers *1–6* on the board and ask for volunteers to write their answers on the board. Point to and say each answer and ask the class: *Is this correct?* Make any necessary corrections on the board.

• Read aloud each line of the story and ask Ss to repeat after you. Answer any questions Ss have about the story.

## Expansion activity (student pairs)

• Have Ss read the completed story aloud to each other in pairs.

## Expansion activity (whole group)

• List on the board the names of Frank's family members: *Marie, Patrick, Annie, Jason.*

• Ask volunteers about each family member, for example: *Who is Marie?* (Frank's wife.)

• Make five columns on the board with the headings *Man, Woman, Boy, Girl, Baby.*

• Have Ss write the names of Frank's family members in the appropriate columns.

# LESSON E Writing

## PRESENTATION

- Ask Ss to turn back to the family pictures on pages 32, 34, 35, and 38. Tell Ss: *These are pictures of families.*

- Draw on the board a simple picture of your family, either posed for a family portrait or doing some activity they like to do. Talk to Ss about your family as you draw the picture.

- Direct Ss' attention to Exercise 2A on page 41 and read the instructions aloud. Reassure Ss that they do not need to be artists to draw a simple picture of their family.

- Give Ss time to draw their pictures. Walk around and ask friendly questions as Ss are drawing, for example: *Who is this?* or *Is this your daughter?*

## PRACTICE

- Direct Ss' attention to Exercise 2B and read the instructions aloud. Point to the title and ask: *What is the title?* or *What will you write about?* (My Wonderful Family.) Read the words in the word bank and ask Ss to repeat. Explain that they can choose the words they need to write about their families.

- Model the task. Direct Ss' attention to the picture you drew on the board. Read aloud the first few prompts in the exercise and write completed sentences on the board about your family. For example, write: *My name is Wendell. This is my family. This is my wife. Her name is Mira.*

- Ss complete the sentences individually. Walk around and help as needed.

> **Teaching Tip**
>
> You may want to walk around and check to see that Ss are completing the sentences with information about their own families, rather than copying the information you wrote about your family.

## COMPREHENSION CHECK

- Direct Ss' attention to Exercise 3 and read the instructions aloud.

- Model the task. Show your book (or paper) to a S and say the sentences in Exercise 2B using your own information. Ask the S to read and show you his or her sentences.

- Ss share their sentences in pairs. Walk around and spot-check Ss' writing.

## Expansion activity *(individual work)*

- Ask each S to write one of their *This is my . . . His / Her name is . . .* sentence pairs on the board. You may want to have several Ss writing at the same time.

- Then have the Ss come back to the board, point to and say their sentences, and hold up the picture they drew as they "introduce" a family member to the class.

## Learner persistence *(whole group)*

- Encourage Ss to attend class regularly and on time. If some Ss are frequently absent or late for class, talk to them and try to find out if there is a problem for which you can suggest a possible solution.

## EVALUATION

- Direct Ss' attention to the first part of the lesson focus on the board. Conduct a spelling test. Ask Ss to close their books and take out a piece of paper. Tell Ss: *Listen. Write the words.* Dictate some or all of the vocabulary from the unit. When you are finished, collect the papers or call on individual Ss to come to the board and write one of the words.

- Direct Ss' attention to the second part of the lesson focus on the board. Since Ss already wrote sentences on the board, simply ask: *Can you write sentences about families?* Point to the sentences Ss wrote on the board to help Ss understand the question. Elicit: *Yes!*

- Check off each part of the lesson focus as Ss demonstrate an understanding of what they have learned in the lesson.

| More Ventures, Unit 3, Lesson E | |
| --- | --- |
| Literacy Workbook, 15–30 min. | |
| Basic Workbook, 15–30 min. | |
| Writing Worksheets, 15–30 min. | www.cambridge.org/ventures/ resources/ |
| Collaborative Worksheets, 30–45 min. | |

## 2 Write

**A  Draw a picture of your family.**

Answers will vary.

**B  Write about your picture.**

daughter   father   husband   mother   son   wife

# My Wonderful Family

My name is ___Answers will vary___ . This is my family.

This is my _____ . _____ name is _____ .
His   Her

This is my _____ . _____ name is _____ .
His   Her

This is my _____ . _____ name is _____ .
His   Her

This is my _____ . _____ name is _____ .
His   Her

I love my family!

## 3 After you write

**Talk with a partner.** Share your writing.

# Lesson F Another view

## 1 Life-skills reading

**KB** **PROPERTY MANAGEMENT COMPANY**
*230 Central Street, Philadelphia, PA 19019 (215) 555-1863*

# HOUSING APPLICATION
### Directions: Complete the form. Please print.

What is your name? Ali Azari

Who will live with you in the house?

| NAME | RELATIONSHIP |
|---|---|
| Shohreh Azari | wife |
| Azam Javadi | mother |
| Omid Azari | son |
| Leila Azari | daughter |
| Soraya Azari | daughter |

**A** **Read the questions.** Look at the housing application. Fill in the answer.

1. Who is Shohreh Azari?
   - (A) Ali's daughter
   - **(B) Ali's wife**
   - (C) Ali's son

2. Who is Soraya Azari?
   - **(A) Ali's daughter**
   - (B) Ali's mother
   - (C) Ali's wife

3. Who is Azam Javadi?
   - **(A) Ali's mother**
   - (B) Ali's wife
   - (C) Ali's daughter

4. Who is Omid Azari?
   - (A) Ali's brother
   - (B) Ali's father
   - **(C) Ali's son**

**B** **Solve the problem.** Which solution is best? Circle your opinion.

Ali has a brother. He will live with Ali for two months. What should Ali do?

1. Write his name on the form.

2. Not write his name on the form.

3. Other: *Answers will vary.*

• Introduce reading a housing application
• Provide practice that develops test-taking skills
• Review vocabulary from the unit

## WARM-UP AND REVIEW

- Before class. Write today's lesson focus on the board.
  *Lesson F:*
  *Read a housing application*
- Before class: Write in random places on the board the vocabulary from the unit: *an aunt, a baby, a boy, a brother, a daughter, a father, a girl, a grandfather, a grandmother, a husband, a man, a mother, a sister, a son, a teenager, an uncle, a wife, a woman.*
- Begin class. Books closed. Review the vocabulary for people and family members by calling on individual Ss to come to the board. Say: *Listen and circle the word.* Call out a word randomly for Ss to locate on the board and circle. When you are finished, practice saying the words with the class.

### Teaching Tip

Ss may not be familiar with the difference between *a* and *an*. It might be helpful to point out that we say "an aunt" because *aunt* starts with a vowel.

## PRESENTATION

- Books open. Direct Ss' attention to the housing application in Exercise 1. Tell Ss: *This is a housing application.* Point to and say the words *Housing Application.*
- Tell Ss: *Sometimes you need to fill out a housing application when you want to rent a house or an apartment.*
- Write on the board: *rent.* Ask Ss: *What is rent?* Encourage Ss to respond to your question, and if they need help, tell them: *"Rent" means you pay money to live in a house or apartment.*

### Teaching Tip

You may need to spend some time explaining the difference between buying and renting a house or apartment in order to help Ss understand the purpose of a housing application.

- Point to the schedule and ask: *Who filled out this application? What's his name?* (Ali Azari.)
- Tell Ss: *Ali Azari has family members. How many family members does he have?* (Five.)

## PRACTICE

- Read the instructions for Exercise 1A aloud. This task helps prepare Ss for standardized-type tests they may have to take.
- Write the first item on the board along with the three answer choices labeled *A, B,* and *C.*
- Read aloud the item and the answer choices and then point to the housing application. Ask Ss: *Who is Shohreh Azari?* Continue to gesture toward the application to show Ss where to look for the information. Elicit: *wife.* Ask Ss: *Whose wife?* (Ali's wife.)
- Point to the three answer choices on the board. Ask Ss: *A, B,* or *C?* (B) Fill in the letter *b* and tell Ss: *Fill in the answer in your book.* Make sure Ss understand the task.
- Have Ss individually scan for and fill in the answers.

## COMPREHENSION CHECK

- Go over the answers to Exercise 1A together. Make sure that Ss followed the instructions and filled in their answers. Ask Ss to point to the information in the housing application.

## APPLICATION

- Read the instructions for Exercise 1B aloud.
- Have Ss discuss what Ali should do. Accept all plausible answers.
- Ss complete the task in pairs. When Ss are finished, ask them to find a new partner and discuss what Ali should do.

### *Expansion activity* (whole group)

- Practice saying the address on the housing application. Write each line of the address on the board. Read the words and numbers aloud and ask Ss to repeat after you. Demonstrate the two common ways of pronouncing *0* – as "zero" and as "oh."

### Literacy Tip

For an alternative activity, refer literacy Ss to pages 40–41 in the *Literacy Workbook* at any time during the lesson.

# LESSON F Another view

## PRESENTATION

- Make three columns on the board with the headings: *Male, Female, Male or female*. Over each heading, draw simplified male and female figures. For the third column, draw both figures with a slash between them.

- Read the column headings aloud and ask Ss to repeat the words after you.

- On a different part of the board, write the first three words from Exercise 2A: *an aunt, a baby, a boy*.

- Ask Ss about each word; for example: *An aunt. Is an aunt male or female?* (Female.) When you get to the word baby, ask: *Is a baby male or female?* Make sure Ss understand that there are male babies and female babies, so the answer is *Male or female*.

## PRACTICE

- Books open. Read aloud the instructions for Exercise 2A. Point to *an aunt* in the word choices and then point to where *an aunt* has been written in the chart as an example.

- Ss complete the chart individually.

- Read aloud the second part of the instructions for Exercise 2A. Ss compare their charts in pairs.

- Check answers with the class. Say each word from the word choices and call on a S to tell you which column he or she chose. Write the words in the columns you made on the board. If there are any errors, ask other Ss if they have a different answer.

> **Teaching Tip**
>
> It might be helpful to give Ss an approximate age range for the terms *boy, girl, man*, and *woman*. Explain that there is no exact definition for these terms, but for many people, boys and girls might range from 0–17 years old whereas men and women might be over 17.

- Direct Ss' attention to Exercise 2B and read the instructions aloud.

- Model the task. Ask a male S to come to the board and to bring his book. Ask the class, *Is (name of S) male or female?* (Male.) Point to the list of male family members in Exercise 2A and ask the S about each term; for example: *Are you a boy? Are you a brother?* Each time the S answers yes, write that term on the board.

- Reproduce the sentence with blanks from Exercise 2B on the board. Ask the same S to fill in the blanks with any of the terms for family members that you wrote on the board; for example: *I am a brother, a man*, and *an uncle*.

- If you think it would be helpful, repeat the modeling procedure with a female S.

- Have Ss fill in the blanks in Exercise 2B individually.

- Read aloud the second part of the instructions for Exercise 2B. Ss use their partner's information to complete the second sentence.

- Ask for several volunteers to tell the class about their partners.

### Expansion activity *(whole group)*

- Teach the words *parent, parents, child, children*. Write and say the words and ask Ss to repeat.

- After the word *parents*, draw an equal sign and the words *mother and father*. Explain that a parent can be either male or female.

- After the word *children*, draw an equal sign and the words *son and daughter*. Explain that a child can be either male or female.

- Give Ss the singular and plural forms of the words by writing on the board: *1 parent, 2 parents; 1 child, 2 children*. Give Ss simple example sentences using the singular and plural forms.

### Evaluation

- Do a quick review of the unit. Have Ss turn to Lesson A. Ask: *What words are on this page? What do you see in the picture?* Continue in this manner to review each lesson quickly.

### Expansion activity

- Before class. Print, for each student, one copy of the Self-assessment for this unit.

- Have Ss complete the Self-assessment either in class or outside of class.

- Provide feedback to Ss such as through a whole-class discussion, partners comparing their worksheets, or T reviewing each S's worksheet.

- If Ss are ready, administer the unit test on page T-160 of this Teacher's Edition. The audio script for the test is available on page T-192.

| *More Ventures, Unit 3, Lesson F* | |
|---|---|
| Literacy Workbook, 15–30 min. | |
| Basic Workbook, 15–30 min. | |
| Writing Worksheets, 15–30 min. | |
| Real-life Document, 15–30 min. | www.cambridge.org/ventures/ resources/ |
| Collaborative Worksheets, 30–45 min. | |
| Self-assessment, 10 min. | |
| CASAS Test Prep Worksheet, 5–10 min. | |

## 2 Fun with vocabulary

### A Complete the chart.

| an aunt | a baby | a boy | a brother | a daughter | a father | a girl |
| a grandfather | a grandmother | a husband | a man | a mother | a sister | a son |
| a teenager | an uncle | a wife | a woman | | | |

| Male | Female | Male or female |
|---|---|---|
| a boy | an aunt | a baby |
| a brother | a daughter | a teenager |
| a father | a girl | |
| a grandfather | a grandmother | |
| a husband | a mother | |
| a man | a sister | |
| a son | a wife | |
| an uncle | a woman | |

**Talk with a partner.** Compare your answers.

### B Write about yourself. Use the words from 2A.

I am _____ Answers will vary. _____, _____,

and _____ .

**Talk with a partner.** Write about your partner.

My partner _____ is _____,

_____ , and _____ .

# UNIT 4 HEALTH

## Lesson A Listening

### 1 Before you listen

A  Look at the picture. What do you see?

B  Listen and point: ■ doctor ■ doctor's office ■ medicine
   ■ nurse ■ patient

🔊 CD1, Track 37

Dr. Brown's Office

Mario

Tony

Tony

# UNIT 4

**Teaching objectives**
- Introduce Ss to the topic
- Find out what Ss know about the topic
- Preview the unit by talking about the picture
- Provide practice of key vocabulary
- Provide practice that develops listening skills

## WARM-UP AND REVIEW

- Before class. Write today's lesson focus on the board.
  *Lesson A:*
  *Health problems*

- Begin class. Books closed. Draw a large human stick figure on the board. Circle different parts of the body and ask Ss: *What is this?* Elicit any vocabulary for body parts that Ss already know, such as: *head, arm, hand, leg, foot.*

- Point to the words *health problems* on the board. Say the words and have Ss repeat after you. Tell Ss: *This unit is about health problems. Problems with the body.*

- Point to a part of the body on the board that your Ss know the word for, for example, *head.* Pretend you have a headache and ask Ss: *What's my health problem?* Elicit or provide: *headache.*

### Teaching Tip

Not all the Ss in your class will know vocabulary for parts of the body or health problems. This warm-up is meant to activate any prior knowledge of the subject that Ss have and to help you assess that knowledge.

### Literacy Tip

If you have literacy Ss in your class, it might be helpful to spend time at the beginning of any activity with art or photos talking about the pictures before focusing Ss' attention on the printed words in the exercise. Have Ss work in pairs. Tell them to ask each other: *What do you see?* Encourage Ss to describe the pictures to each other. Consider pairing literacy Ss with Ss who can help them read the text in the exercise. This will help preview the exercise for literacy Ss and make them more confident as the exercise continues.

## PRESENTATION

- Books open. Set the scene. Hold up the Student's Book. Show Ss the picture on page 44. Tell the class: *These people have health problems. They need a doctor.*

- Ask: *What do you see?* Elicit and write on the board any vocabulary that Ss know, such as: *chairs, desk, teenagers, man, woman, cap.*

### Teaching Tip

If possible, bring in real examples of medicine to show Ss the different forms it can take, for example, tablets, capsules, and liquids. For each example, tell Ss: *This is medicine.*

## PRACTICE

- Direct Ss' attention to the key vocabulary in Exercise **1B**. Read aloud each word or phrase while pointing to the corresponding part of the picture. Ask Ss to repeat and point.

- ▶ *CD1, Track 37* Play or read the audio (see audio script, page T-146). Tell Ss: *Listen and point to the picture.* As Ss hear the key vocabulary, check to see that Ss are pointing to the correct part of the picture. Repeat the audio as needed.

## COMPREHENSION CHECK

- Ask Ss *Yes / No* questions about the picture. Tell Ss: *Listen. Say "yes" or "no."*
  Point to the picture. Ask: *Is this a classroom?* (No.)
  Point to the picture. Ask: *Is this a doctor's office?* (Yes.)
  Point to the nurse. Ask: *Is she a patient?* (No.)
  Point to the doctor. Ask: *Is he a doctor?* (Yes.)
  Point to the woman with the stomachache. Ask: *Is she a patient?* (Yes.)
  Point to the boy with the tissue. Ask: *Is he a doctor?* (No.)
  Point to the medicine. Ask: *Is this medicine?* (Yes.)
  Point to the nurse. Ask: *Is she a nurse?* (Yes.)

### Teaching Tip

Direct Ss' attention to the two teenagers in the picture, Mario and Tony, since they appear again later in the unit. Practice saying the boys' names, ask Ss how old they think the boys are (teenagers in the 13–19-year-old age range), and ask Ss about the boys' clothing (baseball uniforms).

### Literacy Tip

For an alternative activity, refer literacy Ss to pages 42–43 in the *Literacy Workbook* at any time during the lesson.

# LESSON A Listening

## PRESENTATION

- Before class. Bring to class full-page clip-art images to illustrate each of the key vocabulary terms. Save the images to use later in other parts of the unit.
- Direct Ss' attention to Exercise 2A and read the instructions aloud. As you say each word or phrase, hold up the appropriate picture and ask Ss to repeat after you.

## PRACTICE

- ▶ **CD1, Track 38** Play or read the audio (see audio script, page T-146). Ss listen and repeat the vocabulary as you hold up the clip-art images. Repeat the audio as needed.
- Listen carefully to Ss' pronunciation and make corrections as needed.

### Learner persistence *(individual work)*

- ▶ **CD1, Track 38** Ss can listen to the audio for Exercise 2A at home for reinforcement and review. They can also listen to the audio for self-directed learning when class attendance is not possible.

> **Literacy Tip**
>
> Use the clip-art images you found to make smaller flash cards for your literacy Ss.

- Direct Ss' attention to Exercise 2B and read the instructions aloud.
- ▶ **CD1, Track 39** Model the task. Hold up the Student's Book and say: *Number one.* Play or read the audio for number 1 (see audio script, page T-146). Point to the two answer choices in number 1 and ask Ss: *What did you hear – a or b?* Elicit: *b.* Point to the letter *b* next to the second picture and tell Ss: *Circle the letter "b."*
- ▶ **CD1, Track 39** Play or read the complete audio. Ss listen and circle the correct answers. Repeat the audio as needed.
- ▶ **CD1, Track 39** Read aloud the second part of the instructions for Exercise 2B. Play or read the audio again so Ss can listen and check their answers.

### Learner persistence *(individual work)*

- ▶ **CD1, Track 39** Ss can listen to the audio for Exercise 2B at home for reinforcement and review. They can also listen to the audio for self-directed learning when class attendance is not possible.

## COMPREHENSION CHECK

- Write the numbers *1–4* on the board. Ask a few Ss to come to the board and write the correct answers to Exercise 2B next to each number.

- ▶ **CD1, Track 39** Play or read the audio again. Pause the audio after each conversation. Point to the answer on the board and ask: *Is this correct?* Ask another S to make any necessary corrections.

> **Teaching Tip**
>
> Use the same spatial arrangement as the textbook when replicating exercises on the board. This makes the process of checking answers less demanding for Ss and allows them to concentrate on the language.

## APPLICATION

- Direct Ss' attention to Exercise 3 and read the instructions aloud.
- Model the task. Hold up the Student's Book and point to the pictures in Exercise 2B. Say to one S: *Point to a picture.* Say to the first S's partner: *Say the word.*
- Ss complete the exercise in pairs. Walk around and help as needed.

### Expansion activity *(student pairs)*

- Have Ss practice the conversations from Exercise 2B in pairs. Ask Ss to turn to the audio script on page 146 in the Student's Book.
- Ask Ss to choose Role A or B and read aloud the conversations. Then have Ss switch roles and read the conversations again. Walk around and help as needed.

## EVALUATION

- Direct Ss' attention to the lesson focus on the board. Arrange the large clip-art images that you used in Exercise 2A on the board or on a table so Ss can see all of them. Say the key vocabulary in random order and call on individual Ss to select the corresponding image and hold it up for everyone to see. Have Ss replace the image each time so that every S can choose from all five.
- Check off the lesson focus as Ss demonstrate an understanding of what they have learned in the lesson.

| *More Ventures, Unit 4, Lesson A* | |
|---|---|
| **Literacy Workbook,** 15–30 min. **Basic Workbook,** 15–30 min. | |
| **Writing Worksheets,** 15–30 min. **Collaborative Worksheets,** 30–45 min. | www.cambridge.org/ventures/ resources/ |
| **Student Arcade,** time varies | www.cambridge.org/venturesarcade/ |

UNIT GOALS
**Identify** health problems   **Interpret** a medicine label
**Identify** reasons for a visit to a doctor

## 2 Listen

### A  Listen and repeat.

1. doctor     2. doctor's office     3. medicine     4. nurse     5. patient

 CD1, Track 38

### B  Listen and circle.

 CD1, Track 39

1. a.      (b.)

2. (a.)      b.

3. (a.)      b.

4. (a.)      b.

**Listen again.** Check your answers.

## 3 After you listen

**Talk with a partner.** Point to a picture.
Your partner says the word.

# Lesson B Parts of the body

## 1 Vocabulary focus

**Listen and repeat.**

CD1, Track 40

1. head

6. arm

2. hand

5. stomach

3. leg

4. foot

## 2 Practice

**A Read and match.**

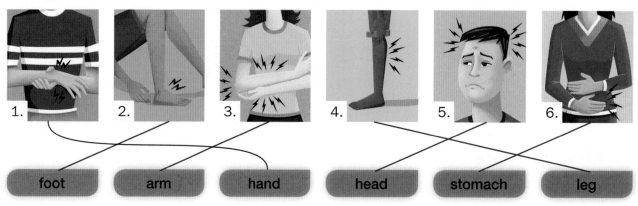

1.
2.
3.
4.
5.
6.

foot   arm   hand   head   stomach   leg

**Teaching objectives**
- Introduce vocabulary for parts of the body
- Provide practice asking and answering questions about health problems

## WARM-UP AND REVIEW

- Before class. Write today's lesson focus on the board.
  *Lesson B:*
  *Parts of the body*
  *What's the matter?*
- Before class. Write the key vocabulary from Lesson A on the board: *doctor, doctor's office, medicine, nurse, patient.*
- Begin class. Books open. Point to and say each of the key vocabulary items from Lesson A and ask Ss to repeat after you.
- Have Ss identify the vocabulary in the picture on page 44. Tell Ss, for example: *Point to the doctor.*
- If you used large clip-art images in Lesson A, hold up the images in random order and have Ss say the corresponding words.

## PRESENTATION

- Point to the words *Parts of the body* at the top of page 46. Say the words aloud and ask Ss to repeat after you. Draw a stick figure on the board and then draw a circle around the whole figure. Tell Ss: *This is the body.* Draw smaller circles around a few body parts, for example, the head, an arm, and a foot. Tell Ss: *These are parts of the body.*
- Direct Ss' attention to the picture in Exercise 1. Tell Ss: *Today, you will learn words for parts of the body.*

## PRACTICE

- Read aloud the instructions for Exercise 1.
- ▷ *CD1, Track 40* Play or read the audio (see audio script, page T-146). Listen and repeat the vocabulary along with Ss. Repeat the audio as needed.
- Listen carefully to Ss' pronunciation and correct as needed.
- Direct Ss' attention to Exercise 2A. As you read aloud the instructions, hold up the Student's Book and indicate that Ss should look at the pictures of body parts and match them to the corresponding words.
- Model the activity. Hold up the Student's Book. Point to the first picture. Ask: *What body part is this?* (Hand.) Say: *Match the picture with the word.*
- Ss complete the exercise individually. Help as needed.

## COMPREHENSION CHECK

- Write the numbers *1–6* on the board. Ask a few Ss to come to the board and write the answers to Exercise 2A on the board.
- Ask different Ss to read the answers on the board. After each answer is read, ask: *Is this correct?* If not, ask a student volunteer to make any necessary corrections on the board.

### *Expansion activity* (individual work)

- Help Ss review the unit vocabulary by preparing a worksheet that lists the new words from Lesson A and Lesson B with all the vowels left out and replaced with blanks; for example:

  d _ c t _ r
  p _ t _ n t
  s t _ m _ c h

  **Option 1** Allow Ss to use their Student's Books to help with spelling.

  **Option 2** Bring in a prize for the S who finishes in the shortest amount of time.
- When Ss are finished, ask volunteers to write the words on the board.

### *Community building*

- Many hospitals, clinics, and doctor's offices provide information in a number of languages. Call local health providers in your area and ask them to send you information such as their hours, their location, and the types of services they provide in English and in your Ss' native languages. You can also ask if they are able to provide translators for patients. Give Ss information about local health providers in English and, whenever possible, in Ss' own languages.

### *Learner persistence*

- Tell Ss what you would like them to do if they have a health problem and can't come to class. For example, give Ss your office phone number or email address and ask them to contact you or have them exchange phone numbers with a specific classmate. You can suggest that Ss use the audio to review what they have already studied and to keep up with any lessons that they miss.

### Literacy Tip

For an alternative activity, refer literacy Ss to pages 44–45 in the *Literacy Workbook* at any time during the lesson.

# LESSON B Parts of the body

## PRESENTATION

- Direct Ss' attention to the picture in Exercise **2B**. Tell the class: *These people have health problems.* Point to the second part of the lesson focus on the board and repeat the words *health problems.*
- Direct Ss' attention to the word bank. Read each word aloud and ask Ss to repeat after you. Then point to the appropriate person in the picture and say, for example: *Her arm hurts.*

### Teaching Tip

Help Ss understand the meaning of the word *hurts* by acting out each health problem in the picture as you go over the vocabulary for body parts. For example, rub your arm and make noises as if you are in pain when you say *Her arm hurts.*

## PRACTICE

- Read aloud the first part of the instructions for Exercise **2B**.
- ▶ **CD1, Track 41** Model the task. Say: *Listen and repeat.* Play or read the audio for number 1 (see audio script, page T-146) and point to the first woman in line in the picture as you repeat. Say: *Then write.* Point to the word *head* written as an example. Make sure Ss understand the task.
- ▶ **CD1, Track 41** Play or read the complete audio. Ss listen and repeat. Encourage Ss to point to the people in the picture as they repeat.
- Ss complete the exercise individually. Repeat the audio as needed. Encourage them to find the words they need in the word bank.
- Check answers with the class. Write the numbers *1–6* on the board. Point to each number and ask Ss: *What hurts?* Elicit, for example: *my head.* Write the words for parts of the body next to the numbers on the board. If Ss give an incorrect answer, ask the class if anyone has a different answer.
- Read aloud the second part of the instructions for Exercise **2B**. Model the exercise by pointing to the woman in the picture with the headache. Then read the conversation aloud using different voices for the two roles and acting as if your head hurts.
- Ask two Ss to read aloud the example conversation and act it out. Ask two different Ss to point to another person in the picture and have a new conversation as they act out his or her health problem.

### Teaching Tip

Write on the board: *What's the matter?* Tell Ss that they can ask this question when someone looks sad, sick, or hurt.

- Have pairs of Ss practice asking and answering questions about the people in the picture as they act out the problems. Walk around and help as needed.
- When Ss are finished, call on different pairs to perform the conversations for the rest of the class.

## APPLICATION

- Direct Ss' attention to Exercise **3** and read the instructions aloud. Read the example question and answer aloud and ask Ss to repeat after you.
- Model the task. Have a S ask you: *What's the matter?* Pretend you have one of the health problems and say, for example: *My stomach hurts.*
- Ss ask and answer questions with new partners. When they are finished, have Ss switch partners and repeat the exercise.

### *Expansion activity* (whole group)

- Practice using possessive pronouns and adjectives by talking about the people in the picture in Exercise **2B**.
- Write on the board:
  *What's the matter with (him / her)?*
  *(His / Her) _____ hurts.*
- Point to and ask Ss about each person in the picture, for example: *What's the matter with her?* Elicit: *Her head hurts.*

## EVALUATION

- Direct Ss' attention to the lesson focus on the board. Indicate parts of your own body and have Ss say the words for the body parts.
- Ask several different Ss: *What's the matter?* Have them pretend to have a sore body part as they did in Exercise **3**. Then have Ss ask their classmates the question.
- Check off each part of the lesson focus as Ss demonstrate an understanding of what they have learned in the lesson.

| More Ventures, Unit 4, Lesson B | |
| --- | --- |
| **Literacy Workbook**, 15–30 min. | |
| **Basic Workbook**, 15–30 min. | |
| **Writing Worksheets**, 15–30 min. **Collaborative Worksheets**, 30–45 min. | www.cambridge.org/ventures/resources/ |
| **Student Arcade**, time varies | www.cambridge.org/venturesarcade/ |

**B** **Listen and repeat.** Then write.

arm   foot   hand   head   leg   stomach

CD1, Track 41

What hurts?

1. My ____head____ .       4. My ____foot____ .
2. My ____hand____ .       5. My ____arm____ .
3. My ___stomach___ .      6. My ____leg____ .

**Talk with a partner.** Ask and answer.

A   What's the matter?

B   My **head** hurts.

My head hurts.

What's the matter?

**3**  **Communicate**

**Talk with a partner.**
Act it out. Ask and answer.

# Lesson C  My feet hurt.

## 1 Grammar focus: singular and plural

1 eye

1 hand

1 foot

2 eyes

2 hands

2 feet

Watch

## 2 Practice

**A  Read and circle.** Then write.

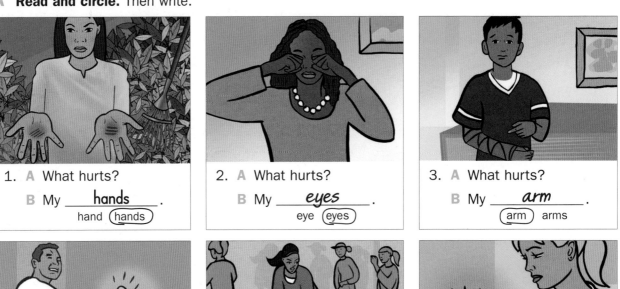

1. **A** What hurts?
   **B** My _____hands_____.
   hand (hands)

2. **A** What hurts?
   **B** My _____eyes_____.
   eye (eyes)

3. **A** What hurts?
   **B** My _____arm_____.
   (arm) arms

4. **A** What hurts?
   **B** My _____foot_____.
   (foot) feet

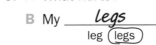

5. **A** What hurts?
   **B** My _____legs_____.
   leg (legs)

6. **A** What hurts?
   **B** My _____hand_____.
   (hand) hands

**Listen and repeat.** Then practice with a partner.

◀) CD1, Track 42

## Teaching objectives
- Introduce singular and plural nouns
- Provide practice asking and answering questions about health problems

## WARM-UP AND REVIEW

- Before class. Write today's lesson focus on the board.
  *Lesson C:*
  *Singular and plural*
  *What hurts?*
- Begin class. Books closed. Draw an outline of your hand on the board. Point to the drawing and ask Ss: *What is this?* Elicit and write on the board: *hand.*
- Draw another hand on the board and circle the two hands. Ask Ss: *What are these?* Elicit or provide the word *hands* and write it on the board. Point to and say the singular and plural forms and ask Ss to repeat after you. Circle the letter *s.*
- Repeat the procedure with *arm / arms, leg / legs,* and *foot / feet.* Direct Ss' attention to the first part of the lesson focus. Say and have Ss repeat: *one hand, two hands; one arm, two arms; one leg, two legs; one foot, two feet.*
- Books closed. Direct Ss' attention to the first part of the lesson focus on the board. Say the words aloud and ask Ss to repeat.

## PRESENTATION

- Use the animated grammar presentation in one or more of the following ways:
  - Preview it before class
  - Show it in class
  - Encourage Ss to watch it outside of class.
- Books closed. Direct Ss' attention to the words *singular* and *plural* in the lesson focus.
- Books open. Direct Ss' attention to the grammar chart in Exercise 1. Read each phrase aloud and ask Ss to repeat after you.

### Teaching Tip

Since the words *eye* and *eyes* may be new to Ss, be sure to practice pronouncing them with the class.

- Use your own body to help Ss practice the singular and plural forms. Hold up one hand and wiggle your fingers to elicit *one hand.* Close one eye to elicit that phrase; then open both eyes wide to elicit *two eyes.* Sit on your desk or table and wiggle one or both of your feet; then continue with your legs, arms, and so on.

### Teaching Tip

You may want to ask a S who is not easily embarrassed to stand next to you as you complete the review of vocabulary for body parts by gesturing to your two heads and your two stomachs.

### Expansion activity *(student pairs)*

- Expand on the presentation of singular and plural nouns and recycle vocabulary for school supplies and classroom objects by asking Ss to count items in the classroom.
- Photocopy and give each pair of Ss a list of items you want them to count, for example: *computer(s), chair(s), desk(s), map(s), eraser(s), ruler(s), stapler(s).* Be sure to include some singular items.
- Increase the difficulty of the task by listing items that are likely to be numerous or that require Ss to talk to their classmates, for example, *pencils* or *notebooks.*
- Have Ss walk around the room and write the quantities on their lists. When Ss are finished, call on Ss to report their numbers to the class. Ask volunteers who disagree on a number to demonstrate how they counted the items.

## PRACTICE

- Direct Ss' attention to the first picture in Exercise 2A. Ask two Ss to read the example conversation aloud.
- Read aloud the instructions for Exercise 2A. Point to where *hands* has been circled and written for number 1.
- Ss complete the exercise individually. Walk around and help as needed.

## COMPREHENSION CHECK

- Read aloud the second part of the instructions for Exercise 2A.
- ▶ *CD1, Track 42* Play or read the audio (see audio script, page T-146). Ss listen and repeat as they check their answers.
- Write the numbers *1–6* on the board. Ask volunteers to come to the board and write the words they circled. Make any necessary corrections on the board.
- Ss in pairs. Ask Ss to choose Role A or B and practice the questions and answers in Exercise 2A. Then have Ss switch roles and practice again. Walk around and help as needed.
- Ask several pairs to act out the situations and say the questions and answers for the rest of the class.

### Literacy Tip

For an alternative activity, refer literacy Ss to pages 46–47 in the *Literacy Workbook* at any time during the lesson.

# LESSON C My feet hurt.

## PRESENTATION

- Direct Ss' attention to the pictures in Exercise 2B. Point to each picture and ask the class: *What hurts?* Elicit the appropriate singular or plural form of each noun. When Ss say the words, ask: *Singular or plural?*

## PRACTICE

- Read aloud the first part of the instructions for Exercise 2B.
- ▶ **CD1, Track 43** Model the task. Say: *Listen and repeat.* Play or read the audio for number 1 (see audio script, pages T-146–T-147) and point to the man in the first picture as you repeat. Make sure Ss understand the task.
- ▶ **CD1, Track 43** Play or read the complete audio. Ss listen and repeat. Encourage Ss to point to the people in the pictures as they repeat.

> ### Teaching Tip
>
> Write on the board the phrase *Oh, I'm sorry.* Tell Ss that they can use the phrase when people tell them about a health problem. Demonstrate the use of the expression by telling Ss that various parts of your body hurt; for example: *My head hurts.* Point to the board and elicit from Ss: *Oh, I'm sorry.*

- Read aloud the second part of the instructions in Exercise 2B. Call on two Ss to read aloud the example conversation. Then, point to one of the pictures in the exercise and ask two Ss to model a new conversation using the appropriate body part.
- Indicate that Ss should ask and answer questions about all six pictures. Make sure Ss understand the task.
- Ss ask and answer questions about the pictures in pairs. When Ss are finished, ask them to switch partners and have new conversations.

### Expansion activity (student pairs)

- Ask pairs of Ss to practice the conversations in Exercise 2A on page 48 again, but this time, have them add the sympathetic expression: *Oh, I'm sorry.*

## APPLICATION

- Direct Ss' attention to Exercise 3 and read the instructions aloud. Read aloud the two column headings in the chart.
- Point to the name *Sasha* in the top line of the chart and tell Ss that it is a first name. Point to the word *head* in the chart and ask Ss: *What hurts?* (Sasha's head.)
- Call on two Ss to read aloud the example question and answer.
- Tell the class: *Write your classmates' names. Ask them the question. Write their answers.* Make sure Ss understand the task.
- Ss complete the exercise in small groups, or alternately Ss walk around and talk to at least five classmates.
- Walk around and help as needed. When Ss are finished, ask for volunteers to perform one of their conversations for the class.

  **Option** Ask the class about several of the Ss, for example: *Tell me about Lor. What's the matter with Lor?* Elicit, for example: *His stomach hurts.*

## EVALUATION

- Direct Ss' attention to the lesson focus on the board. Check Ss' understanding of singular and plural nouns by gesturing toward or wiggling parts of your own body and eliciting the words for those body parts from Ss.
- Direct Ss' attention to the picture in Exercise 2B on page 47 and ask Ss about people in the picture. For example, point to the girl with the hurt hand and ask: *What hurts?* Elicit: *Her hand.* As Ss answer, say: *Oh, I'm sorry.*
- Have student pairs ask and answer questions about this picture. Walk around and monitor Ss' use of the language points.
- Check off each part of the lesson focus as Ss demonstrate an understanding of what they have learned in the lesson.

| More Ventures, Unit 4, Lesson C | |
|---|---|
| Literacy Workbook, 15–30 min. | |
| Basic Workbook, 15–30 min. | |
| Writing Worksheets, 15–30 min. | www.cambridge.org/ventures/resources/ |
| Collaborative Worksheets, 30–45 min. | |
| Student Arcade, time varies | www.cambridge.org/venturesarcade/ |

**B** **Listen and repeat.**

1. legs

CD1, Track 43

2. hand

3. stomach

4. feet

5. eyes

6. head

**Talk with a partner.** Act it out. Ask and answer.

**A** What hurts?

**B** My **legs**.

**A** Oh, I'm sorry.

**3** **Communicate**

**Talk with your classmates.**
Complete the chart.

**A** What hurts, **Sasha**?

**B** My **head**.

**A** Oh, I'm sorry.

| Name | What hurts? |
|------|-------------|
| Sasha | head |
| *Answers will vary.* | |
| | |
| | |
| | |
| | |

# Lesson D Reading

## 1 Before you read

**Talk about the picture.**
What do you see?

## 2 Read

**Listen and read.**

◀)) CD1, Track 44

### At the Doctor's Office

Tony and Mario are at the doctor's office.
They are patients. Tony's leg hurts. His head
hurts, too. He has a headache. Mario's arm
hurts. His hands hurt, too. Tony and Mario are
not happy. It is not a good day.

## 3 After you read

**Read the sentences.** Check (✓) the names.

|  | Tony | Mario |
|---|---|---|
| His arm hurts. |  | ✓ |
| His head hurts. | ✓ |  |
| His leg hurts. | ✓ |  |
| His hands hurt. |  | ✓ |
| He is not happy. | ✓ | ✓ |

## Teaching objectives

- Introduce a paragraph about a doctor's office
- Introduce vocabulary for talking about health problems
- Provide practice using new topic-related words

# WARM-UP AND REVIEW

- Before class. Write today's lesson focus on the board.
  *Lesson D:*
  *Read "At the Doctor's Office"*
  *Learn words for health problems*
- Begin class. Books open. Direct Ss' attention to the picture in Exercise 1. Ask the class: *Who are these boys?* Ss should recognize Mario and Tony from the picture on page 44.
- Ask Ss: *Are Mario and Tony happy?* (No.) Ask: *What's the matter?* Elicit vocabulary and grammar from the unit, for example: *His hands hurt. His leg hurts.*

# PRESENTATION

- Read aloud the instructions for Exercise 1. Ask Ss: *What do you see?* Elicit and write on the board any vocabulary about the picture that Ss know, such as: *doctor*, *patients*, *medicine*.

# PRACTICE

- Direct Ss' attention to Exercise 2. Point to the title of the paragraph and ask: *What's the title?* ("At the Doctor's Office.") Point to the first part of the lesson focus and tell Ss: *Today, you'll read about Mario and Tony at the doctor's office.*

### Literacy Tip

Make a list of the words for body parts that appear in the reading passage (*leg*, *head*, *arm*, *hands*) and give it to the literacy Ss in your class. Have the literacy Ss match the words on the list with the same words in the reading passage while the rest of the class reads the paragraph silently.

- ▶ **CD1, Track 44** Play or read the audio and ask Ss to follow along (see audio script, page T-147). Repeat the audio as needed.
- Read aloud each sentence of the reading and ask Ss to repeat after you.
- Answer any questions Ss have about the reading.

## *Learner persistence* (individual work)

- ▶ **CD1, Track 44** Ss can listen to the audio for Exercise 2 at home for reinforcement and review. They can also listen to the audio for self-directed learning when class attendance is not possible.

# COMPREHENSION CHECK

- Read aloud the instructions for Exercise 3.
- Model the task. Point to and read aloud the two column headings. Then point to and read aloud the first item in the chart: *His arm hurts.* Ask Ss: *Tony? Mario?* (Mario.) Point to the reading and ask: *Where is the answer?* Elicit the appropriate sentence from the reading.
- Ss scan the reading and fill out the chart individually. Walk around and help as needed.
- Go over answers with the class. Write the chart from Exercise 3 on the board. Call on Ss to make a check mark in the appropriate column and tell the class where in the reading they found the answer.

## *Expansion activity* (student pairs)

- Direct Ss' attention to the woman with the stomachache in the picture on page 44. With the class, decide what the woman's name might be. Then ask Ss to rewrite the paragraph about Mario and Tony so that it is about the woman, changing the information as needed.
- Help Ss get started by writing the title on the board: *At the Doctor's Office.* Then begin the first sentence with the woman's name and ask Ss what comes next; for example: *Beatrice is at the doctor's office.*
- Walk around and help as needed, checking to see that Ss write the correct form of *be* for the subject pronoun (she) and the possessive adjective (her). Follow up by asking different pairs to add a sentence to the paragraph on the board. Ask for a volunteer to read the completed paragraph aloud.

### Literacy Tip

For an alternative activity, refer literacy Ss to pages 48–49 in the *Literacy Workbook* at any time during the lesson.

# LESSON D Reading

## PRESENTATION

- Direct Ss' attention to the Picture dictionary in Exercise **4**. Point to and say the words *Health problems* in the book and in the second part of the lesson focus on the board. Tell Ss: *Today, we will learn more words for health problems.*
- Read aloud the instructions for Exercise **4A**.
- ▷ **CD1, Track 45** Play or read the audio (see audio script, page T-147). Listen to Ss' pronunciation as they repeat the words. Correct pronunciation as needed.

### Teaching Tip

Give pairs of Ss additional practice with the Picture dictionary. Ask one S to point to a picture and ask that S's partner to say the health problem. Then have Ss switch roles. Walk around and help with pronunciation.

### *Expansion activity* (student pairs)

- Write on the board the following sentences: *He has a cold. She has a cold.* Say the sentences aloud and ask Ss to repeat after you.
- Point to the first picture in the Picture dictionary and to the sentences on the board. Ask Ss: *Which sentence: "He has a cold." or "She has a cold."?* Elicit: *He has a cold.*
- Write on the board: *He has a headache. She has a headache.* Say the sentences aloud and ask Ss to repeat after you.
- Point to the third picture in the Picture dictionary and to the sentences on the board. Ask Ss which sentence is correct. Elicit: *She has a headache.*
- Write the following example conversation on the board:

  A: *What's the matter?*

  B: *He has a cold.*

- Have pairs of Ss practice the conversation using the pictures in the Picture dictionary. Model the task by asking one S to point to a picture and ask: *What's the matter?* Ask his or her partner to respond with: *He / She has a _____.*

### *Learner persistence* (individual work)

- ▷ **CD1, Track 45** Ss can listen to the audio for Exercise **4A** at home for reinforcement and review. They can also listen to the audio for self-directed learning when class attendance is not possible.

## PRACTICE

- Direct Ss' attention to Exercise **4B** and read the instructions aloud. Read the example conversation aloud using two different voices as you act out having a cold, for example: pretend to cough and sneeze and talk as if your nose is stuffy.
- Hold up your Student's Book and indicate all six pictures. Tell Ss: *Act out the health problem.*
- Ss complete the activity in pairs. Walk around and make sure Ss are practicing all the new vocabulary.
- When Ss are finished, ask them to change partners and have new conversations.

## EVALUATION

- Direct Ss' attention to the lesson focus on the board. Point to the picture of Mario and Tony at the doctor's office on page 50 and ask Ss: *Where are Mario and Tony?* (At the doctor's office.) If Ss don't understand the question, ask: *Is this a doctor's office?* (Yes.)
- Ask Ss: *What's the matter with Mario? What's the matter with Tony?* Elicit information from the reading, for example: *His leg hurts. His hands hurt.*
- Act out the health problems from the Picture dictionary in random order and ask Ss: *What's the matter?* Elicit, for example: *You have a sore throat.*
- Check off each part of the lesson focus as Ss demonstrate understanding of what they have learned in the lesson.

| More Ventures, Unit 4, Lesson D | |
|---|---|
| Literacy Workbook, 15–30 min. | |
| Basic Workbook, 15–30 min. | |
| Picture Dictionary activities, 30–45 min. **Writing Worksheets,** 15–30 min. **Collaborative Worksheets,** 30–45 min. | www.cambridge.org/ventures/ resources/ |
| Student Arcade, time varies | www.cambridge.org/venturesarcade/ |

# 4 Picture dictionary Health problems

1. a cold

2. a fever

3. a headache

4. a sore throat

5. a stomachache

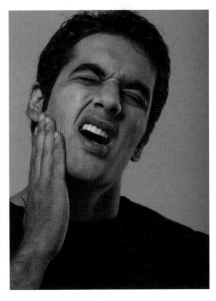

6. a toothache

A **Listen and repeat.** Look at the Picture dictionary.

B **Talk with a partner.** Act it out. Ask and answer questions.

A What's the matter?

B I have **a cold**.

A Oh, I'm sorry.

CD1, Track 45

# Lesson E Writing

## 1 Before you write

**Talk with a partner.** Check (✓) the reason for the visit.

| 1. | Name: **Regina** |
|---|---|
| | Reason for visit: |
| | ☐ cold |
| | ☐ fever |
| | ☐ headache |
| | ☐ sore throat |
| | ☐ stomachache |
| | ✓ toothache |

| 2. | Name: **Isaac** |
|---|---|
| | Reason for visit: |
| | ☐ cold |
| | ☐ fever |
| | ☐ headache |
| | ✓ sore throat |
| | ☐ stomachache |
| | ☐ toothache |

| 3. | Name: **Joe** |
|---|---|
| | Reason for visit: |
| | ☐ cold |
| | ✓ fever |
| | ☐ headache |
| | ☐ sore throat |
| | ☐ stomachache |
| | ☐ toothache |

| 4. | Name: **Esperanza** |
|---|---|
| | Reason for visit: |
| | ✓ cold |
| | ☐ fever |
| | ☐ headache |
| | ☐ sore throat |
| | ☐ stomachache |
| | ☐ toothache |

| 5. | Name: **James** |
|---|---|
| | Reason for visit: |
| | ☐ cold |
| | ☐ fever |
| | ☐ headache |
| | ☐ sore throat |
| | ✓ stomachache |
| | ☐ toothache |

| 6. | Name: **Sue** |
|---|---|
| | Reason for visit: |
| | ☐ cold |
| | ☐ fever |
| | ✓ headache |
| | ☐ sore throat |
| | ☐ stomachache |
| | ☐ toothache |

**Teaching objectives**
- Prepare Ss for completing a sign-in sheet at a doctor's office
- Provide practice writing key vocabulary words

# WARM-UP AND REVIEW

- Before class. Write today's lesson focus on the board.
  *Lesson E:*
  *Review words for health problems*
  *Complete a sign-in sheet at the doctor's office*

- Before class. Write the vocabulary from Lesson D in random order on the board: *a cold, a fever, a headache, a sore throat, a stomachache, a toothache.*

- Begin class. Books closed. Direct Ss' attention to the first part of the lesson focus. Point to and read aloud the vocabulary for health problems on the board. Ask Ss to repeat the words after you.

- Pretend you have one of the health problems; for example, hold your fingers to your temples and look distressed. Ask the class: *What's the matter? or What's my health problem?* Elicit, for example: *A headache.* Say to Ss: *Right. My head hurts. I have a headache.*

- Call on a S to come to the board and circle the word *headache.*

- Repeat the procedure with the rest of the words for health problems.

### Teaching Tip

As you review the vocabulary, encourage Ss to express sympathy with your health problems by saying *Oh, I'm sorry.*

# PRESENTATION

- Books open. Direct Ss' attention to the picture in Exercise 1. Point to each person and ask the class: *What's his / her name? What's his / her health problem?*

- Point to person number 1 and ask: *What's her name?* Point to the name on form #1 below the picture. Say: *name is Regina.*

- Write a sentence about each person on the board, for example: *Regina has a toothache.* Then go over each sentence, reading it aloud and having Ss repeat it in order to practice the pronunciation of the names and the health problems.

# PRACTICE

- Read aloud the instructions for Exercise 1. Explain the meaning of the word *reason*. Write on the board: *Why?* Tell Ss: *This is the question. The "reason" is the answer.* Use the situations in the picture to give examples. Ask Ss: *Why is Regina at the doctor's office?* Elicit: *Regina has a toothache.* Tell Ss: *Right. That's her reason for going to the doctor.*

- Model the task. Point to the first form and ask Ss: *What's her name?* (Regina.) *What's the reason for her visit to the doctor's office?* (A toothache.) Point to where *toothache* has been checked for number 1.

- Ss work alone or in pairs to complete the forms. Walk around and help as needed.

- When Ss are finished, call on different individuals or pairs and say, for example: *Number 2. Isaac. What's the reason for Isaac's visit?* If Ss give any incorrect answers, direct their attention to the appropriate person in the picture, act out the person's symptoms, and say the word for his or her health problem. Make sure Ss have checked the correct boxes.

### Literacy Tip

Pair literacy Ss with higher-level Ss to complete Exercise 1. Have the higher-level Ss ask their partners about the people in the picture. The literacy Ss can say the health problems while their partners check the appropriate boxes.

### Expansion activity *(whole group)*

- Write in large letters on the board: *Doctor's Office.*

- Ask for six volunteers to sit at the front of the room. Give each volunteer a health problem written on a small piece of paper. Indicate that the volunteers shouldn't say or show their problem to anyone.

- Tell the volunteers: *Please act out your health problem.* As the volunteers pretend to have a cold, a sore throat, and so on, ask the class about each person, for example: *What's the matter with Lee? What's the reason for his visit?* Elicit the correct health problem.

### Literacy Tip

For an alternative activity, refer literacy Ss to pages 50–51 in the *Literacy Workbook* at any time during the lesson.

# LESSON E Writing

## PRACTICE

- Direct Ss' attention to Exercise 2A and read the instructions aloud. Indicate the partial words in the exercise and tell Ss: *These words need more letters.*

- Model the task. Point to the first item and ask: *What's the health problem?* (Sore throat.) *What letter did "sore" need?* (O.) *What letter did "throat" need?* (O.) Point to the letters written in number 1.

- Tell Ss that if they need help, they can look at the words on page 52.

- Ss complete the words in pairs. Walk around and help as needed.

- When Ss are finished, ask each pair to join another pair and compare their answers.

## PRESENTATION

- Direct Ss' attention to Exercise 2B and read the instructions aloud.

- Explain the idea of a sign-in sheet. If you use a sign-in sheet to take attendance, show the sheet to Ss and tell them: *At the doctor's office, you write your name and the reason for your visit.* Otherwise, show Ss a clipboard with a piece of paper or just a page in your notebook. Act out a scene in which you arrive at the doctor's office (*Hello. I need to see the doctor.*) and sign in (*Please write your name and the reason for your visit.*).

- Point to and read aloud the parts of the sign-in sheet. Read aloud the example sentence or call on a S to read it aloud. Make sure Ss understand that the information they need can be found in the forms on page 52.

- Point to the last sentence where there is a blank line. Point to students and say: *You have a health problem. Write your name and health problem here.*

## PRACTICE

- Ss complete the sign-in sheet individually or in pairs.

- When Ss are finished, call on Ss using the names on the form, for example: *Regina, what's the reason for your visit?* Elicit, for example: *I have a toothache.*

### Literacy Tip

For Exercise 2B, you might want to write the first letter of each health problem in the appropriate blank in your literacy Ss' books. Then encourage Ss to try to copy the words from Exercise 2A.

## COMPREHENSION CHECK

- Direct Ss' attention to Exercise 3 and read the instructions aloud.

- Model the task. Show your sign-in sheet to a S and say one of the sentences in Exercise 2B. Ask that S to read and show you one of his or her sentences.

- Ss share their sentences in pairs. Walk around and spot-check Ss' writing.

### Community building *(whole group)*

- Write the six health problems from the lesson on the board. Give Ss a chance to show their practical and cultural knowledge by conducting a class discussion about home remedies for each problem.

- Point to each health problem and ask, for example: *What is good for a fever? What can I do?* Help Ss get started by giving a few examples: *Is cold water good for a fever? Can I take a cold shower?* Act out taking a cold shower.

- You may need to help extensively with vocabulary. Allow Ss to use bilingual dictionaries or to draw pictures on the board in order to convey their ideas. Do whatever is necessary to make the discussion comprehensible for all Ss in the class.

## EVALUATION

- Direct Ss' attention to the first part of the lesson focus on the board. Read the phrase aloud and ask Ss to repeat. Point to the people in the picture on page 52 and ask volunteers to say the words for the health problems. Ask different Ss to write the words on the board.

- Direct Ss' attention to the second part of the lesson focus on the board. Read it aloud and ask Ss to repeat. Draw on the board a sign-in sheet similar to the one in Exercise 2B. Call on individual Ss to write their name and the reason for their visit on the board.

- Check off each part of the lesson focus as Ss demonstrate an understanding of what they have learned in the lesson.

| More Ventures, Unit 4, Lesson E | |
|---|---|
| Literacy Workbook, 15–30 min. | |
| Basic Workbook, 15–30 min. | |
| Writing Worksheets, 15–30 min. | www.cambridge.org/ventures/ resources/ |
| Real-life Document, 15–30 min. | |
| Collaborative Worksheets, 30–45 min. | |

## **2** Write

**A** **Talk with a partner.** Complete the words.

1. s __o__ re    thr __o__ at
2. c __o__ ld
3. st __o__ machache
4. h __e__ adache
5. f __e__ ver
6. t __o__ othache
7. s __o__ re    h __a__ nd

**B** **Look at page 52.** Then complete the patient sign-in sheet.

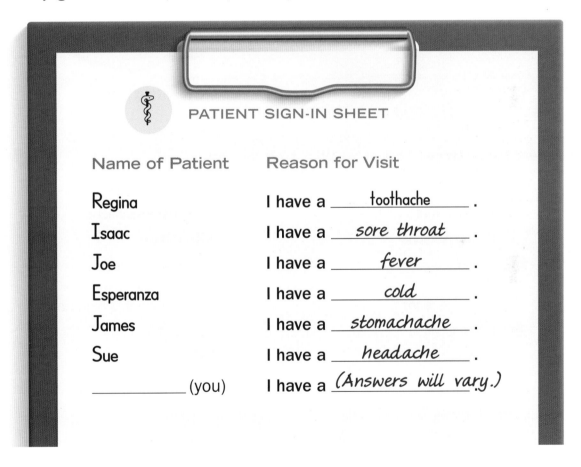

PATIENT SIGN-IN SHEET

| Name of Patient | Reason for Visit |
| --- | --- |
| Regina | I have a ___toothache___ . |
| Isaac | I have a ___sore throat___ . |
| Joe | I have a ___fever___ . |
| Esperanza | I have a ___cold___ . |
| James | I have a ___stomachache___ . |
| Sue | I have a ___headache___ . |
| _____ (you) | I have a _(Answers will vary.)_ |

## **3** After you write

**Talk with a partner.** Share your writing.

## Lesson F Another view

### 1 Life-skills reading

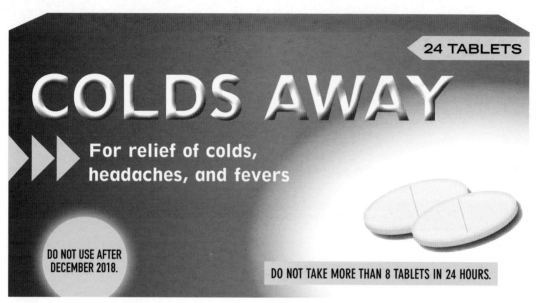

**24 TABLETS**

# COLDS AWAY

**For relief of colds, headaches, and fevers**

DO NOT USE AFTER DECEMBER 2018.

DO NOT TAKE MORE THAN 8 TABLETS IN 24 HOURS.

**A** **Read the sentences.** Look at the label. Fill in the answer.

1. This medicine is for _____ .
   - Ⓐ a sore throat
   - Ⓑ a stomachache
   - **Ⓒ a cold**

2. This medicine is for _____ .
   - **Ⓐ a headache**
   - Ⓑ a backache
   - Ⓒ a toothache

3. This medicine is for _____ .
   - Ⓐ a stomachache
   - **Ⓑ a fever**
   - Ⓒ a sore throat

4. Do not take this medicine after _____ .
   - Ⓐ 2017
   - **Ⓑ 2018**
   - Ⓒ 2019

**B** **Solve the problem.** Which solution is best? Circle your opinion.

Tony has a headache today. He takes Colds Away medicine. He takes 8 tablets. His head still hurts. What should he do?

1. Take another tablet.

2. See a doctor.

3. Other: *Answers will vary.* _____

- Introduce reading the label on a medicine bottle
- Provide practice that develops test-taking skills
- Review vocabulary from the unit

## WARM-UP AND REVIEW

- Before class. Write today's lesson focus on the board.
  *Lesson F:*
  *Read a medicine label*
- Before class. If possible, bring to class real bottles of medicine.
- Begin class. Hold up an example of a real medicine bottle and ask the class: *What is this?* (Medicine.)
- Books closed. Write on the board: *a label.* Say the word aloud and ask Ss to repeat it after you. Ask Ss if they know what a label is. Show Ss the medicine bottles and indicate each bottle's label as you say the word.
- Tell Ss: *You need to read medicine labels. It's very important.* Pretend to read one of the labels.
- Direct Ss' attention to the lesson focus on the board and say: *Today, we will read a medicine label.*

## PRESENTATION

- Books open. Direct Ss' attention to the medicine label in Exercise 1. Tell Ss: *This is a medicine label.* Point to and say the words *Colds Away.* Tell Ss that this is the name of the medicine.
- To help Ss preview the medicine label, go over each section and ask comprehension questions. For example, read aloud: *For relief of colds, headaches, and fevers.* Ask Ss: *What health problems is this medicine for?* (Colds, headaches, and fevers.) Continue in this manner by asking: *How many tablets do we have? When can we use this medicine?*

### Teaching Tip

As with many reading tasks, Ss do not need to understand every word on the medicine label in order to get the main idea and complete the exercises. Give a brief overview of the medicine label. Then let Ss try to answer the questions. They may be surprised by how much they understand.

## PRACTICE

- Read the instructions for Exercise 1A aloud. This task helps prepare Ss for standardized-type tests they may have to take.
- Write the first sentence on the board along with the three answer choices labeled *A, B,* and *C.*

- Read the item and the answer choices aloud and then point to the medicine label. Ask: *Is the medicine for a sore throat?* Show Ss where to look for the information. Elicit: *No.*
- Point to the three answer choices on the board. Ask Ss: *A, B, or C?* (C.) Fill in the letter *c* and tell Ss: *Fill in the answer in your book.* Make sure Ss understand the task.
- Have Ss individually scan and fill in the correct answers.

## COMPREHENSION CHECK

- Go over the answers to Exercise 1A together. Make sure that Ss followed the instructions and filled in their answers. Ask Ss to point to the information on the medicine label.

## APPLICATION

- Read aloud the instructions and the question in Exercise 1B. Tell Ss that they are going to decide what Tony should do.
- Ss complete the task in pairs. When Ss are finished, ask for a volunteer to tell the class what Tony should do. Accept all plausible answers.

### Expansion activity *(whole group)*

- Review and explain the new vocabulary from the medicine label: *away, relief, tablets,* and *Do not use after December 2018.*
- Teach *away* as part of the phrase *go away* using pantomime and gestures.
- Demonstrate *relief* by pretending to have a cold and then feeling better. Tell Ss: *I don't have a cold!*
- Draw a picture of a tablet as a 3-D circle with a line down the middle.
- Draw a timeline on the board with points labeled *now* and *December 2018.* Use shading and words to indicate the periods before December 2018 (between *now* and *December 2018*) and after December 2018. Explain that the medicine is good in the first period of time but bad after that. *Do not use after December 2018* means that people should not take the medicine after that month in that year.

### Literacy Tip

For an alternative activity, refer literacy Ss to pages 52–53 in the *Literacy Workbook* at any time during the lesson.

# LESSON F Another view

## PRESENTATION

- Books closed. Write on the board: *How many?* Point to your eyes and ask Ss: *How many eyes do I have? One eye? Two eyes?* (Two eyes.) Tell Ss: *I have two eyes.*
- Repeat the procedure with *head, arms, legs, hands,* and *feet.* Finish with the word *ears.* Since Ss have not seen the word *ears* previously in the unit, be sure to point to your ears, write the word on the board, and practice pronouncing the word with the class.

## PRACTICE

- Books open. Direct Ss' attention to the picture of the monster in Exercise 2A. Pretend to be frightened and say, for example: *Eek! It's a monster!*
- Read the instructions for Exercise 2A aloud. Write on the board and say the word *monster.* Ask Ss to repeat the word after you.

### Teaching Tip

Feel free to be dramatic and have fun when you talk about the monster in this exercise. Ss will enjoy the creative aspect of the exercise.

- Model the task. Point to and read aloud the two column headings in the chart. Then read aloud the question and the first body part: *How many heads?* Ask Ss: *How many heads does the monster have?* (Two.) Ask Ss: *How many heads do you have?* (One.) Point to where the numbers have been written in the chart.
- Ss complete the chart individually. Walk around and help as needed.
- Read aloud the second part of the instructions for Exercise 2A.
- Write on the board: *The monster has _____. I have _____.* Read aloud each sentence using the numbers in the example from the chart: *The monster has two heads. I have one head.* Ask Ss to repeat the sentences after you. Encourage Ss to use complete sentences as they compare charts with their partners.

### Expansion activity *(student pairs)*

- Ask Ss to take out a piece of paper and draw a picture of a different monster.
- Have Ss share their pictures in pairs and talk about how many of each body part their monsters have.

## PRACTICE

- Direct Ss' attention to Exercise 2B. Ask the class: *What do the words need?* (Letters.) Read the instructions aloud.
- Model the task. Point to the first item and ask: *What's the word?* (Patient.) *What letter does "patient" need?* (i) Point to the letter *i* written for number 1.
- Ss complete the words individually or in pairs. When Ss have finished, ask volunteers to write the words on the board.
- Read aloud the second part of the instructions in Exercise 2B.
- Model the task. Point to the first item and ask Ss: *What letter do we need in number 1?* (i) Read aloud the numbers under the blanks in the new word and stop when you get to number 1. Tell Ss: *Write the letter "i" for number 1.* Make sure Ss understand the task.
- Ask a volunteer to write the new word on the board.

### Evaluation

- Do a quick review of the unit. Have Ss turn to Lesson A. Ask the class to talk about what they remember about this lesson. Prompt Ss, if necessary, with questions, for example: *What words are on this page? What do you see in the picture?* Continue in this manner to review each lesson quickly.

### Expansion activity

- Before class. Print, for each student, one copy of the Self-assessment for this unit.
- Have Ss complete the Self-assessment either in class or outside of class.
- Provide feedback to Ss such as through a whole-class discussion, partners comparing their worksheets, or T reviewing each S's worksheet.
- If Ss are ready, administer the unit test on page T-163 of this Teacher's Edition. The audio script for the test is available on page T-192.

| More Ventures, Unit 4, Lesson F | |
| --- | --- |
| Literacy Workbook, 15–30 min. | |
| Basic Workbook, 15–30 min. | |
| Writing Worksheets, 15–30 min. | |
| Collaborative Worksheets, 30–45 min. | www.cambridge.org/ventures/resources/ |
| Self-assessment, 10 min. | |
| CASAS Test Prep Worksheet, 5–10 min. | |

## 2 Fun with vocabulary

A **Complete the chart.** How many?

|  | The monster | You |
|---|---|---|
| heads | 2 | 1 |
| eyes | 6 | 2 |
| ears | 8 | 2 |
| arms | 5 | 2 |
| legs | 4 | 2 |
| feet | 4 | 2 |

**Talk with a partner.** Compare your answers.

B **Write the missing letters.**

p a t _i_ e n t
      1

f _e_ e t
  2

s t o _m_ a c h
     3

_n_ u r s e
4

t o o t h a _c_ h e
         5

_d_ o c t o r
6

o f f _i_ c e
    7

_e_ y e
8

**Write the letters.** Make a word.

| _m_ | _e_ | _d_ | i | _c_ | _i_ | _n_ | _e_ |
|---|---|---|---|---|---|---|---|
| 3 | 2 | 6 | 1 | 5 | 7 | 4 | 8 |

# REVIEW

## 1 Listening

**Read.** Then listen and circle.

1. Who is Sonya?
   a. Tom's aunt *(circled)*
   b. Tom's brother

2. Who is David?
   a. Tom's aunt
   b. Tom's brother *(circled)*

3. Who is Tina?
   a. Ray's sister
   b. Ray's wife *(circled)*

4. Who is Jay?
   a. Barbara's son *(circled)*
   b. Barbara's brother

5. What hurts?
   a. her hand
   b. her head *(circled)*

6. What hurts?
   a. his leg
   b. his foot *(circled)*

CD1, Track 46

**Talk with a partner.** Ask and answer.

## 2 Vocabulary

**Write.** Complete the story.

cold   doctor's   office   medicine   patients   stomach

# A Visit to the Doctor

Marisa and her family are at the ___doctor's office___.
                                        1

They are ___patients___. Peter is Marisa's son. His ___stomach___
            2                                           3

hurts. Antonia is Marisa's daughter. She has a ___cold___.
                                                    4

They need ___medicine___. Marisa isn't happy. She has a
            5

headache!

Teaching objectives
• Review vocabulary from Units 3 and 4
• Introduce the pronunciation of *e* as in *read*, *i* as in *five*, and *u* as in *June*

# WARM-UP AND REVIEW

• Before class. Write today's lesson focus on the board.
*Review unit:*
*Review vocabulary and grammar from Units 3 and 4*
*Pronounce "e" as in "read," "i" as in "five," and "u" as in "June"*

• Begin class. Books open. Direct Ss' attention to the lesson focus on the board.

• Review vocabulary from Unit 3. Direct Ss' attention to the family picture on page 34. Ask individual Ss, for example:

*What's the grandmother's name?* (Olga.)
*What's the grandfather's name?* (Peter.)
*Who is Vera?* (Sam and Sophie's aunt; Mike and Dave's sister; Peter and Olga's daughter.)
*Who is Mike's mother?* (Olga.)
*Who is Sophie's father?* (Dave.)
*Do Peter and Olga have a son?* (Yes, they have two sons: Mike and Dave.)
*Do Dave and Susan have a daughter?* (Yes: Sophie.)

> **Teaching Tip**
>
> Write the above questions on the board if it would help your Ss' comprehension. On the other hand, if your Ss struggle with reading, present the questions orally. The point of the questions is to help Ss retrieve previously learned vocabulary, so present the questions in the way that is easiest for your Ss to understand.

# PRACTICE

• Direct Ss' attention to Exercise **1** and read the instructions aloud. Read the question and answer choices in number 1 aloud.

▶ **CD1, Track 46** Model the task. Play or read only the first conversation from the audio (see audio script, page T-147). Point to the two answer choices in number 1 and ask: *Tom's aunt or Tom's brother?* (Tom's aunt.) Point to where the letter *a* has been circled.

• Read aloud the remaining questions and answer choices. Say: *Now listen and circle the correct answers.*

▶ **CD1, Track 46** Play or read the complete audio. Ss listen and circle the correct answers. Repeat the audio as needed.

• Check answers with the class. Read each question aloud and call on different Ss to answer.

> **Teaching Tip**
>
> After Ss read their answers to the questions, play the audio again to check their answers.

• Read aloud the second part of the instructions for Exercise **1**. Ss practice asking and answering the questions in pairs. Walk around and help as needed.

• Ask several pairs to ask and answer the questions for the rest of the class.

# PRACTICE

• Direct Ss' attention to Exercise **2**. Point to the title of the story and ask: *What's the title?* (A Visit to the Doctor.) Help Ss by reading the title aloud if necessary.

• Read aloud the instructions for Exercise **2**. Point to the words in the word bank and tell Ss: *Write these words in the story.*

• Model the task. Read aloud the beginning of the first sentence: *Marisa and her family are at the . . .* Elicit: *doctor's office.* Point to *doctor's office* in the word bank and in the blank for number 1.

• Ss read the story and fill in the blanks individually. Walk around and help as needed.

• Write the numbers *1–5* on the board. Ask volunteers to come to the board and write the answers.

• Read the story aloud using Ss' answers. If there is an error, say: *This is not correct. Who has a different answer?* Make any necessary corrections on the board.

# COMPREHENSION CHECK

• Ask Ss comprehension questions about the reading, for example:

*Who is Peter?* (Marisa's son.) *Who is Antonia?* (Marisa's daughter.)
*What's the matter with Peter? What hurts?* (His stomach hurts. / He has a stomachache.)
*What's the matter with Antonia?* (She has a cold.)
*What do the children need?* (Medicine.)
*What's the matter with Marisa?* (She's not happy. She has a headache.)

# REVIEW

## WARM-UP AND REVIEW

- Review singular and plural nouns from Unit 4. Direct Ss' attention to the picture of Mario and Tony on page 50. Ask Ss: *What's the matter with Tony? What hurts?* (His leg, his head.) Ask Ss: *What's the matter with Mario? What hurts?* (His arm, his hands.)

- Draw one side of a human figure on the board with one eye, one arm, one leg, and one foot. Elicit singular nouns by pointing to the body parts and saying: *He / She has one _____.* Then complete the drawing on the board and elicit plural nouns: *He / She has two _____.*

- If your Ss have trouble with grammar, you might want to review the Grammar charts from Units 3 and 4 or show the animated grammar presentations for Units 3 and 4.

## PRACTICE

- Direct Ss to Exercise **3A**. Read the instructions aloud.

- Model the task. Read the question in number 1: *What hurts? His leg or legs?* (Leg.) Point to where *leg* has been circled and written for number 1.

- Ss circle and write their answers individually. Check answers by calling on Ss to read the sentences aloud. As Ss read the sentences, write their answers on the board.

### Teaching Tip

If Ss need to review short answers with *do*, go over the grammar chart on page 36. Then ask questions using *you* (singular) and *you* (plural), for example: *Do you* (a student) *have a brother? Do you* (the class) *have your books?*

- Direct Ss to Exercise **3B**. Read the instructions aloud.

- Model the task. Read the question in number 1 without the first word: *Hmm . . . you have a daughter?* Ask Ss: *Do or don't?* (Do.) Point to where *Do* has been written for number 1 and read the complete question aloud.

- Ss complete the questions individually. Check answers by calling on Ss to read the sentences aloud.

### Expansion activity *(whole group)*

- Before class. Create a chart similar to the one on page 37 in Unit 3, but with words for school supplies in the left-hand column.

- Have Ss walk around and ask at least three classmates the questions from the chart; for example: *Do you have a pencil?* Ask Ss to answer using *Yes, I do. / No, I don't.*

## PRESENTATION

- Direct Ss' attention to the second part of the lesson focus on the board.

- Write on the board: *read, need.* Point to and say each word and ask Ss to repeat. Underline the vowels in each of the words. Say a long e /i:/ sound before repeating each word, for example: /i:/, *read.* Ask Ss to repeat after you.

- Write on the board: *five, write.* Repeat the procedure, underlining the *i* and pronouncing a long i /a:/ sound.

- Write on the board: *June, rule.* Repeat the procedure, underlining the *u* and pronouncing a long u /u:/ sound.

## PRACTICE

- ▶ **CD1, Track 47** Direct Ss' attention to Exercise **4A** and read the instructions aloud. Play or read the audio (see audio script, page T-147). Ss listen to examples of the three vowel sounds.

- ▶ **CD1, Track 48** Direct Ss' attention to Exercise **4B** and read the instructions aloud. Play or read the audio (see audio script, page T-147). Ss listen and repeat what they hear.

- Read aloud the second part of the instructions for Exercise **4B**. Model the task. Point to the three charts and tell one S: *Say a word.* After that S says any word from the charts, tell his or her partner: *Point to the word.*

- Ss complete the task in pairs. Help as needed.

- ▶ **CD1, Track 49** Direct Ss' attention to Exercise **4C** and read the instructions aloud. Model the task. Play or read the first word on the audio (see audio script, page T-147). Ask: *Which letter is it*: e, i, *or* o? (i) Point to where the letter has been checked.

- ▶ **CD1, Track 49** Play or read the complete audio. Ss listen and make a checkmark under the letter they hear.

- ▶ **CD1, Track 49** Reproduce the chart from Exercise **4C** on the board and play or read the audio again. Pause after each word and ask a S to check the appropriate letter in the chart on the board.

## EVALUATION

- Direct Ss' attention to the lesson focus on the board.

- Draw on the board a simple family tree. Identify people by name and whether they are male or female. Ask Ss questions about the people; for example: *Who is Martina?*

- Ask as many Ss as possible: *What hurts?* Have Ss act out and say a health problem; for example: *My feet hurt.*

- Give each S a slip of paper with a number and a part of the body, for example: *2 feet, 3 heads, 1 eye, 2 ears,* and so on. Have each S ask a classmate the question: *Do you have _____?* Classmates should answer: *Yes, I do. / No, I don't.*

- Write on the board: *need, write, rule.* Call on individual Ss as you point to one of the words and ask them to say it. Listen to the vowel sounds and help as needed.

- Check off each part of the lesson focus as Ss demonstrate an understanding of what they have learned in the lesson.

## ③ Grammar

**A** **Read and circle.** Then write.

1. What hurts? His _____leg_____ .
   ( leg ) legs

2. What hurts? His _____arms_____ .
   arm ( arms )

3. What hurts? Her _____hand_____ .
   ( hand ) hands

4. What hurts? Her _____foot_____ .
   ( foot ) feet

Dr. Brady

**B** **Complete the sentences.** Use *do* or *don't*.

A _____Do_____ you have a daughter?
       1

B Yes, we _____do_____ .
            2

A _____Do_____ you have a son?
       3

B Yes, we _____do_____ .
            4

A _____Do_____ you have a sister?
       5

B No, I _____don't_____ .
              6

## ④ Pronunciation

**A** **Listen** to the *e* sound, the *i* sound, and the *u* sound.

| e | i | u |
|---|---|---|
| re**a**d | f**i**ve | J**u**ne |

🔊 CD1, Track 47

**B** **Listen and repeat.**

| e | read | need | | i | five | write | | u | June | rule |
|---|------|------|---|---|------|-------|---|---|------|------|

**Talk with a partner.** Say a word. Your partner points. Take turns.

🔊 CD1, Track 48

**C** **Listen and check (✓).**

|    | e | i | u | | e | i | u | | e | i | u | | e | i | u | | e | i | u |
|----|---|---|---|---|---|---|---|---|---|---|---|---|---|---|---|---|---|---|---|
| 1. |   | ✓ |   | 2. |   |   | ✓ | 3. | ✓ |   |   | 4. | ✓ |   |   | 5. |   | ✓ |   |

🔊 CD1, Track 49

# UNIT 5 AROUND TOWN

## Lesson A Listening

### 1 Before you listen

**A** Look at the picture. What do you see?

**B** Listen and point: ▪ bank ▪ library ▪ restaurant ▪ school
▪ street ▪ supermarket

CD1, Track 50

# UNIT 5

- Introduce Ss to the topic
- Find out what Ss know about the topic
- Preview the unit by talking about the picture
- Provide practice of key vocabulary
- Provide practice that develops listening skills

## WARM-UP AND REVIEW

- Before class. Write today's lesson focus on the board.
  *Lesson A:*
  *Places and locations: on, next to, across from, between*
- Before class. Place a few classroom objects in various places, such as on the table, on the desk, and on the floor.
- Begin class. Books closed. Write on the board: *Where?* Remind Ss of the meaning of this question word and recycle vocabulary for classroom objects by asking questions, such as: *Where's my notebook? Where's my stapler?* Elicit correct responses from Ss.
- Point to the lesson focus *Places and locations* on the board. Say the words and have Ss repeat after you. Tell Ss: *"Where" tells us about places and locations.* Gesture to the room around you and ask: *Where are we?* Elicit: *in the classroom; at school;* etc.
- Write on the board the name of the school or other place where your class is held. Say the name and tell Ss: *This is a "place."* Ask Ss to name other places in your community.

### Literacy Tip

For an alternative activity, refer literacy Ss to pages 54–55 in the *Literacy Workbook* at any time during the lesson.

### Literacy Tip

If you have literacy Ss in your class, it might be helpful to spend time at the beginning of any activity with art or photos talking about the pictures before focusing Ss' attention on the printed words in the exercise. Have Ss work in pairs. Tell them to ask each other: *What do you see?* Encourage Ss to describe the pictures to each other. Consider pairing literacy Ss with Ss who can help them read the text in the exercise. This will help preview the exercise for literacy Ss and make them more confident as the exercise continues.

## PRESENTATION

- Books open. Set the scene. Hold up the Student's Book. Show Ss the picture on page 58. Tell the class: *These are places.*
- Ask: *What do you see?* Elicit and write on the board any vocabulary that Ss know, such as: *school, street, car, bicycle, buildings, bench.*

## PRACTICE

- Direct Ss' attention to the key vocabulary in Exercise 1B. Read aloud each word or phrase while pointing to the corresponding part of the picture. Ask Ss to repeat and point.
- ▶ *CD1, Track 50* Play or read the audio (see audio script, page T-147). Tell Ss: *Listen and point to the picture.* As Ss hear the key vocabulary, check to see that they are pointing to the correct part of the picture. Repeat the audio as needed.

## COMPREHENSION CHECK

- Ask Ss *Yes / No* questions about the picture. Tell Ss: *Listen. Say "yes" or "no."*
  Point to the bank. Ask: *Is this a bank?* (Yes.)
  Point to the school. Ask: *Is this a restaurant?* (No.)
  Point to the woman leaving the bakery. Ask: *Is this a woman?* (Yes.)
  Point to the woman's child. Ask: *Is this a boy?* (No.)
  Point to the school. Ask: *Is this a school?* (Yes.)
  Point to the library. Ask: *Is this a supermarket?* (No.)
  Point to the supermarket. Ask: *Is this a supermarket?* (Yes.)

### Expansion activity *(whole group)*

- Recycle the *'s* possessive from Unit 3, using some of the names for places in the picture.
- Remind Ss of the *'s* possessive form by writing a few phrases for family relationships on the board, for example: *Dave's wife, Sophie's mother, Vera's brother.* Circle the *'s* in each name and ask Ss: *What is this? What does it mean?* Elicit from Ss some explanation of possession – for example, *Dave has a wife.*
- Write on the board: *Jim's Barbershop, Sal's Bakery, Rosie's Restaurant.* Point to and say the name of each business and ask Ss to repeat after you.
- Circle the *'s* in each name and ask Ss: *What is this? What does it mean?* Make sure Ss understand that the businesses in some way belong to the people – for example, that *Jim has a barbershop.*

# LESSON A Listening

## PRESENTATION

- Direct Ss' attention to the words in Exercise 2A. Say each word aloud and ask Ss to repeat after you.
- Ask Ss questions to elicit the new vocabulary.
  Draw a dollar sign ($) on the board. Say: *I need money. Where can I get money?* (Bank.)
  Hold up a book. Say: *I need books. Where can I get books?* (Library; or possibly school.)
  Rub your hand on your stomach. Say: *I'm hungry. Where can I get food?* (Supermarket, restaurant.)
  Pretend to place your hands on a steering wheel. Say: *I'm in my car. Where can I drive my car?* (Street.)
  Say: *I need to learn English. Where can I learn English?* (School.)
- Read aloud the instructions for Exercise 2A.

## PRACTICE

- **CD1, Track 51** Play or read the audio (see audio script, page T-147). Ss listen and repeat the vocabulary. Repeat the audio as needed.
- Listen carefully to Ss' pronunciation and make corrections as needed.

### *Learner persistence* (individual work)
- **CD1, Track 51** Ss can listen to the audio for Exercise 2A at home for reinforcement and review. They can also listen to the audio for self-directed learning when class attendance is not possible.
- Direct Ss' attention to Exercise 2B and read the instructions aloud.
- **CD1, Track 52** Model the task. Hold up the Student's Book and say: *Number one.* Play or read the audio for number 1 (see audio script, page T-147). Point to the two answer choices in number 1 and ask Ss: *What did you hear – a or b?* Elicit: *a.* Point to the letter *a* next to the first picture and tell Ss: *Circle the letter "a."*
- **CD1, Track 52** Play or read the complete audio. Ss listen and circle the correct answers. Repeat the audio as needed.
- **CD1, Track 52** Read aloud the second part of the instructions for Exercise 2B. Play or read the audio again so Ss can listen and check their answers.

### *Learner persistence* (individual work)
- **CD1, Track 52** Ss can listen to the audio for Exercise 2B at home for reinforcement and review. They can also listen to the audio for self-directed learning when class attendance is not possible.

## COMPREHENSION CHECK

- Write the numbers *1–4* on the board. Ask a few Ss to come to the board and write the correct answers to Exercise 2B next to the numbers.
- **CD1, Track 52** Play or read the audio again. Pause the audio after each conversation. Point to the answer on the board and ask: *Is this correct?* Ask a student volunteer to make any necessary corrections.

## APPLICATION

- Direct Ss' attention to Exercise 3 and read the instructions aloud.
- Model the task. Hold up the Student's Book and point to the pictures in Exercise 2B. Say to one S: *Point to a picture.* Say to the first S's partner: *Say the word.*
- Ss complete the exercise in pairs. Walk around and help as needed.

### *Expansion activity* (student pairs)
- Have Ss practice the conversations from Exercise 2B in pairs. Ask Ss to turn to the audio script on page 147 in the Student's Book.
- Ask Ss to choose Role A or B and read aloud the conversations. Then have Ss switch roles and read the conversations again. Walk around and help as needed.

## EVALUATION

- Direct Ss' attention to the lesson focus on the board. Write the key vocabulary words in random places around the board. Then call on Ss to come to the board and point to the word you say.
- Ask Ss questions similar to the ones you used in the presentation of Exercise 2A; for example: *Where can I get money?* (Bank.) *Where can I learn English?* (School.)
- Check off each part of the lesson focus as Ss demonstrate an understanding of what they have learned in the lesson.

| *More Ventures, Unit 5, Lesson A* | |
|---|---|
| Literacy Workbook, 15–30 min. | |
| Basic Workbook, 15–30 min. | |
| Writing Worksheets, 15–30 min. | www.cambridge.org/ventures/ resources/ |
| Collaborative Worksheets, 30–45 min. | |
| Student Arcade, time varies | www.cambridge.org/venturesarcade/ |

## 2 Listen

### A Listen and repeat.

1. bank
2. library
3. restaurant
4. school
5. street
6. supermarket

CD1, Track 51

### B Listen and circle.

CD1, Track 52

1. a.     b.

2. a.     b.

3. a.     b.

4. a.     b.

**Listen again.** Check your answers.

## 3 After you listen

**Talk with a partner.** Point to a picture.
Your partner says the word.

# Lesson B Places around town

## 1 Vocabulary focus

**Listen and repeat.**

🔊 CD1, Track 53

1. pharmacy

2. hospital

3. laundromat

4. post office

5. movie theater

6. gas station

## 2 Practice

**A Read and match.**

post office

movie theater

pharmacy

laundromat

hospital

gas station

60 UNIT 5

## WARM-UP AND REVIEW

- Before class. Write today's lesson focus on the board.
  *Lesson B:*
  *Places around town*
  *Where's Minh?*

- Before class. Find or draw large, simple images that correspond with the key vocabulary from Lesson A, for example: a magazine picture of a plate of spaghetti (for *restaurant*) or a bag of groceries (for *supermarket*).

- Begin class. Books open. Point to and say each of the key vocabulary items from Lesson A and ask Ss to repeat after you. Write each word on the board. Then tape the pictures under the words in random order across the board. Tell the class: *We need to match the words and the pictures. Match.*

- Ask a volunteer to come to the board. Tell the class, for example: *Felipe needs help. Help him match the words and the pictures.* Tell the volunteer: *Listen. Your classmates will help you.*

- Encourage Ss to call out advice as the volunteer draws lines between the words and the pictures. When the class is satisfied with the matches, erase any lines that are incorrect. Ask for a different volunteer to fix the errors.

## PRESENTATION

- Point to the words *Places around town* at the top of page 60 in the Student's Book. Say the words aloud and ask Ss to repeat after you. Point to the vocabulary from Lesson A on the board and tell Ss: *These are places.*

- Explain the meaning of *around town* by writing on the board *town*, *city*, and the name of the community where you live. Hold up your Student's Book and show Ss the picture on page 58. Tell Ss: *A town or a city has places like banks, restaurants, and libraries.*

- Direct Ss' attention to the pictures in Exercise 1 on page 60. Tell Ss: *Today, you will learn more words for places.* Read aloud the instructions for Exercise 1.

- ▶ **CD1, Track 53** Play or read the audio (see audio script, page T-147). Listen and repeat the vocabulary along with Ss. Repeat the audio as needed.

- Listen carefully to Ss' pronunciation and correct as needed.

### Teaching Tip

Exploit the art in this exercise by asking Ss questions similar to the ones you asked for the presentation of Exercise 2A in Lesson A. For example, say: *I need a doctor. Where can I see a doctor?* (Hospital.) *My father needs gas. Where can he go?* (Gas station.)

## PRACTICE

- Direct Ss' attention to Exercise 2A. As you read aloud the instructions, hold up the Student's Book and indicate that Ss should look at the pictures of places and match them to the corresponding words.

- Model the task. Hold up the Student's Book. Point to the first picture. Ask: *What place is this?* (Movie theater.) Say: *Match the picture with the word.*

- Ss complete the exercise individually. Help as needed.

### Literacy Tip

Ask higher-level Ss to work with literacy Ss on Exercise 2A. Have the higher-level Ss point to and read aloud the words while the literacy Ss draw the lines to the pictures.

## COMPREHENSION CHECK

- Write the numbers *1–6* on the board. Ask a few Ss to come to the board and write the answers to Exercise 2A on the board.

- Ask different Ss to read the answers on the board. After each answer is read, ask: *Is this correct?* If not, ask a student volunteer to make corrections on the board.

### *Community building* (small groups)

- Create a matching exercise with the names of local, well-known places in one column and the vocabulary from the unit in the other. Include the names of, for example, a pharmacy, a restaurant, a street, a hospital, a movie theater, and a drugstore. Give each group of 3 or 4 Ss a copy of the handout and ask them to work together to match the names and the places.

- Go over the answers with the class and if possible have Ss share what they know about the places. If a discussion is not possible, ask Ss to point in the direction of the places. Ask, for example: *Which way is Summit Street?* Point in various directions to illustrate the meaning of your question.

### Literacy Tip

For an alternative activity, refer literacy Ss to pages 56–57 in the *Literacy Workbook* at any time during the lesson.

# LESSON B Places around town

## PRESENTATION

- Direct Ss' attention to the pictures in Exercise 2B and to the word bank. Read each word aloud and ask Ss to repeat after you. Indicate the pictures and ask Ss: *Which picture shows the pharmacy?* (Number 3, the picture with Mr. Lopez.) Do the same with the other places and pictures.
- Go over the names by pointing to each picture and saying, for example: *This is Minh. Minh. Please repeat.*

## PRACTICE

- Read aloud the first set of instructions for Exercise 2B.
- ▶ *CD1, Track 54* Model the task. Say: *Listen and repeat.* Play or read the audio for number 1 (see audio script, page T-147) and point to Minh in the picture as you repeat. Say: *Then write.* Point to the words *movie theater* written in the chart. Make sure Ss understand the task.
- ▶ *CD1, Track 54* Play or read the complete audio. Ss listen and repeat. Encourage Ss to point to the people in the pictures as they repeat.
- Ss complete the chart individually, using the words from the word bank. Repeat the audio as needed.
- Check answers with the class. Write the numbers *1–6* on the board and ask for volunteers to write their answers on the board. Make any necessary corrections.

### Literacy Tip

Your literacy Ss may need an alternate assignment to Exercise 2B. You could, for example, photocopy the pictures from Exercise 1 on page 60, covering the labels. Then ask Ss to find the words for the pictures in the word box. Model this process by starting with number 5, the movie theater. Point to the words on the building and then scan the word box and circle *movie theater*.

- Read aloud the second part of the instructions for Exercise 2B. Point to and model the example conversation.
- Call on a pair of volunteers to read the example conversation aloud for the class.
- Point to another person in the pictures on page 61. Ask: *Where's (name)?* Elicit the answer from a volunteer. Repeat with different people and places in the pictures. Indicate that Ss should ask and answer questions about all the people and places in the pictures.
- Ss complete the exercise in pairs. Walk around and help as needed.
- When Ss are finished, ask them where each person is. Make sure Ss answer using the phrase, *At the _____.*

## APPLICATION

- Direct Ss' attention to Exercise 3 and read the instructions aloud.
- Read aloud the example conversation in Exercise 3 as you point to the picture.
- Write on the board the questions: *Where is he? Where is she?* Read each question aloud and ask Ss to repeat after you. Point to the people in the pictures in Exercise 2B as you repeat the questions to reinforce the difference between *he* and *she*.
- Model the task. Ask two Ss to stand beside you. Pretend to be at a movie theater, for example, eating popcorn and staring at an imaginary screen. S1 asks: *Where is she?* S2 guesses: *At the movie theater?* You say: *Right!*
- Ask S1 to act out being at a different place. S2 asks: *Where is he?* You guess. S1 says *Right!* or *No!* Make sure Ss understand the task.
- Ss play the guessing game in small groups. Walk around and help as needed. Then ask each group to act out one place for the rest of the class.

### Expansion activity *(small groups)*

- Before class. Create cards for a "Concentration" game using the six people's names and the six places from the lesson. Each group needs one set of 12 cards.
- Place all of the cards facedown in three rows of four cards on a desk or table where Ss can see the cards easily. The first S turns over two cards. If the cards match, the S must make a sentence with the matching cards, for example: *Isabel is at the gas station.* If the sentence is correct, the S keeps the cards. If the cards don't match, the S puts the cards back. Then the second S tries to find a matching pair. The game continues until all the matching pairs have been found. The winner is the person with the most cards.

## EVALUATION

- Direct Ss' attention to the lesson focus on the board. Point to Exercise 2B and ask individual Ss about the location of people in the exercise: *Where's Minh?* (At the movie theater.) Then have Ss ask their classmates the questions.
- Check off each part of the lesson focus as Ss demonstrate an understanding of what they have learned in the lesson.

| More Ventures, Unit 5, Lesson B | |
| --- | --- |
| Literacy Workbook, 15–30 min. | |
| Basic Workbook, 15–30 min. | |
| Writing Worksheets, 15–30 min. | www.cambridge.org/ventures/ resources/ |
| Collaborative Worksheets, 30–45 min. | |
| Student Arcade, time varies | www.cambridge.org/venturesarcade/ |

B **Listen and repeat.** Then write.

| gas station | hospital | laundromat |
| movie theater | pharmacy | post office |

CD1, Track 54

1. Minh

2. Alan

3. Mr. Lopez

4. Paula

5. Jackie

6. Isabel

| Name | Place | Name | Place |
| --- | --- | --- | --- |
| 1. Minh | movie theater | 4. Paula | laundromat |
| 2. Alan | hospital | 5. Jackie | post office |
| 3. Mr. Lopez | pharmacy | 6. Isabel | gas station |

**Talk with a partner.** Ask and answer.

A Where's **Minh**?

B At the **movie theater**.

## 3 Communicate

**Work in a group.** Play a game.
Ask and guess.

A Where is **he**?

B At the **movie theater**?

C That's right!

# Lesson C The school is on Main Street.

## 1 Grammar focus: *on, next to, across from, between*

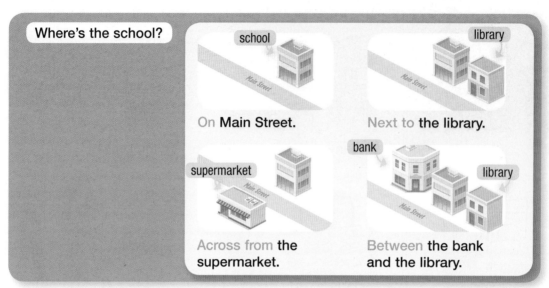

Where's the school?

On **Main Street.**

Next to **the library.**

Across from **the supermarket.**

Between **the bank and the library.**

Watch

## 2 Practice

**A  Read and circle.** Then write.

1. **A** Where's the pharmacy?
   **B** _____**Between**_____ the restaurant
      (Between) Across from
      and the supermarket.

2. **A** Where's the supermarket?
   **B** _____*On*_____ Main Street.
      Across from (On)

3. **A** Where's the restaurant?
   **B** _____*Next to*_____ the pharmacy.
      Between (Next to)

4. **A** Where's the bakery?
   **B** _____*Across from*_____ the restaurant.
      Next to (Across from)

5. **A** Where's the police station?
   **B** _____*Next to*_____ the bakery.
      On (Next to)

**Listen and repeat.**
Then practice with a partner.

restaurant · bakery · pharmacy · MAIN SREET · police station · supermarket

CD1, Track 55

- Introduce prepositions of location (*on, next to, across from, between*)
- Provide practice asking and answering questions about the locations of buildings and places

# WARM-UP AND REVIEW

- Before class. Write today's lesson focus on the board.
  *Lesson C:*
  *on, next to, across from, between*
  *Where's the school?*
- Before class. Write on the board the vocabulary from Lessons A and B: *bank, library, restaurant, school, street, supermarket, pharmacy, hospital, laundromat, movie theater, post office, gas station.*
- Begin class. Books open. Point to and say the vocabulary words and ask Ss to repeat after you.
- Direct Ss' attention to the picture on page 58. Say the first six vocabulary words again and ask Ss to point to the corresponding parts of the picture. Walk around and check to see that Ss are pointing to the correct items in the picture.
- Direct Ss' attention to the six pictures on page 60. Say the next six vocabulary words and ask Ss to point to the corresponding picture. Walk around and check to see that Ss are pointing to the correct pictures.

# PRESENTATION

- Use the animated grammar presentation in one or more of the following ways:
  - Preview it before class
  - Show it in class
  - Encourage Ss to watch it outside of class.
- Direct Ss' attention to the grammar chart in Exercise 1 on page 62. Read the question aloud and ask Ss to repeat after you. Then do the same with the prepositional phrases.
- To show the question-and-answer relationship between the question and the prepositional phrases, say to a S: *Please say the question.* Elicit: *Where's the school?* Answer the question with one of the prepositional phrases.
- Repeat the procedure with at least three more Ss, each time answering with the phrases from the grammar box.
- Finally, have Ss practice asking and answering the question in pairs while pointing to the pictures and phrases in the grammar chart.

## Literacy Tip

Lesson C presents several challenges for literacy Ss. You may want to set up alternate activity stations around the room with, for example, flash cards that have pictures photocopied from the book on one side and the corresponding words on the other or worksheets with the unit vocabulary words followed by the same words with one or two letters missing, for Ss to complete.

## Teaching Tip

Although the meanings of *next to* and *between* are easy to show using physical objects, being *on* a street and *across from* something are more idiomatic. In the first case, buildings are not literally on a street; otherwise they would block traffic. In the second case, there is an implied space between one thing and another, such as a street, a hallway, or an aisle. Since these issues are rather complex, use the pictures in the book to help Ss understand the meanings of these phrases.

# PRACTICE

- Direct Ss' attention to the map in Exercise 2A. Read aloud the example conversation using different voices for Speaker A and Speaker B. When you read Speaker B's line, show Ss the two answer choices under the blank and ask: *"Between"* or *"Across from"*? Elicit: *Between.*
- Read aloud the instructions for Exercise 2A. Point to where *Between* has been circled and written for number 1.
- Ss complete the exercise individually. Walk around and help as needed.

# COMPREHENSION CHECK

- Read aloud the second part of the instructions for Exercise 2A.
- ▶ *CD1, Track 55* Play or read the audio (see audio script, page T-147). Ss listen and repeat as they check their answers.
- Write the numbers *1–5* on the board. Ask volunteers to come to the board and write the answers they circled. Make any necessary corrections on the board.
- Ss in pairs. Ask Ss to choose Role A or B and practice the questions and answers in Exercise 2A. Then have Ss switch roles and practice again. Walk around and help as needed.
- Ask several pairs to say the questions and answers for the rest of the class.

## Literacy Tip

For an alternative activity, refer literacy Ss to pages 58–59 in the *Literacy Workbook* at any time during the lesson.

# LESSON C The school is on Main Street.

## PRESENTATION

- Direct Ss' attention to the pictures in Exercise 2B. Point to each picture and ask the class: *What places do you see?* Elicit the names of the places, for example, *bank* and *supermarket*.

- Point to the prepositional phrase under each picture and say to Ss: *What's this? Please say the words.* Elicit the phrases.

## PRACTICE

- Read aloud the first part of the instructions for Exercise 2B.

- ▶ *CD1, Track 56* Play or read the audio (see audio script, pages T-147–T-148). Ss listen and repeat the conversations.

- Write on the board: *Excuse me. Where's the _____?* Tell Ss that they can use the question to ask people on the street where places are. Model the use of the question by pretending to be a stranger who needs directions.

- Read aloud the second part of the instructions in Exercise 2B. Call on two Ss to read aloud the example conversation. Call on two different Ss to model a new conversation using Picture 2.

- Indicate that Ss should ask and answer questions about all six pictures. Make sure Ss understand the task.

- Ss ask and answer questions in pairs about the pictures. When Ss are finished, ask them to switch partners and repeat the conversations.

### Expansion activity *(student pairs)*

- Before class. Prepare blank maps similar to the map in Exercise 2A on page 62. Include a list of places from the unit that Ss can use to name the places shown on the map. Hand out a map to each S.

- Have Ss work individually to fill in the map with the names of places, or have literacy Ss work with higher-level Ss, pointing to the squares where they would like the places to be written.

- Have Ss in pairs ask and answer questions about each other's maps. The first S shows the map to his or her partner and asks questions, such as: *Where's the school? Where's the pharmacy?*

- The second S answers using prepositional phrases. In many cases, more than one phrase will be correct, so as you walk around, encourage Ss to think of all the ways they can express the location of a place, such as: *Next to the movie theater. Across from the bank.*

- When Ss are finished, ask them to switch roles and talk about the second S's map.

## APPLICATION

- Direct Ss' attention to Exercise 3 and read the instructions and the example conversation aloud.

- Model the task. Say to a S: *Say the question.* Elicit: *Where are you?* Point to the pictures in Exercise 2B and say to the first S's partner: *You are at one of these places. Where?* Elicit one of the prepositional phrases. Ask the first S to guess the place. Make sure Ss understand the task.

- Ss complete the exercise in pairs. Walk around and help as needed.

- When Ss are finished, ask several different Ss: *Where are you?* As Ss answer with prepositional phrases, call on different Ss to guess where their classmate is.

## EVALUATION

- Direct Ss' attention to the lesson focus on the board. Write on the board: *Where's the _____?*

- Direct Ss' attention to the picture on page 58. Call on Ss to ask a classmate the question written on the board about the picture. Have the S who answers ask the next question.

- Repeat the procedure with the map on page 62. Monitor Ss' accuracy using prepositional phrases.

- Check off each part of the lesson focus as Ss demonstrate an understanding of what they have learned in the lesson.

| *More Ventures, Unit 5, Lesson C* | |
|---|---|
| **Literacy Workbook,** 15–30 min. | |
| **Basic Workbook,** 15–30 min. | |
| **Writing Worksheets,** 15–30 min. | www.cambridge.org/ventures/ resources/ |
| **Collaborative Worksheets,** 30–45 min. | |
| **Student Arcade,** time varies | www.cambridge.org/venturesarcade/ |

**B  Listen and repeat.**

CD1, Track 56

1. next to

2. across from

3. between

4. on

5. next to

6. across from

**Talk with a partner.** Ask and answer.

A  Excuse me. Where's the **bank**?

B  **Next to the supermarket.**

A  Thanks.

## 3  Communicate

**Talk with a partner.** Play a game.
Ask and guess.

A  Where are you?

B  **Next to the supermarket.**

A  At the **bank**?

B  Yes, that's right.

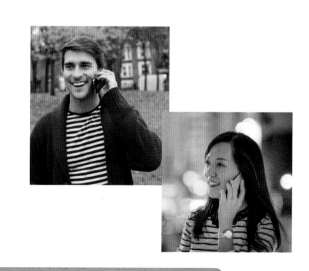

# Lesson D Reading

## 1 Before you read

**Talk about the picture.**
What do you see?

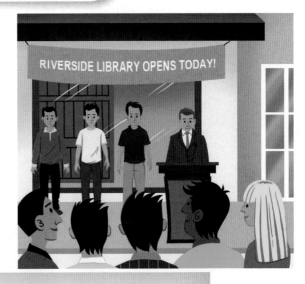

RIVERSIDE LIBRARY OPENS TODAY!

## 2 Read

**Listen and read.**

CD1, Track 57

 **Notice from Riverside Library**

Come and visit Riverside Library. The new library opens today.
The library is on Main Street. It is across from Riverside Adult
School. It is next to K and P Supermarket. It is between K and
P Supermarket and Rosie's Restaurant. The library is open
from 9:00 to 5:00, Monday, Wednesday, and Friday.

## 3 After you read

**Complete the map.** Share your map with a partner.

2. *K and P Supermarket*

Main St.

1. *school*

3. *library*

4. *Rosie's Restaurant*

Teaching objectives
- Introduce a notice about a library
- Introduce transportation vocabulary
- Provide practice using new topic-related words

# WARM-UP AND REVIEW

- Before class. Write today's lesson focus on the board.

  *Lesson D:*
  *Read "Notice from Riverside Library"*
  *Learn transportation words*

- Before class. Take out the six images you used in the Warm-up in Lesson B and find six new images to represent the vocabulary from Lesson B. You will have 12 images in all. For example, you might find a clip-art image of a letter to represent *post office*, a magazine picture of a gas pump to represent *gas station*, and a picture of a box of popcorn to represent *movie theater*.

- Before class: Write on the board the vocabulary from Lessons A and B: *bank, library, restaurant, school, street, supermarket, pharmacy, hospital, laundromat, movie theater, post office, gas station.*

- Begin class. Books closed. Point to and say the vocabulary words and ask Ss to repeat after you.

- One by one, hold up the images and ask Ss: *What's this?* or *Where can I find this?* Elicit the names of the places on the board.

# PRESENTATION

- Read aloud the first part of the lesson focus on the board and ask Ss to repeat after you. Write on the board and say to Ss: *The library opens today!* Ask Ss to repeat.

- Ask: *What does this mean?* Elicit any ideas Ss have. If they need help understanding the meaning, go over the difference between places being *open* and *closed*. Then explain that the library is *new*. This is the first day the library is open.

- Books open. Direct Ss' attention to the picture in Exercise 1. Ask the class: *What is this place?* (The library.) Ask Ss to look for this library in the picture on page 58.

- Read aloud the instructions for Exercise 1 on page 64. Ask: *What do you see?* Elicit and write on the board any vocabulary about the picture that Ss know, such as: *man, woman, bicycle, door.*

# PRACTICE

- Direct Ss' attention to Exercise 2. Point to the title of the paragraph and ask Ss: *What's the title?* ("Notice from Riverside Library.") Explain that a notice is similar to a note, which they saw an example of in Unit 2. A *notice* is for all of the people in town, whereas a *note* is usually for one person.

▶ **CD1, Track 57** Play or read the audio and ask Ss to follow along (see audio script, page T-148). Repeat the audio as needed.

- Read aloud each sentence of the reading and ask Ss to repeat after you.

- Answer any questions Ss have about the reading.

### Literacy Tip

Literacy Ss should be able to talk about the picture and listen to and repeat the lines of the reading passage. They may also be able to assist in the map activity by pointing to the places on the map while a higher-level S writes the names of the places.

### *Learner persistence* (individual work)
▶ **CD1, Track 57** Ss can listen to the audio for Exercise 2 at home for reinforcement and review. They can also listen to the audio for self-directed learning when class attendance is not possible.

# COMPREHENSION CHECK

- Read aloud the instructions for Exercise 3.

- Model the task. Point to where *school* has been written on the map. Ask Ss: *What's this place?* (School or Riverside Adult School.)

- Point to the reading and ask Ss: *Where's the library?* Begin reading aloud with the sentence: *The library is on Main Street. It is across from Riverside Adult School.*

- Point to the map and say: *The school! The library is across from the school.* Ask Ss: *Where do you write "library"?* (Line 3.) Point to line 3 and say: *Write "library" here.*

- Ss scan the reading and fill in the map individually. Walk around and help as needed.

- Go over the answers with the class. Duplicate the map from Exercise 3 on the board. Call on Ss to write the names of the places in the appropriate places and tell the class where they found the answer in the reading.

- Have Ss compare their maps with the picture on page 58.

### Literacy Tip

For an alternative activity, refer literacy Ss to pages 60–61 in the *Literacy Workbook* at any time during the lesson.

# LESSON D Reading

## PRESENTATION

- Direct Ss' attention to the Picture dictionary in Exercise 4. Point to and say the word *transportation* in the Student's Book and in the second part of the lesson focus on the board. Tell Ss: *Today, we will learn transportation words.* Ask Ss to brainstorm some modes of transportation. Write their ideas on the board, such as *bus, plane, car,* etc.
- Read aloud the instructions for Exercise 4A.
- Help Ss preview the pictures by holding up the Student's Book and saying, for example: *Number one. What do you see?* Elicit any vocabulary about the pictures that Ss already know. If Ss know the word for the transportation form pictured, write it on the board; for example: *bicycle.* If Ss don't know the word, tell them the word, write it on the board, say it, and ask them to repeat.

### Teaching Tip

The phrase *on foot* is an exception to the pattern in the Picture dictionary, since it uses a different preposition and there is no mechanical vehicle involved. Ss should know the word *foot,* but they may also know the word *walk* and wonder why it is not being used. If this is the case, teach Ss the phrase *by walking* in addition to *on foot.*

- ▶ **CD1, Track 58** Play or read the audio (see audio script, page T-148). Listen to Ss' pronunciation as they repeat the words. Correct Ss' pronunciation as needed.

### Expansion activity (student pairs)

- Before class. Photocopy and cut out enough of the Picture dictionary cards for Unit 5 to give each S one card.
- Write a story to read in class about someone's busy day in which they go to at least six of the places in the unit, using the six forms of transportation in the Picture dictionary; for example: *Today is Wednesday. Gina goes to the library on foot.*
- Tell Ss to hold up their card when they hear the transportation words in the story.

### Learner persistence (individual work)

- ▶ **CD1, Track 58** Ss can listen to the audio for Exercise 4A at home for reinforcement and review. They can also listen to the audio for self-directed learning when class attendance is not possible.

## PRACTICE

- Direct Ss' attention to Exercise 4B and read the instructions aloud. Read the example conversation aloud or have two Ss read it.
- Point to and read aloud the two column headings in the chart. Point to where Ben's information has been written as an example.

- Ss stand up, walk around, and talk to at least four classmates about how they get to school.
- When Ss are finished, ask them follow-up questions about their classmates, such as: *How does Walter get to school? Who can tell me?*

### Expansion activity (whole group)

- Draw on the board a chart with seven columns. Label the first six columns with the phrases from the Picture dictionary and label the last column *Other.*
- Ask the class: *How do you get to school?* Have Ss come to the board and check the appropriate column to indicate how they get to school. Then have a volunteer add up the checkmarks in each column.

  **Option** Point to each column and ask questions using *How many?* For example, point to the first column and ask: *How many people get to school by bicycle?*

### Expansion activity (whole group)

- Ask Ss who work outside the home to tell the class how they get to work.

## EVALUATION

- Direct Ss' attention to the first part of the lesson focus on the board. Point to the reading passage and ask: *What place did we read about?* (Riverside Library.) Ask: *Is the library opening today?* (Yes.) Ask: *Where is the library?* Elicit prepositional phrases.
- Direct Ss' attention to the second part of the lesson focus. Ask Ss to take out the Picture dictionary cards you gave them in the first expansion activity. Tell Ss: *You are going to the supermarket. Use the words on the cards to tell me how you get there.* Ask individual Ss: *How do you get to the supermarket?* Elicit the phrases from Ss' cards. Then have Ss ask each other the same question.
- Check off each part of the lesson focus as Ss demonstrate understanding of what they have learned in the lesson.

| *More Ventures, Unit 5, Lesson D* | |
|---|---|
| Literacy Workbook, 15–30 min. | |
| Basic Workbook, 15-30 min. | |
| Picture Dictionary activities, 30–45 min. Writing Worksheets, 15–30 min. Collaborative Worksheets, 30–45 min. | www.cambridge.org/ventures/ resources/ |
| Student Arcade, time varies | www.cambridge.org/venturesarcade/ |

## 4 **Picture dictionary** Transportation

1. by bicycle

2. by bus

3. by car

4. by taxi

5. by train

6. on foot

A **Listen and repeat.** Look at the Picture dictionary.

B **Talk with your classmates.** Complete the chart.

A **Ben**, how do you get to school?

B **By car.**

◀))) **CD1, Track** 58

| Name | Transportation |
|------|----------------|
| Ben | by car |
| Answers will vary. | |
| | |
| | |
| | |

# Lesson E Writing

## 1 Before you write

**A** **Talk with a partner.** Complete the words.

1. s u p e r m a r _k_ e t
2. p _h_ a r m a c y
3. p o s t    o f _f_ i c e
4. r e s _t_ a u r a n t
5. l i _b_ r a r y
6. s _c_ h o o l

**B** **Talk with a partner.** Look at the map. Complete the story.

**Reed Street**

Donna lives on Reed _____Street_____ . She lives near a big
1

supermarket. The supermarket is next to a _____pharmacy_____ .
2

A _____restaurant_____ is across from the supermarket. A
3

_post_____office_____ is on Reed Street, too. It is across from
4

the _____library_____ . A _____school_____ is between the
5                                 6

restaurant and the library.

Teaching objectives
• Prepare Ss for completing sentences with directions
• Provide practice writing key vocabulary words

# WARM-UP AND REVIEW

• Before class. Write today's lesson focus on the board.
  *Lesson E:*
  *Review words for places*
  *Review on, next to, across from, between*
  *Complete sentences about directions to your house*

• Before class. Draw on the board a map of a community similar to the map on page 64. Label the places on the map with vocabulary from the unit.

• Begin class. Books closed. Direct Ss' attention to the map on the board. Ask questions, such as: *Where's the post office? Where's the laundromat?* Elicit from Ss prepositional phrases, such as: *Next to the bank* and *Between the supermarket and the library.*

# PRESENTATION

• Books open. Direct Ss' attention to Exercise 1A and read the instructions aloud. Point to the first item and say to Ss: *Number one. What's the word?* (Supermarket.) Ask: *What letter do we need?* (k.) Pretend to write the letter *k* in the blank for number 1.

# PRACTICE

• Ss work individually or in pairs to complete the words.

• When Ss are finished, call on different individuals or pairs to write their completed words on the board. Review the alphabet by asking Ss who write answers on the board to say the letters aloud. Have Ss make any necessary corrections on the board.

### Literacy Tip

Your literacy Ss should be able to handle Exercise 1A without special help, but for the other exercises in the lesson, you may want to provide alternate work such as tracing letters or filling in blanks in the other vocabulary words from the unit. Refer Ss to *Literacy Workbook* (pages 62–63).

• Read the instructions for Exercise 1B aloud.

• Ss work alone or in pairs to fill in the blanks in the story using the map and the words in Exercise 1A.

• Check answers as a class. Write the numbers 1–6 on the board and ask for volunteers to write their answers on the board.

• Read the passage aloud. When you get to each blank, point to and say the answer on the board. Ask the class: *Is this correct?* Make any necessary corrections on the board.

## *Expansion activity* (student pairs)

• Create a fill-in-the-blank exercise using "Directions to Donna's House" with blanks instead of the prepositions.

• Have one S in each pair read aloud the passage from the book while the other fills in the blanks.

• When Ss are finished, ask them to compare their passage with the original in the Student's Book.

## *Expansion activity* (small groups)

• For each group, write the vocabulary for places from the unit on 12 index cards or small pieces of paper.

• Draw a simple map using at least half of the places. Don't show the map to Ss.

• Tell Ss to listen as you make statements about the map you are looking at. Have Ss arrange the "places" on a desk or table. You may need to read through your statements several times.

• When Ss are finished, walk around and see which groups have recreated your map correctly. If a group has made a mistake, give them the relevant information they need to repair it; for example: *The bank is "across from" the restaurant, not "next to" the restaurant.*

## *Expansion activity* (whole group)

• Tell Ss you are going to draw a map of the location of your school on the board. Brainstorm nearby businesses. Write their names on the board.

• Draw a rough map of the area on the board, showing streets. Draw rectangles for nearby buildings.

• Ask volunteers to write the names of nearby streets and businesses on the map.

• Ask volunteers to make statements about the school's location, for example: *The school is next to a gas station. The school is on _____ street.*

# LESSON E Writing

## PRACTICE

- Direct Ss' attention to Exercise **2A** and read the instructions aloud. Tell Ss: *Draw the places on your street. Write the words.*
- Ss draw their maps individually. Walk around and help as needed.
- Read aloud the instructions for Exercise **2B**. Help Ss get started by modeling sentences about your street on the board. Start writing and then say, for example: *I live on . . . What do I need here? (A street.) Correct. I live on Milton Street.*
- Continue in this manner if your Ss need a model to refer to or direct them to the passage on page 66 for help.

### Teaching Tip

Exercises **2A** and **2B** are necessarily open-ended, since Ss live in different places. Be prepared to help Ss think of places in their neighborhoods to put on their maps, but ask Ss not to include places they haven't studied in Unit 5, for example, clothing stores, veterinarians' offices, or any other places that classmates may not know the words for. If any Ss live on a street with only houses, suggest that they draw a different street that they know well. Help them change the wording of the sentences in Exercise **2B** accordingly.

### Literacy Tip

Literacy Ss may have trouble writing the names of buildings and completing the sentences in Exercise **2B**. Instead, assign pages 62–63 from the *Literacy Workbook*.

## COMPREHENSION CHECK

- Direct Ss' attention to Exercise **3** and read the instructions aloud. Hold your Student's Book close to you and tell Ss: *Don't let your partner see your map. Tell your partner about your map.*
- Ss work in pairs. One student reads his/her sentences aloud, and the other listens and draws the map. Students compare their maps with their partners. Then they switch roles.
- Walk around and help as needed and check to see that Ss have written the names of places correctly.

## *Expansion activity* (individual work)

- Ask Ss to write their completed sentences from Exercise **2B** on a piece of paper to hand in.

## *Community building* (whole group)

- Before class. Draw a simple map of the neighborhood where your class is held. Label places on the map with vocabulary from the unit.
- Give each S a copy of the map and ask a few questions about where places are. Then tell Ss anything you know about the places, for example, which restaurant has good food or that the nearby laundromat is very expensive. Encourage Ss to share their information about the places with the class.

## EVALUATION

- Direct Ss' attention to the lesson focus on the board. Read the first two lines aloud and ask Ss to repeat. Ask the class: *Can you do this? Can you talk about where places are?* Elicit: *Yes!*
- Direct Ss' attention to the picture on page 58 and the map on page 62 and have them ask and answer questions about where the places are.
- Direct Ss' attention to the third line of the lesson focus. Read it aloud and ask Ss to repeat. Write sentence prompts on the board similar to the ones in Exercise **2B**. Call on individual Ss to complete the sentences on the board with any appropriate vocabulary from the unit.
- Check off each part of the lesson focus as Ss demonstrate an understanding of what they have learned in the lesson.

| *More Ventures, Unit 5, Lesson E* | |
|---|---|
| Literacy Workbook, 15–30 min. | |
| Basic Workbook, 15–30 min. | |
| Writing Worksheets, 15–30 min. | www.cambridge.org/ventures/ resources/ |
| Collaborative Worksheets, 30–45 min. | |

## 2 Write

**A** Draw a map of your street.

> *Answers will vary.*

**B** Write about your street.

1. I live on _____ *Answers will vary* _____.
2. I live near a _____.
3. A _____ is across from a _____.
4. A _____ is between the _____ and the _____.

## 3 After you write

**Listen to your partner.** Draw your partner's street.

> *Answers will vary.*

# Lesson F Another view

## 1 Life-skills reading

A **Read the sentences.** Look at the map. Fill in the answer.

1. The hospital is ____.

   Ⓐ on Jackson Street

   ⬤Ⓑ on Washington Street

   Ⓒ on Avenue B

2. The post office is ____.

   Ⓐ next to the police station

   Ⓑ next to the school

   ⬤Ⓒ next to the restaurant

3. The post office is ____.

   ⬤Ⓐ between the restaurant and the library

   Ⓑ across from the library

   Ⓒ on Washington Street

4. The hospital is ____.

   Ⓐ across from the school

   ⬤Ⓑ next to the police station

   Ⓒ between the restaurant and the school

B **Solve the problem.** Which solution is best? Circle your answer.

Where's the library? Eva doesn't know. What can she do?

1. Look at a map.

2. Go home.

3. Other: *Answers will vary.*

- Introduce reading a map
- Provide practice that develops test-taking skills
- Review vocabulary from the unit

## WARM-UP AND REVIEW

- Before class. Write today's lesson focus on the board.
  *Lesson F:*
  *Read a map*
- Before class. Draw a simple map on the board. Draw six buildings and label them with the symbols used in the Student's Book: dollar sign for bank, book for library, letter for post office, etc.
- Begin class. Books closed. Review vocabulary and grammar from the unit by pointing to each building on the map and asking Ss: *What's this?* Ask volunteers to come to the board and label the buildings on the map.
- When the map is completed, ask Ss questions with *Where*, for example: *Where's the pharmacy?* Elicit prepositional phrases such as: *Next to the library.*

## PRESENTATION

- Books open. Direct Ss' attention to the map in Exercise 1. Ask Ss: *What places do you see?* As Ss say the names of the places represented with icons on the map, list the words on the board. Repeat and spell words as you list them.

## PRACTICE

- Read aloud the instructions in Exercise 1A. This task helps prepare Ss for standardized-type tests they may have to take.
- Write the first item on the board along with the three answer choices labeled *A*, *B*, and *C*.
- Read the item and answer choices aloud and then point to the map. Ask Ss: *Is the hospital on Jackson Street, Washington Street, or Avenue B?* Show Ss where to look on the map for the information. Elicit: *On Washington Street.*
- Point to the three answer choices on the board. Ask Ss: *A, B, or C?* (*B*) Fill in the letter *B* and tell Ss: *Fill in the answer.* Make sure Ss understand the task.
- Have Ss individually scan for and fill in the answers.

### Literacy Tip

Literacy Ss will likely have trouble with Lesson F, so you may want to provide them alternative activities to work on at their desks or at self-access centers in the classroom.

## COMPREHENSION CHECK

- Go over the answers to Exercise 1A together. Make sure Ss followed the instructions and filled in their answers. Ask Ss to point to the places on the map.

## APPLICATION

- Read aloud the instructions for Exercise 1B. Tell Ss they are going to discuss what Eva can do.
- Ss ask and answer questions in pairs. When Ss are finished, ask them to find a new partner and talk to him or her about what Eva can do.

### Expansion activity *(student pairs)*

- Write on the board: *How do you get to _____?* Say the sentence using the name of a place and ask Ss to repeat after you.
- Have a volunteer ask you the question about any place on the map. Hold up your Student's Book, point to page 65 and answer the question using a phrase from the Picture dictionary.
- Ss ask and answer questions in pairs.

  **Option** Before class. Photocopy and cut out a set of the Picture dictionary cards for each pair of Ss and have them place the cards in a pile facedown. When S1 asks the question, S2 picks up the top card and answers using the form of transportation pictured on the card.

### Literacy Tip

For an alternative activity, refer literacy Ss to pages 64–65 in the *Literacy Workbook* at any time during the lesson.

# LESSON F Another view

## PRACTICE

- Direct Ss' attention to Exercise 2A and read the instructions aloud.
- Model the task. Point to the first picture and ask: *Where is this?* Elicit: *Post office.* Point to the words and the line connecting the picture to *post office.*
- Tell Ss: *Match the pictures and the words.*
- Ss complete the exercise individually. Then Ss compare their answers with a partner's.

### Expansion activity *(whole group)*

- Teach vocabulary for items in the pictures in Exercise 2A.
- Point to each picture in turn and ask Ss: *What do you see?* List on the board any vocabulary Ss know and provide additional words, such as: *stamp, envelope, dollar bill, coins or change, clothes, towels, laundry basket, medicine, tooth brushes, tickets, popcorn, pastries, rolls.*
- Talk about items according to Ss' interest and whenever possible, show Ss real examples of the items.

## PRACTICE

- Direct Ss' attention to the word puzzle in Exercise 2B. Ask the class: *What is this? What do you see?* Ss may say that they see letters.
- Read the instructions for Exercise 2B aloud. Point to the word *puzzle* and tell Ss: *This is a puzzle.* Say the word aloud and ask Ss to repeat after you.
- Model the task. Point to and say the word *foot* in the word box. Point to the puzzle and ask Ss: *Do you see "foot" here?* Ss should point to the circled example.
- Ss find the words individually or in pairs. When most of the Ss have finished, ask Ss if there are words they can't find in the puzzle. Have other Ss show them where the words are.

## EVALUATION

- Do a quick review of the unit. Have Ss turn to Lesson A. Ask the class to talk about what they remember about this lesson. Prompt Ss, if necessary, with questions, such as: *What words are on this page? What do you see in the picture?* Continue in this manner to review each lesson quickly.

### Expansion activity

- Before class. Print, for each student, one copy of the Self-assessment for this unit.
- Have Ss complete the Self-assessment either in class or outside of class.
- Provide feedback to Ss such as through a whole-class discussion, partners comparing their worksheets, or T reviewing each S's worksheet.
- If Ss are ready, administer the unit test on page T-166 of this Teacher's Edition. The audio script for the test is available on page T-192.
- If Ss are ready, administer the midterm test on page T-169 of this Teacher's Edition. The audio script for the test is available on page T-192.

| More Ventures, Unit 5, Lesson F | |
|---|---|
| Literacy Workbook, 15–30 min. | |
| Basic Workbook, 15–30 min. | |
| Writing Worksheets, 15–30 min. | www.cambridge.org/ventures/ resources/ |
| Collaborative Worksheets, 30–45 min. | |
| Self-assessment, 10 min. | |
| CASAS Test Prep Worksheet, 5–10 min. | |

## 2 Fun with vocabulary

### A Read and match.

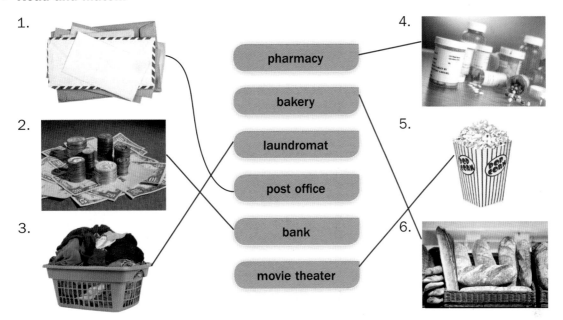

1.
2.
3.

pharmacy
bakery
laundromat
post office
bank
movie theater

4.
5.
6.

**Talk with a partner.** Check your answers.

### B Circle the words in the puzzle.

bicycle   bus   car   foot   taxi   train

k  f  (f  o  o  t)  c  s
v  x  a  m  b  r  a  m
k  a  o  (t  r  a  i  n)
(t  a  x  i)  s  i  g  t
k  a  v  i  (b  u  s)  n
(b  i  c  y  c  l  e)  e
x  r  w  (c  a  r)  k  b

# UNIT 6 TIME

## Lesson A Listening

### 1 Before you listen

**A**  Look at the picture. What do you see?

**B**  Listen and point: ■ 7:00 ■ 9:00 ■ 10:00 ■ 10:30
■ 2:30 ■ 6:30

◄)) CD2, Track 02

# UNIT 6

**Teaching objectives**
- Introduce Ss to the topic
- Find out what Ss know about the topic
- Preview the unit by talking about the picture
- Provide practice of key vocabulary
- Provide practice that develops listening skills

## WARM-UP AND REVIEW

- Before class. Write today's lesson focus on the board.
  *Lesson A:*
  *Time vocabulary*
- Begin class. Books closed. Write the phrase *shopping mall* on the board. Point to the words. Read them aloud and ask Ss to repeat. Ask: *What's this?* Elicit appropriate responses. Ask: *What stores are in the mall?*

### Teaching Tip

Ask Ss to say the names of shopping malls in your area. If you don't have a mall, ask Ss to brainstorm the names of local stores.

- Draw three rectangles on the board and then three more rectangles across from them to represent stores facing each other in a mall. Ask: *What kinds of stores?* Elicit: *clothes store, shoe store,* etc. or use actual names. Write the names of the stores in the rectangles.
- Point to two adjacent stores. Ask: *Where is (name of store)?* (It's next to _____.)
- Continue by asking more questions about the stores. Encourage Ss to use the prepositions *on, next to, across from,* and *between.*

### Literacy Tip

If you have literacy Ss in your class, it might be helpful to spend time at the beginning of any activity with art or photos talking about the pictures before focusing Ss' attention on the printed words in the exercise. Have Ss work in pairs. Tell them to ask each other: *What do you see?* Encourage Ss to describe the pictures to each other. Consider pairing literacy Ss with Ss who can help them read the text in the exercise. This will help preview the exercise for literacy Ss and make them more confident as the exercise continues.

## PRESENTATION

- Books open. Set the scene. Hold up the Student's Book. Show Ss the picture on page 70. Tell Ss: *This is a shopping mall.*

- Ask: *What do you see?* Elicit and write on the board any vocabulary that Ss know, such as: *movie theater, restaurants, woman.*

## PRACTICE

- Direct Ss' attention to the key vocabulary in Exercise 1B. Read each time phrase aloud while pointing to the times in the picture. Ask Ss to repeat and point.
- ▶ *CD2, Track 2* Play or read the audio (see audio script, page T-148). Tell Ss: *Listen and point to the picture.* As Ss hear the key vocabulary, check to see that they are pointing to the correct part of the picture. Repeat the audio as needed.

## COMPREHENSION CHECK

- Ask Ss *Yes / No* questions about the picture. Tell Ss: *Listen. Say "yes" or "no."*

  Point to the picture. Ask: *Is this a shopping mall?* (Yes.)
  Point to the gym. Ask: *Is this a movie theater?* (No.)
  Point to the soup restaurant. Ask: *Is this restaurant next to Brown's Deli?* (Yes.)
  Point to the woman in front of the movie theater. Ask: *Is Teresa next to Brown's Deli?* (No.)
  Point to the woman sitting in front of Brown's Deli. Ask: *Is Joan next to the movie theater?* (No.)
  Point to the sign at the movie theater. Ask: *Is the next movie at 2:30?* (Yes.)
  Point to the sign at Brown's Deli. Ask: *Is the breakfast special from 8:00 a.m. to 10 a.m.?* (No.)
  Point to the clock on the movie theater. Ask: *Is it 10:30?* (Yes.)
  Point to the circled time in the calendar. Ask: *Is this 10:00?* (Yes.)

### Teaching Tip

It might be helpful to explain the difference between *a.m.* and *p.m.* to the class or ask volunteers to explain it for the rest of the class.

### *Expansion activity* (whole group)

- Write different times on the board, such as: *10:00 a.m., 9:30 p.m., 10:00 p.m., 6:30 a.m.,* and *7:30 p.m.* Use only times on the hour or half hour, since Ss will not be familiar with other time phrases yet. Ask a volunteer to come to the board. Say: *Please circle "10:00 p.m."* Ask the rest of the class: *Is that correct?* If it is not correct, ask another S to find the correct answer.

# LESSON A Listening

## PRESENTATION

- Direct Ss' attention to Exercise 2A. Tell Ss: *We are going to practice saying the different times.*
- Read aloud the instructions for Exercise 2A.

## PRACTICE

▶ **CD2, Track 3** Play or read the audio (see audio script, page T-148). Ss listen and repeat the vocabulary. Repeat the audio as needed.

- Listen carefully to Ss' pronunciation and make corrections as needed.

**Learner persistence** *(individual work)*

▶ **CD2, Track 3** Ss can listen to the audio for Exercise 2A at home for reinforcement and review. They can also listen to the audio for self-directed learning when class attendance is not possible.

- Direct Ss' attention to Exercise 2B and read the instructions aloud.

▶ **CD2, Track 4** Model the task. Hold up the Student's Book and say: *Number one.* Play or read the audio for number 1 (see audio script, page T-148). Point to the two answer choices in number 1 and ask Ss: *What did you hear – a or b?* Elicit: *b.* Point to the letter *b* next to the second picture and tell Ss: *Circle the letter "b."*

▶ **CD2, Track 4** Play or read the complete audio. Ss listen and circle the correct answers. Repeat the audio as needed.

▶ **CD2, Track 4** Read aloud the second part of the instructions for Exercise 2B. Play or read the audio again so that Ss can listen and check their answers.

**Learner persistence** *(individual work)*

▶ **CD2, Track 4** Ss can listen to the audio for Exercise 2B at home for reinforcement and review. They can also listen to the audio for self-directed learning when class attendance is not possible.

## COMPREHENSION CHECK

- Write the numbers *1–4* on the board. Ask a few Ss to come to the board and write the correct answers to Exercise 2B next to each number.

▶ **CD2, Track 4** Play or read the audio again. Pause the audio after each conversation. Point to the answer written on the board and ask: *Is this correct?* Ask another S to make any necessary corrections.

### Literacy Tip

For an alternative activity, refer literacy Ss to pages 66–67 in the *Literacy Workbook* at any time during the lesson.

### Useful Language

Read the tip box aloud and ask Ss to repeat the times after you. Write several times (on the hour and half hour) on the board and practice saying them with the class.

## APPLICATION

- Direct Ss' attention to Exercise 3 and read the instructions aloud.
- Model the task. Hold up the Student's Book and point to the answer choices in Exercise 2B. Say to one S: *Point to a picture.* Say to the first S's partner: *Say the word.*
- Ss complete the exercise in pairs. Walk around and help as needed.

**Expansion activity** *(student pairs)*

- Peer dictation. Ask Ss to write five time phrases on a piece of paper. Ask them to write only times that are on the hour or half hour.
- Ss in pairs. Say: *Don't show your paper to your partner. Tell your partner the time phrases in your notebook. Your partner will write them in his or her notebook.*
- When Ss are finished, ask them to switch roles.
- Help as needed. When Ss are finished, ask them to check their work by looking at their partners' notebooks. On the half hour or hour in your class, ask: *What time is it?* Elicit the correct response.

## EVALUATION

- Direct Ss' attention to the lesson focus on the board. Check Ss' understanding of time vocabulary by asking them to point to the times that are written on the signs in the picture on page 70 in the Student's Book: *7:00, 9:00, 10:00, 10:30, 2:30,* and *6:30.* Walk around and check that Ss are pointing to the correct items.
- Check off the lesson focus as Ss demonstrate an understanding of what they have learned in the lesson.

### More Ventures, Unit 6, Lesson A

| Literacy Workbook, 15–30 min. | |
|---|---|
| Basic Workbook, 15–30 min. | |
| Writing Worksheets, 15–30 min. | www.cambridge.org/ventures/ resources/ |
| Collaborative Worksheets, 30–45 min. | |
| Student Arcade, time varies | www.cambridge.org/venturesarcade/ |

**UNIT GOALS**
**Read** clock time   **Make** a schedule
**Identify** parts of an invitation

## 2 Listen

**A** **Listen and repeat.**

1. 7:00     2. 9:00     3. 10:00
4. 10:30    5. 2:30     6. 6:30

◀)) CD2, Track 03

**B** **Listen and circle.**

◀)) CD2, Track 04

1. a.     b.

2. a.     b.

3. a.     b.

4. a.     b.

**Listen again.** Check your answers.

## 3 After you listen

**Talk with a partner.**
Point to a picture and
ask. Your partner says
the time.

**USEFUL LANGUAGE**
Say times like this.
3:00 = *three o'clock*
6:30 = *six-thirty*

What time is it?    It's 10 o'clock.

# Lesson B Events

## 1 Vocabulary focus

**Listen and repeat.**

September

| Sunday | Monday | Tuesday | Wednesday | Thursday | Friday | Saturday |
|--------|--------|---------|-----------|----------|--------|----------|
| | | | 1 | 2 | 3 | 4 |
| 5 | 6 | 7 1:30 | 8 | 9 | 10 3:30 | 11 |
| 12 | 13 | 14 | 15 8:30 | 16 | 17 | 18 7:30 |
| 19 | 20 | 21 | 22 | 23 | 24 | 25 |
| 26 5:00 | 27 | 28 | 29 | 30 4:30 | | |

1. appointment

2. meeting

3. class

4. movie

5. party

6. TV show

## 2 Practice

**A Read and match.**

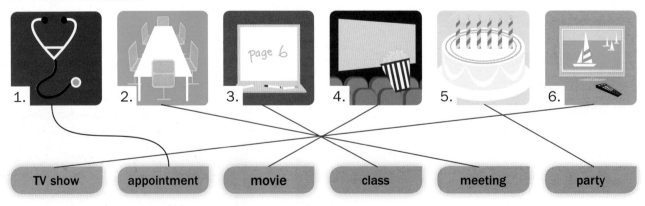

1.    2.    3.    4.    5.    6.

TV show    appointment    movie    class    meeting    party

# WARM-UP AND REVIEW

- Before class. Write today's lesson focus on the board.
  *Lesson B:*
  *Events*
  *What time is the appointment?*
- Begin class. Books open. Direct Ss' attention to the picture on page 70. Review key vocabulary from the unit by asking Ss to point to the following times in their books: *7:00, 9:00, 10:00, 10:30, 2:30, 6:30.*
- Walk around and check to see that Ss are pointing to the correct items in the picture.
- Write the words *calendar* and *schedule* on the board. Ask Ss: *What is a calendar? What is a schedule?* If Ss don't respond, hold up the Student's Book on page 70. Point to Teresa's calendar. Say: *This is a calendar. Teresa has a meeting with Joan on Wednesday at 10:00.*
- Ask Ss what other types of calendars or schedules they use. Many Ss may use a calendar app on their phones or computers.

# PRESENTATION

- Books closed. Direct Ss' attention to the word "Events" on the board under Lesson focus. Write on the board: *appointment, meeting, class, movie, party, TV show.* Say: *These words are names of events.*
- Books open. Point to the word *Events* at the top of page 72 in the Student's Book. Have Ss repeat it after you. Point to the vocabulary on the board and say: *These are events. We often write them on a calendar to remember them.*
- Explain the difference between *appointment* and *meeting.* Say: *A meeting is when people get together. You can have a meeting at work or at your child's school. An appointment is a plan to be at a place at a certain time, like the doctor's office.*
- Direct Ss' attention to the calendar in Exercise **1**. Ask questions about the events on the calendar, pointing to them as you ask: *What time is the appointment?* (1:30.) *What time is the meeting?* (3:30.) *What time is the class?* (8:30.) *What time is the movie?* (7:30.) *What time is the party?* (5:00.) *What time is the TV show?* (4:30.)
- Read aloud the instructions for Exercise **1**.
- ▶ *CD2, Track 5* Play or read the audio (see audio script, page T-148). Listen and repeat the vocabulary along with Ss. Repeat the audio as needed.
- Listen carefully to Ss' pronunciation and correct as needed.

## Expansion activity *(student pairs)*

- Point out to Ss that English has two kinds of numbers. *1, 2, 3,* etc. are cardinal numbers; *first, second, third,* etc. are ordinal numbers. When we use a number with a month, we use an ordinal number. For example, 1 = 1st, 2 = 2nd; 3 = 3rd; etc. For the date September 1, people understand "September one," but they usually say "September first."
- Direct Ss' attention to the calendar in Exercise **1**. Say: *Ask your partner questions.* For example: *When is the meeting?* (September 10.) *When is the class?* (September 15.) *When is the movie?* (September 18.)
- When Ss are finished, ask them to switch roles. Help as needed.

## Community building *(whole class)*

- Show Ss a calendar. (If there isn't one in the classroom, bring one in.) Ask: *What events are happening in our community this month?* Write key words for the events on the calendar. Keep a class calendar at school. Ask Ss to write important events on the calendar as they come up during the school year.

# PRACTICE

- Direct Ss' attention to Exercise **2A**. As you read aloud the instructions, hold up the Student's Book and indicate that Ss should look at the pictures for various events and match them to the corresponding words.
- Model the task. Hold up the Student's Book. Point to the first picture. Ask: *What event is this?* (appointment) Say: *Match the picture with the word.*
- Ss complete the exercise individually. Help as needed.

**Literacy Tip**

For an alternative activity, refer literacy Ss to pages 68–69 in the *Literacy Workbook* at any time during the lesson.

# COMPREHENSION CHECK

- Write the numbers *1–6* on the board. Ask a few Ss to come to the board and write the answers to Exercise **2A** on the board.
- Ask different Ss to read the answers on the board. After each answer is read, ask: *Is this correct?* If not, ask a volunteer to make any necessary corrections on the board.

## Learner persistence *(individual work)*

- Encourage Ss to use calendars or schedules to keep track of their assignments, quizzes, and tests. Show Ss an example of how to use a calendar for the class.

# LESSON B Events

## PRESENTATION

- Direct Ss' attention to the pictures in Exercise 2B. Say: *These are notices about events. What events do you see?* Point to each event in turn. Elicit: *appointment, class, TV show, meeting, movie, party.*

- Ask Ss questions about the events in the pictures. Ask: *What time is the English class?* (8:30.) *What day is the appointment?* (Friday.) *Where is the meeting?* (At Riverside School.)

## PRACTICE

- Read aloud the first part of the instructions in Exercise 2B.
- ▶ *CD2, Track 6* Model the task. Say: *Listen and repeat.* Play or read the audio for number 1 (see audio script, page T-148) and point to the appointment card in the first picture as you repeat. Say: *Then write.* Point to *1:30* and *Friday* written in the chart. Make sure Ss understand the task.
- ▶ *CD2, Track 6* Play or read the complete audio. Ss listen and repeat. Encourage Ss to point to the information in the pictures as they repeat.
- Ss complete the charts individually. Repeat the audio as needed.
- Check answers with the class. Write the numbers *1–6* on the board and ask for volunteers to write their answers on the board. Point to each answer and ask the class: *Yes? Is this correct?* Make corrections on the board.
- Read aloud the second part of the instructions for Exercise 2B. Point to and model the example conversation.
- Call on a pair of volunteers to read aloud the example conversation for the class.
- Point to another event on page 73. Ask: *What time is the TV show?* (At 4:30 on Friday.) Repeat with different events in the pictures. Indicate that Ss should ask and answer questions about all the events in the pictures.
- Ss complete the exercise in pairs. Walk around and help as needed.

### Expansion activity *(student pairs)*

- Draw a rectangle on the board. This represents a page in a calendar. Write today's date at the top of the "page." Write different times on the hour and half hour on the left-hand side of the calendar page. Write events such as *doctor's appointment*, *movie*, *birthday party*, and *meeting* in the time slots.
- Point to one of the events on the page. Ask: *What time is the (name of event)?* Elicit: *It's at (time of event).*

- Encourage Ss to continue asking each other about the events on the board in pairs.
- Ask Ss to draw a calendar page in their notebooks and write events on it. Tell them that the events can be real or imaginary. They can use the events in Exercise 2B as a guide. Encourage them to ask and answer questions about the events with a different partner.

## APPLICATION

- Direct Ss' attention to Exercise 3 and read the instructions aloud. Have Ss write the times and days of a TV show and a party in the chart. They can be real or imaginary.
- Model the task. Ask two Ss to read the question and answer aloud. Hold up the Student's Book and point to the words *movie*, *7:30*, and *Saturday* as the Ss are saying the conversation. Make sure Ss understand the task.
- Ss then circulate and ask other classmates about the events in their charts. Walk around and help as needed.
- Ask several Ss to ask and answer the questions for the rest of the class.

### Learner persistence *(whole group)*

- If you have some Ss who regularly miss class, recycle the words in this lesson to remind them of the days and times your class meets. Ask the class: *What days does this class meet?* Ask: *What times does this class meet?* Elicit appropriate responses.

## EVALUATION

- Direct Ss' attention to the lesson focus written on the board. Check Ss' understanding of the key vocabulary by naming an event and asking them to point to the events in the pictures in Exercise 2B on page 73: *appointment*, *TV show*, *movie*, *class*, *party*, *meeting*. Walk around and check that Ss are pointing to the correct items.
- Check off the lesson focus as Ss demonstrate an understanding of what they have learned in the lesson.

| More Ventures, Unit 6, Lesson B | |
| --- | --- |
| Literacy Workbook, 15–30 min. | |
| Basic Workbook, 15–30 min. | |
| Writing Worksheets, 15–30 min. | www.cambridge.org/ventures/ resources/ |
| Collaborative Worksheets, 30–45 min. | |
| Student Arcade, time varies | www.cambridge.org/venturesarcade/ |

**B** **Listen and repeat.** Then write.

1. **Town Haircuts**

APPOINTMENT INFO:

Day & Time: Friday 1:30

Haircut with: Nick

2. English Class
Friday 8:30

3.

| | 4:30 | Friday |

| Channel 3 | One Life, One Love 1 hour |
| Channel 5 | Dinosaurs 30 minutes |
| Channel 7 | Afternoon Special 1 hour |

CD2, Track 06

4. **RIVERSIDE SCHOOL**
PTA MEETING
SATURDAY 3:00

5. **ATTACK FROM VENUS!!**
NOW PLAYING: SATURDAY 9:00

6. You're Invited!
Gina's Birthday Party
Saturday 5:00

| Event | Time | Day |
|---|---|---|
| appointment | 1:30 | Friday |
| TV show | 4:30 | Friday |
| movie | 9:00 | Saturday |

| Event | Time | Day |
|---|---|---|
| class | 8:30 | Friday |
| party | 5:00 | Saturday |
| meeting | 3:00 | Saturday |

**Talk with a partner.** Ask and answer.

A What time is the **appointment**?

B At **1:30** on **Friday**.

## 3 Communicate

**Complete the chart.** Write a time and day for each event.
Then talk with your classmates.

| Event | Time | Day |
|---|---|---|
| movie | 7:30 | Saturday |
| TV show | Answers will vary. | |
| party | | |
| meeting | | |

A What time is the **movie**?

B At **7:30** on **Saturday**.

# Lesson C  Is your class at 11:00?

## 1  Grammar focus: Yes / No questions with *be*

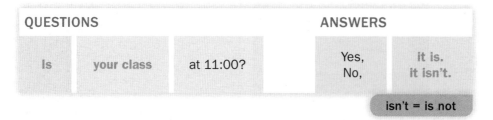

| QUESTIONS | | | ANSWERS | |
|---|---|---|---|---|
| Is | your class | at 11:00? | Yes,<br>No, | it is.<br>it isn't. |

isn't = is not

Watch

## 2  Practice

A  **Read and circle.** Then write.

| Class | Time |
|---|---|
| English | 11:00 |

1.  A  Is your class at 11:00?
   B _____ **Yes, it is.** _____
   ( Yes, it is. )  No, it isn't.

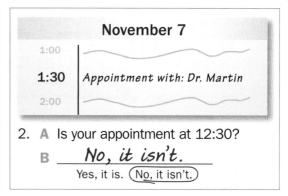

**November 7**

1:00
**1:30**  *Appointment with: Dr. Martin*
2:00

2.  A  Is your appointment at 12:30?
   B _____ *No, it isn't.* _____
   Yes, it is.  ( No, it isn't. )

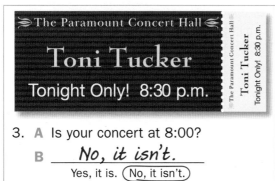

≫ The Paramount Concert Hall ≪
**Toni Tucker**
Tonight Only!  8:30 p.m.

3.  A  Is your concert at 8:00?
   B _____ *No, it isn't.* _____
   Yes, it is.  ( No, it isn't. )

**THE LOST CLUES**
**6:00**

4.  A  Is your movie at 6:00?
   B _____ *Yes, it is.* _____
   ( Yes, it is. )  No, it isn't.

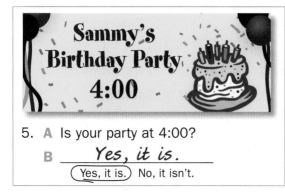

**Sammy's Birthday Party**
**4:00**

5.  A  Is your party at 4:00?
   B _____ *Yes, it is.* _____
   ( Yes, it is. )  No, it isn't.

| Ch. 3<br>7:00 | Singing Stars |
|---|---|
| | Who wins? Final<br>three singers. |

6.  A  Is your TV show at 7:30?
   B _____ *No, it isn't.* _____
   Yes, it is.  ( No, it isn't. )

**Listen and repeat.** Then practice with a partner.

CD2, Track 07

## WARM-UP AND REVIEW

- Before class. Write today's lesson focus on the board:
  *Lesson C:*
  *Yes / No questions with "be"*
- Begin class. Books closed. Write several hour and half hour times on the board. Point to the first one. Ask: *Is this class at (time)?* Elicit: *Yes, it is.* or *No, it isn't.*
- Continue the exercise. Write names of events under the times on the board. Point to each time and event. Ask: *Is the movie at (time)? Is the meeting at (time)?* Elicit appropriate responses.
- If your school has several scheduled weekly classes, ask Ss to brainstorm them by asking: *What classes do we have at this school?* Write the names of the classes on the board. Point to the names of the classes on the board in turn. Ask: *What time is this class?*

## PRESENTATION

- Use the animated grammar presentation in one or more of the following ways:
  - Preview it before class
  - Show it in class
  - Encourage Ss to watch it outside of class.
- Books open. Direct Ss' attention to the grammar chart in Exercise **1**. Read the question and the corresponding answers aloud. Ask Ss to repeat after you.
- Point to the small box beside the grammar chart. Hold up one finger and tell Ss: *One word: isn't.* Hold up two fingers and say: *Two words: is not. They are the same.*
- Ask Ss the question in the grammar chart about the time of their own English class. Ss should answer appropriately.

## PRACTICE

- Direct Ss' attention to the first picture in Exercise **2A**. Ask two Ss to read the example aloud.
- Read aloud the instructions for Exercise **2A**. Point to where *Yes, it is* has been circled and written for number 1. Say: *Circle the correct answer. Then write it in the blank.*
- Ss complete the exercise individually. Walk around and help as needed.

## COMPREHENSION CHECK

- Read aloud the second part of the instructions in Exercise **2A**.
- ▶ *CD2, Track 7* Play or read the audio (see audio script, page T-148). Ss listen and repeat as they check their answers.
- Write the numbers *1–6* on the board. Ask volunteers to come to the board and write the answers they circled. Make any necessary corrections on the board.
- Ss in pairs. Ask Ss to choose Role A or B and practice the questions and answers in Exercise **2A**. Then have Ss switch roles and practice again. Walk around and help as needed.
- Ask several pairs to say the questions and answers for the rest of the class.

### Literacy Tip

Ask literacy Ss to copy the times from Exercise **2A** in their notebooks. Say: *Work with a partner. Say one of the times in your notebook. Your partner will point to it. Then change roles.*

### Expansion activity *(student pairs)*

- Focus Ss' attention on the pictures in Exercise **2A**. Write on the board:
  1. *What kind of class is it?* (Continue writing questions on the board as Ss ask and answer in pairs.)
  2. *What kind of appointment is it?* (A doctor's appointment.)
  3. *What concert is it?* (Toni Tucker.)
  4. *What movie is it?* (The Lost Clues.)
  5. *What kind of party is it?* (A birthday party.)
  6. *What TV show is it?* (Singing Stars.)

### Teaching Tip

Do not expect Ss to answer the questions in complete sentences. The purpose of this exercise is to understand the meaning of the question and answer with the correct information.

### Literacy Tip

For an alternative activity, refer literacy Ss to pages 70–71 in the *Literacy Workbook* at any time during the lesson.

# LESSON C Is your class at 11:00?

## PRESENTATION

- Write on the board: *calendar*. Say the word. Ask Ss to repeat. Ask: *Do you remember what this is?* If Ss don't remember, say: *A calendar tells you the events you have for different days in a week.*

### Teaching Tip

If you have a calendar, it might be helpful to show it to the Ss. Ss learn new vocabulary quickly by visualizing it. Ask Ss if any of them use a calendar. If they do, ask them to hold it up for the class to see.

- Direct Ss' attention to the calendar in Exercise 2B. Say: *This is an example of a page from a calendar.* Ask: *What's the month?* (April.) *What are the days in the calendar?* (Monday, Tuesday, Wednesday, Thursday, Friday, Saturday, Sunday.)
- Ask: *What time is the doctor's appointment in this calendar?* (3:30.) *What time is the concert?* (9:00.)

## PRACTICE

- Read aloud the first part of the instructions for Exercise 2B. Focus Ss' attention on the words below the calendar page. Hold up the Student's Book. Point to the doctor's appointment on Monday in the calendar. Ask: *What time is the appointment?* (3:30.) Point to the line connecting *appointment* to *three-thirty*.
- Ss complete the exercise individually. Walk around and help as needed.

### Teaching Tip

If Ss need help with writing numbers in words, refer them to page 5 in the Welcome Unit. It might be helpful to write the word *thirty* on the board. Tell Ss that this is how *30* is spelled in English.

- Write the numbers *1–6* on the board. Ask a few Ss to come to the board and write the time for each number on the board. Ask: *Are these times correct?* Ask other Ss to make corrections if needed.
- Read aloud the second part of the instructions for Exercise 2B. Model the task. Ask two Ss to read the example conversation. Call on two different Ss to model a new conversation using another event in the calendar.
- Indicate that Ss should ask and answer questions about all the events in the calendar. Make sure Ss understand the task.
- Ss ask and answer questions about the items in the calendar in pairs. When Ss are finished, ask them to switch partners and repeat the conversations.
- Ask several pairs to say their conversations to the rest of the class.

## APPLICATION

- Direct Ss' attention to Exercise 3 and read the instructions aloud.
- Focus Ss' attention on the word bank. Say: *Use these words for the calendar.* Ss complete the task individually. Walk around and help as needed.

### Teaching Tip

It might be helpful to teach Ss the verb *fill in*. Hold up the calendar in Exercise 3. Point to the empty boxes. Tell the Ss that when they write the words, they are filling in the calendar. This is a useful phrase that Ss may encounter when they fill in information on forms.

- Direct Ss' attention to the example conversation below the calendar. Model the task. Ask two Ss to read the example conversation. Point to the information in the calendar as they read.
- Ss complete the exercise in pairs, asking and answering questions about their own calendars. Walk around and help as needed.

### Expansion activity *(student pairs)*

- Ask Ss to draw a calendar of the current month in their notebooks. Say: *Write events from your life in your calendar.* Walk around and help as needed.
- Say: *Now show your calendar to your partner. Your partner will ask questions about your calendar. For example: Is your English class on Tuesday? Is your son's birthday on (date)?*
- Encourage partners to respond appropriately.
- Ask several pairs to ask and answer questions about Ss' real-life calendars for the rest of the class.

## EVALUATION

- Direct Ss' attention to the lesson focus on the board. Write different times and events on the board such as *movie* and *2:00*. Ask Ss to form *Yes / No* questions with these words. Say: *Is the movie at 2:00?* Elicit: *Yes, it is.* or *No, it isn't.*
- Check off the lesson focus as Ss demonstrate an understanding of what they have learned in the lesson.

| *More Ventures, Unit 6, Lesson C* | |
|---|---|
| Literacy Workbook, 15–30 min. | |
| Basic Workbook, 15–30 min. | |
| Writing Worksheets, 15–30 min. | www.cambridge.org/ventures/ resources/ |
| Collaborative Worksheets, 30–45 min. | |
| Student Arcade, time varies | www.cambridge.org/venturesarcade/ |

**B** Read and match.

April

| 2 Monday | 3:30 Doctor's appointment | 5 Thursday | 8:00 Movie with my sister |
| 3 Tuesday | 6:30 English class | 6 Friday | 7:30 Birthday party |
| 4 Wednesday | 12:00 Meeting at work | 7 Saturday | 9:00 Concert: Salsa music |
| | | 8 Sunday | |

1. appointment — seven-thirty
2. class — six-thirty
3. meeting — three-thirty
4. movie — nine o'clock
5. party — twelve o'clock
6. concert — eight o'clock

**Talk with a partner.** Ask and answer.

A Is your **appointment** on **Monday**?

B **Yes, it is.**

A Is your **appointment** at **7:00**?

B **No, it isn't. It's at 3:30.**

## 3 Communicate

**Complete the chart. Write an event and time for each day.**
Then talk with a partner.

appointment   class   concert   meeting   party

| Monday | Tuesday | Wednesday | Thursday | Friday |
|---|---|---|---|---|
| class – 5:00 | *Answers will vary.* | | | |

A Is your **class** on **Tuesday**?

B **No, it isn't. It's on Monday.**

A Is your **class** at **5:00**?

B **Yes, it is.**

# Lesson D Reading

## 1 Before you read

**Talk about the picture.**
What do you see?

## 2 Read

**Listen and read.**

CD2, Track 08

### Teresa's Day

Teresa is busy today. Her meeting with her friend Joan is at 10:00 in the morning. Her doctor's appointment is at 1:00 in the afternoon. Her favorite TV show is at 4:30. Her class is at 6:30 in the evening. Her uncle's birthday party is also at 6:30. Oh, no! What will she do?

## 3 After you read

**Write the answers.**

1. What time is Teresa's meeting? _____ At 10:00 _____ .
2. What time is Teresa's TV show? _____ At 4:30 _____ .
3. What time is Teresa's class? _____ At 6:30 _____ .
4. Is Teresa's appointment at 4:00? _____ No, it isn't _____ .
5. Is her uncle's party at 6:30? _____ Yes, it is _____ .

## Teaching objectives
- Introduce a paragraph about someone's day
- Introduce phrases for times of the day
- Provide practice using new topic-related words

## WARM-UP AND REVIEW

- Before class. Write today's lesson focus on the board.
*Lesson D:*
*Read "Teresa's Day"*
*Discuss the events in Teresa's day*
*Learn phrases for times of the day*

- Begin class. Books closed. Ask: *What are some words for events?* Elicit: *TV show, appointment, party, movie, meeting, concert.* Write the words on the board as Ss say them.

- Point to some of the words on the board. Ask: *Do you have an appointment today? Do you have a meeting today? What time is the appointment or meeting?* Elicit appropriate responses.

- Books open. Direct Ss' attention to the picture on page 70. Hold up the Student's Book. Point to the picture of Teresa. Ask: *What's her name?* (Teresa.) *Where is she?* (At the mall.) *What day is it?* (Wednesday.) *What time is her meeting with Joan?* (At 10:00.)

### Teaching Tip
It might be helpful to point to each part of the picture that corresponds to the answers to the questions you are asking. Doing this gives Ss visual cues that will help them answer the questions correctly.

## PRESENTATION

- Direct Ss' attention to the picture in Exercise 1 on page 76.
- Read aloud the instructions for Exercise 1. Ask: *What do you see?* Elicit and write on the board any vocabulary that Ss know, such as: *her calendar, Wednesday, 10:00.*
- Say: *Now we will read about Teresa's day.*

### Teaching Tip
Do not expect Ss to answer the question in complete sentences. The purpose of this exercise is to prepare Ss for the reading about Teresa's day that follows.

## PRACTICE

- Direct Ss' attention to Exercise 2. Read the instructions aloud.
- **CD2, Track 8** Play or read the audio and ask Ss to follow along (see audio script, page T-148). Repeat the audio as needed.

- Read aloud each sentence of the reading and ask Ss to repeat after you.
- Write *in the morning, in the afternoon,* and *in the evening* on the board. Point to each phrase in turn and say it aloud. Ask Ss to repeat after you. Ask Ss: *What time is the morning? What time is the afternoon? What time is the evening?* (Elicit appropriate responses and correct Ss if necessary.)

### Learner persistence *(individual work)*
- **CD2, Track 8** Ss can listen to the audio for Exercise 2 at home for reinforcement and review. They can also listen to the audio for self-directed learning when class attendance is not possible.

## COMPREHENSION CHECK

- Read aloud the instructions for Exercise 3.
- Model the task. Ask two Ss to read aloud the first question and answer. Ask a S to point to the part of the reading that gives the answer.
- Point out that questions 2 and 3 will have the same kind of answer as number 1. Direct Ss' attention to numbers 4 and 5. Ask: *What kind of answers will these questions have?* Elicit *Yes, it is.* and *No, it isn't.* Write these answers on the board as reference.
- Ss complete the exercise individually. Walk around and help as needed.
- Write the numbers *1–5* on the board. Call on volunteers to write their answers on the board. Go over the answers with the class.
- Read aloud each answer on the board and ask: *Is this correct?* If not, ask a volunteer to correct it.
- Ask several pairs to ask and answer the questions for the class.

### Literacy Tip
For an alternative activity, refer literacy Ss to pages 72–73 in the *Literacy Workbook* at any time during the lesson.

### Learner persistence *(individual work)*
- Encourage Ss to tell you if they have to miss class for any reason. Practice using the vocabulary from this unit to help Ss explain their absences. Write on the board: *I'm sorry. I can't come to class tomorrow. I have a doctor's appointment at 9:00 a.m.*
- Tell Ss to practice writing excuses using the model on the board.

# LESSON D Reading

## PRESENTATION

- Direct Ss' attention to the Picture dictionary in Exercise 4. Point to and say the words *Times of the day* and ask Ss to repeat them after you.
- Write on the board: *morning, afternoon, evening, night.* Ask Ss: *What time of day is it right now?* If Ss are unsure, point to the appropriate picture in the Picture dictionary. Say: *It is (time phrase) right now.* Ask Ss to repeat the sentence after you.
- Direct Ss' attention back to the Picture dictionary. Read the instructions for Exercise 4A aloud.
- ▶ **CD2, Track 9** Play or read the audio (see audio script, page T-148). Listen to Ss' pronunciation as they repeat the times of the day. Correct Ss' pronunciation as needed.

### Teaching Tip

It might be helpful to tell Ss that it is common to refer to 12:00 p.m. as *twelve noon* and 12:00 a.m. as *twelve midnight.* Tell Ss that to avoid confusion, Americans often say *at midnight* or *at noon* as opposed to *at 12:00 a.m.* or *at 12:00 p.m.*

### *Learner persistence* (individual work)

- ▶ **CD2, Track 9** Ss can listen to the audio for Exercise 4A at home for reinforcement and review. They can also listen to the audio for self-directed learning when class attendance is not possible.

### *Expansion activity* (whole group)

- Name That Picture. Before class. Cut out the Picture dictionary cards for this unit. Hold up a picture card and name it incorrectly. For example, hold up the picture card of *in the evening.* Say: *Is this in the morning?* Listen as Ss say *No, it isn't.* and correct the statement. Continue until you have gone through all the cards. Expand questioning to different types of questions besides *Yes / No.* For example, *Is this morning or afternoon? What time of day is this?*

### Useful Language

Read the tip box aloud. Ask: *Is it a.m. or p.m. right now?* Elicit an appropriate answer.

## PRACTICE

- Direct Ss' attention to Exercise 4B and read the instructions aloud. Read the example conversation aloud using two different voices.
- Point to and read aloud the column headings in the chart. Point to the check mark under the "At noon" heading. Say: *Make conversations about the other times. Check the correct boxes.* Make sure Ss understand the task.
- Ss complete the activity in pairs. Walk around and help as needed.
- Ask several pairs to say the conversations for the class.

### *Learner persistence*

- If any of your Ss are having problems learning the new vocabulary from this chapter, make them a set of the Picture dictionary cards from the *Online Teacher's Resource Room.* Tell Ss to use them as flash cards to learn the new words. Say: *Look at the pictures. Say the times of the day. Then look at the backs of the cards to see if you are right.*

## EVALUATION

- Direct Ss' attention to the first part of the lesson focus on the board. Ask: *What were the events in Teresa's day?* Elicit: *doctor's appointment, TV show, class, birthday party.*
- Direct Ss' attention to the third part of the lesson focus. Point to the pictures in Exercise 4A on page 77 in the Student's Book. For each picture, ask: *What time do you think it is?* Elicit answers, such as: *Maybe it's (time).*
- Check off each part of the lesson focus as Ss demonstrate understanding of what they have learned in the lesson.

| More Ventures, Unit 6, Lesson D | |
|---|---|
| Literacy Workbook, 15–30 min. | |
| Basic Workbook, 15–30 min. | |
| Picture Dictionary activities, 30–45 min. | www.cambridge.org/ventures/ resources/ |
| Writing Worksheets, 15–30 min. | |
| Collaborative Worksheets, 30–45 min. | |
| Student Arcade, time varies | www.cambridge.org/venturesarcade/ |

# 4 Picture dictionary Times of the day

1. in the morning

2. in the afternoon

3. in the evening

12:00 p.m.

4. at noon

5. at night

12:00 a.m.

6. at midnight

A **Listen and repeat.** Look at the Picture dictionary.

B **Talk with a partner.** Complete the chart.
Check (✓) the time of the day.

A  It's at **12:00 p.m.**

B  **At noon?**

A  Right.

CD2, Track 09

**USEFUL LANGUAGE**
a.m. = from midnight to noon
p.m. = from noon to midnight

| Event | In the morning | In the afternoon | In the evening | At noon | At midnight |
|---|---|---|---|---|---|
| 12:00 p.m. | | | | ✓ | |
| 3:00 p.m. | | ✓ | | | |
| 6:00 a.m. | ✓ | | | | |
| 12:00 a.m. | | | | | ✓ |
| 6:00 p.m. | | | ✓ | | |

# Lesson E Writing

## 1 Before you write

**A** **Talk with a partner.** Complete the words.

1. m o v _i_ _e_
2. c l a _s_ _s_
3. a p p _o_ _i_ n t m e n t
4. p _a_ _r_ t y
5. T V _s_ _h_ o w
6. m _e_ _e_ t i n g

**B** **Talk with a partner.** Look at the memo. Complete the story.

### MEMO

| TIME | EVENT |
|---|---|
| 8:00 a.m. | meeting – daughter's school |
| 12:00 p.m. | doctor's appointment |
| 1:30 p.m. | class |
| 6:00 p.m. | party – son's class |
| 8:00 p.m. | TV show |

### My Busy Day

Today is a busy day. My ___meeting___ at my daughter's school is at
8:00 in the morning. Then my doctor's _appointment_ is at noon. My English
___class___ is at 1:30. What time is my son's class ___party___? Oh, yes.
At 6:00 in the evening. Dinner with my family is at 7:00. And my favorite TV
___show___ is at 8:00 at night. It's a very busy day.

**Teaching objectives**
- Prepare Ss for writing a paragraph about a busy day
- Provide practice writing key vocabulary words

# WARM-UP AND REVIEW

- Before class. Write today's lesson focus on the board.

  *Lesson E:*

  *Write about a busy day*

- Begin class. Books closed. Write *busy* on the board. Point to the word. Say it aloud. Ask Ss to repeat after you. Ask: *What does this word mean?* Elicit an appropriate response, such as: *having a lot of things to do.*

- Ask: *Do you have a busy day today?* Elicit *Yes / No* responses. If a S responds with yes, ask: *Why?* Elicit an appropriate response, such as a list of things to do that day.

# PRESENTATION

- Direct Ss' attention to Exercise **1A** and read the instructions aloud.

- Point to the first item and say: *Number 1. What's the word?* (Movie.) Ask: *What letters do we need?* (i *and* e) Point to where the letters are written in the blanks. Say: *Now you fill in the missing letters.*

# PRACTICE

- Ss work in pairs to complete the words.

- When Ss are finished, call on different pairs to write their completed words on the board. Review the alphabet by asking Ss who write answers on the board to say the letters aloud.

- Go over the answers with the class. Ask: *Are these words spelled correctly?* Make corrections as needed.

# PRESENTATION

- Books open. Direct Ss' attention to Exercise **1B** and read the instructions aloud.

- Write the word *memo* on the board. Point to the word. Say it aloud and ask Ss to repeat after you. Ask: *What does this word mean?* Elicit an appropriate response, such as: *A short note to help you remember something.*

- Ask five Ss to read each part of the memo aloud.

- Model the exercise. Hold up the Student's Book. Read the first two sentences of the story aloud. Point to the time *8:00* in the story and have Ss find the time in the memo. Ask: *What event is at 8:00 a.m. What word is missing in the memo?* Elicit *meeting*. Then say: *Complete the story.*

- Ss work alone or in pairs to fill in the blanks in the story using the information in the memo. Walk around and help as needed.

- Check answers as a class. Ask several Ss to read sentences from the story aloud. After each sentence, ask: *Is that word correct?* Correct any errors if needed.

  **Option** Ask Ss to read the story to each other in pairs.

- Write the numbers *2–5* on the board and ask volunteers to write their answers on the board. Make any corrections on the board.

### *Community building* (whole class)

- Ask: *Do you often have busy days? What do you do on busy days?*

### *Expansion activity* (whole class)

- Hangman game. Draw on the board the outline for a Hangman game as follows:

- Think of one of the words from Exercise **1A**. Draw a blank to represent each letter of the word under the Hangman outline.

- Ask Ss to guess the word by guessing different letters. If they guess a letter that is in the word, write it in the corresponding blank. If the letter is not in the word, write it on the right side of the outline. Then draw a part of a body hanging from the vertical line on the left of the outline.

- If the Ss guess the word, they win. If an entire figure is drawn in the Hangman outline, the teacher wins.

- Continue the game by asking Ss to think of different words. Draw blanks under the outline to represent each letter in the new words. Encourage Ss to use any word that they have learned in English class up to this point.

### Teaching Tip

This is a good way for Ss to practice saying the names of letters of the alphabet in English. It also reinforces vocabulary learned in the unit.

# LESSON E Writing

## PRESENTATION

- Say: *Remember the memo on page 78? Now you are going to write your own memo about events in your life. They can be real events or imaginary events.*
- Direct Ss' attention to Exercise **2A** and read the instructions aloud. Ask: *What are your plans for today?*
- Draw a vertical line on the board to make two columns. Add *Time* and *Event* as headings.
- Model the task. Ask a S to come to the board and write a time and an event in the columns. Repeat with one or two other Ss.

### Teaching Tip

Remind Ss that they don't have to use real-life events. Give them some examples of imaginary events if they don't know what to write in the memo.

## PRACTICE

- Ss complete the exercise individually. Walk around and help as needed.
- Direct Ss' attention to Exercise **2B** and read the instructions aloud.
- Model the activity. Point to the time and event examples on the board. Say: *Make a sentence about the time and event.* Write on the board: *My_____ is at _____.* beside each line of the memo. Have Ss fill in the blanks on the board.
- Direct Ss' attention to the paragraph in Exercise **2B**. Say: *Now make sentences about the events in your memo.*
- Ss complete the exercise individually. Walk around and help as needed.

### Literacy Tip

For an alternative activity, refer literacy Ss to pages 74–75 in the *Literacy Workbook* at any time during the lesson.

- Direct Ss' attention to Exercise **3**. Read the instructions aloud. Say: *Tell your partner about your busy day.* Encourage Ss to read their paragraphs to their partners. Walk around and help as needed.

### Teaching Tip

This exercise asks Ss to share their writing and work together. Encourage Ss to correct each other's writing if necessary. Say: *Help your partner with any mistakes. Then your partner will help you.*

- Ask several Ss to read their paragraphs aloud for the rest of the class.

   **Option** Ask several Ss to write their memos from Exercise **2A** on the board. Then ask them to explain their schedules to the rest of the class.

### Community building *(whole group)*

- If appropriate for your class, ask Ss to write their daily schedules in their notebooks. Define and discuss carpooling. If any Ss in your class need rides to English class, ask them to compare their schedules to see if carpooling might be a possibility.

### Expansion activity *(whole group)*

- Dictation. Ask Ss to take out a piece of paper and write the numbers *1–5* on it. Dictate the following sentences:
   1. *My meeting is at 10:00 a.m.*
   2. *My TV show is at 11:00 a.m.*
   3. *My appointment is at 12:30 p.m.*
   4. *My English class is at 5:00 p.m.*
   5. *The concert is at 8:00 p.m.*
- Ask volunteers to write their sentences on the board. Ask other Ss: *Are the sentences correct?* Ask different Ss to correct any errors if needed.

## EVALUATION

- Direct Ss' attention to the lesson focus on the board.
- Ask different Ss to come to the board and write sentences about events in their day. They should include the name of the event and the time.
- Check off the lesson focus as Ss demonstrate understanding of what they have learned in the lesson.

| *More Ventures, Unit 6, Lesson E* | |
|---|---|
| **Literacy Workbook,** 15–30 min. | |
| **Basic Workbook,** 15–30 min. | |
| **Writing Worksheets,** 15–30 min. | www.cambridge.org/ventures/ resources/ |
| **Real-life Document,** 15–30 min. | |
| **Collaborative Worksheets,** 30–45 min. | |

**2** **Write**

**A** **Complete the memo.** Write four times and four events for you.

## MEMO

| TIME | EVENT |
|------|-------|
| *Answers will vary.* | |
| | |
| | |
| | |
| | |

**B** **Write about your day.**

## My Busy Day

Today is a busy day.

My ___*Answers will vary.*___ is at _____.

My _____ is at _____.

My _____ is at _____.

And my _____ is at _____.

It's a very busy day.

**3** **After you write**

**Talk with a partner.** Share your writing.

## 1 Life-skills reading

A **Read the sentences.** Look at the invitation. Fill in the answer.

**It's a party!**

**Lily is 50! It's a surprise.
Don't tell her.**

**When:** Saturday, October 2
**What time:** 8:00 p.m.
**Where:** Katya and Alex's house
874 Lake Road
**RSVP:** Call Katya at 555-6188.

1. Who is the party for?

   **(A)** Lily

   (B) Katya and Alex

   (C) Katya

2. When is the party?

   (A) in the morning

   (B) in the afternoon

   **(C)** at night

3. What time is the party?

   (A) 2:00 p.m.

   (B) 4:00 p.m.

   **(C)** 8:00 p.m.

4. What day is the party?

   (A) Friday

   **(B)** Saturday

   (C) Sunday

B **Solve the problem.** Which solution is best? Circle your opinion.

Teresa can't go to the party. What should she do?

1. Call Lily.

2. Call 555-6188.

3. Other: _Answers will vary._

## WARM-UP AND REVIEW

● Before class. Write today's lesson focus on the board.
*Lesson F:*
*Read and answer questions about a party invitation*
*Practice writing times on clocks*
*Complete the Self-assessment*

● Begin class. Books closed. Write the word *invitation* on the board. Point to it and say it aloud. Ask Ss to repeat. Ask: *What kinds of invitations are there?* Elicit appropriate responses, such as: *birthday, graduation, wedding.*

### Teaching Tip

It might be helpful to bring in an example of a blank invitation to show Ss what an invitation is. Alternatively, draw an invitation on the board that says *You're invited to a party!* You could also discuss email invitations, such as evites. Ask Ss if they have ever written or received an evite.

## PRESENTATION

● Books open. Direct Ss' attention to the invitation in Exercise 1A.

● Hold up the Student's Book. Point to the invitation. Ask: *What kind of party is this invitation for?* Elicit: *It's a party for Lily. It's her birthday.*

### Teaching Tip

Make sure Ss know the meaning of the word *surprise.* Say: *A surprise is when you don't know the party is for you.* Ask Ss if they have ever attended a surprise party or had one themselves.

## PRACTICE

● Read the instructions for Exercise 1A aloud. This task helps prepare Ss for standardized-type tests they may have to take.

● Write the first item on the board along with the three answer choices labeled *A, B,* and *C.*

● Read aloud the item and the answer choices and then point to the invitation. Ask Ss: *Who is the party for?* Show Ss where to look for the information. Elicit: *Lily.*

● Point to the three answer choices on the board. Ask Ss: *A, B,* or *C?* (A) Fill in the letter *A* and tell Ss: *Fill in the answer.* Make sure Ss understand the task.

● Have Ss individually scan for and fill in the answers.

## COMPREHENSION CHECK

● Go over the answers to Exercise 1A with the class. Make sure that Ss followed instructions and filled in their answers. Ask Ss to point to the information in the invitation.

## APPLICATION

● Read the instructions for Exercise 1B aloud.

● Model the task. Ask: *What should Teresa do?*

● Ss complete the exercise in pairs. Walk around and help as needed.

### Literacy Tip

For an alternative activity, refer literacy Ss to pages 76–77 in the *Literacy Workbook* at any time during the lesson.

### *Expansion activity* (individual work, student pairs)

● Ask Ss to write in their notebooks an invitation to an imaginary party. Tell them to model their invitation after the one in Exercise 1A. Encourage them to change the information in their invitation to make the party different.

● Ss in pairs. Say: *Look at your partner's invitation. Ask questions about the party. Use these question phrases: What day, What time,* and *Where.*

● Walk around and help as needed.

### *Community building* (whole group)

● If you plan to have a real party in your class in the future (for example, the last day of the course), talk about the party and make an invitation for the party on the board. Ask different Ss to write different parts of the invitation on the board in turn. This might be a good time to teach Ss words like *potluck* and *casual dress.*

# LESSON F Another view

## PRESENTATION

- Books closed. Draw five rectangles on the board to represent five digital clocks.
- Ask a few Ss to come to the board and write different times in the clocks, such as *10:00* or *11:30*.
- Point to each clock in turn. Ask different Ss: *What time is it?* Elicit appropriate responses.

## PRACTICE

- Books open. Direct Ss' attention to Exercise 2A and read the instructions aloud. Hold up the Student's Book. Point to the first row of clocks. Say: *Write times on this row of clocks only.*
- Ss complete the task individually. Walk around and help as needed.
- Direct Ss' attention to the second part of the instructions for Exercise 2A. Model the task. Ask two Ss to read the example conversation. Hold up the Student's Book. Point to the second row of clocks. Say: *Write the time your partner says on these clocks.*
- Ss complete the exercise in pairs. Walk around and help as needed.
- Erase the times on the clocks on the board. Then ask several pairs to say their conversations for the rest of the class. The S who asks the question should write the answer in a clock on the board.

### Expansion activity *(whole class)*

- Competition. Draw a vertical line on the board, dividing the board in half. Draw a large rectangle on each side of the line to represent digital clocks. Divide the class into two teams. Say: *I am going to tell you a time. One person from each team will go to the board and write the time in the clock.*
- Model the activity. Ask a S to stand up. Say: *10:00 a.m.* The S goes to the board and writes the time in the rectangle on his or her side of the board.
- Begin the game. Ask Ss to write the following times or make up other times to match the ability of your class: *9:30 a.m.; 11:00 p.m.; 6:30 a.m.; 8:00 a.m.; 4:30 p.m.*
- The first S who writes the time correctly earns a point. The team with the most points at the end of the game wins.

## PRACTICE

- Direct Ss' attention to Exercise 2B. Read the instructions aloud.
- Model the task. Point to the first item and ask: *What's the word?* (Day.) *What letter does it need?* (d) Point to the letter *d* written in the blank.
- Ss complete the words individually or in pairs. Walk around and help as needed.
- Ask individual Ss to write the words on the board. Point to each word. Ask other Ss: *Is this word correct?* Ask volunteers to correct the spelling if necessary.
- Read aloud the second part of the instructions in Exercise 2B.
- Model the task. Point to the first item and ask: *What letter do we need in number 1?* (d) Read aloud the numbers under the blanks in the puzzle and stop when you get to number 1. Tell Ss: *Write the letter "d" for number 1.* Make sure Ss understand the task.
- Ss complete the task individually.
- Ask a S to write the answer to the puzzle on the board.

## EVALUATION

- Do a quick review of the unit. Have Ss turn to Lesson A. Ask the class to talk about what they remember about this lesson. Prompt Ss, if necessary, with questions, such as: *What words are on this page? What do you see in the picture?* Continue in this manner to review each lesson quickly.

### Expansion activity

- Before class. Print, for each student, one copy of the Self-assessment for this unit.
- Have Ss complete the Self-assessment either in class or outside of class.
- Provide feedback to Ss such as through a whole-class discussion, partners comparing their worksheets, or T reviewing each S's worksheet.
- If Ss are ready, administer the unit test on page T-173 of this Teacher's Edition. The audio script for the test is available on page T-192.

| More Ventures, Unit 6, Lesson F | |
|---|---|
| Literacy Workbook, 15–30 min. | |
| Basic Workbook, 15–30 min. | |
| Writing Worksheets, 15–30 min. | www.cambridge.org/ventures/resources/ |
| Real-life Document, time varies | |
| Collaborative Worksheets, 30–45 min. | |
| Self-assessment, 10 min. | |
| CASAS Test Prep Worksheet, 5–10 min. | |

# REVIEW

## 1 Listening

**Read.** Then listen and circle.

1. Is the meeting on Friday?
   - a. Yes, it is. *(circled)*
   - b. No, it isn't.

2. What time is the meeting?
   - a. at 2:30
   - b. at 10:30 *(circled)*

3. What time is the appointment?
   - a. at 2:00 *(circled)*
   - b. at 4:00

4. Where's the school?
   - a. next to the bank
   - b. across from the bank *(circled)*

5. Where's the movie theater?
   - a. between the supermarket and the pharmacy
   - b. next to the supermarket *(circled)*

6. Is the movie at 7:30?
   - a. Yes, it is. *(circled)*
   - b. No, it isn't.

CD2, Track 10

**Talk with a partner.** Ask and answer.

## 2 Vocabulary

**Write.** Complete the story.

afternoon   class   8:30   hospital   meeting

# Tan's Day

Tan's English ___class___ is at ___8:30___ in the morning.
                    1                2

His ___meeting___ is at 1:00 in the ___afternoon___. The
        3                                   4

meeting is at the ___hospital___, next to the school.
                        5

It's a busy day.

Teaching objectives
● Review vocabulary from Units 5 and 6
● Introduce the pronunciation of *a* as in *at* and *o* as in *on*

# WARM-UP AND REVIEW

● Before class. Write today's lesson focus on the board.
*Review unit:*
*Review vocabulary and grammar from Units 5 and 6*
*Pronounce "a" as in "at" and "o" as in "on"*

● Begin class. Books closed. Ask the following questions and elicit appropriate responses:
*Where is our English class?*
*What time is our English class?*
*What time is our English class over?*
*What building is next to our school?*

# PRACTICE

● Books open. Say: *Listen to conversations about events and places.*

● Direct Ss' attention to Exercise 1 and read the instructions aloud. Ask a S to read aloud the question and answer choices in number 1.

▶ **CD2, Track 10** Model the task. Play or read only the first conversation from the audio (see audio script, page T-148). Point to the two answer choices in number 1 and ask: *Yes, it is or No, it isn't?* (Yes, it is.) Point to where the letter *a* has been circled. Say: *Yes, the meeting is on Friday.*

● Read aloud the remaining questions and answer choices. Say: *Now listen and circle the correct answers.*

▶ **CD2, Track 10** Play or read the complete audio. Ss listen and circle the answers. Repeat the audio as needed.

● Check answers with the class. Read each question aloud and call on different Ss to answer.

● Read aloud the second part of the instructions for Exercise 1. Ss practice asking and answering the questions in pairs. Walk around and help as needed.

● Ask several pairs to ask and answer the questions for the rest of the class.

## *Learner persistence* (student pairs)

● If you have any Ss who are struggling in class, try to pair them with stronger Ss who like to help others. From time to time, ask Ss to pick new partners so everyone gets a chance to practice with Ss of different ability levels.

# PRACTICE

● Direct Ss' attention to Exercise 2. Point to the title of the story and ask: *What's the title?* ("Tan's Day") Ask: *What do you think this story is about?* Elicit any words that Ss might think will be in the story, such as *English class, meeting, morning.*

● Read aloud the instructions for Exercise 2. Point to the words in the word bank and tell Ss: *Write these words in the story.*

● Model the task. Read aloud the first sentence: *Tan's English . . .* Elicit *class.* Point to *class* in the word bank and in the blank for number 1.

● Ss read the story and fill in the blanks individually. Walk around and help as needed.

● Write the numbers *1–5* on the board. Ask volunteers to come to the board and write the answers on the board.

● Ask individual Ss to read sentences from the story aloud. After each sentence, ask: *Is the answer correct?* If not, ask volunteers to correct any errors.

## *Expansion activity* (small groups)

● Before class. Prepare copies of the Picture dictionary cards from Units 5 and 6. Divide the class into small groups. Give each group copies of the cards. Say: *Make sentences. Use one card for time of day. Use one card for type of transportation.*

● Model the activity. Write on the board: *I go _____.*
Ask volunteers to complete the sentence with a place they go every day. Elicit endings, such as: *to school, home, to work.*

● Hold up a Picture dictionary card from Unit 6, for example: *in the morning.* Put it next to a sentence. Say the sentence aloud, for example: *I go to school in the morning.*

● Hold up a Picture dictionary card from Unit 5, for example: *by bus.* Put it next to the card from Unit 6. Form a longer sentence using the two picture dictionary cards. Say the sentence aloud, for example: *I go to school in the morning by bus.*

● Tell Ss to use this order when forming sentences: *I go to school + (card from Unit 6) + (card from Unit 5).*

### Teaching Tip

If appropriate, tell Ss that the order of the phrases in the sentences can be changed, for example: *In the morning I go to school by bus.*

● Ss complete the activity in small groups. Encourage them to make as many sentences as possible. They can write the sentences in their notebooks for further writing practice.

● Ask each group to write a sentence on the board.

# REVIEW

## WARM-UP AND REVIEW

- Books closed. Draw some buildings on the board. Label them with names of places from Unit 5. Make sure they are located across from, between, and next to each other.
- Point to a building. Ask: *What's this?* Elicit the name of the building. Ask: *Where is it?* Elicit an appropriate response. Continue by asking about all the buildings.

## PRACTICE

- Direct Ss' attention to Exercise **3A**. Read the instructions aloud.
- Model the task. Ask a S to read the first example. Ask: *Is it correct to say "The library is on the bank?"* (No.) Say: *No, the library is across from the bank.* Point to where *across from* has been circled and written.
- Ss circle and write their answers individually. Walk around and help as needed.
- Write the numbers *1–4* on the board. Ask volunteers to write the answers from Exercise **3A** on the board. Ask other Ss to read the words aloud. Ask: *Are these words correct?* Ask different Ss to correct any errors.
- Direct Ss' attention to the calendar page in Exercise **3B** and ask: *What do you see?* Elicit any vocabulary that Ss know. Read the instructions aloud.
- Model the task. Ask two Ss to read aloud the example question and answer. Hold up the Student's Book. Point to where it says *movie* in the memo. Ask: *Is the movie at 6:00?* Elicit: *No, it isn't. It's at 6:30.*
- Ss complete the exercise individually. Walk around and help as needed.
- Ss check their answers in pairs. Say: *Ask and answer the questions with your partner. Check to see if your answers are the same or different.*
- Ask several pairs to ask and answer the questions for the rest of the class.

## PRESENTATION

- Direct Ss' attention to the second part of the lesson focus on the board.
- Write on the board: *at, class, map.* Point to and say each word and ask Ss to repeat. Underline the *a* in the words. Say a short a (/æ/) sound before repeating each word, for example: /æ/, *at*. Ask Ss to repeat after you.

- Write on the board: *on, clock, not.* Repeat the procedure, underlining the *o* in the words and pronouncing a short *o* (/ɒ/) sound, for example: /ɒ/, *on.*

## PRACTICE

- ▶ **CD2, Track 11** Direct Ss' attention to Exercise **4A** and read aloud the instructions. Play or read the audio (see audio script, page T-148). Ss listen to examples of the two vowel sounds.

### *Expansion activity* (whole group)

- Draw a vertical line on the board. Write *at* in one column and *on* in the other. Say: *Let's think of other words that have these sounds.* As Ss say words with these sounds, write them in the correct column. Point to each word and ask Ss to repeat.
- ▶ **CD2, Track 12** Direct Ss' attention to Exercise **4B** and read the instructions aloud. Play or read the audio (see audio script, page T-148). Ss listen and repeat what they hear.
- Read aloud the second part of the instructions for Exercise **4B**. Model the task. Point to the two charts and tell one S: *Say a word.* Tell his or her partner: *Point to the word.*
- Ss complete the task in pairs. Walk around and help as needed.
- ▶ **CD2, Track 13** Direct Ss' attention to Exercise **4C** and read the instructions aloud. Model the task. Play or read the first word on the audio (see audio script, page T-148). Ask: *Which letter is it: a or o?* (o) Point to where the letter has been checked in the chart.
- ▶ **CD2, Track 13** Play or read the complete audio. Ss listen and make a checkmark under the letter they hear.
- ▶ **CD2, Track 13** Reproduce the chart from Exercise **4C** on the board and play or read the audio again. Pause after each word and ask a S to check the appropriate letter in the chart.

## EVALUATION

- Direct Ss' attention to the lesson focus.
- Walk around the room. Ask each S to say a sentence about Tan from Exercise **2** on page 82 in the Student's Book.
- Write on the board: *class, clock.* Call on individual Ss as you point to one of the words and ask them to say it. Listen carefully to the vowel sounds and provide help and correction as needed.
- Check off the items in the lesson focus as Ss demonstrate understanding of what they have learned in the lesson.

## 3 Grammar

**A** **Read and circle.** Then write.

1. The library is _____across from_____ the bank.
   on (across from)

2. The post office is _____*between*_____ the bank and the library.
   next to (between)

3. The restaurant is _____*on*_____ Main Street.
   (on) between

4. The hospital is _____*across from*_____ the gas station.
   (across from) between

**B** **Read the memo and answer.** Write *Yes, it is* or *No, it isn't.*

1. Is the movie at 6:00?
   _____No, it isn't_____ .

2. Is the class at 9:00?
   _____Yes, it is_____ .

3. Is the meeting in the morning?
   _____No, it isn't_____ .

4. Is the appointment in the afternoon?
   _____Yes, it is_____ .

| Morning |
| --- |
| 9:00 class |
| **Afternoon** |
| 2:00 – meeting with Ms. Morales |
| 4:30 – appointment with Dr. Morgan |
| **Evening** |
| 6:30 – movie |

## 4 Pronunciation

**A** **Listen to the *a* sound and the *o* sound.**

| a | o |
| --- | --- |
| at | on |

CD2, Track 11

**B** **Listen and repeat.**

| a | at | class | map | | o | on | clock | not |
| --- | --- | --- | --- | --- | --- | --- | --- | --- |

**Talk with a partner.** Say a word. Your partner points. Take turns.

CD2, Track 12

**C** **Listen and check (✓).**

| | a | o | | a | o | | a | o | | a | o | | a | o |
| --- | --- | --- | --- | --- | --- | --- | --- | --- | --- | --- | --- | --- | --- | --- |
| 1. | | ✓ | 2. | | ✓ | 3. | ✓ | | 4. | ✓ | | 5. | | ✓ |

CD2, Track 13

# UNIT 7 SHOPPING

## Lesson A Listening

### 1 Before you listen

**A** Look at the picture. What do you see?

**B** Listen and point: ■ a dress ■ pants ■ a shirt ■ shoes ■ socks ■ a T-shirt

CD2, Track 14

SUMMER SALE!

THE CLOTHES PLACE

$39.99

$27.00

$19.00

$1.99

$24.99

$10.99

Rose

Samuel

# UNIT 7

**Teaching objectives**
- Introduce Ss to the topic
- Find out what Ss know about the topic
- Preview the unit by talking about the picture
- Provide practice of key vocabulary
- Provide practice that devlopes listening skills

## WARM-UP AND REVIEW

- Before class. Write today's lesson focus on the board.
  *Lesson A:*
  *Shopping*
  *Vocabulary for clothes shopping*
- Begin class. Write the word *clothes* on the board. Point to the word. Say it aloud and ask Ss to repeat after you. Ask: *What are some examples of clothes?* Encourage Ss to say the names of clothes that they know or to point to different types of clothes Ss in the classroom are wearing. Write the different types that Ss say on the board. Explain the new words by pointing to examples in the class.
- Say: *Today's class is about shopping for clothes. Where do you go shopping for clothes?* Elicit appropriate responses. Ask: *What clothes stores do you like?* Elicit appropriate responses.

> **Literacy Tip**
>
> If you have literacy Ss in your class, it might be helpful to spend time at the beginning of any activity with art or photos talking about the pictures before focusing Ss' attention on the printed words in the exercise. Have Ss work in pairs. Tell them to ask each other: *What do you see?* Encourage Ss to describe the pictures to each other. Consider pairing literacy Ss with Ss who can help them read the text in the exercise. This will help preview the exercise for literacy Ss and make them more confident as the exercise continues.

## PRESENTATION

- Books open. Set the scene. Hold up the Student's Book. Show Ss the picture on page 84. Ask: *What do you see?* Elicit and write on the board any vocabulary that Ss know, such as: *clothes store, sale, dress, pants, T-shirt.*

> **Teaching Tip**
>
> If Ss don't know the meaning of the word *sale*, say: *"Sale" means a time of lower prices.* If possible, bring in an ad that shows items on sale. Show it to the class. Point to the sale items. Say: *These items are on sale.*

## PRACTICE

- Direct Ss' attention to the key vocabulary in Exercise **1B**. Read each word or phrase aloud while pointing to the corresponding items in the picture. Ask Ss to repeat and point.
- ▶ *CD2, Track 14* Play or read the audio (see audio script, page T-149). Tell Ss: *Listen and point to the picture.* As Ss hear the key vocabulary, check to see that they are pointing to the correct part of the picture. Repeat the audio as needed.

## COMPREHENSION CHECK

- Ask Ss *Yes / No* questions about the picture. Ask about new vocabulary and recycle words learned in previous units. Say: *Listen to the questions. Answer "Yes, it is." or "No, it isn't."*

  Point to the picture. Ask: *Is this a shopping mall?* (No, it isn't.)
  Point to the store. Ask: *Is this a shoe store?* (No, it isn't.)
  Point to the sundress in the store window.
  Ask: *Is this a dress?* (Yes, it is.)
  Point to a T-shirt. Ask: *Is this a pair of pants?* (No, it isn't.)
  Point to a pair of pants. Ask: *Is this a pair of pants?* (Yes, it is.)

> **Teaching Tip**
>
> Review, if necessary, the grammar point learned in Lesson C of Unit 6 on page 74. This grammar point asks questions with the pattern *Is your class at 11:00?* and has the same answers *Yes, it is* and *No, it isn't* as in this exercise.

### *Expansion activity* (whole group)

- Draw a large stick figure on the board. Say: *We are going to put clothes on this person.* Ask a S to come to the board. Say: *Please draw pants on this person.* Continue by asking different Ss to draw other pieces of clothing on the figure.

  **Option** Ask a S to tell the other Ss what to draw. Write: *Draw a _____ on the person.* to help the S with the directions.

> **Literacy Tip**
>
> For an alternative activity, refer literacy Ss to pages 78–79 in the *Literacy Workbook* at any time during the lesson.

# LESSON A Listening

## PRESENTATION

- Direct Ss' attention to Exercise 2A. Tell Ss: *These are different types of clothes.*

- Hold up or point to real examples of the clothing as you read each word aloud. Ask Ss to repeat the words after you. If there is an item that no one is wearing (for example, a dress), draw a quick sketch and label it on the board.

- Read aloud the instructions for Exercise 2A.

## PRACTICE

- ▶ **CD2, Track 15** Play or read the audio (see audio script, page T-149). Ss listen and repeat the vocabulary. Repeat the audio as needed.

- Listen carefully to Ss' pronunciation and make corrections as needed.

### *Learner persistence* (individual work)

- ▶ **CD2, Track 15** Ss can listen to the audio for Exercise 2A at home for reinforcement and review. They can also listen to the audio for self-directed learning when class attendance is not possible.

- Direct Ss' attention to Exercise 2B and read the instructions aloud.

- ▶ **CD2, Track 16** Model the task. Hold up the Student's Book and say: *Number one.* Play or read the audio for number 1 (see audio script, page T-149). Point to the two answer choices in number 1 and ask Ss: *What did you hear – a or b?* Elicit: *a.* Point to the letter *a* next to the first picture and tell Ss: *Circle the letter "a."*

- ▶ **CD2, Track 16** Play or read the complete audio. Ss listen and circle the correct answers. Repeat the audio as needed.

- ▶ **CD2, Track 16** Read aloud the second part of the instructions for Exercise 2B. Play or read the audio again so that Ss can listen and check their answers.

### *Learner persistence* (individual work)

- ▶ **CD2, Track 16** Ss can listen to the audio for Exercise 2B at home for reinforcement and review. They can also listen to the audio for self-directed learning when class attendance is not possible.

## COMPREHENSION CHECK

- Write the numbers *1–4* on the board. Ask a few volunteers to come to the board and write the correct answers to Exercise 2B next to each number.

- ▶ **CD2, Track 16** Play or read the audio again. Pause the audio after each conversation. Point to the answer written on the board and ask: *Is this correct?* If not, ask a volunteer to make any necessary corrections.

## APPLICATION

- Direct Ss' attention to Exercise 3 and read the instructions aloud.

- Model the task. Hold up the Student's Book and point to the answer choices in Exercise 2B. Say to one S: *Point to a picture.* Say to the first S's partner: *Say the word.*

- Ss complete the exercise in pairs. Walk around and help as needed.

## EVALUATION

- Direct Ss' attention to the lesson focus on the board. Check Ss' understanding of clothing vocabulary by asking them to point to the following clothing items in the picture on page 84 in the Student's Book: *dress, pants, shirt, shoes, socks, T-shirt.* Walk around and check that Ss are pointing to the correct items.

- Check off the lesson focus as Ss demonstrate an understanding of what they have learned in the lesson.

| *More Ventures, Unit 7, Lesson A* | |
| --- | --- |
| **Literacy Workbook,** 15–30 min. | |
| **Basic Workbook,** 15–30 min. | |
| **Writing Worksheets,** 15–30 min. **Collaborative Worksheets,** 30–45 min. | www.cambridge.org/ventures/resources/ |
| **Student Arcade,** time varies | www.cambridge.org/venturesarcade/ |

**UNIT GOALS**
**Identify** prices  **Interpret** a receipt
**Complete** a shopping list

## 2 Listen

**A** **Listen and repeat.**

1. a dress     2. pants     3. a shirt

4. shoes     5. socks     6. a T-shirt

CD2, Track 15

CD2, Track 16

**B** **Listen and circle.**

1.  (a.)       b.

2.  a.       (b.)

3.  a.       (b.)

4.  (a.)       b.

**Listen again.** Check your answers.

## 3 After you listen

**Talk with a partner.** Point to a picture.
Your partner says the word.

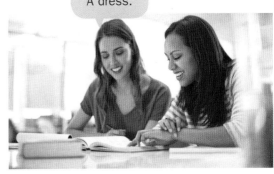

A dress.

Listen for and identify clothing items    **UNIT 7**    **85**

# Lesson B Clothing

## 1 Vocabulary focus

Listen and repeat.

CD2, Track 17

**Back-to-School Sale**

| 1 a tie | $10.00 | 2 a blouse | $19.99 | 3 a sweater | $29.99 |
| 4 a skirt | $24.99 | 5 a jacket | $89.99 | 6 a raincoat | $39.99 |

## 2 Practice

A  Read and match.

1.　2.　3.　4.　5.　6.

a tie　a blouse　a jacket　a skirt　a raincoat　a sweater

- Introduce and provide practice of clothing vocabulary
- Provide practice of questions and answers about prices with *How much?*

# WARM-UP AND REVIEW

- **Before class.** Write today's lesson focus on the board.
  *Lesson B:*
  *Clothing vocabulary*
  *How much?*
  *Prices*
- **Begin class.** Books open. Direct Ss' attention to the picture on page 84. Review key vocabulary from the unit by asking: *What are the names for the clothes in this picture?* Elicit: *dress, pants, shirt, shoes, socks, T-shirt.* Ask Ss to point to these items.
- Walk around and check to see that Ss are pointing to the correct items in the picture.
- Point out to students that *clothes* and *clothing* mean the same thing.
- Write the words *Back-to-School Sale!* on the board. Point to the words. Say them aloud. Ask Ss to repeat them after you. Ask: *What is this?* If necessary, remind Ss of the sale sign in the picture on page 84. If Ss don't know what a back-to-school sale is, say: *It's a sale just before school starts. It's for buying clothes for school.*

### Community building *(whole class)*

- If you have Ss with school-age children, ask if they go to back-to-school sales before the school year starts. Ask: *What store has good back-to-school sales?* Elicit appropriate answers. Ask other Ss if they shop at back-to-school sales for themselves.

# PRESENTATION

- Set the scene. Write on the board: *advertisement.* Point to the word. Say it aloud. Ask: *What's this?* Elicit an appropriate response.

### Teaching Tip

It might be helpful to bring some advertisements to class. Show them to the class. Say: *These are advertisements,* or *"ads" for short.* Erase the letters to show how *advertisement* becomes *ad.*

- Read aloud the instructions for Exercise 1.
- ▶ **CD2, Track 17** Play or read the audio (see audio script, page T-149). Listen and repeat the vocabulary along with Ss. Repeat the audio as needed.
- Listen carefully to Ss' pronunciation and correct as needed.

### Expansion activity *(student pairs)*

- Write on the board: *Is this a (name of clothing item)? Yes, it is. / No, it isn't.*
- Model the activity. Point to the picture of a blouse in Exercise 1. Ask a S: *Is this a blouse?* The S answers: *Yes, it is.* Point to the picture of a raincoat. Ask another S: *Is this a jacket?* The S answers: *No, it isn't.*
- Ss continue pointing and asking about the pictures with their partners.
- Walk around and help as needed.

# PRACTICE

- Direct Ss' attention to Exercise 2A. As you read aloud the instructions, hold up the Student's Book and indicate that Ss should look at the pictures of clothing items and match them to the corresponding words.
- Model the task. Hold up the Student's Book. Point to the first picture. Ask: *What clothing item is this?* (A blouse.) Say: *Match the picture with the word.*
- Ss complete the exercise individually. Help as needed.

### Teaching Tip

Sometimes Ss have difficulty distinguishing between a blouse and a shirt. Draw a frilly blouse on the board or ask a S wearing one to stand up. Draw a plainer shirt on the board or ask a S wearing one to stand up. Point to the blouse and shirt one at a time and say: *This is a blouse. This is a shirt.*

### Literacy Tip

Literacy Ss may be able to complete this activity with help. Pair stronger Ss with literacy Ss. Tell literacy Ss to refer to Exercise 1 when completing Exercise 2A.

# COMPREHENSION CHECK

- Write the numbers *1–6* on the board. Ask volunteers to come to the board and write the answers to Exercise 2A on the board.
- Ask different Ss to read the answers on the board. After each answer is read, ask: *Is this correct?* If not, ask a volunteer to make any necessary corrections on the board.

# LESSON B Clothing

## PRESENTATION

- Direct Ss' attention to the word bank in Exercise 2B. Say: *Repeat these words after me.* Say each word aloud. Listen to Ss' pronunciation as they repeat the words after you.
- Read the instructions for Exercise 2B aloud.
- Say: *You are going to listen to conversations about prices.* Write on the board: *How much?* Point to the words. Say: *When we ask about prices, we say, "How much?"*

## PRACTICE

- ▶ **CD2, Track 18** Model the task. Say: *Listen and repeat.* Play or read the audio for number 1 (see audio script, page T-149) and point to the tie as you repeat. Say: *Then write.* Point to the word *tie* written in the blank. Make sure Ss understand the task.
- ▶ **CD2, Track 18** Play or read the complete audio. Ss listen and repeat. Encourage Ss to point to the clothing pictures as they repeat.
- Ss complete the sentences individually using words from the word bank. Repeat the audio as needed.
- Check answers with the class. Write the numbers *1–6* on the board and ask for volunteers to write their answers on the board. Point to each answer and ask the class: *Yes? Is this correct?* Make any necessary corrections on the board.
- Read aloud the second part of the instructions for Exercise 2B. Point to and model the example conversation.
- Call on a pair of volunteers to read the example conversation aloud for the class.
- Point to another clothing picture on page 87. Ask: *How much is the jacket?* ($48.99.) Repeat with different clothing items. Indicate that Ss should ask and answer questions about all the clothing in the pictures.
- Ss complete the exercise in pairs. Walk around and help as needed.

### Teaching Tip

It might be helpful to go over the different ways prices can be said in English. Write *$9.99* on the board. Say: *In English, we can say this price two ways. One way is "nine ninety-nine." The second way is "nine dollars and ninety-nine cents."* Continue by asking Ss to read the prices in Exercise 2B two ways.

### Literacy Tip

For an alternative activity, refer literacy Ss to pages 80–81 in the *Literacy Workbook* at any time during the lesson.

## *Expansion activity* (student pairs)

- Bring clothing ads from department stores and other stores to class. Ask volunteers to find examples of the clothing items in Lessons A and B in the ads.
- Write: *How much is the _____?* Say: *Point to a clothing item. Ask your partner, "How much is it?"* Walk around and help as needed.
- Ask several pairs to ask and answer questions about the clothing in the ads for the rest of the class.

## APPLICATION

- Direct Ss' attention to Exercise 3 and read the instructions aloud. Have the Ss write their own prices for each of the items.
- Model the task. Ask two Ss to read the question and answer aloud. As Ss are saying the conversation, hold up the Student's Book and point to where $24.99 is written under the skirt. Make sure the Ss understand the task.
- Ss complete the exercise in pairs. Walk around and help as needed.
- Ask several pairs to ask and answer the questions for the rest of the class.

## EVALUATION

- Direct Ss' attention to the lesson focus on the board. Check Ss' understanding of the key vocabulary by asking them to point to the clothing in the pictures in Exercise 2B on page 87: *tie, blouse, jacket, raincoat, skirt, sweater.* Walk around and check that Ss are pointing to the correct items.
- Focus Ss' attention on *How much?* in the lesson focus. Ask Ss to ask questions about the prices of the items in Exercise 2B with *How much?* Ask other Ss to answer the questions.
- Check off each part of the lesson focus as Ss demonstrate an understanding of what they have learned in the lesson.

| More Ventures, Unit 7, Lesson B | |
|---|---|
| Literacy Workbook, 15–30 min. | |
| Basic Workbook, 15–30 min. | |
| Writing Worksheets, 15–30 min. | www.cambridge.org/ventures/ resources/ |
| Collaborative Worksheets, 30–45 min. | |
| Student Arcade, time varies | www.cambridge.org/venturesarcade/ |

**B** **Listen and repeat.** Then write.

blouse   jacket   raincoat   skirt   sweater   tie

CD2, Track 18

1. The ___tie___ is $9.99.   2. The _raincoat_ is $26.95.   3. The _skirt_ is $35.95.

4. The _sweater_ is $39.99.   5. The _jacket_ is $48.99.   6. The _blouse_ is $25.95.

**Talk with a partner.** Ask and answer.

A  How much is the **tie**?
B  **$9.99.**

**USEFUL LANGUAGE**
$9.99 = *nine ninety-nine*
or
*nine dollars and ninety-nine cents*

**3** **Communicate**

**Write prices.** Your partner asks the price. You answer.

$ ___24.99___   $ _Answers will vary._   $ _____   $ _____   $ _____

A  How much is the **skirt**?
B  **$24.99.**

# Lesson C How much are the shoes?

## 1 Grammar focus: *How much is? / How much are?*

| QUESTIONS | | | ANSWERS |
|---|---|---|---|
| How much | **is** | the shirt? | $15.99. |
| | **are** | the shoes? | $68.95. |

Watch

## 2 Practice

**A** **Read and circle.** Then write.

1. **A** How much _____**are**_____ the pants?
   is (are)
   **B** $24.99.

2. **A** How much _____*is*_____ the skirt?
   (is) are
   **B** $18.99.

3. **A** How much _____*is*_____ the raincoat?
   (is) are
   **B** $16.95.

4. **A** How much _____*are*_____ the shoes?
   is (are)
   **B** $58.99.

5. **A** How much _____*is*_____ the sweater?
   (is) are
   **B** $31.99.

6. **A** How much _____*are*_____ the socks?
   is (are)
   **B** $5.95.

**Listen and repeat.** Then practice with a partner.

CD2, Track 19

Teaching objectives
• Provide practice of *How much is?*
• Introduce *How much are?*

## WARM-UP AND REVIEW

• Before class. Write today's lesson focus on the board.
*Lesson C:*
*How much is _____?*
*How much are _____?*

• Begin class. Books closed. Write the names of clothes learned in Lesson B on the board: *blouse, jacket, raincoat, skirt, sweater, tie.* Write a price under each item: *$10.00, $24.99, $32.50, $12.99, $6.99.*

• Point to the word *blouse.* Ask: *What's this?* (A blouse.) Ask: *How much is it?* ($10.00.)

• Remind Ss they learned two ways to say prices. Point out that when the price doesn't have cents, such as with $10.00, there is only one way to say the price. You must say the word *dollars.*

• Continue the exercise. Point to each clothing item on the board. Ask Ss the prices.

## PRESENTATION

• Use the animated grammar presentation in one or more of the following ways:
  • Preview it before class
  • Show it in class
  • Encourage Ss to watch it outside of class.

• Books open. Direct Ss' attention to the *grammar chart* in Exercise 1. Read aloud the questions and corresponding answers. Ask Ss to repeat after you.

• Ask: *Why do we sometimes say "How much is" and sometimes say "How much are"?* If Ss don't know the answer, say: *Use "is" for a singular item (one item) and "are" for a plural item (more than one).*

• Write *singular* and *plural* on the board. Point to each word. Say it aloud. Ask Ss to repeat it after you. Pick up a pen and show it to the class. Ask: *Is this singular or plural?* (Singular.) Pick up two books. Ask: *Are these singular or plural?* (Plural.)

### Teaching Tip

Remind Ss that plurals in English usually have an s on the end of the singular form. Give Ss examples to remind them of the singular and plural forms in English.

## COMPREHENSION CHECK

• Write the words *pants, socks,* and *shoes* on the board. Include a price for each item: *$24.99, $4.99, $62.50.* Point to the word *pants.* Write on the board: *How much is?* and *How much are?* Ask: *Which question do I use with "pants"?* Elicit: *How much are the pants?* If Ss need more explanation, circle the s in pants. Say: *Remember that plural words use "are" in this question.*

• Point to the singular words written on the board at the beginning of the lesson (*blouse, jacket,* etc.). Ask: *Which question do I use with "blouse"?* Elicit: *How much is the blouse?*

• Point to all the words in turn, switching from plural words to singular ones. Check to make sure Ss understand the difference between the two question forms.

## PRACTICE

• Direct Ss' attention to the picture in Exercise 2A. Ask: *Where is this picture?* (In a store.) *What do you see?* Elicit: *pants, a skirt, a raincoat, shoes, a sweater, a shirt, socks.*

### Teaching Tip

Do not expect Ss to answer the questions in complete sentences. The purpose of this exercise is to understand the meaning of the question and answer with the correct information.

• Read aloud the example conversation in number 1. When you read Speaker B's line, show Ss the two answer choices under the blank and ask: *is or are?* Elicit *are.*

• Read aloud the instructions for Exercise 2A. Point to where *are* has been circled and written for number 1.

• Ss complete the exercise individually. Walk around and help as needed.

## COMPREHENSION CHECK

• Read aloud the second part of the instructions in Exercise 2A.

▶ *CD2, Track 19* Play or read the audio (see audio script, page T-149). Ss listen and repeat as they check their answers.

• Write the numbers *1–6* on the board. Ask volunteers to come to the board and write the answers they circled. Make any necessary corrections on the board.

• Ss in pairs. Ask Ss to choose Role A or B and practice the questions and answers in Exercise 2A. Then have Ss switch roles and practice again. Walk around and help as needed.

• Ask several pairs to read the conversations to the rest of the class.

### Literacy Tip

For an alternative activity, refer literacy Ss to pages 82–83 in the *Literacy Workbook* at any time during the lesson.

# LESSON C How much are the shoes?

## PRESENTATION

- Books closed. Write on the board: *yard sale.* Say the words. Ask Ss to repeat. Ask: *What is a yard sale?* If Ss don't know these words, say: *A yard sale is when people sell used items outside their houses.* If Ss still do not understand, ask them to open their books and look at the picture in Exercise 2B for further clarification.

### Culture Tip

If Ss are new to the United States, they may not be familiar with yard sales. It might be interesting to ask them their opinions about yard sales. Ask if any Ss have these types of sales in their countries. Explain that many Americans like to go to yard sales to find bargains or unique items.

## PRACTICE

- Books open. Direct Ss' attention to the picture in Exercise 2B. Say: *This is a picture of a yard sale. What do you see?* Elicit as many vocabulary words as possible.
- Read aloud the first part of the instructions for Exercise 2B. Focus Ss' attention on the shopping list beside the picture.
- *CD2, Track 20* Model the task. Say: *Listen and repeat.* Play or read the audio for number 1 (see audio script, page T-149) and point to the T-shirt in the picture as you repeat. Say: *Then write.* Point to where *$2.00* has been written beside *T-shirt* in the shopping list. Make sure Ss understand the task.
- *CD2, Track 20* Play or read the complete audio. Ss listen and repeat. Encourage Ss to point to the clothing in the picture as they repeat.
- Ss work individually as they write the prices in the shopping list. Repeat the audio as needed.
- Write the numbers *1–8* on the board. Ask a few Ss to come to the board and write the word and the price for each clothing item on the board. Ask volunteers to read each price aloud. Ask: *Are these prices correct?* Ask other Ss to make corrections.
- Read aloud the second part of the instructions for Exercise 2B. Model the task. Ask two Ss to read the first example conversation. Then ask two different Ss to read the second example conversation.

- Indicate that Ss should ask and answer questions about all the clothing. Make sure Ss understand the task.
- Ss ask and answer questions about the clothing in the picture in pairs. When Ss are finished, ask them to switch partners and repeat the conversations.
- Ask several pairs to say their conversations to the rest of the class.

## APPLICATION

- Direct Ss' attention to Exercise 3 and read the instructions aloud. Have Ss write their own prices for the items.
- Model the task. Ask two Ss to read the example conversation aloud. As Ss are saying the conversation, hold up the Student's Book and point to where *$5.00* is written under the socks. Make sure Ss understand the task.
- Ss complete the exercise in pairs. Walk around and help as needed.

### *Community building* (whole group)

- If Ss are interested in visiting a yard sale, tell them how to find out where people are having yard sales. Tell Ss that they can look for yard sale signs in their neighborhoods or look for listings in the classified ads section of their local newspaper or online.

## EVALUATION

- Direct Ss' attention to the lesson focus on the board. Ask Ss to look at the picture on page 84. Ask them to make questions about the clothing items in the picture using *How much is?* and *How much are?* Ask different Ss to answer the questions.
- Check off each part of the lesson focus as Ss demonstrate an understanding of what they have learned in the lesson.

| *More Ventures, Unit 7, Lesson C* | |
|---|---|
| **Literacy Workbook,** 15–30 min. | |
| **Basic Workbook,** 15–30 min. | |
| **Writing Worksheets,** 15–30 min. **Collaborative Worksheets,** 30–45 min. | www.cambridge.org/ventures/ resources/ |
| **Student Arcade,** time varies | www.cambridge.org/venturesarcade/ |

**B** **Listen and repeat.** Then write the price.

 🔊 CD2, Track 20

| | | |
|---|---|---|
| 1. | T-shirt | $2.00 |
| 2. | shoes | $3.00 |
| 3. | jacket | $8.00 |
| 4. | sweater | $4.00 |
| 5. | raincoat | $5.00 |
| 6. | pants | $6.00 |
| 7. | socks | $1.00 |
| 8. | blouse | $7.00 |

**Talk with a partner.** Ask and answer.

A  How much **is the T-shirt**?
B  **$2.00.**
A  **$2.00?** Thanks.

A  How much **are the shoes**?
B  **$3.00.**
A  **$3.00?** Thanks.

## ❸ Communicate

**Write prices.** Your partner asks the price. You answer.

$ ___5.00___   $ _Answers will vary._   $ _____   $ _____   $ _____

A  How much **are the socks**?
B  **$5.00.**

# Lesson D Reading

## 1 Before you read

**Talk about the picture.**
What do you see?

## 2 Read

**Listen and read.**

| From: | Rose | Reply     Forward |
|---|---|---|
| To: | Patty | |
| Subject: | Shopping | |

🔊 CD2, Track 21

Hi Patty,

This morning, Samuel and I are going to The Clothes Place. Samuel needs blue pants. He needs a tie, too. I need a red dress and black shoes. Dresses are on sale. They're $49.99. Shoes are on sale, too. They're $34.99. That's good.

Call you later,
Rose

## 3 After you read

**Read and match.**

1.

Samuel needs blue pants.

Samuel needs a tie.

Dresses are on sale.

Shoes are on sale.

2.

3.

4.

**Teaching objectives**
- Introduce an email about shopping
- Provide practice using new topic-related words

# WARM-UP AND REVIEW

- Before class. Write today's lesson focus on the board.
*Lesson D:*
*Read an email message about shopping*
*Learn new vocabulary about clothes shopping*

- Begin class. Books closed. Write *clothes* on the board. Point to the word. Ask: *What are the names of some clothes?* Elicit appropriate responses and write them on the board. Point to each of the words on the board in turn. Ask: *What is a good price for this item?* Elicit appropriate responses. Write the prices on the board next to the items.

- Write *Sale* on the board. Ask: *Do you remember this word on a sign in the first picture of this unit? What does the sign mean?* Elicit appropriate responses.

## Community building *(whole group)*

- Ask Ss if there are any good sales going on in stores in their neighborhoods. Encourage Ss to tell each other when there are good sales.

# PRESENTATION

- Books open. Direct Ss' attention to the picture in Exercise 1.
- Read the instructions aloud. Ask: *What do you see?* Elicit and write on the board any vocabulary that Ss know, such as: *sale, pants, dress, shoes.*
- Write *email* on the board. Point to the word. Say it aloud and ask Ss to repeat after you. Ask: *What's this?* Elicit an appropriate answer such as: *It's a message on the computer.* Ask: *Do you use email?*
- Say: *Now we will read an email about shopping.*

# PRACTICE

- Direct Ss' attention to Exercise 2. Read the instructions aloud.
- **CD2, Track 21** Play or read the audio and ask Ss to follow along (see audio script, page T-149). Repeat the audio as needed.
- Read aloud each sentence of the email and ask Ss to repeat after you.
- Answer any questions Ss have about the reading.

## Community building

- Ask Ss if they would like to share their email addresses with others in the class. Explain that Ss can practice their writing and get to know their classmates better through email. They can also find out about missed assignments if they are absent from English class.

## Learner persistence *(individual work)*

- **CD2, Track 21** Ss can listen to the audio for Exercise 2 at home for reinforcement and review. They can also listen to the audio for self-directed learning when class attendance is not possible.

# COMPREHENSION CHECK

- Direct Ss' attention to Exercise 3 and read the instructions aloud.
- Hold up the Student's Book. Point to the first picture. Point to the line matching picture 1 to the correct sentence. Ask a S to read the example sentence aloud. Say: *Draw a line to match each picture with the correct sentence.*
- Ss complete the exercise individually. Walk around and help as needed.
- Ask individual Ss to read each sentence aloud and say which picture the sentence matches.

## Expansion activity *(individual)*

- Question-and-answer activity. Say: *Walk around the room. Write down the names of five Ss. Then write their clothing next to their names.*
- Model the activity. Ask a S: *What's your name?* Write the S's name on the board. Ask the class: *What clothes is he / she wearing?* After the class responds, write the S's clothing next to his / her name. For example: *jeans, T-shirt, shoes.*

### Teaching Tip

Tell Ss that they don't have to ask the S what he or she is wearing. They can simply look and write down what the other S is wearing.

# LESSON D Reading

## PRESENTATION

- Books closed. Write the word *colors* on the board. Point to the word and say it aloud. Ask Ss to repeat it after you.
- Ask: *What colors can you say in English?* Write Ss' responses on the board.

### Teaching Tip

It might be helpful to point out examples of the colors in the room as you write the names of the color words on the board.

- Books open. Direct Ss' attention to the Picture dictionary in Exercise **4**. Hold up the Student's Book. Point to the pictures of baseball caps. Say: *These are baseball caps. They are all different colors.* Write *baseball caps* on the board. Say the words aloud and ask Ss to repeat.
- Point to the names of colors under each picture. Read the words aloud and ask Ss to repeat them after you.
- Read the instructions for Exercise **4A** aloud.
- ▶ **CD2, Track 22** Play or read the audio (see audio script, page T-149). Listen to Ss' pronunciation as they repeat the colors. Correct pronunciation as needed.

### *Learner persistence* (individual work)

- ▶ **CD2, Track 22** Ss can listen to the audio for Exercise **4A** at home for reinforcement and review. They can also listen to the audio for self-directed learning when class attendance is not possible.

## PRACTICE

- Direct Ss' attention to Exercise **4B** and read the instructions aloud. Ask two Ss to read the example conversations aloud. Then have them ask about a third S's clothing. Encourage Ss to try to use all the colors in the picture dictionary in their conversations.
- Ss complete the exercise in pairs. Walk around and help as needed.
- Ask several pairs to ask and answer the questions for the rest of the class, indicating who they are talking about. Check that they are using *his* and *her* correctly.

### Teaching Tip

It might be helpful to review possessive adjectives for this exercise. Point to a male and female S in the class. Ask: *What's his name? What's her name?* Write *his* and *her* on the board. Remind Ss to use the correct one when practicing the conversations in Exercise **4B**.

### Literacy Tip

For an alternative activity, refer literacy Ss to pages 84–85 in the *Literacy Workbook* at any time during the lesson.

- Direct Ss' attention to Exercise **4C** and read the instructions aloud.
- Focus Ss' attention on the example in Exercise **4C**. Point to the words written in the chart. Say: *This student's name is Eliza. Her sweater is red. Her socks are yellow. Her blouse is white.* Hold up the Student's Book and point to each item in the chart.
- Model the task. Write *Name* and the colors horizontally across the board in the same order as in the Student's Book. Ask a volunteer to come to the front of the class. Write the S's name on the board under *Name*. Point to the first color on the board. Say: *Look at Stefan's clothes. What is red? Anything? No.* Leave the chart cell blank. Point to the next color on the board. Ask: *What is yellow? His T-shirt. Yes!* Write *T-shirt* under *yellow* on the board. Continue with the rest of the colors: *Is Stefan wearing red?* If the answer is yes, ask: *What clothing item is red?* Elicit an appropriate response. Hold up the Student's Book again. Point to the corresponding cell in the chart. Say: *Write the name of the clothing item in this square.*
- Ss complete the chart in pairs, writing about the clothing of four classmates. Walk around and help as needed. Ss may ask for help with other clothing or color vocabulary.
- Check answers. Ask: *Who is wearing something red?* Write that person's name on board. Tell Ss: *Look at _____. What is red?* Write the name of the item. Repeat for other colors.

## EVALUATION

- Direct Ss' attention to the first part of the lesson focus on the board. Ask: *Where is Rose going shopping?* Elicit: *The Clothes Place.* Ask: *What is Rose going to buy?* Elicit: *Blue pants, a tie, a red dress, black shoes.*
- Direct Ss' attention to the baseball caps in the Picture dictionary. Say: *Please name the color and the item. For example, number one. A black baseball cap.* Continue by asking different Ss to say the colors and names of the items.
- Check off each part of the lesson focus as Ss demonstrate understanding of what they have learned in the lesson.

| *More Ventures, Unit 7, Lesson D* | |
|---|---|
| **Literacy Workbook**, 15–30 min. | |
| **Basic Workbook**, 15–30 min. | |
| **Picture Dictionary activities**, 30–45 min. | www.cambridge.org/ventures/resources/ |
| **Writing Worksheets**, 15–30 min. | |
| **Collaborative Worksheets**, 30–45 min. | |
| **Student Arcade**, time varies | www.cambridge.org/venturesarcade/ |

## 4 Picture dictionary Colors

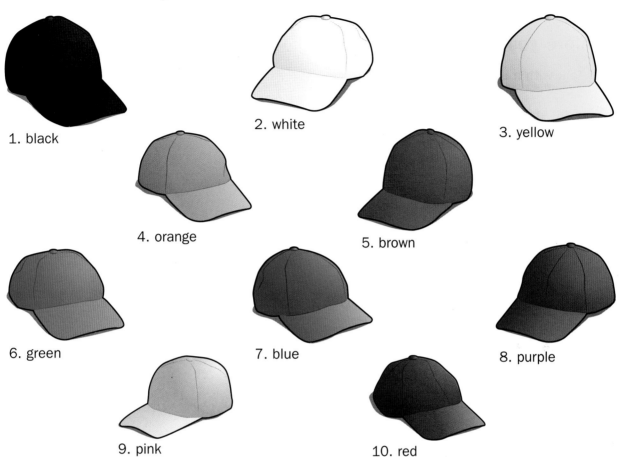

1. black

2. white

3. yellow

4. orange

5. brown

6. green

7. blue

8. purple

9. pink

10. red

A  **Listen and repeat.** Look at the Picture dictionary.

B  **Talk with a partner.** Look around your classroom. Ask and answer.

 A  What color is **her sweater**?

B  **Blue.**

 A  What color are **his shoes**?

B  **Brown.**

 CD2, Track 22

C  **Talk with a partner.** Choose four classmates. Complete the chart.

| Name | red | yellow | green | black | white | brown | blue |
|------|-----|--------|-------|-------|-------|-------|------|
| Eliza | sweater | socks | | | blouse | | |
| Answers will vary. | | | | | | | |
| | | | | | | | |
| | | | | | | | |
| | | | | | | | |

# Lesson E Writing

## 1 Before you write

**A** **Talk with a partner.** Complete the words.

Shopping list
1. _s_ _k_ i r t
2. _d_ _r_ e s s
3. _s_ _h_ o e s
4. _b_ _l_ o u s e
5. _s_ _w_ e a t e r
6. T- _s_ _h_ i r t

**B** **Talk with a partner.** Look at the picture. Complete the story.

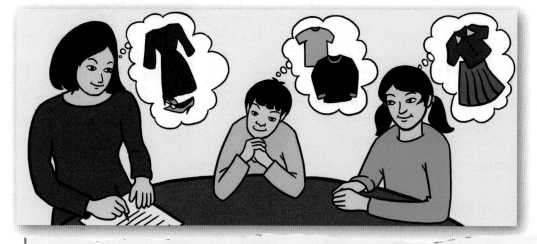

Sun Mi and her children are shopping today. They

need clothes for school. Sun Mi needs a ___dress___ and
1

___shoes___ . Her son Roger needs a ___T-shirt___ and a
2                                                                3

___sweater___ . Her daughter Emily needs a ___blouse___ and
4                                                                          5

a ___skirt___ .
6

- Prepare Ss for writing a shopping list
- Provide practice writing key vocabulary words

## WARM-UP AND REVIEW

- Before class. Write today's lesson focus on the board.
  *Lesson E:*
  *Write about shopping*
  *Write a shopping list*

- Begin class. Books closed. Point to *shopping list* on the board. Say *shopping list* aloud. Ask Ss to repeat after you. Ask: *What does this mean?* Elicit an appropriate response, such as: *A list of things to buy.*

- Ask: *Do you write shopping lists?* Elicit *yes / no* responses. Ask Ss who respond with *yes*: *When do you write shopping lists?* Elicit an appropriate response, such as: *For food shopping, clothes shopping.*

- Ask: *Are you going shopping after English class?* Elicit *yes / no* responses. If a S responds with *yes*, ask: *Do you have a shopping list?* Elicit a *yes / no* response.

## PRESENTATION

- Direct Ss' attention to Exercise 1A.

- Say: *This is an example of a shopping list. What kind of shopping list is it?* Elicit an appropriate response, such as: *A shopping list for clothes.* or *A back-to-school shopping list.*

- Read the instructions aloud.

- Point to the first item and say: *Number 1. What's the word?* (Skirt.) Ask: *What letters do we need?* (s and k) Point to where the letters are written in the blanks. Say: *Now you complete the rest of the words.*

## PRACTICE

- Ss work individually or in pairs to complete the words.

- Write the numbers *1–6* on the board. When Ss are finished, call on volunteers to write their completed words on the board. Review the alphabet by asking the volunteers who write answers on the board to say the letters aloud.

- Go over the answers with the class. Ask: *Are these words spelled correctly?* If not, ask volunteers to make corrections as needed.

- Direct Ss' attention to the picture in Exercise 1B. Ask: *What do you see?* Elicit as much vocabulary about the picture as possible and write the words on the board: *mother, daughter, son, shoes, dress, skirt, blouse, T-shirt, sweater.*

- To confirm that Ss know which is the mother, son, and daughter, review colors and clothing. Ask: *Who is wearing purple?* (The mother.) *Who is wearing green?* (The daughter.) *Who is wearing orange?* (The son.)

### Teaching Tip

Encourage Ss to use language learned in previous lessons. This exercise recycles and reinforces vocabulary learned earlier in the book.

- Read the instructions aloud. Model the exercise. Ask two Ss to read the first two sentences aloud. Ask: *What does Sun Mi need?* Point to Sun Mi's thought bubble in the art and the word *dress* written in the story. (A dress and shoes.) Say: *Now complete the story.* Point out that the words they need are in the list in Exercise 1A.

- Ss work individually or in pairs to fill in the blanks in the story using the information in the art and the words in Exercise 1A. Walk around and help as needed.

- Check answers as a class. Ask several Ss to read sentences from the story aloud. After each sentence ask: *Is that word correct?* Correct any errors if needed.

  **Option** Ask Ss to read the story to each other in pairs.

### Literacy Tip

For an alternative activity, refer literacy Ss to pages 86–87 in the *Literacy Workbook* at any time during the lesson.

### *Expansion activity* (whole class)

- Peer dictation. Before class. Prepare copies of the following lists for your class. Make enough copies so that each S in a pair has one of the lists:

| Student A | Student B |
|---|---|
| 1. a black dress | 1. a pink blouse |
| 2. brown shoes | 2. orange socks |
| 3. a green T-shirt | 3. red pants |
| 4. yellow socks | 4. a purple skirt |
| 5. a white sweater | 5. blue shoes |

- Explain to Ss that one S will dictate words to the other S. Then they will switch roles.

- Walk around and help as needed. Encourage Ss to check their writing after they finish by comparing their words to their partner's list.

# LESSON E Writing

## PRESENTATION

- Say: *Sun Mi was making a shopping list. Now you are going to help complete her shopping list.*
- Direct Ss' attention to Exercise 2A and read the instructions aloud.
- Model the task. Ask: *What clothing does Sun Mi need?* Elicit: *A dress.* Point to *dress* written on the shopping list. Ask: *What else does she need?* Elicit: *Shoes.* Say: *Write "shoes" on the shopping list.*

## PRACTICE

- Ss complete the exercise individually using the information from Exercise 1B. Walk around and help as needed.
- Copy the unfinished list from Exercise 2A on the board. Ask several Ss to complete the list.
- Ask different Ss to read the words on the board. Ask: *Are these items correct?* Ask Ss to correct the list if needed.
- Direct Ss' attention to Exercise 2B. Say: *Now you are going to make your own shopping list.* Read the instructions aloud.
- Model the task. Hold up the Student's Book. Say: *Think about what you need. Then circle the clothing. For example, I need pants, socks, and a raincoat. I'm going to circle those words in this exercise.* Hold up the book and pretend to circle the items. Say: *My son needs a sweater.* Pretend to circle *sweater.*
- Ss complete the exercise individually. Walk around and help as needed.

### Literacy Tip

While Ss are working on Exercise 2B, help literacy Ss by reading the words in this exercise to them. Tell them to circle the items they need.

- Direct Ss' attention to Exercise 2C. Read the instructions aloud. Say: *Write the items you circled on your list.*
- Model the task. Say: *My son needs a sweater. His name is John.* Write on the board: *John: a sweater.*
- Ss write their shopping lists individually, using the list in Exercise 2A as a guide. Walk around and help as needed.
- Focus Ss' attention on Exercise 3. Read the instructions aloud.
- Ss complete the task in pairs. Walk around and help as needed.

### Teaching Tip

This exercise asks Ss to work together to edit their writing. Encourage Ss to correct each other's writing if necessary. Say: *Help your partner with any spelling mistakes. Then your partner will help you.*

- Ask several Ss to read their lists aloud for the whole class.

   **Option** Ask several Ss to write their lists from Exercise 2C on the board. Then ask them to read their lists to the rest of the class.

### *Expansion activity* (student pairs)

- Focus Ss' attention on the picture on page 84. Say: *Look at the items for sale in this picture. Imagine that you are shopping at this store. Make a shopping list. What will you buy?*
- Encourage Ss to use the shopping list in Exercise 2C on page 93 as a guide. They can write the names of people on the list and the items they want to buy for them in the column under *Clothing.*
- Ask several Ss to write their shopping lists on the board.
- Expand this activity more by recycling the grammar points *How much is?* and *How much are?* from Lesson C. Ask Ss to write the prices of the items on their lists. When Ss are finished, ask them *How much is the dress?* and *How much are the shoes?*

## EVALUATION

- Direct Ss' attention to the lesson focus on the board.
- Write *Shopping List* on the board. Ask several Ss to come to the board and write clothing items on the list. Ask them to include the color of the clothing.
- Check off each part of the lesson focus as Ss demonstrate understanding of what they have learned in the lesson.

### More Ventures, Unit 7, Lesson E

| | |
| --- | --- |
| **Literacy Workbook**, 15–30 min. | |
| **Basic Workbook**, 15–30 min. | |
| **Writing Worksheets,** 15–30 min. | www.cambridge.org/ventures/ resources/ |
| **Collaborative Worksheets,** 30–45 min. | |

## 2 Write

**A** Complete the shopping list for Sun Mi's family.

| Name | Clothing |
|------|----------|
| Sun Mi: | a dress, *shoes* |
| Emily: | *a blouse, a skirt* |
| Roger: | *T-shirt, a sweater* |

**B** Circle the clothes you and your family need.

| | | | |
|---|---|---|---|
| a blouse | socks | a tie | a dress |
| a sweater | a jacket | a skirt | a raincoat |
| a T-shirt | a shirt | shoes | pants |

**C** Write a shopping list for your family.

| Name | Clothing |
|------|----------|
| *Answers will vary.* | |

## 3 After you write

**Talk with a partner.** Share your writing.

# Lesson F Another view

## 1 Life-skills reading

THE
*Clothes*
PLACE

271 Center Street
Tampa, Florida 33601
(813) 555-7200

| | |
|---|---|
| Shoes | $29.99 |
| T-shirt | $7.99 |
| Subtotal: | $37.98 |
| 7% Tax: | $2.66 |
| Total: | $40.64 |

**Thank you for shopping at
The Clothes Place.
Have a nice day!**

**A  Read the sentences.** Look at the receipt. Fill in the answer.

1. What is The Clothes Place?

   ● clothing store

   (B) supermarket

   (C) laundromat

2. What's the phone number?

   (A) 555-0072

   ● 555-7200

   (C) 813

3. How much are the shoes?

   ● $29.99

   (B) $19.99

   (C) $40.64

4. How much is the tax?

   (A) $40.64

   (B) $37.98

   ● $2.66

**B  Solve the problem.** Which solution is best? Circle your opinion.

Jimmy wants a black T-shirt. A black T-shirt is $14.99. A blue T-shirt is $7.99.
What should his mother buy?

1. a black T-shirt

2. a blue T-shirt

3. Other: _Answers will vary._

## Teaching objectives
- Introduce reading a store receipt
- Provide practice that develops test-taking skills
- Review vocabulary from the unit

## WARM-UP AND REVIEW

- Before class. Write today's lesson focus on the board.
  *Lesson F:*
  *Read and answer questions about a store receipt*
  *Practice vocabulary on receipts*
  *Complete the Self-assessment*
- Begin class. Books closed. Say: *We are going to make a new shopping list on the board.* Ask Ss to brainstorm clothing items. List them on the board.
- Ask: *How much are these items?* Point to each item in turn and ask Ss to give you a price for it. Write the price to the right of each item in a column. Draw a line under the list of prices.
- Ask: *How much are these items together?* Ask a S to add the prices together on paper or with a calculator. When the S is finished, write the total under all the prices.
- Say: *This is the total amount of money that we will spend on these clothes.* Write the word *Total* beside the total price on the board. Say the word aloud. Ask Ss to repeat it after you.

## PRESENTATION

- Books open. Write on the board: *receipt.* Point to the word. Say it aloud and ask Ss to repeat. Ask: *What is this?* If Ss don't know, show them an example of a receipt from a store. Ask Ss if they have any examples of receipts that they can show to the class.
- Direct Ss' attention to the picture of the receipt in Exercise 1A.
- Hold up the Student's Book. Point to the receipt. Ask: *What store is this receipt from?* (The Clothes Place.) Ask: *Where is the store?* (Tampa, Florida.) Ask: *What clothes are on the receipt?* (Shoes and a T-shirt.) Ask: *What other words do you see on the receipt?* Elicit any other words Ss read on the receipt.
- Write the words *subtotal* and *tax* on the board. Say the words aloud. Ask Ss to repeat them after you. Point to *subtotal.* Ask: *What does this word mean?* If Ss don't know or can't explain the definition in English, say: *It's the total amount before tax.* Point to the word *tax.* Ask: *What does this word mean?* If Ss don't know or can't explain the definition in English, say: *It's extra money you pay when you buy something. It helps pay for government services.*

## PRACTICE

- Read the instructions for Exercise 1A aloud. This task helps prepare Ss for standardized-type tests they may have to take.
- Write the first item on the board along with the two answer choices labeled *A, B,* and *C*.
- Read the item and the answer choices aloud and then point to the receipt. Ask: *Is the Clothes Place a clothing store, a supermarket, or a laundromat?* Show Ss where to look for the information. Elicit: *Clothing store.*
- Point to the three answer choices on the board. Ask Ss: *A, B,* or *C?* (A) Fill in the letter *a* and tell Ss: *Fill in the answer.* Make sure Ss understand the task.
- Have Ss individually scan for and fill in the answers.

## COMPREHENSION CHECK

- Go over the answers to Exercise 1A with the class. Make sure that Ss followed the directions and filled in their answers. Ask Ss to point to the information in the receipt.

## APPLICATION

- Read the instructions for Exercise 1B aloud.
- Tell Ss they will discuss what Jimmy's mother should buy.
- Ss complete the exercise in pairs.
- Ask several pairs to ask and answer the question for the rest of the class.

*Expansion activity* (individual work, student pairs)

- Ask Ss to make a receipt for clothing items that they "bought" in a store. It can be a real store or an imaginary store. The receipt should include the name and address of the store, the names and prices of items bought, the subtotal, the tax, and the total for the purchase.
- When Ss are finished, ask them to work with a partner. Say: *Show your partner your receipt. Then look at your partner's receipt. Ask questions. For example: How much is the _____? How much are the _____?*
- Walk around and help as needed.

Lesson F   T-94

# LESSON F Another view

## PRACTICE

- Books closed. Write *crossword puzzle* on the board. Point to the words. Say them aloud. Ask Ss to repeat the words after you.
- Books open. Focus Ss' attention on Exercise 2. Write the words *across* and *down* on the board. Draw arrows to indicate the directions as shown in the Student's Book. Hold up the Student's Book. Point to the clues on the left side of the page. Say: *These words go across.* Move your finger across the page to show the direction. Point to the clues on the right side of the page. Say: *These words go down.* Move your finger down the page to show the direction.
- Ask Ss: *Do you do crossword puzzles?* Elicit a *yes* or *no* response.
- Read the instructions aloud. Model the task. Hold up the Student's Book. Point to number 1 (*pants*) in the crossword puzzle. Say: *Write the letters of the word in the spaces.*
- Ss complete the exercise individually. Walk around and help as needed.
- Write the numbers *1–10* on the board. Ask volunteers to write their answers on the board.
- Ask different Ss to read the answers aloud. Ask: *Are these answers correct?* Ask different Ss to correct the answers if needed.

### Literacy Tip

For an alternative activity, refer literacy Ss to pages 88–89 in the *Literacy Workbook* at any time during the lesson.

### *Expansion activity* (small groups)

- Scrambled questions and answers. Before class, make enough copies of the following questions for small groups of four Ss in your class:
  1. *How much is the blue shirt?*
  2. *How much are the yellow shoes?*
  3. *How much is the brown sweater?*
  4. *How much are the green socks?*
  5. *How much is the purple blouse?*

- Cut up each question so that the words are separate. Mix up the words in each question. Put them in envelopes with the corresponding number on the envelope.
- Give each small group of Ss a set of five envelopes. Ask them to unscramble the questions. When they are finished, they should write the questions in their notebooks.
- The first group to finish unscrambling the questions wins the game. (Note that each group may make slightly different questions.)
- Write the numbers *1–5* on the board. Ask Ss to write the questions on the board.
- For further practice, ask Ss to ask a partner the questions on the board. Encourage Ss to invent prices for each item in the questions.

## EVALUATION

- Do a quick review of the unit. Have Ss turn to Lesson A. Ask the class to talk about what they remember about this lesson. Prompt Ss, if necessary, with questions, such as: *What words are on this page? What do you see in the picture?* Continue in this manner to review each lesson quickly.

### *Expansion activity*

- Before class. Print, for each student, one copy of the Self-assessment for this unit.
- Have Ss complete the Self-assessment either in class or outside of class.
- Provide feedback to Ss such as through a whole-class discussion, partners comparing their worksheets, or T reviewing each S's worksheet.
- If Ss are ready, administer the unit test on page T-176 of this Teacher's Edition. The audio script for the test is available on page T-192.

| *More Ventures, Unit 7, Lesson F* | |
|---|---|
| **Literacy Workbook**, 15–30 min. | |
| **Basic Workbook**, 15–30 min. | |
| **Writing Worksheets,** 15–30 min. | |
| **Collaborative Worksheets,** 30–45 min. | www.cambridge.org/ventures/ resources/ |
| **Self-assessment**, 10 min. | |
| **CASAS Test Prep Worksheet**, 5–10 min. | |

## 2 Fun with vocabulary

**Write the words in the puzzle.** Some words go across (→).
Some words go down (↓).

**Across →**

1.

9.

5.

10.

8.

**Down ↓**

2.

5.

3.

6.

4.

7.

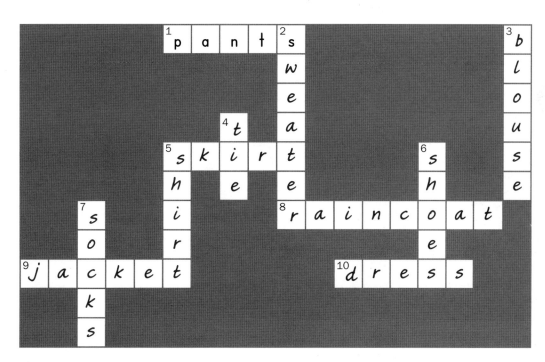

# UNIT 8 WORK

## Lesson A Listening

### 1 Before you listen

**A** Look at the picture. What do you see?

**B** Listen and point: ■ cashier ■ custodian ■ mechanic ■ receptionist ■ salesperson ■ server

◀)) CD2, Track 23

# UNIT 8

- Introduce Ss to the topic
- Find out what Ss know about the topic
- Preview the unit by talking about the picture
- Provide practice of key vocabulary
- Provide practice that develops listening skills

## WARM-UP AND REVIEW

- Before class. Write today's lesson focus on the board.
  *Lesson A:*
  *Work vocabulary*
  *Names of jobs*
- Begin class. Write the word *jobs* on the board. Point to the word. Say it aloud and ask Ss to repeat after you. Say: *Today's class is about jobs. What are some examples of jobs?* As Ss respond, write their examples on the board.
- Ask: *Who has a job?* Ask volunteers who say *yes*: *What's your job?* Write their responses on the board.

### Teaching Tip

If Ss ask, you can explain the difference between *jobs* and *occupations*. Tell Ss that a job is a type of work, and an occupation is a profession or a job you do for a long time.

### Literacy Tip

If you have literacy Ss in your class, it might be helpful to spend time at the beginning of any activity with art or photos talking about the pictures before focusing Ss' attention on the printed words in the exercise. Have Ss work in pairs. Tell them to ask each other: *What do you see?* Encourage Ss to describe the pictures to each other. Consider pairing literacy Ss with Ss who can help them read the text in the exercise. This will help preview the exercise for literacy Ss and make them more confident as the exercise continues.

## PRESENTATION

- Books open. Set the scene. Direct Ss' attention to the picture on page 96. Ask: *Where is this?* (a big store with a restaurant, an office, a car garage, etc.)
- Hold up the Student's Book. Show Ss the picture. Ask: *What do you see?* Elicit and write on the board any vocabulary that Ss know, such as: *people, a salesperson, a customer, a computer, a server, a mechanic.*

### Teaching Tip

Do not expect Ss to know all the new vocabulary words. These questions are intended to find out what Ss already know about work vocabulary.

## PRACTICE

- Direct Ss' attention to the key vocabulary in Exercise **1B**. Read each word aloud while pointing to the corresponding person in the picture. Ask Ss to repeat and point.
- ▶ *CD2, Track 23* Play or read the audio (see audio script, page T-149). Tell Ss: *Listen and point to the picture.* As Ss hear the key vocabulary, check to see that they are pointing to the correct part of the picture. Repeat the audio as needed.

### Expansion activity *(student pairs)*

- If your Ss would benefit from answering more questions about the picture using a different form for the question and answer, write the following on the board: *What's his job? What's her job? He's a _____. She's a _____.*
- Ss in pairs. Say: *Look at the questions on the board. Point to different people in the picture. Ask your partner the questions.* Point to the answers on the board. Say: *Answer the questions like this.*
- Model the activity. Point to Sara. Ask: *What's her job?* Elicit: *She's a salesperson.*
- Ss complete the activity in pairs. Walk around and help as needed.
- Ask several pairs to ask and answer the questions for the rest of the class.

## COMPREHENSION CHECK

- Ask Ss *Yes / No* questions about the picture. Ask about new vocabulary and recycle words learned in previous units. Say: *Listen to the questions. Answer "Yes" or "No."*
  Point to the picture. Ask: *Is this a school?* (No, it isn't.)
  Point to the store sign. Ask: *Is this a store?* (Yes, it is.)
  Point to the cashier. Ask: *Is she a cashier?* (Yes, she is.)
  Point to the woman sitting at the desk. Ask: *Is she a mechanic?* (No, she isn't.)
  Point to the mechanic. Ask: *Is he a server?* (No, he isn't.)
  Point to Sara. Ask: *Is she a salesperson?* (Yes, she is.)
  Point to the server. Ask: *Is he a server?* (Yes, he is.)

### Literacy Tip

For an alternative activity, refer literacy Ss to pages 90–91 in the *Literacy Workbook* at any time during the lesson.

# LESSON A Listening

## PRESENTATION

- Direct Ss' attention to the jobs in Exercise 2A. Read them aloud. Ask Ss to repeat them after you.
- Ask Ss questions about the jobs. Focus their attention on the picture on page 96. Ask Ss to point when you ask: *Where is the cashier?* Continue with all the words in Exercise 2A.
- Focus Ss' attention on Exercise 2A again. Read the instructions aloud.

## PRACTICE

- ▶ **CD2, Track 24** Play or read the audio (see audio script, page T-149). Ss listen and repeat the vocabulary. Repeat the audio as needed.
- Listen carefully to Ss' pronunciation and make corrections as needed.

### *Learner persistence* (individual work)

- ▶ **CD2, Track 24** Ss can listen to the audio for Exercise 2A at home for reinforcement and review. They can also listen to the audio for self-directed learning when class attendance is not possible.
- Direct Ss' attention to Exercise 2B and read the instructions aloud.
- ▶ **CD2, Track 25** Model the task. Hold up the Student's Book and say: *Number one.* Play or read the audio for number 1 (see audio script, page T-149). Point to the two answer choices in number 1 and ask Ss: *What did you hear – a or b?* Elicit: *b.* Point to the letter *b* next to the second picture and tell Ss: *Circle the letter "b."*
- ▶ **CD2, Track 25** Play or read the complete audio. Ss listen and circle the correct answers. Repeat the audio as needed.
- ▶ **CD2, Track 25** Read aloud the second part of the instructions for Exercise 2B. Play or read the audio again so that Ss can listen and check their answers.

### *Learner persistence* (individual work)

- ▶ **CD2, Track 25** Ss can listen to the audio for Exercise 2B at home for reinforcement and review. They can also listen to the audio for self-directed learning when class attendance is not possible.

## COMPREHENSION CHECK

- Write the numbers *1–4* on the board. Ask volunteers to come to the board and write the correct answers to Exercise 2B next to each number.
- ▶ **CD2, Track 25** Play or read the audio again. Pause the audio after each conversation. Point to the answers written on the board and ask: *Is this correct?* Ask another S to make any necessary corrections.

## APPLICATION

- Direct Ss' attention to Exercise 3 and read the instructions aloud.
- Model the task. Hold up the Student's Book and point to the answer choices in Exercise 2B. Say to one S: *Point to a picture.* Say to that S's partner: *Say the word.*
- Ss complete the exercise in pairs. Walk around and help as needed.

### *Expansion activity* (whole group)

- Before class. Make copies of a two-row chart (one row for Ss' names and one row for their jobs) or draw one on the board.
- Hold up the chart or point to the one on the board. Say: *You are going to ask two questions. What are the questions?* Point to *Name.* Elicit: *What's your name?* Point to *Job.* Elicit: *What's your job?* Write the questions on the board.
- Say: *Stand up. Walk around and ask five students for their names. Then ask about their jobs. Write their names and jobs in the chart.* You may have to assist Ss with additional job vocabulary.

### Teaching Tip

Encourage non-working Ss to say, as applicable: *I'm a student. I'm a homemaker. I'm a stay-at-home parent.* Define these words for Ss if necessary.

- When everyone is finished, ask several Ss to make sentences with the information in their charts, such as: *Rosa is a student. Arif is a mechanic.*

## EVALUATION

- Direct Ss' attention to the lesson focus on the board. Hold up the Student's Book and point to jobs in the picture on page 96. Ask Ss to tell you the jobs as you point to them (*cashier, custodian, mechanic, receptionist, salesperson, server*). Walk around and check that Ss are pointing to the correct jobs.
- Check off the lesson focus as Ss demonstrate an understanding of what they have learned in the lesson.

| *More Ventures, Unit 8, Lesson A* | |
|---|---|
| **Literacy Workbook**, 15–30 min. | |
| **Basic Workbook**, 15–30 min. | |
| **Writing Worksheets**, 15–30 min. **Collaborative Worksheets**, 30–45 min. | www.cambridge.org/ventures/ resources/ |
| **Student Arcade**, time varies | www.cambridge.org/venturesarcade/ |

**UNIT GOALS**
**Identify** jobs   **Identify** job duties
**Interpret** help wanted ads

## 2 Listen

**A** **Listen and repeat.**

1. cashier
2. custodian
3. mechanic
4. receptionist
5. salesperson
6. server

CD2, Track 24

CD2, Track 25

**B** **Listen and circle.**

1. a.    b.

2. a.    b.

3. a.    b.

4. a.    b.

**Listen again.** Check your answers.

## 3 After you listen

**Talk with a partner.** Point to a picture.
Your partner says the word.

# Lesson B Job duties

## 1 Vocabulary focus

**Listen and repeat.**

CD2, Track 26

1. She answers the phone.

2. She counts money.

3. He fixes cars.

4. He cleans buildings.

5. She sells clothes.

6. He serves food.

## 2 Practice

**A Read and match.**

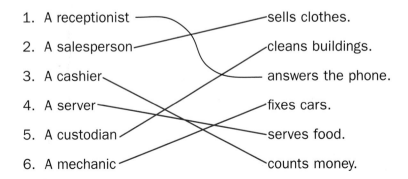

1. A receptionist — sells clothes.
2. A salesperson — cleans buildings.
3. A cashier — answers the phone.
4. A server — fixes cars.
5. A custodian — serves food.
6. A mechanic — counts money.

- Introduce and provide practice of work-related vocabulary
- Introduce and provide practice writing sentences in the simple present

## WARM-UP AND REVIEW

- Before class. Write today's lesson focus on the board.
  *Lesson B:*
  *Work vocabulary*
  *Job duties*

- Begin class. Books open. Direct Ss' attention to the picture on page 96. Review key vocabulary from the unit by asking: *What are the different jobs in this picture?* Elicit: *salesperson, cashier, receptionist, server, custodian, mechanic.* Ask Ss to point to the people with these jobs.

- Walk around and check to see that Ss are pointing to the correct people in the picture.

## PRESENTATION

- Set the scene. Point to *Job duties* on the board. Say the words aloud. Ask Ss to repeat the words after you. Say: *Job duties tell what people in different jobs do at work.*

- Focus Ss' attention on the sentences below the pictures in Exercise 1. Say: *These are some examples of job duties. They describe the jobs in the pictures.*

- Read aloud the instructions for Exercise 1.

- ▶ *CD2, Track 26* Play or read the audio (see audio script, page T-149). Listen and repeat the sentences along with Ss. Repeat the audio as needed.

- Listen carefully to Ss' pronunciation and correct as needed.

### Literacy Tip

It might be helpful to hold up the Student's Book and point to each picture as Ss listen to the audio. This will help literacy Ss if they are unable to read the text as they listen to the audio.

## Expansion activity *(student pairs)*

- Put Ss in pairs. Try to pair more advanced Ss with less advanced Ss or advanced Ss with literacy Ss. Tell Ss to practice reading the job duties. They will read one of the sentences, and their partner will point to the picture that matches the description. After that, encourage Ss to switch roles.

### Multilevel Tip

To make this activity more challenging for advanced Ss, ask them to put a piece of paper over the job descriptions. Say: *Describe the pictures. What do these people do every day at work?* Literacy Ss who have good oral skills may like the challenge of this activity as well.

## PRACTICE

- Direct Ss' attention to Exercise 2A. As you read aloud the instructions, hold up the Student's Book and indicate that Ss should match the words for jobs with the corresponding duties.

- Model the task. Hold up the Student's Book. Point to the word *receptionist* in the example. Ask: *What does a receptionist do?* (Answers the phone.) Say: *Match the job with the job duty.*

- Ss complete the exercise individually. Help as needed.

### Literacy Tip

For an alternative activity, refer literacy Ss to pages 92–93 in the *Literacy Workbook* at any time during the lesson.

## COMPREHENSION CHECK

- Write the numbers *1–6* on the board. Ask volunteers to come to the board and write the answers to Exercise 2A.

- Ask different Ss to read the answers written on the board. After each answer is read, ask: *Is this correct?* Ask another S to make any necessary corrections on the board.

# LESSON B  Job duties

## PRESENTATION

- Direct Ss' attention to the word bank in Exercise 2B. Say: *Repeat these words after me.* Say each phrase aloud. Listen to Ss' pronunciation as they repeat the phrases.

- Direct Ss' attention to the pictures below the word bank. Read aloud the names and ask Ss to repeat after you.

- Hold up the Student's Book. Point to different people and ask: *What is his or her job?* Elicit: *cashier, server, receptionist, salesperson, custodian, mechanic.*

- Read the instructions for Exercise 2B aloud.

## PRACTICE

- ▶ **CD2, Track 27** Model the task. Say: *Listen and repeat.* Play or read the audio for number 1 (see audio script, page T-149) and point to Sandra in the first picture as you repeat. Say: *Then write.* Point to the phrase *counts money* in the Duty column beside Sandra in the chart. Make sure Ss understand the task.

- ▶ **CD2, Track 27** Play or read the complete audio. Ss listen and repeat. Encourage Ss to point to the people in the pictures as they repeat.

- Ss complete the charts individually using words from the word bank. Repeat the audio as needed.

- Check answers with the class. Write the numbers *1–6* on the board and ask volunteers to write their answers on the board. Point to each answer and ask the class: *Yes? Is this correct?* Make any necessary corrections.

- Read aloud the second part of the instructions for Exercise 2B. Point to and model the example conversation.

- Call on a pair of volunteers to read the example conversation aloud for the class. Then ask the same Ss to make up a new conversation about another person in the pictures on page 99. Indicate that Ss should ask and answer questions about all the people in the pictures.

- Ss complete the exercise in pairs. Walk around and help as needed.

### Multilevel Tip

Some Ss may wish to expand on the job duties of the jobs in this lesson. If you feel it is appropriate for your class, encourage Ss to say more job duties for these jobs if they already know them.

## APPLICATION

- Direct Ss' attention to Exercise 3 and read the instructions aloud.

- Model the task. Ask two Ss to read the conversation aloud.

### Useful Language

Read the tip box aloud. Ask Ss to repeat the two questions after you. Tell Ss that the two questions have the same meaning.

- Ss walk around and practice the conversation with as many classmates as possible in the time allotted. Encourage them to use both of the questions in the Useful language box.

- Ask several pairs to ask and answer the questions for the rest of the class.

### *Expansion activity* (whole group)

- Password. Prepare a list of jobs that Ss have learned in this unit. Write them in list form on a piece of paper.

- Divide the class into two teams. Explain to Ss that the game is called Password. One person from each team will come to the front of the class. You will show them a job written on a piece of paper. The Ss will give one- or two-word clues to their team. Their team will guess the job.

- Model the game. Write *student* on the board. Ask: *What words describe this job?* Elicit: *school, study, English, books,* etc.

- Start the game. Encourage Ss to use only one or two words as clues. If Ss get stuck, help them think of words.

- Teams take turns giving clues. Whenever someone on the team guesses the job, the team gets a point. The team with the most points wins.

## EVALUATION

- Direct Ss' attention to the lesson focus on the board. Check Ss' understanding of the key vocabulary by asking them to explain the job duties for the jobs in the pictures in Exercise 2B on page 99.

- Check off the lesson focus as Ss demonstrate an understanding of what they have learned in the lesson.

| More Ventures, Unit 8, Lesson B | |
| --- | --- |
| **Literacy Workbook,** 15–30 min. | |
| **Basic Workbook,** 15–30 min. | |
| **Writing Worksheets,** 15–30 min. **Collaborative Worksheets,** 30–45 min. | www.cambridge.org/ventures/ resources/ |
| **Student Arcade,** time varies | www.cambridge.org/venturesarcade/ |

**B** **Listen and repeat.** Then write.

| answers the phone | cleans buildings | counts money |
|---|---|---|
| fixes cars | sells clothes | serves food |

CD2, Track 27

Stephanie

Sandra

DOCTOR'S OFFICE

Alba

Tim

Oscar

Ahmad

| Name | Duty | Name | Duty |
|---|---|---|---|
| 1. Sandra | She ___counts money___. | 4. Oscar | He ___sells clothes___. |
| 2. Stephanie | She ___serves food___. | 5. Tim | He ___cleans buildings___. |
| 3. Alba | She ___answers the phone___. | 6. Ahmad | He ___fixes cars___. |

**Talk with a partner.** Ask and answer.

A What does **Sandra** do?

B **She counts money.**

## 3 Communicate

**Talk with your classmates.** Ask and answer.

A What do you do?

B I'm a **cashier. I count money.**

**USEFUL LANGUAGE**
*What do you do?* =
*What's your job?*

Use vocabulary for jobs and job duties  UNIT 8  **99**

## 1 Grammar focus: *does* and *doesn't*

| QUESTIONS | | | ANSWERS | | | | | |
|---|---|---|---|---|---|---|---|---|
| Does | he / she | sell clothes? | Yes, | he / she | does. | No, | he / she | doesn't. |

Watch

doesn't = does not

## 2 Practice

**A** **Read and circle.** Then write.

1.  **A** Does he serve food?
    **B** No, he ___doesn't___.
    does (doesn't)

2.  **A** Does he clean buildings?
    **B** No, he ___doesn't___.
    does (doesn't)

3.  **A** Does she answer the phone?
    **B** Yes, she ___does___.
    (does) doesn't

4.  **A** Does he sell clothes?
    **B** Yes, he ___does___.
    (does) doesn't

5.  **A** Does she fix cars?
    **B** No, she ___doesn't___.
    does (doesn't)

**Listen and repeat.** Then practice with a partner.

CD2, Track 28

## WARM-UP AND REVIEW

- Before class. Write today's lesson focus on the board.
  *Lesson C:*
  *does*
  *doesn't*

- Begin class. Books closed. Write a question mark on the board. Tell Ss you are going to practice making questions about jobs. Ask volunteers to say the names of some jobs they have learned in this unit. Elicit any jobs Ss remember from the unit. Write them on the board (*receptionist, mechanic, server,* etc.).

- Write on the board: *What does a _____ do?* Point to one of the jobs on the board. Say: *Make a question.* Point to the question mark on the board. Elicit: *What does a receptionist do?* Continue until Ss make questions about each of the jobs on the board.

- Point to the word *does* on the board. Say it aloud. Ask Ss to repeat it after you.

## PRESENTATION

- Use the animated grammar presentation in one or more of the following ways:
  - Preview it before class
  - Show it in class
  - Encourage Ss to watch it outside of class.

- Books open. Say: *Here are some Yes / No questions with "does."* Direct Ss' attention to the grammar chart in Exercise 1. Read the questions and the corresponding answers aloud. Ask Ss to repeat after you.

- Say: *When the answer is negative, we say "doesn't."* Hold up the Student's Book. Point to the word *doesn't.* Say it aloud. Ask Ss to repeat it after you.

- Point to the small box beside the grammar chart. Hold up one finger and tell Ss: *One word: doesn't.* Hold up two fingers and say: *Two words: does not. They are the same.*

## PRACTICE

- Direct Ss' attention to the pictures in Exercise 2A. Hold up the Student's Book. Point to the first picture. Ask: *What's his job?* (He's a salesperson.) Ask: *What does he do?* (He sells TVs.) Ask: *Does he serve food?* (No, he doesn't.) Review the jobs in the other pictures.

- Read aloud the instructions for Exercise 2A. Model the task. Read aloud the example conversation in number 1. When you read Speaker B's line, show Ss the two answer choices under the blank and ask: *does or doesn't?* Elicit *doesn't.*

- Point to where *doesn't* has been circled and written for number 1. Say: *Circle the correct answer. Then write it in the blank.*

- Ss complete the exercise individually. Walk around and help as needed.

## COMPREHENSION CHECK

- Read aloud the second part of the instructions in Exercise 2A.

- ▶ *CD2, Track 28* Play or read the audio (see audio script, page T-150). Ss listen and repeat as they check their answers.

- Write the numbers 2–5 on the board. Ask volunteers to come to the board and write the answers they circled. Make any necessary corrections on the board.

- Ss in pairs. Ask Ss to choose Role A or B and practice the questions and answers in Exercise 2A. Then have Ss switch roles and practice again. Walk around and help as needed.

- Ask several pairs to read the conversations to the rest of the class.

### *Expansion activity* (student pairs)

- Direct Ss' attention to page 98 in the Student's Book. Say: *Look at the pictures. Ask Yes / No questions about them. Use the questions and answers in Exercise 2A on page 100 as a guide.*

> **Teaching Tip**
>
> It might be helpful to remind Ss of the question form in the simple present tense. Point to the questions in the grammar chart on page 100. Remind Ss that the base form of the verb doesn't change in a question. Tell Ss that they can ask questions with *yes* or *no* answers as they look at the pictures on page 98.

- Model the activity. Hold up the Student's Book. Point to picture 1. Ask: *Does she answer the phone?* (Yes, she does.) Ask: *Does she count money?* (No, she doesn't.)

- Ss complete the activity in pairs. Walk around and help as needed.

- Ask several pairs to ask and answer questions about the pictures for the rest of the class.

- If Ss need more practice, they can continue this expansion activity by asking *Yes / No* questions about the pictures on page 96, 97, and 99 in the Student's Book.

# LESSON C  Does he sell clothes?

## PRESENTATION

- Books open. Direct Ss' attention to the picture in Exercise 2B. Ask: *What do you see?* Elicit as many vocabulary words as possible, such as: *man, job, pants, shirt, tie, coffee.*

### Teaching Tip

Do not expect Ss to answer in complete sentences. The purpose of this question is to recycle any vocabulary Ss already know and to find out any new words Ss may know about the topic.

## PRACTICE

- Read aloud the first part of instructions for Exercise 2B.
- ▶ **CD2, Track 29** Model the task. Say: *Listen and repeat.* Play or read the audio for number 1 (see audio script, page T-150) and point to the man in the picture as you repeat. Say: *Then write.* Point to where the words have been written in the blanks in number 1. Make sure Ss understand the task.
- ▶ **CD2, Track 29** Play or read the complete audio. Ss listen and repeat. Encourage Ss to focus on the man in the picture as they repeat.
- Ss work individually as they fill in the blanks in the exercise. Repeat the audio as needed.

### Literacy Tip

For an alternative activity, refer literacy Ss to pages 94–95 in the *Literacy Workbook* at any time during the lesson.

- Write the numbers *1–6* on the board. Ask volunteers to come to the board and write the words missing from the blanks for each number on the board. Ask: *Are these words correct?* Ask other Ss to make corrections if needed.
- Read aloud the second part of the instructions for Exercise 2B.
- Model the activity. Ask: *What's his job?* Tell Ss to guess the man's job. Tell them to choose one of the jobs in the word bank.
- Ss complete the exercise in pairs. Walk around and help as needed.
- Ask for a show of hands to see how many Ss agree about the man's job.

## APPLICATION

- Direct Ss' attention to Exercise 3 and read the instructions aloud.
- Focus Ss' attention on the picture in Exercise 3. Say: *They are playing a game.*
- Model the task. Ask a S to read part A of the example conversation with you. Act out fixing a car engine as you read the conversation. Make sure Ss understand the task.
- In small groups, Ss take turns acting out and guessing different jobs. Walk around and help as needed.

### *Expansion activity* (student pairs)

- Before class. Find pictures of different jobs in magazines or online. Bring the pictures to class. You should have one for each pair of Ss. Give each pair a picture. Say: *Ask questions about the jobs in the pictures. Use "Yes, he / she does." or "No, he / she doesn't." in your answers.*
- Ss complete the activity in pairs. Walk around and help as needed.
- Ask several pairs to hold up their pictures and ask and answer questions for the class.

## EVALUATION

- Direct Ss' attention to the lesson focus on the board. Ask Ss to look at the picture on page 96. Ask them to ask and answer questions about the jobs in the picture using *does* and *doesn't.*
- Check off the lesson focus as Ss demonstrate an understanding of what they have learned in the lesson.

| More Ventures, Unit 8, Lesson C | |
|---|---|
| Literacy Workbook, 15–30 min. | |
| Basic Workbook, 15–30 min. | |
| Writing Worksheets, 15–30 min. | www.cambridge.org/ventures/ resources/ |
| Collaborative Worksheets, 30–45 min. | |
| Student Arcade, time varies | www.cambridge.org/venturesarcade/ |

**B** **Listen and repeat.** Then write.

CD2, Track 29

1. **A** _____ Does _____ he _____ sell _____ clothes?
   **B** _____ No _____, he _____ doesn't _____.

2. **A** _____ Does _____ he _____ fix _____ cars?
   **B** _____ No _____, he _____ doesn't _____.

3. **A** _____ Does _____ he _____ clean _____ buildings?
   **B** _____ No _____, he _____ doesn't _____.

4. **A** _____ Does _____ he _____ serve _____ food?
   **B** _____ No _____, he _____ doesn't _____.

5. **A** _____ Does _____ he _____ count _____ money?
   **B** _____ No _____, he _____ doesn't _____.

6. **A** _____ Does _____ he _____ answer _____ the phone?
   **B** _____ Yes _____, he _____ does _____.

**Talk with a partner.** Ask and guess his job.

| | | |
|---|---|---|
| cashier | custodian | mechanic |
| receptionist | salesperson | server |

**A** What's his job?

**B** He's a _____.

## 3 Communicate

**Talk with your classmates.** Play a game.
Ask and guess.

**A** Do you **sell clothes**?

**B** **No.**

**A** Do you **fix cars**?

**B** **Yes.**

**A** You're a **mechanic**?

**B** **Yes, that's right.**

# Lesson D Reading

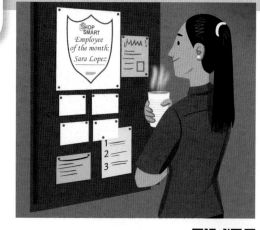

## 1 Before you read

**Talk about the picture.**
What do you see?

## 2 Read

**Listen and read.**

CD2, Track 30

EMPLOYEE of the MONTH

## Sara Lopez

Congratulations, Sara Lopez – Employee of the Month! Sara is a salesperson. She sells clothes. Sara's whole family works here at Shop Smart. Her father is a custodian, and her mother is a receptionist. Her uncle Eduardo is a server. He serves food. Her sister Lucy is a cashier. She counts money. Her brother Leo fixes cars. He's a mechanic. Everybody in the store knows the Lopez family!

## 3 After you read

**Write the job and the job duty.**

1.
**Name**          **Job**
Leo Lopez          mechanic

**Job duty**
He fixes cars.          $hop $mart

2.
**Name**          **Job**
Lucy Lopez          cashier

**Job duty**
She counts money.          $hop $mart

3.
**Name**          **Job**
Eduardo Lopez          server

**Job duty**
He serves food.          $hop $mart

4.
**Name**          **Job**
Sara Lopez          salesperson

**Job duty**
She sells clothes.          $hop $mart

Teaching objectives
- Introduce a paragrah about the employee of the month
- Provide practice using new topic-related words

# WARM-UP AND REVIEW

- Before class. Write today's lesson focus on the board.
*Lesson D:*
*Read "Employee of the Month: Sara Lopez"*
*Learn new vocabulary about work*

- Begin class. Books closed. Write *jobs* on the board. Point to the word. Ask: *Do any of you work right now? Do you have jobs?* If any S says yes, ask: *What do you do at your job every day?* Elicit short answers, such as: *I cook. I fix cars. I serve food.*

### Teaching Tip

Do not expect Ss to know many words to describe their jobs. If appropriate, teach them a few words to describe their work. The purpose of this exercise is to prepare Ss for the reading about work that follows.

# PRESENTATION

- Books open. Direct Ss' attention to the picture in Exercise 1.
- Read the instructions aloud. Ask: *What do you see?* Elicit and write on the board any vocabulary that Ss know, such as: *salesperson, notice, coffee.*
- Write on the board: *Employee of the Month.* Say the words aloud. Ask Ss to repeat them after you. Ask: *What's an employee?* If Ss don't know, say: *An employee is a person who works at a company.*
- Point to the words on the board. Ask: *What's an employee of the month?* If Ss don't know, say: *It's a person who is a good worker. This person gets an award.* If Ss don't know the meaning of the word *award*, point to the plaque in the picture. Say: *This is her award.*

## Community building *(whole group)*

- If appropriate for your class, ask working Ss if they have an "Employee of the Month" award at their jobs. Ask Ss with school-age children if their children's schools have a "Student of the Month / Week" award.

# PRACTICE

- Direct Ss' attention to Exercise 2. Ask a S to read aloud the title of the reading. Read the instructions aloud.

- ▶ **CD2, Track 30** Play or read the audio and ask Ss to follow along (see audio script, page T-150). Repeat the audio as needed.
- Read aloud each sentence of the reading and ask Ss to repeat after you.
- Ask: *Are there any words you don't understand?* Write the words on the board. Give definitions or ask volunteers if they can define the words for the rest of the class.

## Expansion activity *(student pairs)*

- Bring in pictures of famous celebrities from magazines or the Internet. If you don't have pictures, write the celebrities' names on index cards.
- Ss in pairs. Give each pair of Ss a few pictures or index cards with celebrities on them. Say: *Ask your partner questions about the celebrities.* Model the activity. Show a picture of a famous actor. Ask: *Who is he? What does he do?* Elicit appropriate responses.

## Learner persistence *(individual work)*

- ▶ **CD2, Track 30** Ss can listen to the audio for Exercise 2 at home for reinforcement and review. They can also listen to the audio for self-directed learning when class attendance is not possible.

# COMPREHENSION CHECK

- Direct Ss' attention to Exercise 3 and read the instructions aloud.
- Hold up the Student's Book. Draw Ss' attention to the first job card. Point to the word *name.* Ask: *What's his name?* (Leo Lopez.) Ask: *What's his job?* (He's a mechanic.) Ask: *What does he do?* (He fixes cars.) Point to the words written under *Name, Job,* and *Job duty.*
- Ss complete the exercise individually. Walk around and help as needed.
- Write the numbers *1–4* on the board. Ask volunteers to write their answers to Exercise 3 on the board. Ask different Ss to ask the questions: *What's his / her name? What's his / her job? What does he / she do?* for all three employees. The S who wrote the answers must answer the questions for his or her example.

### Literacy Tip

For an alternative activity, refer literacy Ss to pages 96–97 in the *Literacy Workbook* at any time during the lesson.

# LESSON D Reading

## PRESENTATION

- Books closed. Write the word *jobs* on the board. Point to the word. Say: *We have learned the names of some jobs in this unit. What other job names do you know?* Write Ss' responses on the board.

- Books open. Direct Ss' attention to the Picture dictionary in Exercise 4. Hold up the Student's Book. Point to the names of job under each picture. Read the words aloud and ask Ss to repeat them after you.

> ### Teaching Tip
> It might be helpful to point out that *aide* means helper. Tell Ss that a teacher's aide helps the teacher.

- Read the instructions for Exercise 4A aloud.
- ▶ **CD2, Track 31** Play or read the audio (see audio script, page T-150). Listen to Ss' pronunciation as they repeat the jobs. Correct pronunciation as needed.

### *Learner persistence* (individual work)
- ▶ **CD2, Track 31** Ss can listen to the audio for Exercise 4A at home for reinforcement and review. They can also listen to the audio for self-directed learning when class attendance is not possible.

### *Expansion activity* (whole group)
- Memory game. Say: *Think of the name of a job. Write the name in your notebook.* Write on the board: *I'm a _____.* Tell Ss: *Use your imagination. Maybe this isn't your real job.*

- Model the game. Say: *I'm a painter.* Ask a S to continue. Say: *Say your job. Then say my job.* The S says: *I'm a (name of job). She's a painter.* Point to yourself as the S says your job.

- Continue by asking the S next to the first S to continue saying the jobs. Ss must remember all the previous jobs that have been said. If a S doesn't remember, help him or her so that the game can continue.

> ### Multilevel Tip
> If this game seems too challenging, put Ss in groups of six. This way Ss will only have to remember six jobs for the game.

## PRACTICE

- Direct Ss' attention to Exercise 4B. Read the instructions aloud. Ask two Ss to read the conversation aloud and point to the picture in number 5 as they read. Then ask them to change the conversation to ask about another picture. Make sure Ss understand the task.

- Ss complete the exercise in pairs. Walk around and help as needed.
- Ask several pairs to ask and answer the questions for the rest of the class.

### *Expansion activity* (small groups)
- Concentration. Before class. Copy and cut out the Picture dictionary cards for this unit. Make two sets of cards for each small group of four Ss.

- Ss in groups of four. Give each group two sets of picture cards. Tell Ss to mix up the cards and spread them out facedown on a desk.

- Tell Ss to divide each group into two teams of two Ss. One person from the first team will pick up two cards and put them faceup on the desk. If the cards match, the S must ask his or her teammate the name of the job on the card. If the teammate answers correctly, he or she keeps the cards. If the teammate doesn't answer correctly, the cards must be put back in their original places, and the other team can have a chance to say the name of the job.

- The game continues until all matches have been found and names of jobs identified correctly. The teams count their cards. The team with the most cards wins the game.

> ### Teaching Tip
> It might be helpful to write on the board as a guideline: *What's his / her job? He's / She's a _____.*

## EVALUATION

- Direct Ss' attention to the first part of the lesson focus on the board. Turn Ss' attention to the story on page 102. Call on several Ss to answer comprehension questions about the reading.

- Direct Ss' attention to the jobs in the Picture dictionary. Ask different Ss the names of the different jobs.

- Check off each part of the lesson focus as Ss demonstrate understanding of what they have learned in the lesson.

| *More Ventures, Unit 8, Lesson D* | |
| --- | --- |
| **Literacy Workbook**, 15–30 min. | |
| **Basic Workbook**, 15–30 min. | |
| **Picture Dictionary activities**, 30–45 min. <br> **Writing Worksheets**, 15–30 min. <br> **Collaborative Worksheets**, 30–45 min. | www.cambridge.org/ventures/resources/ |
| **Student Arcade**, time varies | www.cambridge.org/venturesarcade/ |

## 4 **Picture dictionary** Jobs

1. bus driver

2. homemaker

3. painter

4. plumber

5. teacher's aide

6. truck driver

A **Listen and repeat.** Look at the Picture dictionary.

B **Talk with a partner.** Point and ask. Your partner answers.

A What does **he** do?

B **He's a teacher's aide.**

CD2, Track 31

# Lesson E Writing

## 1 Before you write

**A** **Talk with a partner.** Check (✓) the job duty.

|  | Counts money | Drives a bus | Cleans buildings | Answers the phone | Serves food |
|---|---|---|---|---|---|
| cashier | ✓ |  |  |  |  |
| custodian |  |  | ✓ |  |  |
| server |  |  |  |  | ✓ |
| bus driver |  | ✓ |  |  |  |
| receptionist |  |  |  | ✓ |  |

**B** **Talk with a partner.** Complete the words.

1. s a l e s p _e_ _r_ s o n
2. s e l l s _c_ _l_ o t h e s
3. m e _c_ _h_ a n i c
4. f i x _e_ _s_ c a r s
5. a n _s_ _w_ e r s t h e p h o n e
6. c _o_ _u_ n t s m o n e y

**C** **Read the letter.**

Dear Grandpa,

How are you? We are all well here. Luis and Maria have new jobs! Luis is a server. He serves food. Maria is a receptionist. She answers the phone. I'm a homemaker. I work at home. Write soon.

Love,
Rosa

Teaching objectives
• Prepare Ss for writing a letter about jobs
• Provide practice writing key vocabulary words

# WARM-UP AND REVIEW

• Before class. Write today's lesson focus on the board.
*Lesson E:*
*Write about family, friends, and jobs*

• Begin class. Books closed. Write *job duties* on the board.
Point to the word. Ask: *What are some examples of job
duties?* Elicit appropriate responses, such as: *serve food,
count money, make appointments.*

## Teaching Tip

If Ss can't think of any job duties, ask: *What are some
things people do at work?* Give Ss an example if needed.

# PRESENTATION

• Direct Ss' attention to Exercise 1A and read the instructions
aloud.

• Model the activity. Ask a S: *What does a cashier do?*
(He / She counts money.) Ask: *Does a cashier drive a bus?*
(No.) Hold up the Student's Book. Point to the check mark
under *Counts money.* Continue with questions for the other
columns. Make sure Ss understand the task.

# PRACTICE

• Ss complete the chart in pairs. Walk around and help
as needed.

• Check Ss' answers by calling on individual Ss. Ask about
each job in turn: *What does a custodian do?* (Cleans
buildings.) Have Ss check each other's charts.

• Direct Ss' attention to Exercise 1B and read the instructions
aloud.

• Point to the first item and say: *Number 1. What's the word?*
(Salesperson.) Ask: *What letters do we need?*
(e and r) Point to where the letters are written in the blanks.
Say: *Now you complete the rest of the words.*

• Ss work individually or in pairs to complete the words.

• When Ss are finished, have volunteers write their completed
words on the board. Review the alphabet by asking Ss who
write answers on the board to say the letters aloud.

• Go over the answers with the class. Ask: *Are these words
spelled correctly?* Make corrections as needed.

## Literacy Tip

Pair literacy Ss with more advanced Ss for Exercise 1B.
Encourage the Ss to work together to fill in the blanks.
The literacy S can help with oral clues while the other S
can help the literacy S write the letters correctly. This kind
of teamwork will make literacy Ss feel more comfortable
asking other Ss questions in class.

• Say: *The word "letter" has more than one meaning. A, B, and C
are letters. Look at Exercise 1C. This is also a letter.*

• Write the word *letter* on the board. Point to the word. Say it
aloud. Ask Ss to repeat it after you. Ask: *Do you write letters?*
If Ss don't know what a letter is, say: *It's a note that you write
someone.* Show Ss the letter in Exercise 1C as an example.
If any Ss answer *yes* to your question, ask: *Who do you write
letters to? Where does this person live?* Say: *Today, many
people write emails. Emails often leave out the greeting ("Dear
Grandpa") and the closing ("Love, Rosa").*

• Direct Ss' attention to the letter in Exercise 1C. Ask: *Who is
the letter to?* (Grandpa.) *Who is the letter from?* (Rosa.) *How
do you begin a letter in English?* (Dear [name].) *How do you
finish a letter in English?* (Elicit an appropriate answer, such
as *Love* or *Sincerely.*)

• Read the instructions aloud. Ask Ss to read the letter
silently. Then ask a volunteer to read the letter aloud.

## Literacy Tip

It might be helpful to explain the differences between
different ways to sign a letter. Tell Ss that *Love* is used for
people you are close to and *Sincerely* is formal. It is used
for business.

## Expansion activity *(student pairs)*

• Say: *Ask and answer questions about the letter.* Write on the
board: *What is Luis's job? What does he do? What is Maria's
job? What does she do?*

• Ss in pairs. Say: *Ask your partner the questions. Then your
partner will ask you the questions.*

• Walk around and help as needed.

• Ask several pairs to ask and answer the questions for the
rest of the class.

# LESSON E Writing

## PRESENTATION

- Direct Ss' attention to Exercise 2A and read the instructions aloud.
- Model the task. Ask a S to read the first part of the letter aloud. Ask the S to stop after the example word *salesperson*.
- Remind Ss to look at Exercise 1B on the previous page for the words to write in the blanks.

## PRACTICE

- Ss complete the exercise individually or in pairs, using the words from Exercise 1B. Walk around and help as needed.

### Teaching Tip

It might be helpful to give Ss examples of how to talk with their partner about completing the exercise. Tell Ss to read the sentences aloud. Then they can ask their partner: *What is this word? What do you think?* Write the questions on the board so Ss can refer to them as they work with their partners.

- Write the numbers *1–6* on the board. Ask volunteers to write their answers on the board.
- Ask different Ss to read the answers aloud. Ask: *Are these words correct?* Ss can correct the list if needed. Then ask a S to read the letter aloud.
- Direct Ss' attention to Exercise 2B and read the instructions aloud.
- Model the task. Hold up the Student's Book. Say: *I'm going to write about my friend. My friend's name is _____.* Use a real or imaginary friend's name for the example. Continue by telling the class about your friend's job and job duties. For example: *My friend's name is Mary. She is a receptionist. She answers the phone.*
- Ss complete the exercise individually. Walk around and help as needed.

### Teaching Tip

Tell Ss that they can write about real or imaginary friends and family. If Ss choose to write about real people, they may need help with names of other jobs and job duties in English. Encourage Ss to use bilingual dictionaries to find the words they are trying to use in this exercise.

### Literacy Tip

For an alternative activity, refer literacy Ss to pages 98–99 in the *Literacy Workbook* at any time during the lesson.

## APPLICATION

- Focus Ss' attention on Exercise 3. Read the instructions aloud. Encourage Ss to read what they wrote in Exercise 2B to their partners.
- Ss complete the task in pairs. Walk around and help as needed.
- Ask several volunteers to read their sentences aloud to the class.

### Teaching Tip

This exercise asks Ss to work together to edit their writing. Encourage Ss to correct each other's writing if necessary. Say: *Help your partner with any spelling mistakes. Then your partner will help you.*

### Expansion activity *(student pairs)*

- Give each S two index cards. Tell them to write the name of a job they learned in this unit on one side of the card and the job duty on the back of the card. For example: *cashier* on one side and *counts money* on the other side.
- When Ss are finished, collect the cards. Mix them up, and hand out four cards to each pair of Ss.
- Ss in pairs. Say: *Show your partner the job on one of your cards. Your partner will tell you the job duty.*
- Walk around and help as needed. When Ss are finished with their four cards, encourage them to exchange cards with other Ss.

## EVALUATION

- Direct Ss' attention to the lesson focus on the board.
- Ask volunteers to write the names of the jobs they reviewed in this lesson on the board (*cashier, custodian, server, bus driver, receptionist, salesperson, mechanic*). Point to each job in turn. Ask individual Ss to tell you the job duty for each job.
- Check off each part of the lesson focus as Ss demonstrate understanding of what they have learned in the lesson.

| *More Ventures, Unit 8, Lesson E* | |
|---|---|
| **Literacy Workbook**, 15–30 min. | |
| **Basic Workbook**, 15–30 min. | |
| **Writing Worksheets**, 15–30 min. | www.cambridge.org/ventures/ resources/ |
| **Collaborative Worksheets**, 30–45 min. | |

## 2 Write

A **Talk with a partner.** Complete the letter. Use the words from 1B.

Dear Grandma,

How are you? We are all well here. Janie and Walter have new jobs!

Janie is a __salesperson__ . She __sells__ clothes. She also __answers__
              1                     2                            3

the phone at work, and she __counts__ money. Walter is a __mechanic__ . He
                                 4                           5

__fixes__ cars.
    6

Write soon.

Love,
Meg

B **Write about your family and friends.** Write about their jobs.

My ___friend's___ name is ___Sandra___ .
She is a ___receptionist___ . She ___answers the phone___ .

1. My _Answers will vary._'s name is _____.
He is a _____ . He _____ .

2. My _____'s name is _____.
She is a _____ . She _____ .

3. My _____'s name is _____.
_____ is a _____ .
_____ .

## 3 After you write

**Talk with a partner.** Share your writing.

# Lesson F Another view

## 1 Life-skills reading

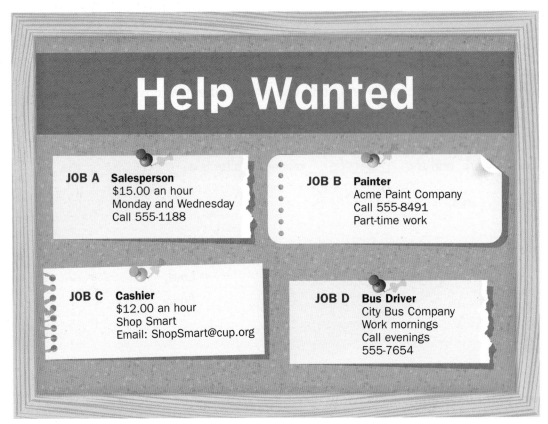

# Help Wanted

**JOB A  Salesperson**
$15.00 an hour
Monday and Wednesday
Call 555-1188

**JOB B  Painter**
Acme Paint Company
Call 555-8491
Part-time work

**JOB C  Cashier**
$12.00 an hour
Shop Smart
Email: ShopSmart@cup.org

**JOB D  Bus Driver**
City Bus Company
Work mornings
Call evenings
555-7654

**A  Read the sentences.** Look at the ads. Fill in the answer.

1. What is Job A for?

   Ⓐ cashier

   Ⓑ receptionist

   **Ⓒ** salesperson

2. What is Job B for?

   Ⓐ driver

   **Ⓑ** painter

   Ⓒ plumber

3. You want the cashier job. What should you do?

   **Ⓐ** write to Shop Smart

   Ⓑ go to Shop Smart

   Ⓒ call Shop Smart

4. You want the bus driver job. What should you do?

   Ⓐ call in the morning

   Ⓑ call in the afternoon

   **Ⓒ** call in the evening

**B  Solve the problem.** Which solution is best? Circle your opinion.

Ana wants to apply for Job C, but she doesn't have a computer. What should she do?

1. Use a computer at the library.

2. Borrow a friend's computer.

3. Other: _Answers will vary._

Teaching objectives
- Introduce reading job ads
- Provide practice that develops test-taking skills
- Review vocabulary from the unit

## WARM-UP AND REVIEW

- Before class. Write today's lesson focus on the board.
*Lesson F:*
*Read and answer questions about job ads*
*Practice vocabulary about jobs*
*Complete the Self-assessment*
- Begin class. Books closed. Write on the board: *job advertisements.* Point to the words. Say them aloud and ask Ss to repeat. Cross out *-vertisements.* Say: *These are also called ads. "Ad" is the short form for "advertisement."*
- Ask: *Where can you find job ads?* If Ss don't know, say: *You can find them in the newspaper and online.*

### Teaching Tip
It might be helpful to bring in examples of job ads from your local newspaper or the Internet.

## PRESENTATION

- Books open. Direct Ss' attention to the job ads in Exercise 1A.
- Hold up the Student's Book. Point to the words *Help Wanted.* Say the words aloud. Ask Ss to repeat them after you. Ask Ss what they think this means. Say: *This means that a company needs help. If you see this sign in a workplace, it means they are looking for workers.*

## PRACTICE

- Read aloud the instructions in Exercise 1A. This task helps prepare Ss for standardized-type tests they may have to take.
- Write the first item on the board along with three answer choices labeled *A, B,* and *C.*
- Read the item and the answer choices aloud and then point to the help-wanted ads. Ask Ss: *What job is Job A?* Show Ss where to look for the information. Elicit: *Salesperson.*
- Point to the three answer choices on the board. Ask Ss: *A, B, or C?* (C) Fill in the letter *C* and tell Ss: *Fill in the answer.* Make sure Ss understand the task.
- Have Ss individually scan for and fill in the answers.

## COMPREHENSION CHECK

- Go over the answers to Exercise 1A with the class. Make sure Ss followed the directions and filled in their answers. Ask Ss to point to the information in the job ads.

### Literacy Tip
For an alternative activity, refer literacy Ss to pages 100–101 in the *Literacy Workbook* at any time during the lesson.

## APPLICATION

- Read aloud the instructions for Exercise 1B.
- Tell Ss that they will discuss what Ana can do.
- Ss complete the task in pairs.
- Ask several pairs to ask and answer the question for the rest of the class.

### Teaching Tip
If you do not want to limit your Ss to one of the jobs in the help-wanted ads on this page, explain that they can choose a different job that they would like to have in the future. List any new jobs that Ss come up with on the board and ask the Ss who chose them to define them for the class.

### Expansion activity *(individual work, student pairs)*
- Ask Ss to write ads for different jobs. Encourage them to use the ads in Exercise 1 as a guide.
- When Ss are finished, ask them to work with a partner. Say: *Show your partner your ad. Then look at your partner's ad. Ask questions. For example: How much is the salary? What's the phone number? Is it part-time or full-time?*
- Ask Ss: *Do you want any of the jobs in the ads? Why or why not?*

### Community building *(whole group)*
- Do the expansion activity using real job ads from a local newspaper or the Internet. Discuss which ads are the most interesting to Ss in your class and why they feel that way. Help Ss understand any unfamiliar words in the ads.

# LESSON F Another view

## PRACTICE

- Direct Ss' attention to Exercise 2A. Read the instructions aloud.

- Focus Ss' attention on the pictures. Say: *These are things that people need for their jobs.*

- Ask a S to read the names of the jobs aloud.

- Model the task. Hold up the Student's Book. Point to the first picture (a truck). Ask: *Who needs this?* (A truck driver.) Point to the line drawn from picture number 1 to *a truck driver.* Say: *A truck driver needs a truck.*

- Ss complete the exercise individually. Walk around and help as needed.

### Teaching Tip

Some Ss may want to know how to say the names of the items in the pictures in Exercise 2A. If your Ss express interest in this, write the names of the items on the board: *1. a truck; 2. a car; 3. a cash register; 4. paints and a roller; 5. books; 6. a phone.*

- Direct Ss' attention to the second set of instructions in Exercise 2A. Read the instructions aloud.

- Ss complete the exercise in pairs. Ask: *Are your answers the same as your partner's?*

- Go over the answers with the class. Ask individual Ss to read their answers to the class. Ask: *Are the answers correct?* Ask different Ss to make corrections if needed.

### Expansion activity *(individual work)*

- Dictation. Books closed. Ask Ss to take out a piece of paper and write the numbers *1–5* on it. Tell them they will listen to five sentences and write them on their papers. Dictate the following sentences:
  *1. A truck driver needs a truck.*
  *2. A mechanic fixes cars.*
  *3. A receptionist answers the phone.*
  *4. A custodian cleans buildings.*
  *5. A cashier counts money.*

- Write the numbers *1–5* on the board. Ask five volunteers to come to the board and write one sentence each. Ask different Ss to read the sentences aloud. Ask: *Are the sentences correct?* Ask different Ss to make corrections if needed.

## PRACTICE

- Direct Ss' attention to Exercise 2B. Read the instructions aloud.

- Hold up the Student's Book. Point to where the word *fix* has been circled in the puzzle. Focus Ss' attention on the words in the word bank. Say: *Find the rest of the words in the puzzle.*

- Ss complete the exercise individually or in pairs. Walk around and help as needed.

### Expansion activity *(individual work)*

- Ask Ss to write sentences using the words in the word search.

  **Option** Ask Ss to erase the words from the word bank in their sentences and draw a blank line in each word's place. Ask them to trade papers with a partner. Their partners fill in the blanks with the words from the word bank. When they are finished, they can give their papers back to their partners. The partners will check to see if the correct words were chosen.

## EVALUATION

- Do a quick review of the unit. Have Ss turn to Lesson A. Ask the class to talk about what they remember about this lesson. Prompt Ss, if necessary, with questions such as: *What words are on this page? What do you see in the picture?* Continue in this manner to review each lesson quickly.

### Expansion activity

- Before class. Print, for each student, one copy of the Self-assessment for this unit.

- Have Ss complete the Self-assessment either in class or outside of class.

- Provide feedback to Ss such as through a whole-class discussion, partners comparing their worksheets, or T reviewing each S's worksheet.

- If Ss are ready, administer the unit test on page T-179 of this Teacher's Edition. The audio script for the test is available on page T-193.

| *More Ventures, Unit 8, Lesson F* | |
|---|---|
| Literacy Workbook, 15–30 min. | |
| Basic Workbook, 15–30 min. | |
| Writing Worksheets, 15–30 min. | www.cambridge.org/ventures/ resources/ |
| Collaborative Worksheets, 30–45 min. | |
| Self-assessment, 10 min. | |
| CASAS Test Prep Worksheet, 5–10 min. | |

## 2 Fun with vocabulary

### A Read and match.

1.

2.

3.

a cashier

a mechanic

a teacher's aide

a receptionist

a painter

a truck driver

4.

5.

6.

**Talk with a partner.** Check your answers.

### B Circle the words in the puzzle.

| answer | cashier | clean | count | custodian |
|--------|---------|-------|-------|-----------|
| fix | mechanic | sell | server | |

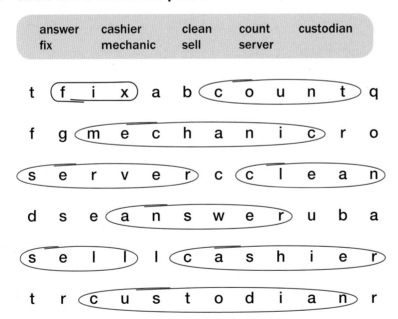

t  f  i  x  a  b  c  o  u  n  t  q

f  g  m  e  c  h  a  n  i  c  r  o

s  e  r  v  e  r  c  c  l  e  a  n

d  s  e  a  n  s  w  e  r  u  b  a

s  e  l  l  l  c  a  s  h  i  e  r

t  r  c  u  s  t  o  d  i  a  n  r

# REVIEW

## 1 Listening

**Read.** Then listen and circle.

CD2, Track 32

1. What does Chul do?
   - **a.** He's a cashier.
   - b. He's a custodian.

2. Does he serve food?
   - a. Yes, he does.
   - **b.** No, he doesn't.

3. What does Luz do?
   - a. She's a salesperson.
   - **b.** She's a receptionist.

4. Does she answer the phone?
   - **a.** Yes, she does.
   - b. No, she doesn't.

5. What color are the pants?
   - **a.** blue
   - b. green

6. How much are the pants?
   - a. $9.99
   - **b.** $19.99

**Talk with a partner.** Ask and answer.

## 2 Vocabulary

**Write.** Complete the story.

> cars   clothes   mechanic   $9.99   salesperson   shirt

# A New Shirt

Sam is a ___mechanic___ . He fixes ___cars___ . Today he
         1             2

is at Shop Smart. He needs a blue ___shirt___ . Shirts are
         3

on sale. Brenda is a _salesperson_ . She sells ___clothes___ at
        4           5

Shop Smart. How much is the shirt? It's ___$9.99___ .
        6

**Teaching objectives**
- Review vocabulary from Units 7 and 8
- Introduce pronunciation of e as in *red*, i as in *six*, and u as in *bus*

# WARM-UP AND REVIEW

- Before class. Write today's lesson focus on the board.
  *Review unit:*
  *Review vocabulary and grammar from Units 7 and 8*
  *Pronounce "e" as in "red," "i" as in "six," and "u" as in "bus"*
- Begin class. Books closed. Ask a volunteer to come to the front of the class. Ask another S: *What color is her (clothing item)?* Elicit an appropriate response.
- Point to another item of clothing the volunteer is wearing. Ask: *What's this?* Elicit an appropriate response.
- Write the words *mechanic*, *teacher's aide*, and *receptionist* on the board. Point to each word in turn. Ask Ss: *What does a mechanic do?* (He / She fixes cars.) *What does a teacher's aide do?* (He / She helps teachers and students.) *What does a receptionist do?* (He / She answers the phone.)
- Draw a simple drawing of a T-shirt and shoes on the board. Write a price next to each clothing item, such as: *$10.99* and *$29.99*, respectively. Point to each item. Ask: *How much is the T-shirt?* ($10.99) *How much are the shoes?* ($29.99)

# PRACTICE

- Books open. Direct Ss' attention to Exercise 1 and read the instructions aloud.
- Ask a S to read the question and answer choices in number 1 aloud.
- ▶ **CD2, Track 32** Model the task. Play or read only the first conversation on the audio (see audio script, page T-150). Point to the two answer choices in number 1 and ask: *Is Chul a cashier or a custodian?* (He's a cashier.) Point to where the answer *a* is circled.
- ▶ **CD2, Track 32** Play or read the complete audio. Ss listen and circle the correct answers. Repeat the audio as needed.
- Check answers with the class. Read each question aloud and call on different Ss to answer.

**Teaching Tip**

You may need to play the audio several times in order to give Ss a chance to extract the information they need. Then, to check comprehension and help Ss who may be struggling, play the audio again and ask Ss to repeat the parts of the conversation that contain the answers to the questions.

- Read aloud the second part of the instructions for Exercise 1. Ss practice asking and answering the questions in pairs. Walk around and help as needed.
- Ask several pairs to ask and answer the questions for the rest of the class.

## *Expansion activity* (small groups)

- Tell Ss to write questions about their group members. Then they will ask the rest of the class the questions. They should use Exercise 1 as a guide.
- Model the activity. Point to a small group. Say: *I will give you some examples of questions about this group.* Point to one S. Ask: *What does Maria do?* Elicit an appropriate response such as *Maria is a student.* Ask: *Does she fix cars?* Elicit a yes / no response. Point to a different S in the group. Ask: *What color is her (name of clothing item S is wearing)?*
- Ss write questions in their groups. Ask them to ask the questions to other Ss in the class.

**Teaching Tip**

You may need to remind Ss to look at the questions in Exercise 1 as a guide while they are writing questions about their group members.

# PRACTICE

- Direct Ss' attention to Exercise 2. Point to the title of the story and ask Ss: *What's the title?* ("A New Shirt") Help Ss by reading the title aloud if necessary.
- Direct Ss' attention to the words in the word bank. Say each word aloud. Ask Ss to repeat them after you.
- Read aloud the instructions for Exercise 2. Point to the words in the word bank and tell Ss: *Write these words in the story.*
- Model the task. Read aloud the first two sentences of the story. Point to *mechanic* in the word bank and in the blank for number 1.
- Ss read the story and fill in the blanks individually. Walk around and help as needed.
- Write the numbers *1–6* on the board. Ask volunteers to come to the board to write the answers.
- Ask several Ss to read different sentences of the story aloud using the words on the board. Ask: *Are these words correct?* Ask different Ss to correct any errors.

**Review: Units 7 & 8**  **T-108**

# REVIEW

## WARM-UP AND REVIEW

- Books closed. Draw an example of a store receipt on the board. Use the following information or create your own:

  *The Clothes Shop*
  | | |
  |---|---|
  | *pants* | *$16.95* |
  | *socks* | *$9.95* |
  | *T-shirt* | *$12.00* |
  | *Subtotal* | *$38.90* |
  | *Tax* | *$3.15* |
  | *Total* | *$42.05* |

- Ask Ss: *How much is the T-shirt?* ($12) *How much are the socks?* ($9.95) *How much are the pants?* ($16.95) *How much is the tax?* ($3.15) *How much is the total price?* ($42.05)

## PRACTICE

- Direct Ss' attention to the picture in Exercise 3A. Ask: *What do you see?*
- Read the instructions aloud. Model the task. Read number 1: *How much is or are the T-shirt?* (is) Point to where *is* has been written for number 1 and read the complete sentence aloud. Ask: *Why "is" and not "are"?* (T-shirt is singular.) Ask: *When do we use "are"?* (With plurals.)
- Ss write their answers individually. Check answers by calling on Ss to read the sentences aloud. After each question, ask: *Is this question correct?* Ask different Ss to make corrections.
- Direct Ss' attention to Exercise 3B and read the instructions aloud.
- Model the task. Ask two Ss to read the example question and answer aloud. Ask: *Is it "Yes, she does" or "Yes, she doesn't"?* (Yes, she does.) Point to where *does* has been written for number 1. Ask: *Why is it "does"?* (It's a *Yes* answer.) Ask: *When do we use "doesn't"?* (With *No* answers.)
- Ss complete the exercise individually. Check answers by calling on Ss to read the questions and answers aloud.

### Expansion activity *(whole group)*

- Expand on Exercise 3B by asking questions about Ss' lives. Point to a S. Ask another S: *Does (student's name) come from Mexico?* Elicit an appropriate response. Continue by asking more questions about other Ss, *such as Does _____ (student's name) have children? Does _____ (student's name) have a job?*

## PRESENTATION

- Direct Ss' attention to the second part of the lesson focus on the board.
- Draw two vertical lines on the board, making a three-column chart. Write *e*, *i*, and *u* as headings in each column.

- Write in the *e* column: *red, when.* Point to and say each word and ask Ss to repeat. Underline the *e* in the words. Say a short *e* (/e/) sound before repeating each word, for example: /e/, *red*. Ask Ss to repeat.
- Write in the *i* column: *six, his.* Repeat the procedure. Underline the *i* in the words and pronounce a short *i* sound, for example: /i/, *six*.
- Write in the *u* column: *bus, much.* Repeat the procedure. Underline the *u* in the words and pronounce a short *u* sound, for example: /u/, *bus*.

## PRACTICE

- ▶ **CD2, Track 33** Direct Ss' attention to Exercise 4A and read the instructions aloud. Play or read the audio (see audio script, page T-150). Ss listen to examples of the three vowel sounds.
- ▶ **CD2, Track 34** Direct Ss' attention to Exercise 4B and read the instructions aloud. Play or read the audio (see audio script, page T-150). Ss listen and repeat what they hear.
- Read aloud the second part of the instructions for Exercise 4B. Model the task. Point to the three charts and tell one S: *Say a word.* After that S says any word from the charts, tell his or her partner: *Point to the word.*
- Ss complete the task in pairs. Help as needed.
- ▶ **CD2, Track 35** Direct Ss' attention to Exercise 4C and read the instructions aloud. Model the task. Play or read the first word from the audio (see audio script, page T-150). Ask: *Which letter is it: e, i, or u?* Point to where the letter has been checked in the chart.
- ▶ **CD2, Track 35** Play or read the complete audio. Ss listen and make a check mark under the letter they hear.
- ▶ **CD2, Track 35** Reproduce the chart from Exercise 4C on the board and play or read the audio again. Pause after each word and ask a S to check the appropriate letter in the chart.

## EVALUATION

- Direct Ss' attention to the lesson focus on the board.
- Ask individual Ss questions similar to the ones in Exercise 1. Ask real questions about Ss in the class.
- Write on the board: *red, six, bus.* Call on individual Ss as you point to one of the words and ask them to say the word. Listen carefully to the vowel sounds and provide help and correction as needed.
- Check off each part of the lesson focus as Ss demonstrate an understanding of what they have learned in the lesson.

## 3 Grammar

**A** **Complete the sentences.** Use *is* or *are*.

1. **A** How much _____is_____ the T-shirt?
   **B** $10.99.

2. **A** How much _____*are*_____ the pants?
   **B** $28.99.

3. **A** How much _____*are*_____ the shoes?
   **B** $39.95.

4. **A** How much _____*is*_____ the sweater?
   **B** $22.95.

**B** **Read and circle.** Then write.

1. **A** Does Kayla count money?
   **B** Yes, she _____**does**_____ .
   (does) doesn't

2. **A** Does she clean buildings?
   **B** No, she _____*doesn't*_____ .
   does (doesn't)

3. **A** Does Allen fix cars?
   **B** No, he _____*doesn't*_____ .
   does (doesn't)

4. **A** Does he serve food?
   **B** Yes, he _____*does*_____ .
   (does) doesn't

## 4 Pronunciation

**A** **Listen** to the *e* sound, the *i* sound, and the *u* sound.

| e | i | u |
|---|---|---|
| red | six | bus |

CD2, Track 33

**B** **Listen and repeat.**

| e | red | when | | i | six | his | | u | bus | much |
|---|-----|------|---|---|-----|-----|---|---|-----|------|

**Talk with a partner.** Say a word. Your partner points. Take turns.

CD2, Track 34

**C** **Listen and check (✓).**

|    | e | i | u | e | i | u | e | i | u | e | i | u | e | i | u |
|----|---|---|---|---|---|---|---|---|---|---|---|---|---|---|---|
| 1. | ✓ |   |   |   |   |   |   |   |   |   |   |   |   |   |   |
| 2. |   |   |   |   |   | ✓ |   |   |   |   |   |   |   |   |   |
| 3. |   |   |   |   | ✓ |   |   |   |   |   |   |   |   |   |   |
| 4. |   |   |   |   | ✓ |   |   |   |   |   |   |   |   |   |   |
| 5. |   |   |   | ✓ |   |   |   |   |   |   |   |   |   |   |   |

CD2, Track 35

# UNIT 9 DAILY LIVING

## Lesson A Listening

### 1 Before you listen

**A** Look at the picture. What do you see?

**B** Listen and point: ■ doing homework ■ doing the laundry
■ drying the dishes ■ making lunch
■ making the bed ■ washing the dishes

CD2, Track 36

# UNIT 9

**Teaching objectives**
- Introduce Ss to the topic
- Find out what Ss know about the topic
- Preview the unit by talking about the picture
- Provide practice of key vocabulary
- Provide practice that develops listening skills

## WARM-UP AND REVIEW

- Before class. Write today's lesson focus on the board.
  *Lesson A:*
  *Daily living*
  *Vocabulary for daily activities*
- Begin class. Books closed. Point to the words *daily activities* in the lesson focus. Say each word aloud. Ask Ss to repeat them after you. Tell Ss some daily activities that you do in your house, such as: *washing the dishes, making the bed.*
- Ask: *What are some activities you do at home every day?* Write Ss' responses on the board. Elicit any appropriate responses, such as: *cooking, doing the laundry.* Say: *These types of activities are called household chores.* Write *chores* on the board. Say the word and ask Ss to repeat it after you.

### Teaching Tip

Do not expect Ss to know the vocabulary for all their daily activities. This warm-up will help you to find out what Ss know before you present the vocabulary for daily activities in this lesson.

### Literacy Tip

If you have literacy Ss in your class, it might be helpful to spend time at the beginning of any activity with art or photos talking about the pictures before focusing Ss' attention on the printed words in the exercise. Have Ss work in pairs. Tell them to ask each other: *What do you see?* Encourage Ss to describe the pictures to each other. Consider pairing literacy Ss with Ss who can help them read the text in the exercise. This will help preview the exercise for literacy Ss and make them more confident as the exercise continues.

## PRESENTATION

- Books open. Set the scene. Hold up the Student's Book. Show Ss the picture on page 110. Ask: *What do you see?* Elicit and write on the board any vocabulary that Ss know, such as: *a kitchen, a family, food, father, mother, daughter, son.*
- Ask: *What are the people's names?* (Huan, Quan, Li, Tao, Mei, Ping.)

## PRACTICE

- Direct Ss' attention to the key vocabulary in Exercise **1B**. Say: *These are some daily activities or chores.* Read each phrase aloud while pointing to the corresponding chore in the picture. Ask Ss to repeat and point.
- Read the instructions for Exercise **1B** aloud.
- ▶ **CD2, Track 36** Play or read the audio (see audio script, page T-150). Tell Ss: *Listen and point to the picture.* As Ss hear the key vocabulary, check to see that they are pointing to the correct part of the picture. Repeat the audio as needed.

## COMPREHENSION CHECK

- Ask Ss *Yes / No* questions about the picture. Tell Ss: *Listen. Say "yes" or "no."*

  Point to the mother. Ask: *Is she making lunch?* (Yes.)

  Point to the father. Ask: *Is he drying the dishes?* (No.)

  Point to the boy drying dishes. Ask: *Is he washing the dishes?* (No.)

  Point to the boy doing the laundry. Ask: *Is he doing the laundry?* (Yes.)

  Point to the girl making her bed. Ask: *Is she doing her homework?* (No.)

  Point to the girl doing her homework. Ask: *Is she making the bed?* (No.)

### Expansion activity *(student pairs)*

- Write on the board: *Do you do this chore at home?* Hold up the Student's Book. Point to one of the activities. Ask a S: *Do you do this chore at home?* Elicit *Yes, I do* or *No, I don't.* Write this question and these responses on the board as a guide.
- Ss in pairs. Say: *Point to different activities in the picture. Ask your partner the question on the board.* Your partner answers. Take turns.
- Walk around and help as needed.

  **Option** Write on the board: *Who does this activity at your house?* Model the task. Point to an activity in the picture. Tell Ss who does the activity at your house, for example: *My husband washes the dishes.* Ask Ss to point to activities in the picture. Elicit short responses to the question on the board, such as: *My brother / sister / roommate / daughter.*

# LESSON A Listening

## PRESENTATION

- Direct Ss' attention to the phrases in Exercise 2A. Tell Ss: *We are going to practice pronouncing these daily activities.* Read them aloud. Ask Ss to repeat them after you.
- Read aloud the instructions for Exercise 2A.

## PRACTICE

- ▶ **CD2, Track 37** Play or read the audio (see audio script, page T-150). Ss listen and repeat the vocabulary. Repeat the audio as needed.
- Listen carefully to Ss' pronunciation and make corrections as needed.

### *Learner persistence* (individual work)
- ▶ **CD2, Track 37** Ss can listen to the audio for Exercise 2A at home for reinforcement and review. They can also listen to the audio for self-directed learning when class attendance is not possible.

> **Literacy Tip**
>
> For an alternative activity, refer literacy Ss to pages 102–103 in the *Literacy Workbook* at any time during the lesson.

- Direct Ss' attention to Exercise 2B and read the instructions aloud.
- ▶ **CD2, Track 38** Model the task. Hold up the Student's Book and say: *Number one.* Play or read the audio for number 1 (see audio script, page T-150). Point to the two answer choices in number 1 and ask Ss: *What did you hear – a or b?* Elicit: *a.* Point to the letter *a* next to the first picture and tell Ss: *Circle the letter "a."*
- ▶ **CD2, Track 38** Play or read the complete audio. Ss listen and circle the correct answers. Repeat the audio as needed.
- ▶ **CD2, Track 38** Read aloud the second part of the instructions in Exercise 2B. Play or read the audio again so Ss can listen and check their answers.

### *Learner persistence* (individual work)
- ▶ **CD2, Track 38** Ss can listen to the audio for Exercise 2B at home for reinforcement and review. They can also listen to the audio for self-directed learning when class attendance is not possible.

## COMPREHENSION CHECK

- Write the numbers *1–4* on the board. Ask volunteers to come to the board and write the correct answers to Exercise 2B next to each number.

- ▶ **CD2, Track 38** Play or read the audio again. Pause the audio after each conversation. Point to the answer written on the board and ask: *Is this correct?* If not, ask another S to make any necessary corrections.

## APPLICATION

- Direct Ss' attention to Exercise 3 and read the instructions aloud.
- Model the task. Hold up the Student's Book and point to the pictures in Exercise 2B. Say to one S: *Point to a picture.* Say to the S's partner: *Say the word.*
- Ss complete the exercise in pairs. Walk around and help as needed.

### *Expansion activity* (student pairs)
- Write on the board: *Do you like _____?* Point to the question. Say it aloud. Ask Ss to repeat it after you. Tell Ss to ask each other the question on the board using the household chores in Exercises 2A and 2B.
- Model the activity. Hold up the Student's Book. Point to the first picture in number 1 in Exercise 2B. Ask a S: *Do you like doing homework?* Elicit a *yes* or *no* response.
- Ss in pairs. Say: *Point to the pictures in Exercise 2B. Ask your partner the question on the board.* Tell Ss to switch roles when they are finished.
- Walk around and help as needed.

## EVALUATION

- Direct Ss' attention to the lesson focus on the board. Check Ss' understanding of vocabulary for daily activities by asking them to point to the activities in the picture on page 110: *doing homework, doing the laundry, drying the dishes, making lunch, making the bed, washing the dishes.*
- Walk around and check that Ss are pointing to the correct parts of the picture.
- Check off the lesson focus as Ss demonstrate an understanding of what they have learned in the lesson.

| More Ventures, Unit 9, Lesson A | |
|---|---|
| Literacy Workbook, 15–30 min. | |
| Basic Workbook, 15–30 min. | |
| Writing Worksheets, 15–30 min. | |
| Real-life Document, 15–30 min. | www.cambridge.org/ventures/resources/ |
| Collaborative Worksheets, 30–45 min. | |
| Student Arcade, time varies | www.cambridge.org/venturesarcade/ |

## 2 Listen

### A Listen and repeat.

| | | |
|---|---|---|
| 1. doing homework | 2. doing the laundry | 3. drying the dishes |
| 4. making lunch | 5. making the bed | 6. washing the dishes |

◀)) CD2, Track 37

### B Listen and circle.

◀)) CD2, Track 38

1. (a.)    b.

2. a.    (b.)

3. (a.)    b.

4. (a.)    b.

**Listen again.** Check your answers.

## 3 After you listen

**Talk with a partner.** Point to a picture.
Your partner says the words.

# Lesson B Outside chores

## 1 Vocabulary focus

**Listen and repeat.**

 CD2, Track 39

1. cutting the grass

2. getting the mail

3. taking out the trash

4. walking the dog

5. washing the car

6. watering the grass

## 2 Practice

**A Read and match.**

taking out the trash    washing the car    cutting the grass

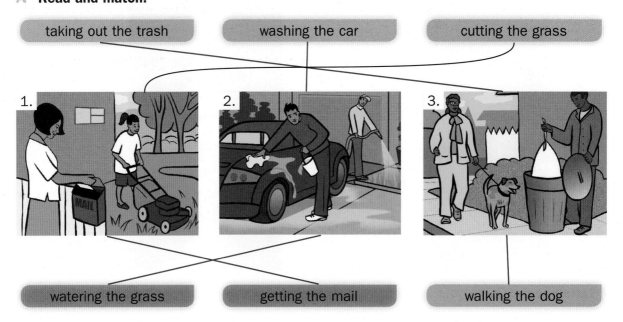

1.    2.    3.

watering the grass    getting the mail    walking the dog

## WARM-UP AND REVIEW

- Before class. Write today's lesson focus on the board.
  *Lesson B:*
  *Vocabulary about outside chores*
  *Ask and answer questions about outside chores*
- Begin class. Books open. Direct Ss' attention to the picture on page 110. Ask Ss to cover the words in Exercise 1B. Review key vocabulary from the unit by asking: *What are the names of daily activities in this picture?* Elicit: *doing homework, doing the laundry, drying the dishes, making lunch, making the bed,* and *washing the dishes.* Ask Ss to point to these activities.

### Teaching Tip

If you feel that covering the words in Exercise 1B is too challenging for your Ss, allow them to look at the words while pointing to the activities in the picture.

- Walk around and check to see that Ss are pointing to the correct items in the picture.
- Point to the words *outside chores* on the board. Say them aloud. Ask Ss to repeat them after you. Ask Ss: *What are these?* Tell Ss that chores are work you do at home. If Ss don't know what *outside* means, point out the window and say: *That's outside.* If your classroom doesn't have a window, explain that *outside* is the opposite of *inside.* Use hand gestures to indicate the meanings of the two words. Direct Ss' attention to the picture on page 110. Ask: *Is this outside?* (No.) *Is it inside* (Yes.) Direct Ss' attention to the pictures on page 112. Ask: *Is this inside?* (No.) *Is it outside?* (Yes.)

## PRESENTATION

- Set the scene. Point to the words *outside chores* on the board again. Ask: *What are some examples of outside chores?* Elicit appropriate examples, such as cutting the grass. If Ss don't know any examples, direct Ss' attention to the pictures in Exercise 1. Say: *Here are some examples of outside chores.*
- Read aloud the instructions for Exercise 1.
- ▶ *CD2, Track 39* Play or read the audio (see audio script, page T-150). Listen and repeat the vocabulary along with Ss. Repeat the audio as needed.
- Listen carefully to Ss' pronunciation and correct as needed.

### Expansion activity *(student pairs)*

- Write on the board: *What are your chores at home?* Point to the words. Say them aloud. Ask Ss to repeat them after you.

- Ss in pairs. Say: *Ask your partner the question on the board.* Model the activity. Ask a S the question. Elicit an appropriate response, for example: *taking out the trash, walking the dog, washing the dishes.*
- Ss continue asking the questions in pairs. Walk around and help as needed.
- Have several pairs ask and answer the question for the rest of the class.

### Teaching Tip

Encourage Ss to use the chores in Lesson A as well as the chores in Lesson B for this expansion activity.

## PRACTICE

- Direct Ss' attention to Exercise 2A. As you read aloud the instructions, hold up the Student's Book and indicate that Ss should look at the pictures of outside chores and match them with the corresponding phrases.
- Model the task. Hold up the Student's Book. Point to the daughter in the first picture. Ask: *What is she doing?* Elicit: *Cutting the grass.* Point to the mother. Ask: *What is she doing?* Elicit: *Getting the mail.* Hold up the Student's Book. Point to the lines connecting the first picture to the phrases *cutting the grass* and *getting the mail.* Say: *Match the pictures and the words.*
- Ss complete the exercise individually. Help as needed.

### Literacy Tip

Literacy Ss may be able to complete this activity with help. Pair stronger Ss with literacy Ss. Tell literacy Ss to refer to Exercise 1 when completing Exercise 2A.

## COMPREHENSION CHECK

- Ask different Ss to point to each picture in Exercise 2A and read the phrases that match the picture. After each phrase is read, ask: *Is this correct?* Ask another S to make any corrections if needed.

### Community building *(whole group)*

- If your school has a custodian, ask: *What are the custodian's chores?* Brainstorm his or her chores. Write them on the board. Elicit appropriate responses, such as: *taking out the trash, cleaning the boards, cleaning the classroom.*

# LESSON B Outside chores

## PRESENTATION

- Direct Ss' attention to the picture in Exercise 2B. Ask: *What do you see?* Elicit any words that Ss know, such as: *family chores, cutting the grass, getting the mail, walking the dog, watering the grass.*

- Tell Ss that this picture shows the Navarro family. Ask volunteers to tell you the names of the people in the family (*Mr. and Mrs. Navarro, Roberto, Diego, Norma, and Rita*). Say: *Mr. and Mrs. Navarro are the father and mother. Who are Roberto and Diego?* (brothers or sons) *Who are Norma and Rita?* (sisters or daughters)

- Read the instructions for Exercise 2B aloud.

- ▶ **CD2, Track 40** Model the task. Say: *Listen and repeat.* Play or read the audio for number 1 (see audio script, page T-150) and point to Mrs. Navarro in the picture as you repeat. Say: *Then write.* Point to where *watering* has been written in the chart. Make sure Ss understand the task.

- ▶ **CD2, Track 40** Play or read the complete audio. Ss listen and repeat. Encourage Ss to point to the people in the picture as they repeat.

- Ss complete the chart individually using words from Exercises 1 and 2A. Repeat the audio as needed.

- Check answers with the class. Write the numbers *2–6* on the board and ask volunteers to write their answers on the board. Point to each answer and ask the class: *Is this correct?* Make any necessary corrections.

- Read aloud the second part of the instructions for Exercise 2B. Point to and model the example conversation.

- Call on a pair of volunteers to read aloud the example conversation for the class. Then ask the same Ss to make up a new conversation about another person in the Navarro family. Indicate that Ss should ask and answer questions about all the people in the family.

- Ss complete the exercise in pairs, first asking and then answering. Remind Ss to switch roles. Walk around and help as needed.

### Literacy Tip

For an alternative activity, refer literacy Ss to pages 104–105 in the *Literacy Workbook* at any time during the lesson.

## APPLICATION

- Direct Ss' attention to Exercise 3 and read the instructions aloud.

- Model the task. Act out taking out the trash. Ask: *What am I doing?* Elicit: *taking out the trash.*

- Ss complete the exercise in pairs. Have Ss act out as many chores as they can in the time allotted.

- Ask several pairs to act out the chores for the rest of the class. Encourage Ss to act out the chores learned in both Lessons A and B of this unit.

### Expansion activity *(whole group)*

- Competition. Divide the class into two teams. Ask one S from each team to come to the board. Say: *I will start saying a chore. You have to finish it by writing on the board.* Model the activity. Ask a S to come to the board. Say: *Watering _____.* The S has to write *the grass* on the board. If the S doesn't understand the prompt, model the game by writing *the grass* on the board for the S. Say: *The chore is "watering the grass."*

- Start the game. Use all the chores in Lessons A, B, and C. Use the following as prompts:
  *cutting _____* (the grass)
  *walking _____* (the dog)
  *washing _____* (the dishes or the car)
  *doing _____* (homework or the laundry)
  *making _____* (lunch or the bed)
  *taking out _____* (the trash)
  *watering _____* (the grass)
  *drying _____* (the dishes)
  *getting _____* (the mail)

- The first S who completes the phrase correctly earns a point. The team with the most points wins.

## EVALUATION

- Direct Ss' attention to the lesson focus on the board. Check Ss' understanding of the key vocabulary by asking them to point to the outdoor chores in the pictures in Exercise 2B on page 113: *cutting the grass, getting the mail, taking out the trash, walking the dog, washing the car,* and *watering the grass.* Walk around and check that Ss are pointing to the correct items.

- Check off the lesson focus as Ss demonstrate an understanding of what they have learned in the lesson.

| More Ventures, Unit 9, Lesson B | |
|---|---|
| Literacy Workbook, 15–30 min. | |
| Basic Workbook, 15–30 min. | |
| Writing Worksheets, 15–30 min. | www.cambridge.org/ventures/resources/ |
| Collaborative Worksheets, 30–45 min. | |
| Student Arcade, time varies | www.cambridge.org/venturesarcade/ |

**B** **Listen and repeat.** Then write.

CD2, Track 40

| Name | Chore | |
|---|---|---|
| 1. Mrs. Navarro | _watering_ the grass | |
| 2. Mr. Navarro | _cutting_ the grass | |
| 3. Roberto | _washing_ the car | |
| 4. Diego | _taking_ _out_ the trash | |
| 5. Norma | _getting_ the mail | |
| 6. Rita | _walking_ the dog | |

**Talk with a partner.** Ask and answer.

A What is **Mrs. Navarro** doing?

B **Watering the grass.**

**3** **Communicate**

**Talk with a partner.** Act and guess.

Watering the grass?

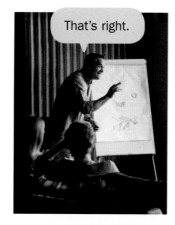

That's right.

# Lesson C What are they doing?

## 1 Grammar focus: questions with *What*

| QUESTIONS | | | | ANSWERS |
|---|---|---|---|---|
| | Is | he | | Cutting the grass. |
| What | is | she | doing? | Walking the dog. |
| | are | they | | Washing the dishes. |

Watch

## 2 Practice

**A Read and circle.** Then write.

1. A What _____are_____ they doing?
      is (are)
   B Making dinner.

   A What _____is_____ he doing?
      (is) are
   B Washing the dishes.

2. A What _____are_____ they doing?
      is (are)
   B Making the bed.

   A What _____is_____ he doing?
      (is) are
   B Taking out the trash.

3. A What _____is_____ he doing?
      (is)  are
   B Washing the car.

   A What _____is_____ she doing?
      (is) are
   B Watering the grass.

**Listen and repeat.** Then practice with a partner.

CD2, Track 41

Teaching objectives
- Provide practice of the present continuous tense
- Introduce questions with *What*

## WARM-UP AND REVIEW

- Before class. Write today's lesson focus on the board.
  *Lesson C:*
  *What is he doing?*
  *What is she doing?*
  *What are they doing?*

- Begin class. Direct Ss' attention to the picture on page 110. Ask Ss to review the names of the activities in the picture. Model the task. Hold up the Student's Book. Point to the mother. Say: *She is making lunch.*

- Ss continue the exercise in pairs. One S should point, and the other names the activity. Walk around and help as needed.

- Continue by reviewing the activities in the pictures in Exercises 1 and 2A on page 112. This time the second S points, and the first S names the activity.

## PRESENTATION

- Use the animated grammar presentation in one or more of the following ways:
  - Preview it before class
  - Show it in class
  - Encourage Ss to watch it outside of class.

- Books open. Direct Ss' attention to the grammar chart in Exercise 1. Read the questions and the corresponding answers aloud. Ask Ss to repeat after you.

### Teaching Tip

It might be helpful to review the verb *to be*. Write *I, you, he, she, it, we, you,* and *they* on the board in list form. Ask Ss for the correct forms of the verb *to be* (*I am, you are, he is, she is, it is, we are, you are, they are*).

### *Expansion activity* (student pairs)

- Focus Ss' attention on the picture in Exercise 2B on page 113. Point to the questions in the lesson focus. Point to people in the picture and say: *Ask your partner the questions on the board.*

- Ss complete the exercise in pairs. Walk around and help as needed.

- Ask several pairs to ask and answer the questions for the rest of the class.

## PRACTICE

- Read aloud the instructions for Exercise 2A. Model the task. Read aloud the example conversation in number 1. When you read Speaker A's first line, show Ss the two answer choices under the blank and ask: *is* or *are*? Elicit *are*.

- Point to where *are* has been circled and written for number 1. Say: *Circle the correct answer. Then write it in the blank.*

- Ss complete the exercise individually. Walk around and help as needed.

## COMPREHENSION CHECK

- Read aloud the second part of the instructions for Exercise 2A.

- ▶ **CD2, Track 41** Play or read the audio (see audio script, page T-151). Ss listen and repeat as they check their answers.

- Write the numbers *1–3* on the board. Ask volunteers to come to the board and write the answers they circled. Tell Ss to write two answers for each number. Remind Ss to write only the words they circled, not the complete sentences. Make any necessary corrections on the board.

- Ss in pairs. Ask Ss to choose Role A or B and practice the questions and answers in Exercise 2A. Then have Ss switch roles and practice again. Walk around and help as needed.

- Ask several pairs to read the conversations to the rest of the class.

### *Expansion activity* (student pairs)

- Focus Ss' attention on Exercise 2B on page 111. Say: *Look at the pictures. Ask your partner questions.*

- Point to the lesson focus questions on the board. Tell Ss to use these questions as a guide to talk about the pictures.

# LESSON C What are they doing?

## PRESENTATION

- Books open. Direct Ss' attention to the word bank in Exercise 2B. Say the words aloud. Ask Ss to repeat them after you.
- Focus Ss' attention on the pictures in Exercise 2B. Ask: *What do you see?* Elicit: *People doing chores.*
- Read the instructions aloud.

## PRACTICE

- ▶ *CD2, Track 42* Model the task. Say: *Listen and repeat.* Play or read the audio for number 1 (see audio script, page T-151) and point to the people in picture number 1 as you repeat. Say: *Then write.* Point to where the word *getting* has been written in number 1. Make sure Ss understand the task.
- ▶ *CD2, Track 42* Play or read the complete audio. Ss listen and repeat. Encourage Ss to point to the people in the pictures as they repeat.
- Ss work individually as they fill in the blanks. Repeat the audio as needed.
- Write the numbers 2–6 on the board. Ask volunteers to come to the board and write the answers for each number. Ask: *Are these words correct?* Ask other Ss to make corrections if needed.
- Read aloud the second part of the instructions for Exercise 2B. Model the task. Ask two pairs of Ss to read aloud the example conversations. Point to numbers 1 and 2 as they are reading.
- Indicate that Ss should ask and answer questions about all the pictures. Make sure Ss understand the task.
- Ss ask and answer questions about the pictures in pairs. Walk around and help as needed.
- When Ss are finished, ask them to switch partners and repeat the conversations.
- Ask several pairs to say their conversations to the rest of the class.

## APPLICATION

- Direct Ss' attention to Exercise 3 and read the instructions aloud.
- Model the task. Draw on the board two stick figures, each with a dish towel and dish. Point to the stick figures. Ask: *What are they doing?* (Drying the dishes.) Make sure Ss understand the task.
- Ss complete the exercise in pairs. Walk around and help as needed.

- Ask several volunteers to come to the board and draw one of the chores from Lessons A, B, or C. Encourage the other Ss to guess what the S is drawing.

### Literacy Tip

For an alternative activity, refer literacy Ss to pages 106–107 in the *Literacy Workbook* at any time during the lesson.

### *Expansion activity* (student pairs)

- Ss in pairs. Bring enough magazines to class for each pair of Ss to share. Tell Ss to look through the magazines for pictures of people doing something. Point to the lesson focus on the board: *What is he doing? What is she doing? What are they doing?*
- Tell Ss to ask their partners the questions on the board about the magazine pictures. Their partners will answer the questions. Then encourage them to switch roles.
- Walk around and listen to Ss' questions and answers. Help as needed.
- Ask several pairs to hold up their magazine pictures and ask and answer questions about them for the class.

### *Community building* (whole class)

- Before class. Ask Ss to bring in a photo of themselves or a friend or family member doing something. There can be other people in the picture, such as friends or family members. Ask volunteers to show the pictures to the rest of the class and name everyone in the picture. The other Ss will ask: *What are you doing in the picture? What is (name) doing?* This exercise helps Ss practice talking about their friends and family members.

## EVALUATION

- Direct Ss' attention to the lesson focus on the board. Ask Ss to look at the pictures on pages 110 and 114. Ask them to make questions about the chores in the pictures using the questions in the lesson focus on the board. Ask different Ss to answer the questions.
- Check off the lesson focus as Ss demonstrate an understanding of what they have learned in the lesson.

| More Ventures, Unit 9, Lesson C | |
|---|---|
| Literacy Workbook, 15–30 min. | |
| Basic Workbook, 15–30 min. | |
| Writing Worksheets, 15–30 min.<br>Collaborative Worksheets, 30–45 min. | www.cambridge.org/ventures/resources/ |
| Student Arcade, time varies | www.cambridge.org/venturesarcade/ |

B **Listen and repeat.** Then write.

| cutting | doing | drying | getting | making | taking |

CD2, Track 42

1. _**Getting**_ the mail.

2. _**Making**_ lunch.

3. _**Cutting**_ the grass.

4. _**Doing**_ the laundry.

5. _**Drying**_ the dishes.

6. _**Taking**_ out the trash.

**Talk with a partner.** Ask and answer.

A  What **are they** doing?
B  **Getting the mail.**

A  What **is he** doing?
B  **Making lunch.**

3 # Communicate

**Talk with a partner.** Make a picture. Ask and guess.

What are they doing?

Drying the dishes.

Ask and answer questions with *What* (*What is she doing?*)  UNIT 9  **115**

# Lesson D Reading

## 1 Before you read

**Talk about the picture.**
What do you see?

## 2 Read

**Listen and read.**

CD2, Track 43

> ● ● ●                                    Reply      Forward
>
> From:     Huan
> To:       Susie
> Subject:  Help
>
> Dear Susie,
>
> It's after dinner. My family is working in the kitchen. My daughter Li is washing the dishes. My daughter Mei is drying the dishes. My husband and Tao are taking out the trash. Where is my oldest son? He isn't in the kitchen. He is sleeping in the living room! I am not happy.
>
> I need help. What can I do?
>
> Huan

## 3 After you read

**Read and match.**

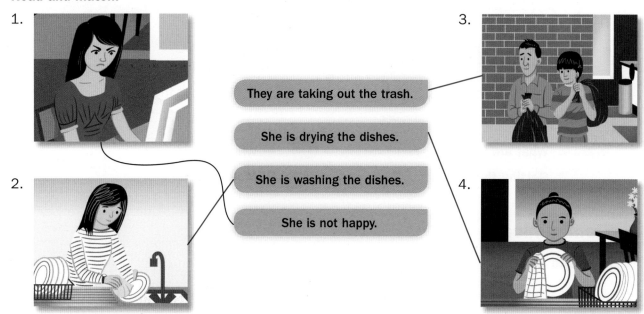

1.

They are taking out the trash.

She is drying the dishes.

She is washing the dishes.

She is not happy.

2.

3.

4.

Teaching objectives
● Introduce an email about chores
● Provide practice using new topic-related words

# WARM-UP AND REVIEW

● Before class. Write today's lesson focus on the board.
*Lesson D:*
*Read an email about chores*
*Learn vocabulary about rooms in the house*
● Begin class. Books open. Hold up the Student's Book to the picture on page 110. Ask: *Remember this family? What are they doing in this picture?* (Chores.) Or elicit the specific names of the chores the family is doing. Say: *Now we will see another picture of this family.*

# PRESENTATION

● Direct Ss' attention to the picture in Exercise **1**. Read the instructions aloud. Ask: *What do you see?* Elicit: *teenage son, mother, house.*
● Ask: *Is the mother happy?* If Ss don't know what this word means, draw a happy face on the board to illustrate the meaning. Elicit: *No, she's not.*

### Teaching Tip

If appropriate for your class, teach Ss the word *angry*. Point to the picture of Huan in Exercise **1**. Say: *She is angry.* Make your face angry or draw an angry face on the board to illustrate the meaning of the word. Write the word on the board. Ask Ss to repeat it after you.

# PRACTICE

● Direct Ss' attention to the email under the picture. Ask: *What's this?* (An email.) Ask: *Who is the email to?* (Susie.)

### Culture Tip

Explain that Susie is an advice columnist and that people in the United States sometimes write letters or emails to advice columnists asking for help with their problems. Ask Ss if they know about these columnists. If possible, bring an example of an advice column in your local newspaper to class. Show Ss the letters. Ask Ss if they have advice columns in newspapers in their countries.

● Say: *Now we will read an email to Susie from Huan. It's about family chores.* Direct Ss' attention to Exercise **2**. Read the instructions aloud.
● ▶ **CD2, Track 43** Play or read the audio and ask Ss to follow along (see audio script, page T-151). Repeat the audio as needed.
● Read aloud each sentence of the email and ask Ss to repeat after you. Answer any questions Ss have about new words in the reading.

### Learner persistence *(individual work)*

● ▶ **CD2, Track 43** Ss can listen to the audio for Exercise **2** at home for reinforcement and review. They can also listen to the audio for self-directed learning when class attendance is not possible.

### Expansion Activity *(individual work)*

● Tell Ss that they are going to write an email to a friend, similar to the one to Susie in Exercise **2** but without a problem. Say: *Write an email to a friend.*
*Tell your friend what you and your classmates and your teacher are doing in English class.*
● Walk around the room and make sure that Ss are using the salutation "Dear _____."
● When Ss are finished, ask a few of them to read their emails to the rest of the class.

# COMPREHENSION CHECK

● Direct Ss' attention to Exercise **3** and read the instructions aloud.
● Hold up the Student's Book. Direct Ss' attention to the first picture. Ask: *Is Huan happy?* (No.) Point to the line matching the first picture to the last sentence. Say: *She is not happy. Draw a line to match the picture with the correct sentence.*
● Ss complete the exercise individually. Walk around and help as needed.
● Ask individual Ss to read each sentence aloud and say which picture matches it.
● After each sentence, ask: *Is that correct?* Ask different Ss to make corrections if needed.

# LESSON D Reading

## PRESENTATION

- Books closed. Write the phrase *rooms of a house* on the board. Point to the words. Say them aloud. Ask Ss to repeat them after you.
- Draw on the board a simple floor plan for a house. Tell Ss that it is a house with rooms. Ask Ss: *Do you know the names of the rooms in a house?* If Ss know the names, write their responses in the spaces that represent rooms on the board.
- Books open. Direct Ss' attention to the Picture dictionary in Exercise 4. Hold up the Student's Book. Point to the pictures of individual rooms. Say: *These are different rooms in a house.* Say the words aloud. Ask Ss to repeat them after you.
- Read the instructions for Exercise 4A aloud.
- ▶ **CD2, Track 44** Play or read the audio (see audio script, page T-151). Listen to Ss' pronunciation as they repeat the names of rooms in a house. Correct pronunciation as needed.

### Learner persistence *(individual work)*

- ▶ **CD2, Track 44** Ss can listen to the audio for Exercise 4A at home for reinforcement and review. They can also listen to the audio for self-directed learning when class attendance is not possible.

### Expansion activity *(small groups)*

- Copy and cut out the Picture dictionary cards that correspond to this unit. You will need one set for each group of four or five Ss. Make the sets with pictures on one side of the cards and the names of the rooms on the other side.
- Ss in small groups. Have Ss show each other the pictures on the flash cards and say the names of the rooms in the pictures.
- Ss complete the exercise in small groups. Walk around and help as needed.

## PRACTICE

- Direct Ss' attention to Exercise 4B. Read the instructions aloud. Model the conversation. Ask two Ss to read the conversation aloud and point to the kitchen in the picture as they read. Then ask them to change the conversation to ask about a different room. Make sure Ss understand the task.
- Ss complete the exercise in pairs, asking and answering questions about the rooms in the house. Walk around and help as needed.
- Ask several pairs to ask and answer the questions for the rest of the class.

### Literacy Tip

For an alternative activity, refer literacy Ss to pages 108–109 in the *Literacy Workbook* at any time during the lesson.

### Expansion activity *(individual work)*

- Ask Ss to draw a floor plan of their house or apartment. Model the activity. Draw a simple outline of your house or apartment on the board. Label each room with the appropriate name.
- Give each S a large blank piece of paper. Say: *You can draw your real house or an imaginary house. The house can be big or small.*
- When Ss are finished, ask several volunteers to show their floor plans to the rest of the class. Encourage them to point to each room and say: *This is the living room. This is the bedroom.*

  **Option** Put Ss in pairs. Ask them to describe their house floor plans to each other.

## EVALUATION

- Direct Ss' attention to the first part of the lesson focus on the board. Turn Ss' attention to the email on page 116. Call on several Ss to ask and answer questions about the reading.
- Direct Ss' attention to the rooms in the Picture dictionary. Say: *Please name the rooms in the house.* Ask different Ss to say the names of the rooms as you point to them.

  **Option** Show Ss the Picture dictionary cards. Ask them to identify the different rooms in the house as you show them each card in turn.

- Check off each part of the lesson focus as Ss demonstrate understanding of what they have learned in the lesson.

| More Ventures, Unit 9, Lesson D | |
|---|---|
| Literacy Workbook, 15–30 min. | |
| Basic Workbook, 15–30 min. | |
| Picture Dictionary activities, 30–45 min. Writing Worksheets, 15–30 min. Collaborative Worksheets, 30–45 min. | www.cambridge.org/ventures/resources/ |
| Student Arcade, time varies | www.cambridge.org/venturesarcade/ |

**4** **Picture dictionary** Rooms of a house

1. bathroom

2. bedroom

3. living room

4. laundry room

5. kitchen

6. dining room

**A** **Listen and repeat.** Look at the Picture dictionary.

**B** **Talk with a partner.** Point to a room and ask. Your partner answers.

   A What room is this?

   B **The kitchen.**

◀) CD2, Track 44

# Lesson E Writing

## 1 Before you write

**A** **Talk with a partner.** Complete the words.

1. d _o_ i _n_ _g_    the    l aun _d_ r _y_
2. m _a_ k _i_ ng    the    _b_ e _d_ s
3. w _a_ l _k_ ing    the    _d_ o _g_
4. c _u_ tt _i_ ng    the    _g_ ra _s_ s
5. w _a_ s _h_ ing    the    _d_ is _h_ es
6. t _a_ king    out    the    _t_ ras _h_

**B** **Talk with a partner.** Read the chart. Complete the sentences.

### Walker Family's Weekend Chores

| Chore | Dad | Mom | Max | Iris | Charlie |
|---|---|---|---|---|---|
| Do the laundry. | | ✔ | | ✔ | |
| Take out the trash. | | | | | ✔ |
| Wash the dishes. | | | ✔ | | |
| Cut the grass. | ✔ | | | | |
| Make the beds. | | ✔ | | | |
| Walk the dog. | | | ✔ | | ✔ |

It is the weekend. We are doing chores.

1. Charlie is ___taking___ ___out___ ___the___ ___trash___ .

2. Mom and Iris are ___doing___ ___the___ ___laundry___ .

3. Dad is ___cutting___ ___the___ ___grass___ .

4. Max is ___washing___ ___the___ ___dishes___ .

5. Mom is ___making___ ___the___ ___beds___ .

6. Charlie and Max are ___walking___ ___the___ ___dog___ .

Teaching objectives
- Prepare Ss for writing a chore chart
- Provide practice writing key vocabulary words

# WARM-UP AND REVIEW

- Before class. Write today's lesson focus on the board.
  *Lesson E:*
  *Write about chores*
  *Write a chore chart*
- Begin class. Books closed. Write *chores* on the board. Ask: *What are some chores that we learned about in this unit?* Elicit the names of chores from previous lessons in this unit.
- Ask: *What chores do you like?* Elicit an appropriate response, such as: *walking the dog.*
- Ask: *What chores don't you like?* Elicit an appropriate response, such as: *doing the laundry.*

# PRESENTATION

- Read the instructions aloud. Model the activity.
- Point to the first item and say: *Number 1. What's the chore?* (Doing the laundry.) Ask: *What letters do we need?* (o, n, g, l, d, and y) Point to where the letters are written in the blanks. Say: *Now you complete the rest of the words.*

## Teaching Tip

It might be helpful to write on the board questions and answers that will help Ss as they work with a partner, such as: *What chore is this? Do you think this is right?*

- Ss work in pairs to complete the words. Encourage Ss to figure out the chores together.
- When Ss are finished, call on different pairs to write their completed words on the board. Review the alphabet by asking Ss who write answers on the board to say the letters aloud.
- Go over the answers with the class. Ask: *Are these words spelled correctly?* Ask different Ss to make corrections as needed.

## Teaching Tip

This is a good opportunity to review the names of the letters in English. Ask the Ss who write the answers on the board to say the names of the missing letters for the class. Make corrections if needed.

- Focus Ss' attention on the chart in Exercise **1B**. Ask: *What do you see?* Elicit as much vocabulary about the chart as possible and write the words on the board: *Weekend chores, Walker family, Dad, Mom,* etc.
- Read the instructions aloud. Hold up the Student's Book. Point to the chart. Say: *This is a chart. It tells who does the chores on the weekend.* Ask: *What days are the weekend?* (Saturday and Sunday.)

## Culture Tip

Explain that American families sometimes use charts to show different responsibilities in a family. Ask Ss if they use charts like this in their own homes.

- Ask questions about the chart. Hold up the Student's Book and point to the corresponding areas in the chart as you ask: *Who is in the Walker family?* (Dad, Mom, Max, Iris, and Charlie.) Say: *It's the weekend. Who is doing the laundry?* (Mom.) *Who is taking out the trash?* (Charlie.)
- Model the exercise. Focus Ss' attention on the sentences below the chart. Ask a S to read aloud the first two sentences. Ask: *What is Charlie doing?* (Taking out the trash.) Point to the words written in the blanks.
- Say: *Now you complete the sentences. Use the information in the chart and the phrases in Exercise* **1A**.
- Ss complete the exercise in pairs. Walk around and help as needed.

# COMPREHENSION CHECK

- Write the numbers *1–6* on the board. Ask individual Ss to write their answers on the board. Ask: *Is this answer correct?* Different Ss can correct the answers if needed.

## *Expansion activity* (student pairs)

- Direct Ss' attention to the sentences in Exercise **1B**. Say: *Now read your sentences to your partner. Then your partner will read his / her sentences to you.*
- Walk around and listen to Ss' pronunciation. Write any errors that you hear. When Ss are finished reading, write on the board any words that Ss are having difficulties with. Read the words aloud. Ask Ss to repeat. Correct their pronunciation if needed.

# LESSON E Writing

## PRESENTATION

- Ask: *What are your chores at home?* Elicit appropriate responses.
- Direct Ss' attention to Exercise **2A** and read the instructions aloud. Say: *You can write different people's names if you don't want to use your family's real names.*
- Model the task. Hold up the Student's Book. Point to the *name* category. Say: *Write the names here.* Point to the *chore* category. Say: *Write the chores here.*

## PRACTICE

- Ss complete the exercise individually. Walk around and help as needed.
- Ask several S volunteers to write their chore charts on the board. Ask questions to preview Exercise **2B**. Ask: *Who is (name of family member)? What is (name of person) doing?*
- Direct Ss' attention to Exercise **2B**. Say: *Now you are going to write about your family's chores.*
- Model the task. Point to one of the chore charts on the board. Make sentences about it, such as: *(Name of person) is (chore).*
- Ss complete the exercise individually. Walk around and help as needed.

### Literacy Tip

For an alternative activity, refer literacy Ss to pages 110–111 in the *Literacy Workbook* at any time during the lesson.

## APPLICATION

- Direct Ss' attention to Exercise **3**. Read the instructions aloud. Encourage Ss to read what they wrote in Exercise **2B** to their partners.
- Ss complete the task in pairs. Walk around and help as needed.
- Ask several Ss to read their sentences aloud for the whole class.

### Teaching Tip

This exercise asks Ss to work together to edit their writing. Encourage Ss to correct each other's writing if necessary. Say: *Help your partner with any mistakes. Then your partner will help you.*

### Expansion activity *(student pairs)*

- Student dictation. Ask Ss to write the numbers *1–5* in list form in their notebooks. Ask five Ss to volunteer to read the sentences to the class. Explain that the other Ss will listen and write the sentences in their notebooks.
- Ask the five Ss to come up one at a time and read the following sentences to the class:
  1. *Mom is doing the laundry.*
  2. *Dad is taking out the trash.*
  3. *Max is walking the dog.*
  4. *Sarah is cutting the grass.*
  5. *John is making the beds.*

### Teaching Tip

Each S should read the sentence more than once so Ss who are slower writers have the opportunity to complete the exercise.

- Write the numbers *1–5* on the board. Ask different Ss to write the dictated sentences on the board. Read each sentence aloud. Ask: *Is it correct?* Have different Ss make corrections if needed.

## EVALUATION

- Direct Ss' attention to the lesson focus on the board.
- Draw a chore chart on the board. Include names on the chart. Ask different Ss to come to the board and write chores on it. Check off chores for each name on your chart.
- Ask Ss questions about the chart, for example: *What is (name) doing?* Make sure Ss answer correctly.
- Check off each part of the lesson focus as Ss demonstrate understanding of what they have learned in the lesson.

| *More Ventures, Unit 9, Lesson E* | |
|---|---|
| **Literacy Workbook**, 15–30 min. | |
| **Basic Workbook**, 15–30 min. | |
| **Writing Worksheets**, 15–30 min. **Collaborative Worksheets**, 30–45 min. | www.cambridge.org/ventures/resources/ |

## 2 Write

A **Complete the chart.** Write the weekend chores at your house. Write your family's names. Check (✓) the names.

# My Family's Weekend Chores

| Chore | Answers | will vary. | | |
|---|---|---|---|---|
| | | | | |
| | | | | |
| | | | | |
| | | | | |
| | | | | |

B **Write.** It is the weekend. Tell about your family's chores. Look at 1B for help.

It is the weekend. We are doing chores.

1. I am _Answers will vary_____.

2. _____ is _____.

3. _____ is _____.

4. _____ is _____.

5. _____ and _____ are _____.

## 3 After you write

**Talk with a partner.** Share your writing.

# Lesson F Another view

## 1 Life-skills reading

## Friendly Cleaning Service, Inc.
### We do your chores with a smile!  Madison, WI 53714

| Work Order for:<br>1812 Franklin Street<br><br>Madison, WI 53714<br><br>**Date:**<br>Monday, August 27 | Name | Chore |
|---|---|---|
| | Alma | dishes |
| | Kay | beds |
| | Ramiro | grass |
| | Binh | laundry |

### Questions or Problems? Call Elena Sanchez at 555-1234.

**A** **Read the sentences.** Look at the work order. Fill in the answer.

1. What is Alma's chore?
   - Ⓐ cutting the grass
   - ⬤Ⓑ washing the dishes
   - Ⓒ making the beds

2. What is Kay's chore?
   - ⬤Ⓐ making the beds
   - Ⓑ doing the laundry
   - Ⓒ washing the dishes

3. What is Ramiro's chore?
   - Ⓐ doing the laundry
   - Ⓑ taking out the trash
   - ⬤Ⓒ cutting the grass

4. What is Binh's chore?
   - ⬤Ⓐ doing the laundry
   - Ⓑ cutting the grass
   - Ⓒ taking out the trash

**B** **Solve the problem.** Which solution is best? Circle your opinion.

Alma is sick. What should she do?

1. Call Elena.
2. Go to work sick.
3. Other: *Answers will vary.*

- Introduce reading a work order
- Provide practice that develops test-taking skills
- Review vocabulary from the unit

## WARM-UP AND REVIEW

- Before class. Write today's lesson focus on the board.
  *Lesson F:*
  *Read and answer questions about a work order*
  *Review vocabulary about chores*
  *Complete the Self-assessment*

- Begin class. Books closed. Write *cleaning service* on the board. Point to the words. Say them aloud. Ask Ss to repeat them after you. Say: *This is a company that cleans for people who can't or don't want to clean the house or the office themselves.*

- Ask: *What are some chores that cleaning companies do?* Elicit: *cleaning the house or office, taking out the trash, making the beds, doing the laundry, doing the dishes.*

## PRESENTATION

- Books open. Write on the board: *work order.* Point to the words. Say them aloud and ask Ss to repeat. Ask: *What is this?* If Ss don't know, direct their attention to the example of a work order in Exercise 1. Say: *This is a work order for Friendly Cleaning Service, Inc. This shows the work the cleaning company will do on Monday, August 27.*

- Hold up the Student's Book. Point to the work order. Ask: *Where is the Friendly Cleaning Service?* (Madison, Wisconsin.) Ask: *What address is the work order for?* (1812 Franklin Street, Madison, WI 53714.) Ask: *How many people are working at this house?* (Four.) *Who are the workers on the work order?* (Alma, Kay, Ramiro, and Binh.)

## PRACTICE

- Read aloud the instructions in Exercise 1A. This task helps prepare Ss for standardized-type tests they may have to take.

- Write the first item on the board along with the three answer choices labeled *A, B,* and *C.*

- Read the item and the answer choices aloud and then point to the work order. Ask Ss: *What is Alma's chore?* Show Ss where to look for the information. Elicit: *washing the dishes.*

- Point to the three answer choices on the board. Ask Ss: *A, B, or C?* (B) Fill in the letter *b* and tell Ss: *Fill in "B."* Make sure Ss understand the task.

- Have Ss individually scan for and fill in the answers.

## COMPREHENSION CHECK

- Go over the answers to Exercise 1A with the class. Make sure that Ss followed the directions and filled in their answers. Ask Ss to point to the information in the work order.

## APPLICATION

- Read aloud the instructions for Exercise 1B.
- Tell Ss they will discuss what Alma should do.
- Ss complete the task in pairs.
- Ask several pairs to ask and answer the question for the rest of the class.

### *Expansion activity* (small groups)

- Ask Ss to form groups of four or five Ss. Say: *Imagine that you are a cleaning service. Each of you has a job. Make a work order for your company for today.*

- Remind Ss to use the work order in Exercise 1 as a guide. Encourage Ss to think of an interesting name for their company and to change the date and address on their work orders. They should have a chore listed for each member of the group.

- Ask several groups to come to the front of the class and write their work orders on the board. Ask one of the group members to describe the work order to the rest of the class. For example: *We are the (name of cleaning service). This is a work order for today (date). This work order is for (address). Our group is doing these chores: (names of each person and that person's chore).*

# LESSON F Another view

## PRACTICE

- Direct Ss' attention to Exercise 2A. Read the instructions aloud.
- Focus Ss' attention on the word bank. Say: *Use these words to complete the chores in the chart.*
- Model the exercise. Hold up the Student's Book. Point to the column with *make* as the heading. Ask: *What chores begin with "make"?* (Make the bed, make lunch.) Point out that there are two extra blanks, one under *wash* and one under *do*. See if Ss can come up with two more chores. (Do the dishes, wash the dog.)
- Ss complete the exercise individually. Walk around and help as needed.
- Write the words *cut, wash, do, make,* and *dry* in list form on the board. Ask individual Ss to write their answers on the board in the correct column.
- Ask different Ss to read the answers aloud. Ask: *Are these answers correct?* Have different Ss correct the answers if needed.

### Expansion activity *(individual work)*

- Make copies of the following chart for each S in the class.
  **Option** Draw the chart on the board and ask Ss to copy it into their notebooks.

| Name | | | | |
|---|---|---|---|---|
| What chores do you do every day? | | | | |

- Tell Ss they need to talk to four Ss in the class. They will write the names of the Ss in the first row of their chart and the answers to the question in the second row of the chart.
- Model the activity. Draw the chart on the board. Ask a S: *What chores do you do every day?* Elicit chores such as: *I wash the dishes. I make lunch.* Write the S's name in the first row and his or her answers in the second row.
- Ss complete the exercise individually. Walk around and help as needed.
- Direct Ss' attention to the puzzle in Exercise 2B. Read the instructions aloud. Ask Ss: *What are some "-ing" words?* Write Ss' examples on the board, such as: *writing, doing, making.*
- Model the exercise. Hold up the Student's Book. Show Ss where *walking* has been circled in the puzzle. Tell Ss that all the words can be found horizontally. Draw a line on the board to show what *horizontally* means.

- Ss complete the activity individually. Walk around and help as needed.
- Ask seven Ss to write the words they found on the board. Ask different Ss to read the words aloud. Make sure the words on the board are spelled correctly. Make corrections if needed.

  **Option** Ask Ss to make sentences with the words they found in the word search.

### Literacy Tip

For an alternative activity, refer literacy Ss to pages 112–113 in the *Literacy Workbook* at any time during the lesson.

## EVALUATION

- Do a quick review of the unit. Have Ss turn to Lesson A. Ask the class to talk about what they remember about this lesson. If necessary, prompt Ss with questions, such as: *What words are on this page? What do you see in the picture?* Continue in this manner to review each lesson quickly.

### Expansion activity

- Before class. Print, for each student, one copy of the Self-assessment for this unit.
- Have Ss complete the Self-assessment either in class or outside of class.
- Provide feedback to Ss such as through a whole-class discussion, partners comparing their worksheets, or T reviewing each S's worksheet.
- If Ss are ready, administer the unit test on page T-182 of this Teacher's Edition. The audio script for the test is available on page T-193.

### More Ventures, Unit 9, Lesson F

| | |
|---|---|
| **Literacy Workbook,** 15–30 min. | |
| **Basic Workbook,** 15–30 min. | |
| **Writing Worksheets,** 15–30 min. **Real-life Document,** 15–30 min. **Collaborative Worksheets,** 30–45 min. **Self-assessment,** 10 min. **CASAS Test Prep Worksheet,** 5–10 min. | www.cambridge.org/ventures/resources/ |

## **2** Fun with vocabulary

A **Talk with a partner.** Complete the chart.

> the bed     the car     the dishes     the dog     the grass
> homework     the laundry     lunch     mail

| cut | wash | do | make | get |
|---|---|---|---|---|
| the grass | the car | homework | the bed | the mail |
| | the dishes | the dishes | lunch | |
| | the dog | the laundry | | |

B Circle eight **-ing** words in the puzzle.

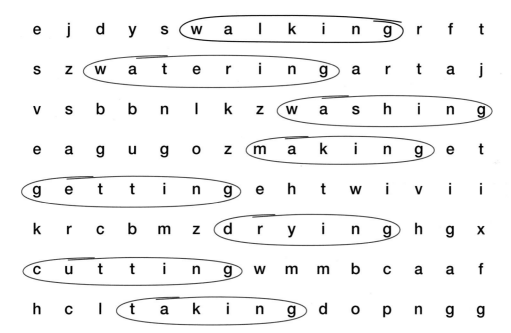

# UNIT 10 FREE TIME

## Lesson A Listening

### 1 Before you listen

A Look at the picture. What do you see?

B Listen and point: ■ dance ■ exercise ■ fish ■ play basketball
■ play cards ■ swim

CD2, Track 45

# UNIT 10

## Teaching objectives
- Introduce Ss to the topic
- Find out what Ss know about the topic
- Preview the unit by talking about the picture
- Provide practice of key vocabulary
- Provide practice that develops listening skills

## WARM-UP AND REVIEW

- Before class. Write today's lesson focus on the board.
  *Lesson A:*
  *Vocabulary for free-time activities*
- Begin class. Books closed. Point to the words *free-time activities* on the board. Read them aloud and ask Ss to repeat after you. Explain that free-time activities are what you do in your extra time. Say: *Free time is when you don't work or go to school.* Ask: *When do you have free time?* Elicit appropriate responses, such as: *Saturday, Sunday, the weekend.* Ask: *What do you do in your free time?* Elicit appropriate responses.

### Teaching Tip

If Ss still don't understand the words *free time*, show them a calendar. Point to the days you work. Say: *I work on these days.* Point to your days off. Say: *I don't work on these days. I have free time.*

### Literacy Tip

If you have literacy Ss in your class, it might be helpful to spend time at the beginning of any activity that contains art or photos talking about the pictures before focusing Ss' attention on the printed words in the exercise. Have Ss work in pairs. Tell them to ask each other: *What do you see?* Encourage Ss to describe the pictures to each other. Consider pairing literacy Ss with Ss who can help them read the text in the exercise. This will help preview the exercise for literacy Ss and make them more confident as the exercise continues.

## PRESENTATION

- Books open. Set the scene. Show Ss the picture on page 122. Ask: *What do you see?* Elicit and write on the board any vocabulary that Ss know, such as: *park, people, boys, basketball, music.*
- Hold up the Student's Book. Point to each labeled person in turn. Ask: *What is his / her name?* Elicit the appropriate responses.

## PRACTICE

- Direct Ss' attention to the key vocabulary in Exercise **1B**. Hold up the Student's Book. Read each word aloud while pointing to the corresponding activity in the picture. Ask Ss to repeat and point.
- ▶ *CD2, Track 45* Play or read the audio (see audio script, page T-151). Tell Ss: *Listen and point to the picture.* As Ss hear the key vocabulary, check to see that they are pointing to the people doing the activity. Repeat the audio as needed.

## COMPREHENSION CHECK

- Ask Ss *Yes / No* questions about the picture. Tell Ss: *Listen. Say "yes" or "no."*

  Point to the picture. Ask: *Is this a park?* (Yes.)

  Point to the two teenage boys. Ask: *Are they playing baseball?* (No.)

  Point to the people dancing. Ask: *Are they dancing?* (Yes.)

  Point to the man fishing. Ask: *Is he fishing?* (Yes.)

  Point to the people swimming. Ask: *Are they fishing?* (No.)

  Point to the people playing cards. Ask: *Are they playing cards?* (Yes.)

  Point to the woman running. Ask: *Is she walking?* (No.)

### Expansion activity *(student pairs)*

- Write on the board:
  *What is he doing? He is _____.*
  *What is she doing? She is _____.*
  *What are they doing? They are _____.*
- Point to the questions and incomplete answers on the board. Say: *Ask your partner questions about the people in the picture.*
- Model the activity. Hold up the Student's Book. Point to the people playing cards. Ask a S: *What are they doing?* Elicit: *They are playing cards.*
- Ss complete the activity in pairs. Encourage Ss to ask about all the people in the picture. Then tell them to switch roles.
- Ask several pairs to ask and answer questions about different people in the picture for the rest of the class.

### Community building *(whole group)*

- Ask Ss to make a list of possible free-time activities in your local community. Write the activities on the board. Ss new to your city or town will appreciate learning about different activities to do in their free time.

# LESSON A Listening

## PRESENTATION

- Direct Ss' attention to Exercise 2A. Tell Ss: *We are going to practice saying these free-time activities.* Read the words aloud. Ask Ss to repeat them after you.
- Read aloud the instructions for Exercise 2A.

## PRACTICE

- ▶ *CD2, Track 46* Play or read the audio (see audio script, page T-151). Ss listen and repeat the vocabulary. Repeat the audio as needed.
- Listen carefully to Ss' pronunciation and make corrections as needed.

### Learner persistence *(individual work)*

- ▶ *CD2, Track 46* Ss can listen to the audio for Exercise 2A at home for reinforcement and review. They can also listen to the audio for self-directed learning when class attendance is not possible.

## PRACTICE

- Direct Ss' attention to Exercise 2B and read the instructions aloud.
- ▶ *CD2, Track 47* Model the task. Hold up the Student's Book and say: *Number one.* Play or read the audio for number 1 (see audio script, page T-151). Point to the two answer choices in number 1 and ask: *What did you hear – a or b?* Elicit: *a.* Point to the letter *a* next to the first picture and tell Ss: *Circle the letter "a."*
- ▶ *CD2, Track 47* Play or read the complete audio. Ss listen and circle the correct answers. Repeat the audio as needed.
- ▶ *CD2, Track 47* Read aloud the second part of the instructions for Exercise 2B. Play or read the audio again so that Ss can listen and check their answers.

### Learner persistence *(individual work)*

- ▶ *CD2, Track 47* Ss can listen to the audio for Exercise 2B at home for reinforcement and review. They can also listen to the audio for self-directed learning when class attendance is not possible.

## COMPREHENSION CHECK

- Write the numbers *1–4* on the board. Ask a few Ss to come to the board and write the correct answers to Exercise 2B next to each number.
- ▶ *CD2, Track 47* Play or read the audio again. Pause the audio after each conversation. Point to the answer written on the board and ask: *Is this correct?* If not, have a volunteer make any necessary corrections.

## APPLICATION

- Direct Ss' attention to Exercise 3 and read the instructions aloud.
- Model the task. Hold up the Student's Book and point to the pictures in Exercise 2B. Say to one S: *Point to a picture.* Say to the first S's partner: *Say the word.*
- Ss complete the exercise in pairs. Walk around and help as needed.

### Literacy Tip

For an alternative activity, refer literacy Ss to pages 114–115 in the *Literacy Workbook* at any time during the lesson.

### Community building *(whole class)*

- Draw a vertical line on the board, making two columns. Above the first column, write *free-time activity.* Above the second column, write *Where?*
- Ask volunteers to tell you the activities they learned in this lesson (*dance, exercise, fish, play basketball, play cards, swim*). Write them in list form in the first column.
- Point to the word *Where?* in the second column. Ask: *Where can you dance in (name of your city or town)?* Write Ss' answers in the second column. Write only the names of local places or draw a line to indicate that no place for dancing exists where Ss live.
- Continue by asking about the other activities. By talking about local places to socialize, Ss can learn more about their community.

## EVALUATION

- Direct Ss' attention to the lesson focus on the board and then to the picture on page 122. Check Ss' understanding of vocabulary for free-time activities by asking them to point to the activities that are listed at the top of the page. Walk around and check that Ss are pointing to the correct parts of the picture.
- Check off the lesson focus as Ss demonstrate an understanding of what they have learned in the lesson.

| More Ventures, Unit 10, Lesson A | |
|---|---|
| Literacy Workbook, 15–30 min. | |
| Basic Workbook, 15–30 min. | |
| Writing Worksheets, 15–30 min. | www.cambridge.org/ventures/ resources/ |
| Collaborative Worksheets, 30–45 min. | |
| Student Arcade, time varies | www.cambridge.org/venturesarcade/ |

UNIT GOALS
**Identify** free-time activities   **Describe** what people like to do
**Interpret** information on a class flyer

## 2 Listen

**A  Listen and repeat.**

1. dance
2. exercise
3. fish
4. play basketball
5. play cards
6. swim

 CD2, Track 46

**B  Listen and circle.**

 CD2, Track 47

1. (a.)    b.

2. a.    (b.)

3. (a.)    b.

4. a.    (b.)

**Listen again.** Check your answers.

## 3 After you listen

**Talk with a partner.** Point to a picture.
Your partner says the words.

# Lesson B Around the house

## 1 Vocabulary focus

**Listen and repeat.**

 CD2, Track 48

1. cook

2. play the guitar

3. listen to music

4. watch TV

5. read magazines

6. work in the garden

## 2 Practice

**A  Read and match.**

work in the garden          play the guitar          cook

1.          2.          3.

watch TV          listen to music          read magazines

## WARM-UP AND REVIEW

● Before class. Write today's lesson focus on the board.
*Lesson B:*
*More vocabulary about free-time activities*

● Begin class. Books open. Write on the board: *lake, basketball
court, home, party, gym, pool.* Point to each word in turn. Say
it aloud and ask Ss to repeat after you. Define any words if
needed. You can do this by drawing pictures on the board.

● Point to *free-time activities* in the lesson focus. Ask: *What
free-time activities did we learn about in the last lesson?* Elicit
and write on the board: *dance, exercise, fish, play basketball,
play cards, swim.*

● Ask: *What activity can you do at the lake?* (Fish, swim.)
Continue asking about the other places on the board.

● Ask Ss: *What other activities do you like to do in your free
time?* If Ss know the names of any other activities, write
them on the board. Ask Ss who say the words to convey
them with gestures. If Ss don't know any other names of
activities, say: *We will learn more in this lesson.*

> **Teaching Tip**
>
> If Ss need help remembering the vocabulary for free-time
> activities learned in Lesson A, hold up the Student's
> Book. Point to each activity on page 122 or 123 as you
> say the words.

## PRESENTATION

● Set the scene. Books open. Direct Ss' attention to the
picture in Exercise 1. Say: *These people are at home. It is
their free-time. They like doing these things.* Read aloud the
instructions.

▶ **CD2, Track 48** Play or read the audio (see audio script,
page T-151). Listen and repeat the vocabulary along with Ss.
Repeat the audio as needed.

● Listen carefully to Ss' pronunciation and correct as needed.

### Expansion activity *(student pairs)*

● Ask Ss to review the names of different rooms in a house.
Write the names of the rooms on the board: *bedroom,
kitchen, living room, bathroom, dining room, laundry room.*

● Direct Ss' attention to the picture in Exercise 1. Write on the
board:
*Where is the _____?*
*She / He is in the _____.*

● Ss in pairs. Say: *Ask your partner questions about the people
in Exercise 1.* Encourage Ss to use the question and answer
on the board as a guide. Model the task. Say: *Where is the
woman?* Elicit: *In the kitchen.*

● Ss complete the exercise in pairs. Walk around and help as
needed.

● Ask several pairs to ask and answer questions about each
person and where he / she is.

> **Teaching Tip**
>
> Ss may not know the meaning of the word *garden.* Point to
> picture 6 in Exercise 1. Tell Ss that the woman is working
> in the garden outside the house.

## PRACTICE

● Direct Ss' attention to Exercise 2A. Read the instructions
aloud.

● Focus Ss' attention on the first picture. Model the task. Ask:
*What are the activities in this picture?* Elicit: *play the guitar*
and *read magazines.* Hold up the Student's Book. Point to
the lines connecting the first picture to the phrases *play the
guitar* and *read magazines.* Say: *Match the pictures and the
words.*

● Ss complete the exercise individually. Help as needed.

> **Literacy Tip**
>
> For an alternative activity, refer literacy Ss to pages
> 116–117 in the *Literacy Workbook* at any time during
> the lesson.

## COMPREHENSION CHECK

● Ask volunteers to say a picture number, point to the picture,
and say the phrase that matches the picture.

● Write the number of the picture and the phrase that the
student says.

● Ask different Ss to read the answers written on the board.
After each phrase is read, ask: *Is this correct?* Ask another S
to make any corrections if needed.

# LESSON B Around the house

## PRESENTATION

- Direct Ss' attention to the pictures in Exercise 2B. Say: *These are pictures of free-time activities. What activities do you see?* Point to each activity in turn. Elicit: *watch TV, listen to music, play the guitar, cook, work in the garden, read magazines.* Point to each person and say the person's name. Ask Ss to repeat.

- Focus Ss' attention on the words in the word bank. Say aloud each word or phrase. Ask Ss to repeat them after you. Read the instructions for Exercise 2B aloud.

- ▶ **CD2, Track 49** Model the task. Say: *Listen and repeat.* Play or read the audio for number 1 (see audio script, page T-151) and point to Pablo in the picture as you repeat. Say: *Then write.* Point to where *watch TV* has been written in the "Activity" column of the chart. Make sure Ss understand the task.

- ▶ **CD2, Track 49** Play or read the complete audio. Ss listen and repeat. Encourage Ss to point to the people in the pictures as they repeat.

- Ss complete the charts individually using words from the word bank. Repeat the audio as needed.

- Check answers with the class. Draw the charts from Exercise 2B on the board. Ask five Ss to fill in the blanks in the charts.

- Point to each answer and ask the class: *Yes? Is this correct?* Ask other Ss to make any necessary corrections on the board.

- Read aloud the second part of the instructions for Exercise 2B. Point to and model the example conversation.

- Call on a pair of volunteers to read the example conversation aloud for the class. Then ask the same Ss to make up a new conversation about another person in the pictures in Exercise 2B. Indicate that Ss should ask and answer questions about all the people in the pictures.

- Ss complete the exercise in pairs. Walk around and help as needed.

### Literacy Tip

Be sure to give literacy Ss extra time to do Exercise 2B. Ask them to work with a partner. Literacy Ss should be able to do this exercise with extra time and help from a classmate.

### Expansion activity *(student pairs)*

- Before class. Prepare the following chart and give each S a copy.

| Name | | | | |
|-----------|---|---|---|---|
| morning | | | | |
| afternoon | | | | |
| evening | | | | |

- Write *Saturday* on the board. Point to the word. Say it aloud. Tell Ss to talk to four other Ss in the class. They will ask the questions in the chart about what other Ss do on Saturday morning, afternoon, and evening.

- Model the activity. Ask a S the questions. Hold up the chart. Write the S's answers in short form in the chart, for example: *clean the house, listen to music, watch TV.*

- Ss complete the exercise. Walk around and help as needed.

## APPLICATION

- Direct Ss' attention to Exercise 3 and read the instructions aloud. Direct Ss' attention to the picture. Tell them that one person in the picture is acting out an activity and the other S is guessing what it is.

- Model the task. Ask one S to read part A of the conversation with you. Pretend to play the electric guitar while you read the conversation.

- Ss complete the exercise in pairs. Walk around and help as needed.

- Ask several Ss to act out free-time activities learned in this unit for the rest of the class.

## EVALUATION

- Direct Ss' attention to the lesson focus on the board. Check Ss' understanding of the key vocabulary by asking them to point to the free-time activities in the pictures in Exercise 2B on page 125: *cook, listen to music, play the guitar, read magazines, watch TV,* and *work in the garden.* Walk around and check that Ss are pointing to the correct items.

- Check off the lesson focus as Ss demonstrate an understanding of what they have learned in the lesson.

| *More Ventures, Unit 10, Lesson B* | |
|---|---|
| **Literacy Workbook,** 15–30 min. | |
| **Basic Workbook,** 15–30 min. | |
| **Writing Worksheets,** 15–30 min. | www.cambridge.org/ventures/ resources/ |
| **Collaborative Worksheets,** 30-45 min. | |
| **Student Arcade,** time varies | www.cambridge.org/venturesarcade/ |

**B** **Listen and repeat.** Then write.

🔊 CD2, Track 49

| cook | listen to music | play the guitar |
|------|-----------------|-----------------|
| read magazines | watch TV | work in the garden |

| Name | Activity |
|------|----------|
| 1. Pablo | watch TV |
| 2. Tom | work in the garden |
| 3. Rashid | play the guitar |

| Name | Activity |
|------|----------|
| 4. Estela | listen to music |
| 5. Ling | read magazines |
| 6. Farah | cook |

**Talk with a partner.** Ask and answer.

   A  What does **Pablo** like to do?

   B  **Watch TV.**

**3** **Communicate**

**Talk with a partner.** Act and guess.

   A  **Dance?**

   B  **No.**

   A  **Play the guitar?**

   B  **That's right.**

# Lesson C | I like to watch TV.

## 1 Grammar focus: *like to*

| QUESTIONS | | | | ANSWERS | | |
|---|---|---|---|---|---|---|
| | do | you | | I | like | |
| | do | they | like to do? | They | like | to watch TV. |
| What | does | he | | He | likes | |
| | does | she | | She | likes | |

Watch

## 2 Practice

**A Read and circle.** Then write.

1. A What do they like to do?
   B They _____**like**_____ to play basketball.
   ( like ) likes

2. A What does she like to do?
   B She _____*likes*_____ to swim.
   like ( likes )

3. A What does he like to do?
   B He _____*likes*_____ to play cards.
   like ( likes )

4. A What does she like to do?
   B She _____*likes*_____ to fish.
   like ( likes )

5. A What do they like to do?
   B They _____*like*_____ to dance.
   ( like ) likes

**Listen and repeat.** Then practice with a partner.

CD2, Track 50

# WARM-UP AND REVIEW

- Before class. Write today's lesson focus on the board.
  *Lesson C:*
  *Questions and answers with "like to"*
- Begin class. Books closed. Write *like* on the board. Point to it. Say it aloud. Ask Ss to repeat after you. Draw a smiley-face on the board. Say: *"Like" means something you enjoy or something that makes you happy. For example: I like pizza. I like ice cream. I like books.* Ask Ss: *What do you like?* Allow Ss to give one-word responses.

**Teaching Tip**

If Ss have a difficult time thinking of what they like, ask *Yes / No* questions, such as: *Do you like English class? Do you like movies? Do you like TV?* Ss can give simple *Yes / No* responses.

# PRESENTATION

- Use the animated grammar presentation in one or more of the following ways:
  - Preview it before class
  - Show it in class
  - Encourage Ss to watch it outside of class.
- Books open. Direct Ss' attention to the grammar chart in Exercise 1. Read the questions and the corresponding answers aloud. Ask Ss to repeat after you.

**Teaching Tip**

It might be helpful to point out the *s* in the third-person singular for *he likes* and *she likes.* Tell Ss to put an *s* on the verb for *he* and *she.* Then point out that the verb in the question never takes an *s.* Tell Ss that the *s* in the question form is part of the word *does.*

- Ask the questions in the grammar chart about the Ss in the class. Point to two Ss and ask: *What do they like to do?* Point to a male S and ask: *What does he like to do?* Point to a female S and ask: *What does she like to do?* Ss should answer appropriately using examples they learned in Lessons A and B.

# PRACTICE

- Read aloud the instructions for Exercise 2A. Model the task. Read aloud the example conversation in number 1. When you read Speaker A's first line, show Ss the two answer choices under the blank and ask: *"Like" or "likes"?* Elicit *like.*
- Point to where *like* has been circled and written for number 1. Say: *Circle the correct answer. Then write it in the blank.*
- Ss complete the exercise in pairs. Walk around and help as needed.
- Ask several pairs to read the conversations to the rest of the class. After each conversation write on the board the conversation number and the correct answer.

# COMPREHENSION CHECK

- Read aloud the second part of the instructions for Exercise 2A.
- ▶ *CD2, Track 50* Play or read the audio (see audio script, page T-151). Ss listen and repeat.
- Ss in pairs. Ask Ss to choose Role A or B and practice the questions and answers in Exercise 2A. Then have Ss switch roles and practice again. Walk around and help as needed.
- Ask several pairs to read the conversations to the rest of the class.

**Teaching Tip**

If appropriate for your class, ask the Ss why the answers on the board are correct. Ss should respond that the verb after *they* and *you* is *like* and the verb after *he* and *she* is *likes.*

### *Expansion activity* (student pairs)

- Direct Ss' attention to the picture on page 122. Say: *Ask your partner questions about this picture. Use the questions and answers on page 126 to help.*
- Encourage Ss to point to people in the picture and ask: *What do they like to do? What does he like to do? What does she like to do?* Partners answer appropriately about the pictures. (They like to play basketball. She likes to exercise. They like to dance. etc.)
- Ask several pairs to hold up the Student's Book and point to people in the picture. Have them ask and answer questions about the picture for the rest of the class.

# LESSON C | I like to watch TV.

## PRESENTATION

- Write on the board: *What _____ he like to do? What _____ she like to do? What _____ they like to do?*
- Point to the sentences. Ask Ss what words are missing. Write the missing words in the blanks (*does*, *does*, and *do*). Say the questions aloud. Ask Ss to repeat after you.
- Direct Ss' attention to Exercise 2B. Read aloud the instructions.

## PRACTICE

- ▶ *CD2, Track 51* Model the task. Say: *Listen and repeat.* Play or read the audio for number 1 (see audio script, page T-151) and point to the man in picture number 1 as you repeat.
- ▶ *CD2, Track 51* Play or read the complete audio. Ss listen and repeat. Encourage Ss to point to the people in the pictures as they repeat.
- Read aloud the second part of the instructions in Exercise 2B. Model the activity. Ask two Ss to read the example question and answer aloud.
- Ss complete the exercise in pairs, asking and answering questions about the people in the pictures. Walk around and listen to Ss' pronunciation. Write down any errors that you hear. Write the words that were pronounced incorrectly on the board. When Ss are finished, point to the words and say them aloud. Ask Ss to repeat them after you.

## COMPREHENSION CHECK

- Ask several pairs to say the conversations for pictures *1–6* in order for the rest of the class. When a pair finishes one conversation, ask: *Is the answer correct?* Ask other Ss to make corrections if needed.

## APPLICATION

- Direct Ss' attention to Exercise 3 and read the instructions aloud.
- Model the task. Ask two Ss to read the conversation aloud. Hold up the Student's Book. Point to the first line in the chart. Tell Ss to use their classmate's name and to fill in the information that they hear from their classmates.
- Ss complete the exercise by talking to six different Ss in the class. Encourage Ss to stand up and walk around the room.

**Teaching Tip**

It is helpful to encourage Ss to speak to more than one partner in the classroom. Ask Ss to find new partners periodically. This gives them a chance to practice with Ss of all abilities.

### *Expansion activity* (student pairs)

- Expand on Exercise 3 by asking Ss to talk to a new partner. Tell Ss to talk about the answers on their charts with the new partner.
- Write on the board: *What does _____ like to do? He / She likes to _____.* Tell Ss to ask their new partners the question on the board. They will ask about the names on their partner's chart.
- Model the activity. Direct Ss' attention to the example of Vinh in Exercise 3. Ask a S: *What does Vinh like to do?* (He likes to play basketball.)
- Ss complete the activity in pairs. Walk around and make sure Ss are answering with the *s* added to the verb.

**Literacy Tip**

For an alternative activity, refer literacy Ss to pages 118–119 in the *Literacy Workbook* at any time during the lesson.

## EVALUATION

- Direct Ss' attention to the lesson focus on the board. Point to different Ss in the class. Ask: *What do you like to do? What do they like to do? What does he like to do? What does she like to do?* Listen as other Ss answer the questions. Make sure they answer with the correct form of the verb.
- Check off the lesson focus as Ss demonstrate an understanding of what they have learned in the lesson.

| *More Ventures, Unit 10, Lesson C* | |
|---|---|
| Literacy Workbook, 15–30 min. | |
| Basic Workbook, 15–30 min. | |
| Writing Worksheets, 15–30 min. | www.cambridge.org/ventures/ resources/ |
| Collaborative Worksheets, 30–45 min. | |
| Student Arcade, time varies | www.cambridge.org/venturesarcade/ |

B **Listen and repeat.**

CD2, Track 51

1. exercise

2. cook

3. play cards

4. work in the garden

5. swim

6. play soccer

**Talk with a partner.** Ask and answer.

A  What **does he** like to do?

B  **He likes to exercise.**

## 3 Communicate

**Talk with your classmates.** Complete the chart.

A  What do you like to do, **Vinh**?

B  I like to **play basketball**.

| Name | What do you like to do? |
|------|-------------------------|
| Vinh | play basketball |
| Answers will vary. | |
| | |
| | |
| | |

# Lesson D Reading

## 1 Before you read

**Talk about the picture.**
What do you see?

## 2 Read

**Listen and read.**

CD2, Track 52

●●●●● LTE       1:20       100% ▬

‹ Messages     Lupe     Details

Hi Miriam,

I'm not working today. It's my day off. Are you busy? Come and visit me!

What do you like to do? I like to cook. I like to play cards. I like to listen to music and dance. I like to watch TV. Do you like to watch TV?

Please call me at 10:00.

## 3 After you read

**Check (✓) the answers.** What does Lupe like to do?

1.       2.       3.       4.       5.

☑       ☐       ☑       ☑       ☑

Teaching objectives
• Introduce an email about free-time activities
• Provide practice using new topic-related words

# WARM-UP AND REVIEW

- Before class. Write today's lesson focus on the board.
  *Lesson D:*
  *Read and discuss an email message*
  *Learn more vocabulary about free-time activities*

- Begin class. Books closed. Ask Ss to review by saying the activities they like to do in their free time. Write any activities that Ss say on the board. These can include activities learned in Lessons A, B, and C and any other activities that Ss already know.

- Ask Ss who they do these activities with. Elicit short answers such as: *my mother, my father, my husband, my friend, my daughter, my son.*

# PRESENTATION

- Books open. Direct Ss' attention to the picture in Exercise **1**. Read the instructions aloud. Ask: *What do you see?* Elicit and write on the board any vocabulary that Ss know, such as: *computer, woman, cell phone.* Ask: *What is the woman doing?*

### Teaching Tip

Do not expect Ss to answer the question in complete sentences. The purpose of this exercise is to prepare Ss for the reading that follows.

# PRACTICE

- Write *email* on the board. Point to the word. Say it aloud and ask Ss to repeat it after you. Ask: *Do you remember the email message you read in Unit 7?* Explain to Ss that they will read another email message in this lesson.

- Direct Ss' attention to Exercise **2**. Read the instructions aloud.

- **CD2, Track 52** Play or read the audio and ask Ss to follow along (see audio script, page T-151). Repeat the audio as needed.

- Read aloud each sentence of the reading and ask Ss to repeat after you. Answer any questions Ss have about new words in the reading.

### Learner persistence *(individual work)*

- **CD2, Track 52** Ss can listen to the audio for Exercise **2** at home for reinforcement and review. They can also listen to the audio for self-directed learning when class attendance is not possible.

# COMPREHENSION CHECK

- Direct Ss' attention to Exercise **3** and read the instructions aloud.

- Model the task. Hold up the Student's Book. Point to the first picture. Ask Ss to identify it. Elicit: *Cards* or *playing cards.* Point to the next pictures in turn. Elicit the names of the items. (*Magazines, TV, food, music player.*) Focus Ss' attention on picture 1 again. Ask: *Does Lupe like to play cards?* (Yes.) Ask Ss the questions for the next four pictures. Say: *Check the boxes for the "yes" answers.*

- Ss complete the exercise individually. Walk around and help as needed.

- Ask volunteers which pictures they checked. Walk around and make sure they checked pictures 1, 3, 4, and 5.

### Expansion activity *(student pairs)*

- Direct Ss' attention to the pictures in Exercise **3**. Write on the board: *Does Lupe like to _____? Yes, she does. / No, she doesn't.*

- Ss in pairs. Say: *Ask your partner the question on the board. Point to the pictures in Exercise **3**. Your partner will answer the questions.*

- When Ss are finished, ask them to switch roles.

- Walk around and help as needed.

### Community building *(whole class)*

- Ask Ss if they use email. Ask them who they usually send emails to and receive emails from. If appropriate for your class, encourage Ss to write emails to each other to practice writing in English.

# LESSON D Reading

## PRESENTATION

- Direct Ss' attention to the Picture dictionary in Exercise 4. Tell Ss that they are going to learn the names of more free-time activities in English. Hold up the Student's Book. Point to each picture in turn and read aloud the words corresponding to them. Ask Ss to repeat the words after you.

### Teaching Tip

Ss may not understand the word *volunteer* from the illustration alone. Explain that a volunteer works without pay. Point to Picture 6. Tell Ss that the people in the picture are working to make their neighborhood better because they like to help and they won't get paid for this work.

▶ **CD2, Track 53** Play or read the audio (see audio script, page T-151). Listen to Ss' pronunciation as they repeat the leisure activities. Correct pronunciation as needed.

### Learner persistence *(individual work)*

▶ **CD2, Track 53** Ss can listen to the audio for Exercise 4A at home for reinforcement and review. They can also listen to the audio for self-directed learning when class attendance is not possible.

### Expansion activity *(student pairs)*

- Cut out the Picture dictionary cards that correspond to this unit. Make enough copies for each pair of Ss in your class. The picture should be on the front of the card and the description of the activity on the back.

- Ss in pairs. Tell Ss to show their partner the pictures. Their partners need to identify the pictures. Then Ss can check to see if their partners are right by looking at the back of the picture card.

- Ask Ss to practice with these flash cards until they know all the names of the activities without looking at the words on the back of the cards.

## PRACTICE

- Direct Ss' attention to Exercise 4B. Read the instructions aloud. Model the conversation. Hold up the Student's Book and point to the first picture. Ask two Ss to read the conversation aloud.

- Ss complete the exercise in pairs, asking and answering questions about the Picture dictionary pictures. Walk around and help as needed.

- Ask several pairs to ask and answer the questions for the rest of the class.

### Literacy Tip

For an alternative activity, refer literacy Ss to pages 120–121 in the *Literacy Workbook* at any time during the lesson.

## EVALUATION

- Direct Ss' attention to the first part of the lesson focus on the board. Ask: *What does Lupe like to do?* Elicit: *cook, play cards, listen to music, dance,* and *watch TV.*

- Direct Ss' attention to the pictures in the Picture dictionary. Ask Ss to cover the names of the activities with a piece of paper and then identify them one by one.

- Check off each part of the lesson focus as Ss demonstrate understanding of what they have learned in the lesson.

| *More Ventures, Unit 10, Lesson D* | |
|---|---|
| **Literacy Workbook,** 15–30 min. **Basic Workbook,** 15–30 min. | |
| **Picture Dictionary activities,** 30–45 min. **Writing Worksheets,** 15–30 min. **Collaborative Worksheets,** 30–45 min. | www.cambridge.org/ventures/resources/ |
| **Student Arcade,** time varies | www.cambridge.org/venturesarcade/ |

**4** **Picture dictionary** Free-time activities

1. go to the movies

2. go online

3. shop

4. travel

5. visit friends

6. volunteer

**A** **Listen and repeat.** Look at the Picture dictionary.

**B** **Talk with a partner.** Point and ask. Your partner answers.

A  What do they like to do?

B  **Go to the movies.**

CD2, Track 53

# Lesson E Writing

## 1 Before you write

**A** **Talk with a partner.** Complete the words.

1. r _e_ _a_ d    m _a_ g a z i n e s
2. p l _a_ y    b _a_ s k _e_ t b a l l
3. w _a_ t c h    T V
4. v _i_ s _i_ t    f r i _e_ n d s
5. _e_ x _e_ r c _i_ s e
6. w _o_ r k    _i_ n    t h e    g a r d _e_ n

**B** **Talk with a partner.** Write the words.

1. ____exercise____

2. ____read____ magazines

3. ____play____ basketball

4. ____work____ in the garden

5. ____visit____ friends

6. ____watch____ TV

Teaching objectives
● Prepare Ss for writing about free-time activities
● Provide practice writing key vocabulary words

# WARM-UP AND REVIEW

● Before class. Write today's lesson focus on the board.
*Lesson E:*
*Write about free-time activities*

● Begin class. Books closed. Ask volunteers to recall some of the free-time activities that they have learned in the unit so far. Emphasize that they are not supposed to look in their books for the answers but should try to remember the names of the activities. Write on the board the activities: *go to the movies, visit friends, shop, travel,* etc.

● Point to the activities on the board. Ask individual Ss: *Do you like to (the activity you are pointing to)?* Elicit appropriate responses.

# PRESENTATION

● Direct Ss' attention to Exercise 1A. Read aloud the instructions.

● Point to the first item and say: *Number 1. What's the activity?* (Read magazines.) Ask: *What letters do we need?* (e, a and a) Point to where the letters are written in the blanks. Say: *Now you complete the rest of the words.*

● Ss work in pairs to complete the words. Encourage Ss to figure out the activities together.

● Write the numbers 2–6 on the board. Ask individual Ss to write the completed words from Exercise 1A on the board. Ask different Ss: *Are the words correct?* Make corrections if needed.

## Expansion activity *(individual work)*

● Write on the board: *I like to _____. I don't like to _____.*

● Say: *Look at the activities in Exercise 1A. Make sentences about yourself. Use the words on the board. For example: I like to read magazines. I don't like to work in the garden.*

● Ss complete the activity individually. Walk around and help as needed.

● Ask several Ss to read their likes and dislikes to the rest of the class.

# PRACTICE

● Focus Ss' attention on Exercise 1B and read the instructions aloud.

● Model the task. Direct Ss' attention to picture 1. Ask: *What does he like to do?* (exercise) Say: *Now you complete the rest of the phrases. Use the words in Exercise 1A.*

● Ss complete the exercise individually or in pairs. Walk around and help as needed.

● Write the numbers 2–6 on the board. Ask individual Ss to write the answers on the board.

● Go over the answers. Ask: *Are these words spelled correctly?* Correct any errors if needed.

## Expansion activity *(student pairs)*

● Write on the board: *What does he like to do? He likes to _____.*

● Direct Ss' attention to the pictures in Exercise 1B. Say: *Ask your partner the question on the board about each picture.*

● Ss complete the exercise in pairs. Walk around and help as needed.

● Ask several pairs to ask and answer the questions for the rest of the class.

## Community building *(whole class)*

● Brainstorm free-time activities students like and dislike. If any Ss have common interests, encourage them to get together and try some of these activities together on the weekend or whenever they have free time.

### Literacy Tip

For an alternative activity, refer literacy Ss to pages 122–123 in the *Literacy Workbook* at any time during the lesson.

# LESSON E Writing

## PRESENTATION

- Write *day off* on the board. Point to the words. Say them aloud and ask Ss to repeat them after you. Ask: *What's a day off?* If Ss don't know, say: *It's a day when you don't work or go to school.*

- Hold up the Student's Book. Point to the pictures in Exercise **1B** on page 130. Say: *This man's name is Brian. He likes to do different activities on his day off.*

- Direct Ss' attention to Exercise **2A** and read the instructions aloud. Ask a S to read the statement *My name is Brian. Saturday is my day off.*

- Model the task. Explain that the sentences in Exercise **2A** go with the pictures in Exercise **1B**. Hold up the Student's Book. Point to picture 1 in Exercise **1B**. Ask: *What does Brian like to do on his day off?*

- Ask a S to read aloud the first sentence in Exercise **2A**. Say: *That's right. Brian likes to exercise in the morning.*

- Ss complete the exercise individually. Walk around and help as needed.

## COMPREHENSION CHECK

- Write the numbers 2–6 on the board. Ask S volunteers to write their answers on the board. Ask: *Is this answer correct?*

## APPLICATION

- Direct Ss' attention to Exercise **2B**. Read the instructions aloud.

- Model the task. Tell Ss what you like to do on your day off. Hold up the Student's Book and pretend to check off the activities as you say them. Point to the word *other*. Say: *I like to sing.* Write *sing* on the board and check it off.

- Ss complete the exercise individually. Walk around and help as needed.

### Literacy Tip

Literacy Ss should be able to complete this exercise with some help from a more advanced S. Ask a more advanced S to read the activities to the literacy Ss to make sure that they understand the activities.

## PRACTICE

- Direct Ss' attention to the second part of Exercise **2B**. Read the instructions aloud.

- Model the task. Write on the board: *I like to _____.* Say: *Remember, I like to sing.* Write *sing* in the blank. Continue with the activities you mentioned in Exercise **2B**.

- Ss complete the exercise individually. Walk around and help as needed.

## APPLICATION

- Direct Ss' attention to Exercise **3**. Read aloud the instructions. Tell Ss to read aloud their lists to their partners. Walk around and help as needed.

### Teaching Tip

This exercise asks Ss to work together to edit their writing. Encourage Ss to correct each other's writing if necessary. Say: *Help your partner with any mistakes. Then your partner will help you.*

- Ask several Ss to read their sentences aloud for the whole class.

### *Expansion activity* (whole group)

- Dictation. Books closed. Ask Ss to take out a piece of paper and write the numbers *1–5* on it. Dictate the following sentences: *1. I like to volunteer. 2. He likes to go to the movies. 3. She likes to exercise. 4. I like to cook. 5. They like to swim.*

- Ask volunteers to write their sentences on the board. Ask other Ss: *Are the sentences correct?* Have different Ss correct any errors if needed.

## EVALUATION

- Direct Ss' attention to the lesson focus on the board.

- Ask different Ss to come to the board and write sentences about leisure activities that they enjoy. They should use the form *I like to _____.*

- Check off the lesson focus as Ss demonstrate understanding of what they have learned in the lesson.

| *More Ventures, Unit 10, Lesson E* | |
|---|---|
| Literacy Workbook, 15–30 min. | |
| Basic Workbook, 15–30 min. | |
| Writing Worksheets, 15–30 min.<br>Collaborative Worksheets, 30–45 min. | www.cambridge.org/ventures/resources/ |

## 2 **Write**

A **Complete the sentences.** Look at 1B.

My name is Brian.

Saturday is my day off.

1. I like to _____exercise_____ in the morning.
2. I like to _____*read*_____ magazines, too.
3. I like to _____*play*_____ basketball with my son in the afternoon.
4. I also like to _____*work*_____ in the garden.
5. I like to _____*visit*_____ friends in the evening.
6. I like to _____*watch*_____ TV at night.

B **Check (✓).** What do you like to do on your day off?

☐ cook          ☐ play cards
☐ dance         ☐ shop
☐ exercise      ☐ swim
☐ fish          ☐ volunteer
☐ go to the movies   ☐ other: *Answers will vary.*

**Write about yourself.**

### My Day Off

My name is *Answers will vary.*_____.

_____ is my day off.

I like to _____.

I like to _____.

I like to _____.

I like to _____.

## 3 **After you write**

**Talk with a partner.** Share your writing.

## 1 Life-skills reading

**Valley Community Center Evening Classes**
## GUITAR CLASS
**Learn to play the guitar.**
September 3 to November 21
Monday and Wednesday
7:00 p.m. to 9:00 p.m.
Room 101
$100.00

A **Read the questions.** Look at the class ad. Fill in the answer.

1. What is this class?

   (A) a guitar class

   (B) an exercise class

   (C) an ESL class

2. Where is this class?

   (A) room 100

   (B) room 101

   (C) room 901

3. When is this class?

   (A) morning

   (B) afternoon

   (C) evening

4. How much is this class?

   (A) $10.00

   (B) $100.00

   (C) $101.00

B **Solve the problem.** Which solution is best? Circle your opinion.

Pablo wants to study guitar. He doesn't have $100. What can he do?

1. Talk to the teacher.

2. Save money and take the class later.

3. Other: *Answers will vary.*

Teaching objectives
- Introduce a descriptive paragraph about a class
- Provide practice that develops test-taking skills
- Review vocabulary from the unit

# WARM-UP AND REVIEW

- Before class. Write today's lesson focus on the board.
  *Lesson F:*
  *Read and answer questions about a class description*
  *Talk about free-time activities*
  *Complete the Self-assessment*

- Begin class. Books closed. Write the words *class description* on the board. Point to the words. Say them aloud and ask Ss to repeat. Ask: *What kinds of classes are there?* Elicit appropriate responses, such as: *English classes, music classes, sports classes.*

### Teaching Tip

If your school has a catalog with class descriptions in it, bring it to class to show Ss a real-life example.

- Ask: *Are you taking any other classes?* If any Ss say *yes*, ask them what classes they are taking. If you have Ss with children, ask if the children are taking any classes after school. If any Ss say *yes*, ask them to say the names of the classes.

# PRESENTATION

- Books open. Direct Ss' attention to the class description in Exercise 1A.

- Hold up the Student's Book. Point to the class description. Ask questions about the class:

  *What kind of class is this?* (A guitar class.)

  *Where is the class?* (Valley Community Center.)

  *When is the class?* (September 3 to November 21.)

  *What day is the class?* (Monday and Wednesday.)

  *What time is the class?* (7:00 p.m. to 9:00 p.m.)

# PRACTICE

- Read aloud the instructions in Exercise 1A. This task helps prepare Ss for standardized-type tests they may have to take.

- Write the first item on the board along with the three answer choices labeled *A, B,* and *C.*

- Read aloud the item and answer choices and then point to the class description. Ask Ss: *What is this class for?* Show Ss where to find the information. Elicit: *a guitar class.*

- Point to the three answer choices on the board. Ask Ss: *A, B,* or *C? (A)* Fill in the letter *a* and tell Ss: *Fill in the answer.* Make sure Ss understand the task.

- Have Ss individually scan for and fill in the answers.

# COMPREHENSION CHECK

- Go over the answers to Exercise 1A with the class. Make sure that Ss followed the directions and filled in their answers. Ask Ss to point to the information in the class description.

# APPLICATION

- Read the instructions aloud for Exercise 1B.
- Tell Ss that they will discuss what Pablo can do.
- Ss ask and answer the question in pairs.

### Expansion activity *(individual work)*

- Ask Ss to write a description for an imaginary class in their notebooks. Tell them to model their class description after the one in Exercise 1A. Encourage them to change the information in their description to make the class different. Remind Ss of the classes they brainstormed at the beginning of the lesson.

- Ask several Ss to write their class descriptions on the board. Encourage Ss to ask questions about the class using the question words in Exercise 1A.

### Community building *(whole group)*

- If possible, bring several copies of a local continuing education course catalog to your class. Tell Ss about courses they can take that don't require a lot of English, such as art, music, and exercise classes. Tell Ss that this is a great way to meet other people and practice English outside of class.

# LESSON F Another view

## PRACTICE

- Direct Ss' attention to Exercise 2A and read the instructions aloud.
- Model the task. Point to the first picture and ask: *What is this?* Elicit: *guitar*. Ask: *What's the activity?* (Play the guitar.) Point to the line connecting the picture to the word *play*.
- Tell Ss: *Match the pictures and the words.*
- Ss complete the task in pairs. Help as needed.
- Go over the answers to Exercise 2A with the class. Ask Ss to say aloud the full verb phrase for each picture for example, *play guitar*.
- Write the numbers *2–8* on the board. Ask volunteers to come to the board to write their answers. Then ask different Ss to complete each verb phrase on the board.
- Ask: *Are the answers correct?* Have other Ss correct any errors on the board.

### Expansion activity (whole group)

- Before class. Make copies of the following chart for each S in your class:

| Do you like to . . . | | | | | | |
|---|---|---|---|---|---|---|
| Name | play the guitar? | watch TV? | work in the garden? | read magazines? | go to the movies? | play basketball? |
| | | | | | | |
| | | | | | | |
| | | | | | | |
| | | | | | | |

- Write on the board: *Yes, I do. / No, I don't.* Tell Ss to use these answers as guidelines for this activity.
- Ask Ss to stand up and talk to five other Ss. Ask them to choose Ss they are not usually partners with.
- Tell Ss to write in the chart the names of the people they speak with as well as the answers these Ss give them for each question. Point to the answers on the board to remind Ss of the correct spelling and help as needed.

## PRACTICE

- Direct Ss' attention to Exercise 2B. Read the instructions aloud.
- Write *inside* and *outside* on the board. Point to each word. Say them aloud. Ask Ss to repeat the words after you. Say: *We are inside now.* Point to a window or in the direction of the outdoors. Say: *That's outside.*
- Ask: *What else do you do inside?* Elicit: *watch TV, cook, play the guitar*, etc. Ask: *What do you do outside?* Elicit: *play basketball, work in the garden*, etc.
- Model the activity. Hold up the Student's Book. Point to the chart in Exercise 2B. Ask: *Do you cook inside the house?* (Yes.)

- Ask: *Do you cook outside the house?* Elicit *Yes / No* responses. Point to the check marks in both columns of the chart.
- Ss complete the activity in pairs. Walk around and help as needed.
- Go over the answers to Exercise 2B with the class. Ask questions about Exercise 2B. Ask about each activity: *Can you _____ inside the house? Can you _____ outside the house?*
- If Ss disagree, ask them to explain their opinions. For example, you can cook inside the house and outside at a picnic.
- Reproduce the chart in Exercise 2B on the board. Ask different Ss to check the columns for each activity. Ss compare their own charts to the one on the board.

**Literacy Tip**

For an alternative activity, refer literacy Ss to pages 124–125 in the *Literacy Workbook* at any time during the lesson.

## EVALUATION

- Do a quick review of the unit. Have Ss turn to Lesson A. Ask the class to talk about what they remember about this lesson. Prompt Ss, if necessary, with questions, for example: *What words are on this page? What do you see in the picture?* Continue in this manner to review each lesson quickly.

### Expansion activity

- Before class. Print, for each student, one copy of the Self-assessment for this unit.
- Have Ss complete the Self-assessment either in class or outside of class.
- Provide feedback to Ss such as through a whole-class discussion, partners comparing their worksheets, or T reviewing each S's worksheet.
- If Ss are ready, administer the unit test on page T-185 of this Teacher's Edition. The audio script for the test is available on page T-193.
- If Ss are ready, administer the final test on page T-188 of this Teacher's Edition. The audio script for the test is available on page T-193.

**More Ventures, Unit 10, Lesson F**

| | |
|---|---|
| **Literacy Workbook,** 15–30 min. | |
| **Basic Workbook,** 15–30 min. | |
| **Writing Worksheets,** 15–30 min. | |
| **Collaborative Worksheets,** 30–45 min. | www.cambridge.org/ventures/ resources/ |
| **Self-assessment,** 10 min. | |
| **CASAS Test Prep Worksheet,** 5–10 min. | |

## 2 Fun with vocabulary

A **Talk with a partner.** Read and match.

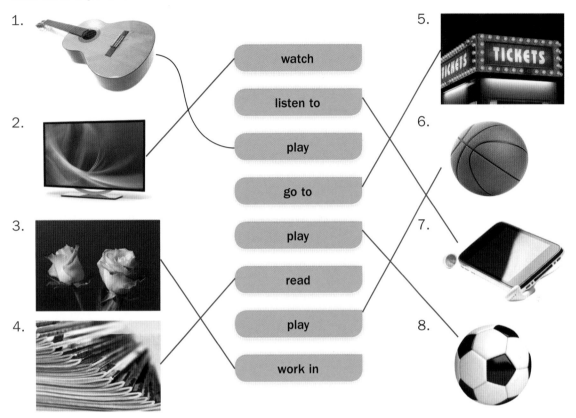

1.

2.

3.

4.

watch

listen to

play

go to

play

read

play

work in

5.

6.

7.

8.

B **Talk with a partner.** Complete the chart.

| | Inside the house | Outside the house |
|---|---|---|
| cook | ✓ | ✓ |
| fish | | ✓ |
| dance | ✓ | ✓ |
| shop | | ✓ |
| swim | | ✓ |
| watch TV | ✓ | |

# REVIEW

## 1 Listening

**Read.** Then listen and circle.

■)) CD2, Track 54

1. What is Marco doing?
   a. washing the car
   b. playing the guitar

2. What does he like to do?
   a. wash the car
   b. play the guitar

3. What is Ricky doing?
   a. making lunch
   b. making the bed

4. What is Fred doing?
   a. reading magazines
   b. watching TV

5. What does Tina like to do?
   a. cook
   b. exercise

6. What does she like to do on the weekend?
   a. fish
   b. dance

**Talk with a partner.** Ask and answer.

## 2 Vocabulary

**Write.** Complete the story.

bedroom    kitchen    playing    watching    work

# Sunday at Home

Today is Sunday. My son is ___watching___ TV in the living room.
                              1

My daughter is ___playing___ the guitar in her ___bedroom___ .
                    2                                3

My wife is in the ___kitchen___ . She likes to cook. I am in the
                      4

garden. I like to ___work___ in the garden. Sunday is our
                     5

favorite day of the week. We like to relax.

Teaching objectives
- Review vocabulary from Units 9 and 10
- Review pronunciation of *a, e, i, o,* and *u*

# WARM-UP AND REVIEW

- Before class. Write today's lesson focus on the board.
  *Review unit:*
  *Review vocabulary and grammar from Units 9 and 10*
  *Review pronunciation of "a," "e," "i," "o," and "u"*

- Begin class. Books closed. Draw a simple floor plan of a house on the board. Include a bedroom, kitchen, living room, dining room, and laundry room.

- Ask a S to come to the board. Say: *Draw Rosa. She is in the living room.* Encourage the S to draw a stick figure in the living room by pointing to that room on the board. Write *Rosa* under the stick figure.

- Ask other Ss to draw people in the other rooms. Use the names *Ali, Sara, Mike,* and *Sally* or other names that you choose. Write the names under the stick figures.

- Point to the people in the house and ask questions. For example, point to Rosa. Ask: *Where is she?* (In the living room.) Ask: *What's she doing?* Elicit an appropriate response, such as: *She's watching TV.* Encourage Ss to make up activities for the stick figures.

- Continue asking about the other people in the house. Ss can invent answers about activities in the house.

# PRACTICE

- Books open. Direct Ss' attention to Exercise 1 and read the instructions aloud.

- Ask individual Ss to read aloud the questions and answers. Say: *Now listen to the conversations. Circle the correct answers.*

- ▶ *CD2, Track 54* Model the task. Play or read the first conversation from the audio (see audio script, page T-152). Point to the two answer choices in number 1 and ask: *Is Marco washing the car or playing the guitar?* (Washing the car.) Point to where the answer *a* has been circled.

- ▶ *CD2, Track 54* Play or read the complete audio. Ss listen and circle the correct answers. Repeat the audio as needed.

- Check answers with the class. Read each question aloud and call on different Ss to answer.

### Teaching Tip

You may need to play the audio several times in order to give Ss a chance to extract the information they need. Then, to check comprehension and to help Ss who may be struggling, play the audio again and ask Ss to repeat the parts of the conversation that contain the answers to the questions.

- Read aloud the second part of the instructions for Exercise 1. Ss complete the exercise in pairs. Walk around and help as needed.

- Ask several pairs to ask and answer the questions for the rest of the class.

### Multilevel Tip (*small groups*)

If you have Ss who are struggling in class, put them in a group with more advanced Ss who like to help others. In this way, struggling Ss will have the help of someone who knows the target language better than they do.

# PRACTICE

- Direct Ss' attention to Exercise 2. Point to the title of the story and ask Ss: *What is the title of this story?* ("Sunday at Home")

- Direct Ss' attention to the words in the word bank. Say each word aloud. Ask Ss to repeat them after you.

- Read aloud the instructions in Exercise 2. Ask a S to read the first and second sentences in the story aloud. Say: *Use the words from the word bank to complete the story.*

- Ss read the story and fill in the blanks individually. Walk around and help as needed.

- Write the numbers *1–5* on the board. Ask volunteers to come to the board to write the answers.

- Ask several Ss to read different sentences from the story aloud using the words on the board. Ask: *Are these words correct?* Ask different Ss to correct any errors.

### *Expansion activity* (individual work, student pairs)

- Tell Ss: *Write this story again. Use information about you. What do you like to do on Sunday?* Elicit appropriate responses.

### Teaching Tip

If some of your Ss work on Sundays, ask them to change the day in the title to reflect a day when they don't have to work. If they work every day, ask them to write about a morning or afternoon when they have free time.

- Ss complete the story individually. Walk around and help as needed.

- Ask Ss to read their stories to a partner. Tell the partners to check the stories for errors and help correct the errors.

- Ask several Ss to read their stories to the rest of the class.

# REVIEW

## WARM-UP AND REVIEW

- Books closed. Ask Ss to brainstorm free-time activities that they learned in Unit 10. Write the names of the activities on the board.

- Ask a S to stand up. Ask: *What do you like to do in your free time?* Elicit an appropriate response, such as: *I like to cook.* Ask another S: *What does (first S) like to do?* Elicit: *He / She likes to cook.*

- Continue by asking other Ss what they like to do in their free time and have classmates tell what that S likes to do.

## PRACTICE

- Direct Ss' attention to Exercise 3A. Read the instructions aloud.

- Model the task. Write *they*, *he*, and *she* on the board. Point to *they*. Ask: *Is it "they is" or "they are"?* (They are.) Continue by asking about *she* and *he*. (He is / She is.)

- Direct Ss' attention to question number 1. Ask two Ss to read aloud the question and answer.

- Ss complete the exercise individually. Walk around and help as needed.

- Check answers to Exercise 3A with the class. Ask different pairs of Ss to read the questions and answers aloud. After each question, ask: *Is that correct?* Ask different Ss to make corrections if needed.

- Direct Ss' attention to Exercise 3B. Read the instructions aloud.

- Model the task. Ask two Ss to read aloud the example question and answer. Ask: *Is it "does" or "do"?* (Does.) Hold up the Student's Book. Point to where *does* has been written for number 1. Ask: *Why is it "does" and not "do"?* Elicit: *Because we use "does" with "he" and "she."* Ask: *When do we use "do"?* Elicit: *Use "do" with "I," "you," or "they."*

- Ss complete the exercise individually.

- Check answers to Exercise 3B with the class. Ask different pairs of Ss to read the questions and answers aloud. After each question and answer, ask: *Is that correct?* Different Ss can make corrections if needed.

## PRESENTATION

- Direct Ss' attention to the second part of the lesson focus on the board.

- Ask: *What are the vowels in English?* (a, e, i, o, u) Write the vowels on the board.

- Say each vowel aloud while pointing to it. Ask Ss to repeat after you. Say: *Each of these letters has two sounds.* Ask Ss to say the two sounds for each letter.

## PRACTICE

- ▷ **CD2, Track 55** Direct Ss' attention to Exercise 4A and read aloud the instructions. Play or read the audio (see audio script, page T-152). Ss listen to examples of the two sounds for each vowel.

- ▷ **CD2, Track 56** Direct Ss' attention to Exercise 4B and read aloud the instructions. Play or read the audio (see audio script, page T-152). Ss listen and repeat what they hear.

- Read aloud the second part of the instructions for Exercise 4B. Model the task. Point to the charts in the exercise and tell one S: *Say a word.* After that S says any word in the chart, tell his or her partner: *Point to the word.*

- Ss complete the task in pairs. Then they switch roles. Walk around and help as needed.

### *Expansion activity* (whole group)

- Draw eleven vertical lines on the board to make a chart with 10 columns. Write the vowels twice, so that the headings of the columns will be like this: *a, a, e, e, i, i, o, o, u, u.*

- Write the example words from Exercise 4A in the corresponding columns.

- Ask Ss to brainstorm more words that belong in each column. For example: *say, cat, need, red, drive, fix, go, Tom, tune, cut.*

    **Option** Ask Ss to look up words in Units 9 and 10 that belong in the categories.

## EVALUATION

- Direct Ss' attention to the lesson focus on the board.

- Ask individual Ss questions similar to the ones in Exercise 3B. Ask real questions about Ss in the class. Make sure Ss answer the questions with correct English.

- Write on the board: *name, at, read, red, five, six, phone, on, June, bus.* Call on individual Ss as you point to one of the words and ask them to say the word. Listen carefully to Ss' pronunciation and provide help and correction as needed.

- Check off each part of the lesson focus as Ss demonstrate an understanding of what they have learned in the lesson.

## 3 Grammar

**A** **Complete the sentences.** Use *is* or *are*.

1. **A** What _____are_____ they doing?
   **B** Drying the dishes.

2. **A** What _____is_____ she doing?
   **B** Taking out the trash.

3. **A** What _____is_____ he doing?
   **B** Washing the clothes.

4. **A** What _____are_____ they doing?
   **B** Getting the mail.

**B** **Read and circle.** Then write.

1. **A** What _____does_____ Pai like to do?
   do (does)

   **B** He _____likes to_____ listen to music.
   like to (likes to)

2. **A** What _____do_____ Vance and Anh like to do?
   (do) does

   **B** They _____like to_____ read magazines.
   (like to) likes to

3. **A** What _____do_____ you like to do?
   (do) does

   **B** I _____like to_____ travel.
   (like to) likes to

## 4 Pronunciation

**A** **Listen** to the two sounds of *a, e, i, o,* and *u*.

| a | | e | | i | | o | | u | |
|---|---|---|---|---|---|---|---|---|---|
| name | **a**t | r**ea**d | r**e**d | f**i**ve | s**i**x | ph**o**ne | **o**n | J**u**ne | b**u**s |

◄)) CD2, Track 55

**B** **Listen and repeat.**

| a | name | at |
|---|------|-----|

| e | read | red |
|---|------|-----|

| i | five | six |
|---|------|-----|

| o | phone | on |
|---|-------|-----|

| u | June | bus |
|---|------|-----|

◄)) CD2, Track 56

**Talk with a partner.** Say a word. Your partner points. Take turns.

# REFERENCE

## Possessive adjectives

| QUESTIONS | | | ANSWERS | |
|---|---|---|---|---|
| | my | | Your | |
| | your | | My | |
| | his | | His | |
| | her | | Her | |
| What's | its | phone number? | Its | phone number is 555–3348. |
| | our | | Your | |
| | your | | Our | |
| | their | | Their | |

## Present of *be*

| QUESTIONS | | | SHORT ANSWERS | | | | | |
|---|---|---|---|---|---|---|---|---|
| Am | I | | | you | are. | | you aren't. | |
| Are | you | | | I | am. | | I'm not. | |
| Is | he | | | he | is. | | he isn't. | |
| Is | she | | | she | is. | | she isn't. | |
| Is | it | from Somalia? | Yes, | it | is. | No, | it isn't. | |
| Are | we | | | you | are. | | you aren't. | |
| Are | you | | | we | are. | | we aren't. | |
| Are | they | | | they | are. | | they aren't. | |

**Contractions**
| | | |
|---|---|---|
| I'm | = | I am |
| You're | = | You are |
| He's | = | He is |
| She's | = | She is |
| It's | = | It is |
| We're | = | We are |
| You're | = | You are |
| They're | = | They are |

| | | |
|---|---|---|
| aren't | = | are not |
| isn't | = | is not |

# Simple present

| YES / NO QUESTIONS | | | SHORT ANSWERS | | | | | | |
|---|---|---|---|---|---|---|---|---|---|
| Do | I | | | you | do. | | you | don't. |
| Do | you | | | I | do. | | I | don't. |
| Does | he | | | he | does. | | he | doesn't. |
| Does | she | | | she | does. | | she | doesn't. |
| Does | it | sell clothes? | Yes, | it | does. | No, | it | doesn't. |
| Do | we | | | you | do. | | you | don't. |
| Do | you | | | we | do. | | we | don't. |
| Do | they | | | they | do. | | they | don't. |

don't = do not
doesn't = does not

# Present continuous

| QUESTIONS WITH WHAT | | | | SHORT ANSWERS |
|---|---|---|---|---|
| | am | I | | |
| | are | you | | |
| | is | he | | |
| | is | she | | |
| What | is | it | doing? | Working. |
| | are | we | | |
| | are | you | | |
| | are | they | | |

# Simple present of *like to* + verb

## QUESTIONS WITH *WHAT*

| | | | | |
|---|---|---|---|---|
| | do | I | | |
| | do | you | | |
| | does | he | | |
| | does | she | | |
| What | does | it | like to do? | |
| | do | we | | |
| | do | you | | |
| | do | they | | |

## ANSWERS

| | | |
|---|---|---|
| You | like | |
| I | like | |
| He | likes | |
| She | likes | |
| It | likes | to swim. |
| You | like | |
| We | like | |
| They | like | |

## YES / NO QUESTIONS

| | | |
|---|---|---|
| Do | I | |
| Do | you | |
| Does | he | |
| Does | she | |
| Does | it | like to swim? |
| Do | we | |
| Do | you | |
| Do | they | |

## SHORT ANSWERS

| | | | | | |
|---|---|---|---|---|---|
| | you | do. | | you | don't. |
| | I | do. | | I | don't. |
| | he | does. | | he | doesn't. |
| | she | does. | | she | doesn't. |
| Yes, | it | does. | No, | it | doesn't. |
| | you | do. | | you | don't. |
| | we | do. | | we | don't. |
| | they | do. | | they | don't. |

# Simple present of *have*

## YES / NO QUESTIONS

| | | |
|---|---|---|
| Do | I | |
| Do | you | |
| Does | he | |
| Does | she | have a sister? |
| Do | we | |
| Do | you | |
| Do | they | |

## SHORT ANSWERS

| | | | | | |
|---|---|---|---|---|---|
| Yes, | you | do. | No, | you | don't. |
| | I | do. | | I | don't. |
| | he | does. | | he | doesn't. |
| | she | does. | | she | doesn't. |
| | you | do. | | you | don't. |
| | we | do. | | we | don't. |
| | they | do. | | they | don't. |

## AFFIRMATIVE STATEMENTS

| | | |
|---|---|---|
| I | have | |
| You | have | |
| He | has | |
| She | has | a sister. |
| We | have | |
| You | have | |
| They | have | |

## NEGATIVE STATEMENTS

| | | | |
|---|---|---|---|
| I | don't | | |
| You | don't | | |
| He | doesn't | | |
| She | doesn't | have | a sister. |
| We | don't | | |
| You | don't | | |
| They | don't | | |

## Capitalization rules

| | |
|---|---|
| Begin the first word in a sentence or question with a capital letter. | **M**y name is Nancy.<br>**W**here is Ivan from? |
| Begin the names of months and days of the week with a capital letter. | **J**anuary<br>**S**unday |
| Begin the names of countries, states/provinces, cities, streets, and other places with a capital letter. | **M**exico      **F**lorida      **T**ampa<br>**P**ine **A**venue      **T**he **C**lothes **P**lace |
| Begin the names of people with a capital letter. | **S**ara **G**arza<br>**E**rnesto **D**elgado |
| Begin family relationship words with a capital when they are part of a name.<br>Do not begin family relationship words with a capital when they are not part of a name. | I like **U**ncle Eduardo.<br><br>My uncle is Eduardo. |
| Begin a title with a capital when it is part of the name. | **M**rs. Navarro<br>**D**r. Martin |

## Punctuation rules

| | |
|---|---|
| Use a period to end a sentence. | My name is Nancy. |
| Use a question mark at the end of a question. | What's your name? |
| Use an exclamation point to show emotion, emphasis, or surprise. It replaces a period. | It's Monday, your first day of English class!<br>I love my family! |
| Use commas after the salutation and closing of a note, letter, or email. | Dear Grandma,<br>Love, Meg |
| Use an apostrophe + an s to show possession. | the doctor's office = the office of the doctor<br>Maria's son = the son of Maria<br>a teacher's aide = an aide for a teacher |

## Cardinal numbers

| | | | | |
|---|---|---|---|---|
| 0 zero | 10 ten | 20 twenty | 30 thirty | 40 forty |
| 1 one | 11 eleven | 21 twenty-one | 31 thirty-one | 50 fifty |
| 2 two | 12 twelve | 22 twenty-two | 32 thirty-two | 60 sixty |
| 3 three | 13 thirteen | 23 twenty-three | 33 thirty-three | 70 seventy |
| 4 four | 14 fourteen | 24 twenty-four | 34 thirty-four | 80 eighty |
| 5 five | 15 fifteen | 25 twenty-five | 35 thirty-five | 90 ninety |
| 6 six | 16 sixteen | 26 twenty-six | 36 thirty-six | 100 one hundred |
| 7 seven | 17 seventeen | 27 twenty-seven | 37 thirty-seven | 1,000 one thousand |
| 8 eight | 18 eighteen | 28 twenty-eight | 38 thirty-eight | |
| 9 nine | 19 nineteen | 29 twenty-nine | 39 thirty-nine | |

## Ordinal numbers

| | | | |
|---|---|---|---|
| 1st first | 11th eleventh | 21st twenty-first | 31st thirty-first |
| 2nd second | 12th twelfth | 22nd twenty-second | |
| 3rd third | 13th thirteenth | 23rd twenty-third | |
| 4th fourth | 14th fourteenth | 24th twenty-fourth | |
| 5th fifth | 15th fifteenth | 25th twenty-fifth | |
| 6th sixth | 16th sixteenth | 26th twenty-sixth | |
| 7th seventh | 17th seventeenth | 27th twenty-seventh | |
| 8th eighth | 18th eighteenth | 28th twenty-eighth | |
| 9th ninth | 19th nineteenth | 29th twenty-ninth | |
| 10th tenth | 20th twentieth | 30th thirtieth | |

## Metric equivalents

| | | |
|---|---|---|
| 1 inch = 25 millimeters | 1 dry ounce = 28 grams | 1 fluid ounce = 30 milliliters |
| 1 foot = 30 centimeters | 1 pound = .45 kilograms | 1 quart = .95 liters |
| 1 yard = .9 meters | 1 mile = 1.6 kilometers | 1 gallon = 3.8 liters |

## Converting Fahrenheit temperatures to Celsius

Subtract 30 and divide by 2.

Example: 80°F – 30 = 50; divided by 2 = 25

80°F = approximately 25°C

## Countries and nationalities

| | | | | | |
|---|---|---|---|---|---|
| Afghanistan | Afghan | Germany | German | Portugal | Portuguese |
| Albania | Albanian | Ghana | Ghanaian | Puerto Rico | Puerto Rican |
| Algeria | Algerian | Greece | Greek | Republic of | Congolese |
| Angola | Angolan | Grenada | Grenadian | the Congo | |
| Argentina | Argentine | Guatemala | Guatemalan | Romania | Romanian |
| Armenia | Armenian | Guyana | Guyanese | Russia | Russian |
| Australia | Australian | Haiti | Haitian | Saudi Arabia | Saudi |
| Austria | Austrian | Herzegovina | Herzegovinian | Senegal | Senegalese |
| Azerbaijan | Azerbaijani | Honduras | Honduran | Serbia | Serbian |
| Bahamas | Bahamian | Hungary | Hungarian | Sierra Leone | Sierra Leonean |
| Bahrain | Bahraini | India | Indian | Singapore | Singaporean |
| Bangladesh | Bangladeshi | Indonesia | Indonesian | Slovakia | Slovak |
| Barbados | Barbadian | Iran | Iranian | Somalia | Somali |
| Belarus | Belarusian | Iraq | Iraqi | South Africa | South African |
| Belgium | Belgian | Ireland | Irish | South Korea | Korean |
| Belize | Belizean | Israel | Israeli | Spain | Spanish |
| Benin | Beninese | Italy | Italian | Sri Lanka | Sri Lankan |
| Bolivia | Bolivian | Jamaica | Jamaican | Sudan | Sudanese |
| Bosnia | Bosnian | Japan | Japanese | Sweden | Swedish |
| Brazil | Brazilian | Jordan | Jordanian | Switzerland | Swiss |
| Bulgaria | Bulgarian | Kazakhstan | Kazakhstani | Syria | Syrian |
| Cambodia | Cambodian | Kenya | Kenyan | Tajikistan | Tajikistani |
| Cameroon | Cameroonian | Kuwait | Kuwaiti | Tanzania | Tanzanian |
| Canada | Canadian | Laos | Laotian | Thailand | Thai |
| Cape Verde | Cape Verdean | Lebanon | Lebanese | Togo | Togolese |
| Chile | Chilean | Liberia | Liberian | Tonga | Tongan |
| China | Chinese | Lithuania | Lithuanian | Trinidad | Trinidadian |
| Colombia | Colombian | Macedonia | Macedonian | Tunisia | Tunisian |
| Comoros | Comoran | Malaysia | Malaysian | Turkey | Turkish |
| Costa Rica | Costa Rican | Mexico | Mexican | Turkmenistan | Turkmen |
| Côte d'Ivoire | Ivoirian | Morocco | Moroccan | Uganda | Ugandan |
| Croatia | Croatian | Myanmar | Myanmar | Ukraine | Ukrainian |
| Cuba | Cuban | (Burma) | (Burmese) | United Arab | Emirati |
| Dominica | Dominican | Nepal | Nepali | Emirates | |
| Dominican | Dominican | Netherlands | Dutch | United | British |
| Republic | | New Zealand | New Zealander | Kingdom | |
| Ecuador | Ecuadorian | Nicaragua | Nicaraguan | United States | American |
| Egypt | Egyptian | Niger | Nigerien | Uruguay | Uruguayan |
| El Salvador | Salvadoran | Nigeria | Nigerian | Uzbekistan | Uzbekistani |
| Equatorial | Equatorial | Norway | Norwegian | Venezuela | Venezuelan |
| Guinea | Guinean | Pakistan | Pakistani | Vietnam | Vietnamese |
| Eritrea | Eritrean | Panama | Panamanian | Yemen | Yemeni |
| Ethiopia | Ethiopian | Paraguay | Paraguayan | Zambia | Zambian |
| Fiji | Fijian | Peru | Peruvian | Zimbabwe | Zimbabwean |
| France | French | Philippines | Filipino | | |
| Georgia | Georgia | Poland | Polish | | |

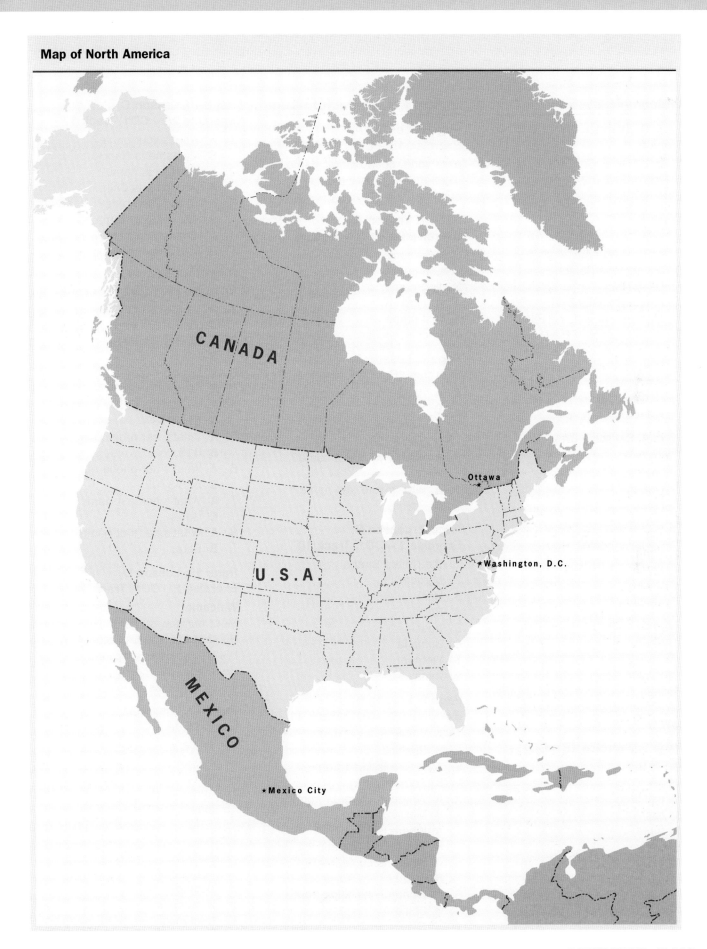

CANADA

Ottawa

U.S.A.

★Washington, D.C.

MEXICO

★Mexico City

# AUDIO SCRIPT

## Welcome Unit

### Page 3, Exercise 2A – CD1, Track 2

A, B, C, D, E, F, G, H, I, J, K, L, M, N, O, P, Q, R, S, T, U, V, W, X, Y, Z

### Page 3, Exercise 2B – CD1, Track 3

1. Hello, my name is Anita. A-N-I-T-A.
2. My name is Daniel. D-A-N-I-E-L.
3. I'm Peizhi. P-E-I-Z-H-I.
4. My name is Yuri. Y-U-R-I.
5. Hi, I'm Franco. F-R-A-N-C-O.
6. Hi, my name is Lee. L-E-E.
7. Hello, my name is Hakim. H-A-K-I-M.
8. Hi there. My name is Karla. K-A-R-L-A.

### Page 4, Exercise 3A – CD1, Track 4

1. Look.
2. Listen.
3. Point.
4. Repeat.
5. Talk.
6. Write.
7. Read.
8. Circle.
9. Match.

### Page 5, Exercise 4A – CD1, Track 5

one, two, three, four, five, six, seven, eight, nine, ten, eleven, twelve, thirteen, fourteen, fifteen, sixteen, seventeen, eighteen, nineteen, twenty

### Page 5, Exercise 4B – CD1, Track 6

1. six
2. eighteen
3. five
4. three
5. twelve
6. eleven
7. fifteen
8. nine

## Unit 1: Personal information

### Page 6, Lesson A, Exercise 1B – CD1, Track 7

area code, country, first name, ID card, last name, phone number

### Page 7, Lesson A, Exercise 2A – CD1, Track 8

1. area code
2. country
3. first name
4. ID card
5. last name
6. phone number

### Page 7, Lesson A, Exercise 2B – CD1, Track 9

1. **A** What's your area code?
   **B** 201.
2. **A** What's your phone number?
   **B** 555-5983.
3. **A** What's your first name?
   **B** Glen.
4. **A** What's your last name?
   **B** Reyna.

### Page 8, Lesson B, Exercise 1 – CD1, Track 10

1. the United States
2. Mexico
3. Haiti
4. Brazil
5. Russia
6. Somalia
7. Vietnam
8. China

### Page 9, Lesson B, Exercise 2B – CD1, Track 11

1. **A** Where is Ivan from?
   **B** Russia.
2. **A** Where is Asad from?
   **B** Somalia.
3. **A** Where is Eduardo from?
   **B** Mexico.
4. **A** Where is Elsa from?
   **B** The United States.
5. **A** Where is Luisa from?
   **B** Brazil.
6. **A** Where is Jun-Ming from?
   **B** China.

### Page 10, Lesson C, Exercise 2A – CD1, Track 12

1. **A** What's your name?
   **B** My name is Nancy.
2. **A** What's his name?
   **B** His name is Chin.
3. **A** What's her name?
   **B** Her name is Alima.
4. **A** What's your name?
   **B** My name is Vincent.

### Page 11, Lesson C, Exercise 2B – CD1, Track 13

1. **A** What's his first name?
   **B** Jack.
2. **A** What's his last name?
   **B** Lee.
3. **A** What's his area code?
   **B** 203.
4. **A** What's his phone number?
   **B** 555-9687.
5. **A** What's her area code?
   **B** 415.
6. **A** What's her phone number?
   **B** 555-3702.
7. **A** What's her last name?
   **B** Garza.
8. **A** What's her first name?
   **B** Sara.

### Page 12, Lesson D, Exercise 2 – CD1, Track 14

**Welcome!**

Meet our new student.
His first name is Ernesto.
His last name is Delgado.
He is from Mexico.
Welcome, Ernesto Delgado!

### Page 13, Lesson D, Exercise 4A – CD1, Track 15

1. January
2. February
3. March
4. April
5. May
6. June
7. July
8. August
9. September
10. October
11. November
12. December

## Unit 2: At school

**Page 18, Lesson A,**
**Exercise 1B – CD1, Track 16**

a book, a chair, a computer, a desk, a notebook, a pencil

**Page 19, Lesson A,**
**Exercise 2A – CD1, Track 17**

1. a book
2. a chair
3. a computer
4. a desk
5. a notebook
6. a pencil

**Page 19, Lesson A,**
**Exercise 2B – CD1, Track 18**

1. **A** What do you need?
   **B** A pencil.
   **A** Here. Take this one.
2. **A** What do you need?
   **B** A notebook.
   **A** Here. Take this one.
3. **A** What do you need?
   **B** A book.
   **A** Here. Take this one.
4. **A** What do you need?
   **B** A chair.
   **A** Here. Take this one.

**Page 20, Lesson B,**
**Exercise 1 – CD1, Track 19**

1. a dictionary
2. paper
3. a pen
4. an eraser
5. a stapler
6. a ruler

**Page 21, Lesson B,**
**Exercise 2B – CD1, Track 20**

1. **A** What do you need, Carla?
   **B** A dictionary.
   **A** Here you are.
2. **A** What do you need, Daw?
   **B** An eraser.
   **A** Here you are.
3. **A** What do you need, Stefan?
   **B** A ruler.
   **A** Here you are.
4. **A** What do you need, Felicia?
   **B** Paper.
   **A** Here you are.
5. **A** What do you need, Kim?
   **B** A pen.
   **A** Here you are.

6. **A** What do you need, Pablo?
   **B** A stapler.
   **A** Here you are.

**Page 22, Lesson C,**
**Exercise 2A – CD1, Track 21**

1. **A** Where's my pencil?
   **B** In the desk.
2. **A** Where's my notebook?
   **B** On the desk.
3. **A** Where's my pen?
   **B** On the floor.
4. **A** Where's my dictionary?
   **B** Under the table.
5. **A** Where's my ruler?
   **B** On the table.
6. **A** Where's my paper?
   **B** Under the desk.

**Page 24, Lesson D,**
**Exercise 2 – CD1, Track 22**

Sue,

It's Monday, your first day of English class! You need a pencil, eraser, notebook, and dictionary. The pencil is in the desk. The eraser is on the desk. The notebook is on my computer. And the dictionary is under the chair.
Have fun at school!

Mom

**Page 25, Lesson D,**
**Exercise 4A – CD1, Track 23**

1. Sunday
2. Monday
3. Tuesday
4. Wednesday
5. Thursday
6. Friday
7. Saturday

## Review: Units 1 and 2

**Page 30, Exercise 1 – CD1,**
**Track 24**

1. **A** Welcome to class. What's your name?
   **B** My name is Hassan.
   **A** Your first name?
   **B** Yes.
2. **A** And what's your last name?
   **B** My last name is Ali.
3. **A** Where are you from, Hassan?
   **B** Somalia.

4. **A** And when's your birthday?
   **B** In August.
5. **A** What do you need, Hassan?
   **B** A notebook.
   **A** The notebook is on the desk.
6. **A** Ms. Garcia?
   **B** Yes, Hassan? What do you need?
   **A** Paper.
   **B** The paper is in the notebook.

**Page 31, Exercise 4A – CD1,**
**Track 25**

/eɪ/
name

/oʊ/
phone

**Page 31, Exercise 4B – CD1,**
**Track 26**

/eɪ/
name
day
say

/oʊ/
phone
code
note

**Page 31, Exercise 4C – CD1,**
**Track 27**

1. say
2. code
3. name
4. phone
5. day

## Unit 3: Friends and family

**Page 32, Lesson A,**
**Exercise 1B – CD1, Track 28**

daughter, father, grandfather, grandmother, mother, son

**Page 33, Lesson A,**
**Exercise 2A – CD1, Track 29**

1. daughter
2. father
3. grandfather
4. grandmother
5. mother
6. son

**Page 33, Lesson A,**
**Exercise 2B – CD1, Track 30**

1. **A** Who's that?
   **B** The grandmother.
2. **A** Who's that?
   **B** The daughter.
3. **A** Who's that?
   **B** The father.
4. **A** Who's that?
   **B** The grandfather.

**Page 34, Lesson B,**
**Exercise 1 – CD1, Track 31**

1. husband
2. wife
3. uncle
4. aunt
5. brother
6. sister

**Page 35, Lesson B,**
**Exercise 2B – Class audio,**
**CD1 Track 32**

1. **A** Who is Vera?
   **B** Sam's aunt.
2. **A** Who is Mike?
   **B** Sam's uncle.
3. **A** Who is Sophie?
   **B** Sam's sister.
4. **A** Who is Susan?
   **B** Dave's wife.
5. **A** Who is Sam?
   **B** Sophie's brother.
6. **A** Who is Dave?
   **B** Susan's husband.

**Page 36, Lesson C,**
**Exercise 2A – CD1, Track 33**

1. **A** Do you have a brother?
   **B** Yes, I do.
2. **A** Do you have a sister?
   **B** No, we don't.
3. **A** Do you have a son?
   **B** Yes, I do.
4. **A** Do you have a daughter?
   **B** Yes, we do.
5. **A** Do you have a wife?
   **B** No, I don't.

**Page 37, Lesson C,**
**Exercise 2B – CD1, Track 34**

1. **A** Do you have a sister?
   **B** Yes, I do.
   **A** What's her name?
   **B** Diana.
2. **A** Do you have a brother?
   **B** No, I don't.

3. **A** Do you have a husband?
   **B** Yes, I do.
   **A** What's his name?
   **B** Ken.
4. **A** Do you have a son?
   **B** Yes, we do.
   **A** What's his name?
   **B** Danny.
5. **A** Do you have a daughter?
   **B** No, we don't.
6. **A** Do you have a grandmother?
   **B** Yes, I do.
   **A** What's her name?
   **B** Rose.

**Page 38, Lesson D,**
**Exercise 2 – CD1, Track 35**
**My Family**

My name is Gloria. This is my family.
This is my mother. Her name is
Natalia. It is her birthday. This is
my father. His name is Enrico. This
is my husband, Luis. This is our
daughter, Lisa. This is our son, Tony.
I love my family.

**Page 39, Lesson D,**
**Exercise 4A – CD1, Track 36**

1. baby
2. girl
3. boy
4. teenager
5. woman
6. man

## Unit 4: Health

**Page 44, Lesson A,**
**Exercise 1B – CD1, Track 37**

doctor, doctor's office, medicine,
nurse, patient

**Page 45, Lesson A,**
**Exercise 2A – CD1, Track 38**

1. doctor
2. doctor's office
3. medicine
4. nurse
5. patient

**Page 45, Lesson A,**
**Exercise 2B – CD1, Track 39**

1. **A** What's the matter?
   **B** I need a nurse.
2. **A** What's the matter?
   **B** I need a doctor.
3. **A** What's the matter?
   **B** I need a nurse.

4. **A** What's the matter?
   **B** I need some medicine.

**Page 46, Lesson B,**
**Exercise 1 – CD1, Track 40**

1. head
2. hand
3. leg
4. foot
5. stomach
6. arm

**Page 47, Lesson B,**
**Exercise 2B – CD1, Track 41**

1. **A** What hurts?
   **B** My head.
2. **A** What hurts?
   **B** My hand.
3. **A** What hurts?
   **B** My stomach.
4. **A** What hurts?
   **B** My foot.
5. **A** What hurts?
   **B** My arm.
6. **A** What hurts?
   **B** My leg.

**Page 48, Lesson C,**
**Exercise 2A – CD1, Track 42**

1. **A** What hurts?
   **B** My hands.
2. **A** What hurts?
   **B** My eyes.
3. **A** What hurts?
   **B** My arm.
4. **A** What hurts?
   **B** My foot.
5. **A** What hurts?
   **B** My legs.
6. **A** What hurts?
   **B** My hand.

**Page 49, Lesson C,**
**Exercise 2B – CD1, Track 43**

1. **A** What hurts?
   **B** My legs.
   **A** Oh, I'm sorry.
2. **A** What hurts?
   **B** My hand.
   **A** Oh, I'm sorry.
3. **A** What hurts?
   **B** My stomach.
   **A** Oh, I'm sorry.
4. **A** What hurts?
   **B** My feet.
   **A** Oh, I'm sorry.

5. **A** What hurts?
   **B** My eyes.
   **A** Oh, I'm sorry.
6. **A** What hurts?
   **B** My head.
   **A** Oh, I'm sorry.

### Page 50, Lesson D, Exercise 2 – CD1, Track 44

**At the Doctor's Office**

Tony and Mario are at the doctor's office. They are patients. Tony's leg hurts. His head hurts, too. He has a headache. Mario's arm hurts. His hands hurt, too. Tony and Mario are not happy. It is not a good day.

### Page 51, Lesson D, Exercise 4A – CD1, Track 45

1. a cold
2. a fever
3. a headache
4. a sore throat
5. a stomachache
6. a toothache

## Review: Units 3 and 4

### Page 56, Exercise 1 – CD1, Track 46

1. **A** Tom, who is Sonya?
   **B** My aunt.
2. **A** Tom, do you have a brother?
   **B** Yes, I do. His name is David.
3. **A** Ray, do you have a wife?
   **B** Yes, I do. Her name is Tina.
4. **A** Barbara, do you have a son?
   **B** Yes, I do. His name is Jay.
5. **A** What's the matter?
   **B** My head hurts.
   **A** Oh, I'm sorry.
6. **A** What's the matter?
   **B** My foot hurts.
   **A** Oh, I'm sorry.

### Page 57, Exercise 4A – CD1, Track 47

/iː/
read

/aɪ/
five

/uː/
June

### Page 57, Exercise 4B – CD1, Track 48

/iː/
read
need

/aɪ/
five
write

/uː/
June
rule

### Page 57, Exercise 4C – CD1, Track 49

1. write
2. June
3. need
4. read
5. five

## Unit 5: Around town

### Page 58, Lesson A, Exercise 1B – CD1, Track 50

bank, library, restaurant, school, street, supermarket

### Page 59, Lesson A, Exercise 2A – CD1, Track 51

1. bank
2. library
3. restaurant
4. school
5. street
6. supermarket

### Page 59, Lesson A, Exercise 2B – CD1, Track 52

1. **A** Where's the school?
   **B** The school? It's on Main Street.
   **A** Thanks.
2. **A** Where's the restaurant?
   **B** The restaurant? I don't know.
   **A** OK. Thank you.
3. **A** Where's the library?
   **B** The library's on Market Street.
   **A** Thanks a lot.
4. **A** Where's the supermarket?
   **B** Sorry, I don't know.
   **A** Thanks, anyway.

### Page 60, Lesson B, Exercise 1 – CD1, Track 53

1. pharmacy
2. hospital
3. laundromat
4. post office
5. movie theater
6. gas station

### Page 61, Lesson B, Exercise 2B – CD1, Track 54

1. **A** Where's Minh?
   **B** At the movie theater.
2. **A** Where's Alan?
   **B** At the hospital.
3. **A** Where's Mr. Lopez?
   **B** At the pharmacy.
4. **A** Where's Paula?
   **B** At the laundromat.
5. **A** Where's Jackie?
   **B** At the post office.
6. **A** Where's Isabel?
   **B** At the gas station.

### Page 62, Lesson C, Exercise 2A – CD1, Track 55

1. **A** Where's the pharmacy?
   **B** Between the restaurant and the supermarket.
2. **A** Where's the supermarket?
   **B** On Main Street.
3. **A** Where's the restaurant?
   **B** Next to the pharmacy.
4. **A** Where's the bakery?
   **B** Across from the restaurant.
5. **A** Where's the police station?
   **B** Next to the bakery.

### Page 63, Lesson C, Exercise 2B – CD1, Track 56

1. **A** Excuse me. Where's the bank?
   **B** Next to the supermarket.
   **A** Thanks.
2. **A** Excuse me. Where's the restaurant?
   **B** Across from the bank.
   **A** Thanks.
3. **A** Excuse me. Where's the bank?
   **B** Between the pharmacy and the supermarket.
   **A** Thanks.
4. **A** Excuse me. Where's the police station?
   **B** On Park Street.
   **A** Thanks.
5. **A** Excuse me. Where's the bakery?
   **B** Next to the restaurant.
   **A** Thanks.

6. **A** Excuse me. Where's the supermarket?
   **B** Across from the bakery.
   **A** Thanks.

### Page 64, Lesson D, Exercise 2 – CD1, Track 57
**Notice from Riverside Library**
Come and visit Riverside Library. The new library opens today. The library is on Main Street. It is across from Riverside Adult School. It is next to K and P Supermarket. It is between K and P Supermarket and Rosie's Restaurant. The library is open from 9:00 to 5:00, Monday, Wednesday, and Friday.

### Page 65, Lesson D, Exercise 4A – CD1, Track 58
1. by bicycle
2. by bus
3. by car
4. by taxi
5. by train
6. on foot

## Unit 6: Time

### Page 70, Lesson A, Exercise 1B – CD2 ,Track 2
seven o'clock, nine o'clock, ten o'clock, ten-thirty, two-thirty, six-thirty

### Page 71, Lesson A, Exercise 2A – CD2, Track 3
1. seven o'clock
2. nine o'clock
3. ten o'clock
4. ten-thirty
5. two-thirty
6. six-thirty

### Page 71, Lesson A, Exercise 2B – CD2, Track 4
1. **A** What time is it?
   **B** It's nine o'clock.
2. **A** Excuse me. What time is it?
   **B** It's ten-thirty.
3. **A** What time is it?
   **B** It's two-thirty.
4. **A** Excuse me. What time is it?
   **B** It's ten o'clock.

### Page 72, Lesson B, Exercise 1 – CD2, Track 5
1. appointment
2. meeting
3. class
4. movie
5. party
6. TV show

### Page 73, Lesson B, Exercise 2B – CD2, Track 6
1. **A** What time is the appointment?
   **B** At one-thirty on Friday.
2. **A** What time is the class?
   **B** At eight-thirty on Friday.
3. **A** What time is the TV show?
   **B** At four-thirty on Friday.
4. **A** What time is the meeting?
   **B** At three o'clock on Saturday.
5. **A** What time is the movie?
   **B** At nine o'clock on Saturday.
6. **A** What time is the party?
   **B** At five o'clock on Saturday.

### Page 74, Lesson C, Exercise 2A – CD2, Track 7
1. **A** Is your class at eleven o'clock?
   **B** Yes, it is.
2. **A** Is your appointment at twelve-thirty?
   **B** No, it isn't.
3. **A** Is your concert at eight o'clock?
   **B** No, it isn't.
4. **A** Is your movie at six o'clock?
   **B** Yes, it is.
5. **A** Is your party at four o'clock?
   **B** Yes, it is.
6. **A** Is your TV show at seven thirty?
   **B** No, it isn't.

### Page 76, Lesson D, Exercise 2 – CD2, Track 8
**Teresa's Day**
Teresa is busy today. Her meeting with her friend Joan is at 10:00 in the morning. Her doctor's appointment is at 1:00 in the afternoon. Her favorite TV show is at 4:30. Her class is at 6:30 in the evening. Her uncle's birthday party is also at 6:30. Oh, no! What will she do?

### Page 77, Lesson D, Exercise 4A – CD2, Track 9
1. in the morning
2. in the afternoon
3. in the evening
4. at noon
5. at night
6. at midnight

## Review: Units 5 and 6

### Page 82, Exercise 1 – CD2, Track 10
1. **A** When is the meeting with Mr. Johnson?
   **B** On Friday.
2. **A** Is the meeting at two-thirty?
   **B** No, it isn't. It's at ten-thirty.
3. **A** Is your appointment at two o'clock?
   **B** Yes, It is.
4. **A** Excuse me. Where's the school?
   **B** Across from the bank.
   **A** Thanks.
5. **A** Where are you?
   **B** At the movie theater.
   **A** Next to the supermarket?
   **B** Right.
6. **A** What time is the movie?
   **B** Seven-thirty.

### Page 83, Exercise 4A – CD2, Track 11
/æ/
at

/ɒ/
on

### Page 83, Exercise 4B – CD2, Track 12
/æ/
at
class
map

/ɒ/
on
clock
not

### Page 83, Exercise 4C – CD2, Track 13
1. not
2. clock
3. at
4. class
5. on

## Unit 7: Shopping

**Page 84, Lesson A,
Exercise 1B – CD2, Track 14**

a dress, pants, a shirt, shoes, socks, a T-shirt

**Page 85, Lesson A,
Exercise 2A – CD2, Track 15**

1. a dress
2. pants
3. a shirt
4. shoes
5. socks
6. a T-shirt

**Page 85, Lesson A,
Exercise 2B – CD2, Track 16**

1. **A** How much is the shirt?
   **B** The shirt? $19.00.
2. **A** How much are the socks?
   **B** The socks? $1.99.
3. **A** How much is the dress?
   **B** The dress? $39.99.
4. **A** How much are the pants?
   **B** The pants? $24.99.

**Page 86, Lesson B,
Exercise 1 – CD2, Track 17**

1. a tie
2. a blouse
3. a sweater
4. a skirt
5. a jacket
6. a raincoat

**Page 87, Lesson B,
Exercise 2B – CD2, Track 18**

1. **A** How much is the tie?
   **B** The tie is $9.99.
2. **A** How much is the raincoat?
   **B** The raincoat is $26.95.
3. **A** How much is the skirt?
   **B** The skirt is $35.95.
4. **A** How much is the sweater?
   **B** The sweater is $39.99.
5. **A** How much is the jacket?
   **B** The jacket is $48.99.
6. **A** How much is the blouse?
   **B** The blouse is $25.95.

**Page 88, Lesson C, Exercise 2A –
CD2, Track 19**

1. **A** How much are the pants?
   **B** $24.99.
2. **A** How much is the skirt?
   **B** $18.99.

3. **A** How much is the raincoat?
   **B** $16.95.
4. **A** How much are the shoes?
   **B** $58.99.
5. **A** How much is the sweater?
   **B** $31.99.
6. **A** How much are the socks?
   **B** $5.95.

**Page 89, Lesson C,
Exercise 2B – CD2, Track 20**

1. **A** How much is the T-shirt?
   **B** $2.00.
   **A** $2.00? Thanks.
2. **A** How much are the shoes?
   **B** $3.00.
   **A** $3.00? Thanks.
3. **A** How much is the jacket?
   **B** $8.00.
   **A** $8.00? Thanks.
4. **A** How much is the sweater?
   **B** $4.00.
   **A** $4.00? Thanks.
5. **A** How much is the raincoat?
   **B** $5.00.
   **A** $5.00? Thanks.
6. **A** How much are the pants?
   **B** $6.00.
   **A** $6.00? Thanks.
7. **A** How much are the socks?
   **B** $1.00.
   **A** $1.00? Thanks.
8. **A** How much is the blouse?
   **B** $7.00.
   **A** $7.00? Thanks.

**Page 90, Lesson D,
Exercise 2 – CD2, Track 21**

Hi Patty,

This morning, Samuel and I are going to The Clothes Place. Samuel needs blue pants. He needs a tie, too. I need a red dress and black shoes. Dresses are on sale. They're $49.99. Shoes are on sale, too. They're $34.99. That's good. Call you later,

Rose

**Page 91, Lesson D,
Exercise 4A – CD2, Track 22**

1. black
2. white
3. yellow
4. orange
5. brown

6. green
7. blue
8. purple
9. pink
10. red

## Unit 8: Work

**Page 96, Lesson A,
Exercise 1B – CD2, Track 23**

cashier, custodian, mechanic, receptionist, salesperson, server

**Page 97, Lesson A,
Exercise 2A – CD2, Track 24**

1. cashier
2. custodian
3. mechanic
4. receptionist
5. salesperson
6. server

**Page 97, Lesson A,
Exercise 2B – CD2, Track 25**

1. **A** What does he do?
   **B** He's a server.
2. **A** What does she do?
   **B** She's a receptionist.
3. **A** What's his job?
   **B** He's a custodian.
4. **A** What's her job?
   **B** She's a mechanic.

**Page 98, Lesson B,
Exercise 1 – CD2, Track 26**

1. She answers the phone.
2. She counts money.
3. He fixes cars.
4. He cleans buildings.
5. She sells clothes.
6. He serves food.

**Page 99, Lesson B,
Exercise 2B – CD2, Track 27**

1. **A** What does Sandra do?
   **B** She counts money.
2. **A** What does Stephanie do?
   **B** She serves food.
3. **A** What does Alba do?
   **B** She answers the phone.
4. **A** What does Oscar do?
   **B** He sells clothes.
5. **A** What does Tim do?
   **B** He cleans buildings.
6. **A** What does Ahmad do?
   **B** He fixes cars.

## Page 100, Lesson C, Exercise 2A – CD2, Track 28

1. **A** Does he serve food?
   **B** No, he doesn't.
2. **A** Does he clean buildings?
   **B** Yes, he does.
3. **A** Does she answer the phone?
   **B** Yes, she does.
4. **A** Does he sell clothes?
   **B** Yes, he does.
5. **A** Does she fix cars?
   **B** No, she doesn't.

## Page 101, Exercise 2B – CD2, Track 29

1. **A** Does he sell clothes?
   **B** No, he doesn't.
2. **A** Does he fix cars?
   **B** No, he doesn't.
3. **A** Does he clean buildings?
   **B** No, he doesn't.
4. **A** Does he serve food?
   **B** No, he doesn't.
5. **A** Does he count money?
   **B** No, he doesn't.
6. **A** Does he answer the phone?
   **B** Yes, he does.

## Page 102, Lesson D, Exercise 2 – CD2, Track 30

**Employee of the Month: Sara Lopez**

Congratulations, Sara Lopez – Employee of the Month! Sara is a salesperson. She sells clothes. Sara's whole family works here at Shop Smart. Her father is a custodian, and her mother is a receptionist. Her uncle Eduardo is a server. He serves food. Her sister Lucy is a cashier. She counts money. Her brother Leo fixes cars. He's a mechanic. Everybody in the store knows the Lopez family!

## Page 103, Lesson D, Exercise 4A – CD2, Track 31

1. bus driver
2. homemaker
3. painter
4. plumber
5. teacher's aide
6. truck driver

## Review: Units 7 and 8

### Page 108, Exercise 1 – CD2, Track 32

1. **A** Chul, what's your job?
   **B** I'm a cashier at City Café.
2. **A** What do you do, Chul?
   **B** I count money.
3. **A** Luz, what's your job?
   **B** I'm a receptionist at Shop Smart.
4. **A** What do you do, Luz?
   **B** I answer phones.
5. **A** Look! Pants are on sale.
   **B** What color are the pants?
   **A** They're blue.
6. **A** Excuse me. How much are the pants?
   **B** They're $19.99.
   **A** $19.99? Thanks.

### Page 109, Exercise 4A – CD2, Track 33

/e/
red

/ɪ/
six

/ʌ/
bus

### Page 109, Exercise 4B – CD2, Track 34

/e/
red
when

/ɪ/
six
his

/ʌ/
bus
much

### Page 109, Exercise 4C – CD2, Track 35

1. red
2. much
3. his
4. six
5. when

## Unit 9: Daily living

### Page 110, Lesson A, Exercise 1B – CD2, Track 36

doing homework, doing the laundry, drying the dishes, making lunch, making the bed, washing the dishes

### Page 111, Lesson A, Exercise 2A – CD2, Track 37

1. doing homework
2. doing the laundry
3. drying the dishes
4. making lunch
5. making the bed
6. washing the dishes

### Page 111, Lesson A, Exercise 2B – CD2, Track 38

1. **A** What's she doing?
   **B** She's doing homework.
2. **A** What's he doing?
   **B** He's washing the dishes.
3. **A** What's she doing?
   **B** She's making the bed.
4. **A** What's he doing?
   **B** He's making lunch.

### Page 112, Lesson B, Exercise 1 – CD2, Track 39

1. cutting the grass
2. getting the mail
3. taking out the trash
4. walking the dog
5. washing the car
6. watering the grass

### Page 113, Lesson B, Exercise 2B – CD2, Track 40

1. **A** What is Mrs. Navarro doing?
   **B** Watering the grass.
2. **A** What is Mr. Navarro doing?
   **B** Cutting the grass.
3. **A** What is Roberto doing?
   **B** Washing the car.
4. **A** What is Diego doing?
   **B** Taking out the trash.
5. **A** What is Norma doing?
   **B** Getting the mail.
6. **A** What is Rita doing?
   **B** Walking the dog.

**Page 114, Lesson C,**
**Exercise 2A – CD2, Track 41**

1. **A** What are they doing?
   **B** Making dinner.
   **A** What is he doing?
   **B** Washing the dishes.
2. **A** What are they doing?
   **B** Making the bed.
   **A** What is he doing?
   **B** Taking out the trash.
3. **A** What is he doing?
   **B** Washing the car.
   **A** What is she doing?
   **B** Watering the grass.

**Page 115, Lesson C,**
**Exercise 2B – CD2, Track 42**

1. **A** What are they doing?
   **B** Getting the mail.
2. **A** What is he doing?
   **B** Making lunch.
3. **A** What are they doing?
   **B** Cutting the grass.
4. **A** What is she doing?
   **B** Doing the laundry.
5. **A** What is she doing?
   **B** Drying the dishes.
6. **A** What are they doing?
   **B** Taking out the trash.

**Page 116, Lesson D,**
**Exercise 2 – CD2, Track 43**

Dear Susie,

It's after dinner. My family is working in the kitchen. My daughter Li is washing the dishes. My daughter Mei is drying the dishes. My husband and Tao are taking out the trash. Where is my oldest son? He isn't in the kitchen. He is sleeping in the living room! I am not happy.
I need help. What can I do?
Huan

**Page 117, Lesson D,**
**Exercise 4A – CD2, Track 44**

1. bathroom
2. bedroom
3. living room
4. laundry room
5. kitchen
6. dining room

**Unit 10: Free time**

**Page 122, Lesson A,**
**Exercise 1B – CD2, Track 45**

dance, exercise, fish, play basketball, play cards, swim

**Page 123, Lesson A,**
**Exercise 2A – CD2, Track 46**

1. dance
2. exercise
3. fish
4. play basketball
5. play cards
6. swim

**Page 123, Lesson A,**
**Exercise 2B – CD2, Track 47**

1. **A** Do you like to dance?
   **B** Yes, we do.
2. **A** Do you like to play cards?
   **B** Yes, we do.
3. **A** What do you like to do?
   **B** I like to fish.
4. **A** What do you like to do?
   **B** I like to swim.

**Page 124, Lesson B,**
**Exercise 1 – CD2, Track 48**

1. cook
2. play the guitar
3. listen to music
4. watch TV
5. read magazines
6. work in the garden

**Page 125, Lesson B,**
**Exercise 2B – CD2, Track 49**

1. **A** What does Pablo like to do?
   **B** Watch TV.
2. **A** What does Tom like to do?
   **B** Work in the garden.
3. **A** What does Rashid like to do?
   **B** Play the guitar.
4. **A** What does Estela like to do?
   **B** Listen to music.
5. **A** What does Ling like to do?
   **B** Read magazines.
6. **A** What does Farah like to do?
   **B** Cook.

**Page 126, Lesson C,**
**Exercise 2A – CD2, Track 50**

1. **A** What do they like to do?
   **B** They like to play basketball.
2. **A** What does she like to do?
   **B** She likes to swim.
3. **A** What does he like to do?
   **B** He likes to play cards.
4. **A** What does she like to do?
   **B** She likes to fish.
5. **A** What do they like to do?
   **B** They like to dance.

**Page 127, Lesson C,**
**Exercise 2B – CD2, Track 51**

1. **A** What does he like to do?
   **B** He likes to exercise.
2. **A** What does he like to do?
   **B** He likes to cook.
3. **A** What do they like to do?
   **B** They like to play cards.
4. **A** What does she like to do?
   **B** She likes to work in the garden.
5. **A** What does he like to do?
   **B** He likes to swim.
6. **A** What do they like to do?
   **B** They like to play soccer.

**Page 128, Lesson D,**
**Exercise 2 – CD2, Track 52**

Hi Miriam,

I'm not working today. It's my day off. Are you busy? Come and visit me!
What do you like to do? I like to cook. I like to play cards. I like to listen to music and dance. I like to watch TV. Do you like to watch TV? Please call me at 10:00.

**Page 129, Lesson D,**
**Exercise 4A – CD2, Track 53**

1. go to the movies
2. go online
3. shop
4. travel
5. visit friends
6. volunteer

## Review: Units 9 and 10

### Page 134, Exercise 1 – CD2, Track 54

1. **A** What are you doing, Marco?
   **B** Washing the car.
   **A** It's your day off! You need to relax.
2. **A** Marco, what do you like to do?
   **B** I like to play the guitar.
3. **A** Ricky, are you busy?
   **B** Yes. I'm making the bed.
4. **A** Fred, what are you doing?
   **B** I'm reading magazines in the living room.
5. **A** What do you like to do, Tina?
   **B** I like to cook.
6. **A** Tina, what do you like to do on the weekend?
   **B** I like to dance.

### Page 135, Exercise 4A – CD2, Track 55

| /eɪ/ | /æ/ |
|------|-----|
| name | at |

| /iː/ | /e/ |
|------|-----|
| read | red |

| /aɪ/ | /ɪ/ |
|------|-----|
| five | six |

| /oʊ/ | /ɒ/ |
|-------|-----|
| phone | on |

| /uː/ | /ʌ/ |
|------|-----|
| June | bus |

### Page 135, Exercise 4B – CD2, Track 56

| /eɪ/ | /æ/ |
|------|-----|
| name | at |

| /iː/ | /e/ |
|------|-----|
| read | red |

| /aɪ/ | /ɪ/ |
|------|-----|
| five | six |

| /oʊ/ | /ɒ/ |
|-------|-----|
| phone | on |

| /uː/ | /ʌ/ |
|------|-----|
| June | bus |

# TESTS

## Overview

The unit tests, midterm test, and final test help teachers assess students' mastery of the material in the *Ventures Basic* Student's Book.

- Each of the ten unit tests covers one unit.
- The midterm test covers Units 1–5.
- The final test covers Units 6–10.
- Each test assesses listening, grammar, reading, and writing, with real-life documents incorporated into the reading and writing sections.

Students' performance on the tests helps to determine what has been successfully learned and what may need more attention. Successful completion of a test can also give students a sense of accomplishment.

## Getting ready for a test

- Plan to give a unit test shortly after students have completed a unit and have had time for a review. The midterm should follow completion of Unit 5 and the review lesson for Units 5 and 6. The final test should follow completion of Unit 10 and the review lesson for Units 9 and 10. Tell students when the test will be given. Encourage students to study together and to ask you for help if needed.
- Explain the purpose of the test and how students' scores will be used.
- Prepare one test for each student. The tests may be photocopied from the Teacher's Edition, starting on page T-155, or printed from the *Ventures* Online Teacher's Resources.
- Schedule approximately 30 minutes for each unit test and 1 hour for the midterm and final tests. Allow more time if needed.
- Locate the audio for each test's listening section in the Online Teacher's Resources.

## Giving a test

- During the test, have students use a pencil and an eraser. Tell students to put away their Student's Books and dictionaries before the test.
- Hand out one copy of the test to each student.
- Encourage students to take a few minutes to look through the test without answering any of the items. Go through the instructions to make sure students understand them.

- Tell students that approximately 5 minutes of the unit test (10 minutes of the midterm and final tests) will be used for the listening section.
- When playing the audio for the listening section of the test, you may choose to pause or repeat the audio if you feel that students require more time to answer. The audio script for the *Ventures* Basic tests appears in the Teacher's Edition on pages T-192 – T-193. The script can also be printed from the Online Teacher's Resources and read aloud in class.
- Customizable tests and test audio are available via a secure download site. Contact your Cambridge ESL Specialist (www.cambridge.org/cambridgeenglish/contact) for more information.

## Scoring

- You can collect the tests and grade them on your own. Alternatively, you can have students correct their own tests by going over the answers in class or by having students exchange tests with a partner and correcting each other's answers. The answer key for the *Ventures* Basic tests located in the Teacher's Edition on pages T-194–T-195. It can also be printed from the Online Teacher's Resources.
- Each test has a total score of 100 points. Each unit test has five sections worth 20 points each. The midterm and final tests have eight sections worth 10 or 15 points each.

## Track list for test audio program

Track 2:    Unit 1 Test
Track 3:    Unit 2 Test
Track 4:    Unit 3 Test
Track 5:    Unit 4 Test
Track 6:    Unit 5 Test
Track 7:    Midterm Test, Section A
Track 8:    Midterm Test, Section B
Track 9:    Unit 6 Test
Track 10:   Unit 7 Test
Track 11:   Unit 8 Test
Track 12:   Unit 9 Test
Track 13:   Unit 10 Test
Track 14:   Final Test, Section A
Track 15:   Final Test, Section B

Name: _____

Date: _____ Score: _____

# UNIT 1 PERSONAL INFORMATION

## A Listening

TRACK 2 Listen and circle.

1. a.  b. Class Sign Up / First name Last name / Pilar Mendez

2. a.  b.

3. a.  b.

4. a. July  b. June

5. a.  China b.  Somalia

## B Vocabulary

Read and write.

| Name | Country |
|------|---------|
| 1. Ivan | |
| 2. Asad | |
| 3. Eduardo | |

| Name | Country |
|------|---------|
| 4. Elsa | |
| 5. Luisa | |
| 6. Jun-Ming | |

## C Grammar

Read and circle. Then write.

1. **A** What's her name?

   **B** _____ name is Luisa.
   <u>Her    His</u>

2. **A** What's my area code?

   **B** _____ area code is 415.
   <u>Your    My</u>

3. **A** What's his last name?

   **B** _____ last name is Delgado.
   <u>Her    His</u>

4. **A** _____ your name?
   <u>What    What's</u>

   **B** My name is Nancy.

5. **A** What's your name?

   **B** _____ name is Angela.
   <u>My    Your</u>

## D Reading

# A New Student

Meet our new student. Her first name is Ling. Her last name is Lee. She is from China. Her birthday is in May. Welcome, Ling!

Read the sentences. Circle *Yes* or *No*.

1. Her name is Ling Chin.          Yes     No
2. Her first name is Chin.         Yes     No
3. Her last name is Lee.           Yes     No
4. She is from China.              Yes     No
5. Her birthday is in March.       Yes     No

## E Writing

Read the ID Card. Then complete the sentences.

MIDTOWN
ADULT SCHOOL

Name: Samir Ahmed

Address: 1432 Woodrow Street
Tampa, FL 33612

Phone: (813) 555-6978

Birthday: February 8, 1995

*Samir Ahmed*
SIGNATURE

1. His first name is _____.

2. His last name is _____.

3. His area code is _____.

4. His telephone number is _____.

5. His birthday is in _____.

# UNIT 2 AT SCHOOL

Name: _____

Date: _____    Score: _____

## A Listening

TRACK 3   Listen and circle.

1. a.    b.

2. a.    b.

3. a.    b.

4. a.    b.

5. a.    b.

## B Vocabulary

Read and match.

1.

2.

3.

dictionary

Friday

computer

Tuesday

desk

4.

5.

## C Grammar

Read the sentences. Choose *in*, *on*, or *under*.

1. The dictionary is in / on / under the floor.

2. The paper is in / on / under the desk.

3. The chair is in / on / under the notebook.

4. The pencil is in / on / under the desk.

5. The notebook is in / on / under the eraser.

## D Reading

**Welcome to Community Adult School!**

Your teacher is Ms. Angela Delgado.
Your first day of class is Tuesday.
Your class is in Room 203.
For class, you need:
    a notebook
    a pencil
    an eraser
    a dictionary

Read the sentences. Circle *Yes* or *No*.

| | | |
|---|---|---|
| 1. The teacher is Mr. Delgado. | Yes | No |
| 2. The first day of class is Tuesday. | Yes | No |
| 3. The class is in Room 302. | Yes | No |
| 4. You need a pencil. | Yes | No |
| 5. You need a ruler. | Yes | No |

## E Writing

Look at the picture. Complete the letter to Carla.

chair    desk    dictionary    floor    notebook

Carla,

   You need a dictionary. It's on the _____. You
need a stapler. It's on the _____. You need an
eraser. It's on the _____. You need a ruler. It's in
the _____. You need a notebook. It's under the
_____. Have fun at school!

                    Love,

                    Mom

# TEST

# UNIT 3 FRIENDS AND FAMILY

### A  Listening

TRACK 4  Listen and circle.

1. a.     b.         4. a.     b.

2. a.     b.         5. a.     b.

3. a.     b.

### B  Vocabulary

Look at the picture. Read and match.

1. Ramona is             Ramona's grandmother.

2. Pilar is              Pilar's husband.

3. Hugo is               Geraldo's daughter.

4. Magdalena is          Ramona's mother.

5. Geraldo is            Geraldo's father.

## C Grammar

Read and circle. Then write.

1. **A** Do you have a brother?

   **B** Yes, we _____.
   <br>do   don't

2. **A** Do you have a grandfather?

   **B** Yes, I _____.
   <br>do   don't

3. **A** Do you have a daughter?

   **B** No, I _____.
   <br>do   don't

4. **A** Do you have a wife?

   **B** Yes, I _____.
   <br>do   don't

5. **A** Do you have a son?

   **B** No, we _____.
   <br>do   don't

## D Reading

### About My Family

My name is Ken. I have a nice family. I have a daughter. Her name is Cindy. I have a son, Danny. I have a wife. Her name is Felicia. I have a brother, too. His name is Mark. Mark has a wife. Her name is Diana. I love my family!

Read the sentences. Circle *Yes* or *No*.

| | | |
|---|---|---|
| 1. Cindy is Ken's daughter. | Yes | No |
| 2. Ken is Danny's father. | Yes | No |
| 3. Felicia is Ken's husband. | Yes | No |
| 4. Ken and Mark are brothers. | Yes | No |
| 5. Mark is Felicia's husband. | Yes | No |

## E Writing

Look at the picture. Complete the story.

| daughter | family | husband | sister | son |

My name is Carla. This is my _____ .
                                        1

His name is Roberto. This is my _____ ,
                                           2

Alfredo. This is my _____ . Her name is
                              3

Inez. This is my _____ , Gabriela. I love
                          4

my _____ !
          5

# TEST
# UNIT 4 HEALTH

## A Listening

TRACK 5 Listen and circle.

1. a.  b.

2. a.  b.

3. a.  b.

4. a.  b.

5. a.  b.

## B Vocabulary

Read and match.

1.

2.

3.

leg

foot

hand

eye

arm

4.

5.

## C Grammar

Read and circle. Then write.

1. **A** What hurts?

   **B** My _____.
   arm   arms

2. **A** What hurts?

   **B** My _____.
   leg   legs

3. **A** What hurts?

   **B** My _____.
   eye   eyes

4. **A** What hurts?

   **B** My _____.
   foot   feet

5. **A** What hurts?

   **B** My _____.
   hand   hands

## D Reading

### At the Doctor's Office

Regina's tooth hurts. Isaac's throat hurts. Joe has a fever. Esperanza has a cold. James has a stomachache. Sue's head hurts. It's not a good day at the doctor's office!

Read the sentences. Circle *Yes* or *No*.

1. Regina has a toothache.          Yes    No
2. Isaac has a sore throat.          Yes    No
3. Esperanza has a fever.            Yes    No
4. James has a toothache.            Yes    No
5. Sue has a headache.               Yes    No

**E  Writing**

Look at the picture. Then complete the patient sign-in sheet.

cold    fever    sore throat    stomachache    toothache

### Patient Sign-In Sheet

Name of Patient:     Reason for Visit:

1. _Matt_      I have a _____ .

2. _Ella_      I have a _____ .

3. _Stefano_   I have a _____ .

4. _Reyna_     I have a _____ .

5. _Minh_      I have a _____ .

Name: _____

Date: _____     Score: _____

## A Listening

TRACK 6  Listen and circle.

1. a.

1. b.

2. a.      b.

3. a.      b.

4. a.      b.

5. a.      b.

## B Vocabulary

Read and match.

1.

2.

3.

 movie theater

 by car

 hospital

pharmacy

by train

4.

5.

## C Grammar

Look at the picture.

Read and circle. Then write.

1. **A** Where's the post office?

   **B** _____ the supermarket.

      Between   Next to

2. **A** Where's the school?

   **B** _____ the library.

      Next to   Across from

3. **A** Where's the pharmacy?

   **B** _____ Main Street.

      Next to   On

4. **A** Where's the supermarket?

   **B** _____ the post office and the pharmacy.

      On   Between

5. **A** Where's the bank?

   **B** Between the movie theater and the _____.

      pharmacy   restaurant

##  Reading

---
### Notice from Enrico's Restaurant

Come and visit Enrico's Restaurant. The new restaurant opens today. Enrico's Restaurant is on Third Street. It is across from the library. It is next to the bank. The restaurant is open from 8:00 a.m. to 9:00 p.m., Monday, Tuesday, Wednesday, Thursday, and Friday. Welcome!
---

Read the sentences. Circle *Yes* or *No*.

1. Enrico's Restaurant is a new restaurant.                           Yes   No

2. Enrico's Restaurant opens today.                                   Yes   No

3. The restaurant is next to Third Street.                            Yes   No

4. The restaurant is between the library and the bank.               Yes   No

5. The restaurant is open from 8:00 in the morning to 9:00 at night.  Yes   No

## E Writing

Look at the picture. Complete the sentences.

| by bicycle | by bus | by taxi | by train | on foot |

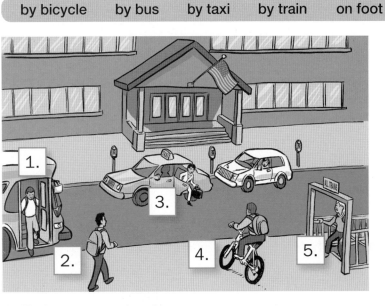

1. Ted gets to school _____

2. Sam gets to school _____

3. Yoko gets to school _____

4. Martin gets to school _____

5. Katia gets to school _____

# MIDTERM TEST
## UNITS 1–5

Name: _____

Date: _____   Score: _____

### A Listening

TRACK 7  Listen and circle.

1. a.    b.

2. a.    b.

3. a.    b.

4. a.    b.

5. a.    b.

### B Listening

TRACK 8  Listen and circle the answer.

1. a. Anita.                b. Brazil.
2. a. My arm.              b. Kim.
3. a. A patient.           b. A pen.
4. a. On the desk.         b. The United States.
5. a. Natalia's brother.   b. By train.

### C Vocabulary

Read and match.

1.

2.

3.

paper

headache

woman

school

car

4.

5.

## D Grammar

Read and match. Write the letter.

1. Where's my pencil? ____
2. Who is Vincent? ____
3. Do you have a son? ____
4. What hurts? ____
5. Where's the library? ____

a. Yes, I do.
b. On First Street.
c. On the desk.
d. My son.
e. My hand.

## E Reading

**FAST RELIEF**

*For relief of headaches and toothaches*

20 tablets
Do not use after February 2020.

**PPC Pharmacy**

Read the sentences. Look at the label. Circle *Yes* or *No*.

1. This medicine is for headaches.            Yes    No
2. This medicine is for stomachaches.         Yes    No
3. This medicine is for toothaches.           Yes    No
4. Use after February 2020.                   Yes    No
5. The name of the pharmacy is PPC.           Yes    No

**F** Reading

**PROPERTY MANAGEMENT COMPANY**
*230 Central Street, Philadelphia, PA 19019 (215) 555-1863*

# HOUSING APPLICATION

**Directions: Complete the form. Please print.**

What is your name? _Ivan Mendoza_____

Who will live with you in the house?

| NAME | RELATIONSHIP |
|---|---|
| Elsa Mendoza | wife |
| Eduardo Mendoza | mother |
| Ernesto Mendoza | son |
| Rosa Mendoza | daughter |
| Luisa Mendoza | daughter |

Read the questions. Look at the housing application. Circle the answers.

1. Who is Elsa Mendoza?

   a. Ivan's wife          b. Ivan's husband

2. Who is Ivan's father?

   a. Ernesto          b. Eduardo

3. Who is Rosa Mendoza?

   a. Ivan's sister          b. Ivan's daughter

4. Who is Ernesto's sister?

   a. Luisa          b. Elsa

5. Who is Luisa's grandfather?

   a. Ivan          b. Eduardo

## G Writing

Write the missing letters.

1. J a ___ u a ___ y
2. T u ___ ___ d a y
3. U n ___ t e d   S t a t e ___
4. l ___ b r a ___ y
5. h ___ s p ___ t a l

## H Writing

Complete the note.

eye    mother    needs    November    office

_____ 15, 2019
                    1

Dear Mr. Garza,

   I am Chi's _____. He is at the doctor's
                        2

_____ today. His _____ hurts.
        3                              4

He _____ medicine.
        5

                    Thank you,

                    Mrs. Tran

Name:

Date:                          Score:

## A Listening

TRACK 9  Listen and circle.

1. a.  b.

2. a.  b.

3. a.  b.

4. a.  b.

5. a.  b.

## B Vocabulary

Read and match.

1.

2.

3.

midnight

class

TV show

party

movie

4.

5.

## C Grammar

Read and circle. Then write.

1. **A** Is your appointment at 10:00?

   **B** _____, it isn't.
   <u>No   Yes</u>

2. **A** Is your class at 1:00?

   **B** _____, it is.
   <u>No   Yes</u>

3. **A** Is your concert at night?

   **B** No, _____.
   <u>it is   it isn't</u>

4. **A** Is your TV show at 5:00?

   **B** Yes, _____.
   <u>it is   it isn't</u>

5. **A** Is your party in the afternoon?

   **B** _____, it is.
   <u>No   Yes</u>

## D Reading

*IT'S A PARTY!*
**Vincent is 40!**

**When:  Friday, May 6**
**What time:  7:00 p.m.**
**Where:  Jack's apartment**

**581 Spring Street**
**Apt. 5**

**RSVP: Call Alex at 555-3107.**

Read the sentences. Look at the invitation. Circle *Yes* or *No*.

1. It's Vincent's birthday party.          Yes   No
2. The party is for Jack.                  Yes   No
3. The party is in the morning.            Yes   No
4. The party is at seven o'clock.          Yes   No
5. The party is at Jack's apartment.       Yes   No

## E Writing

Complete the story.

afternoon    appointment    at    birthday    busy

Asad is busy today. His doctor's _____ is
                                          1
at 8:00 a.m. His meeting with his friend Glen is at 10:30 a.m.

His class is at 2:00 in the _____. His meeting
                                     2
with his teacher is _____ 4:00 p.m. His wife's
                              3
_____ party is at 6:00 p.m. He needs to go
        4
shopping! Asad is very _____ today!
                                    5

Name: _____

Date: _____     Score: _____

**A** Listening

TRACK 10  Listen and circle.

1. a.      b.      4. a.      b.

2. a.      b.      5. a.      b.

3. a.      b.

**B** Vocabulary

Read and match.

1.

2.

3.

socks

sweater

blouse

skirt

tie

4.

5.

## C Grammar

Read and circle. Then write.

1. How much _____ the brown shoes?
   is   are

2. How much _____ the jacket?
   is   are

3. How much _____ the black dress?
   is   are

4. How much _____ the blue pants?
   is   are

5. How much _____ the skirt?
   is   are

## D Reading

New Message

TO: Natalia
FROM: Sophie
Subject: Sale at The Clothes Place

Hi Natalia,
This afternoon, Dave and I are going to The Clothes Place. I need a pink dress and white shoes. Dave needs shoes, too. Dresses are on sale! They're $35.00. Raincoats are on sale, too. They're $30.00. That's a good sale!

Call you later,
Sophie

Read the sentences. Circle *Yes* or *No*.

| | | |
|---|---|---|
| 1. Natalia and Dave are going to The Clothes Place today. | Yes | No |
| 2. Sophie needs a pink dress. | Yes | No |
| 3. Dave and Sophie need shoes. | Yes | No |
| 4. Dresses are $30.00. | Yes | No |
| 5. Raincoats are $30.00. | Yes | No |

## E Writing

Complete the story.

are    black    blouse    children    tie

Sheila and her _____ are going to The Clothes
                        1
Place today. Her son needs a shirt and a _____.
                                                        2
Her daughter needs a _____ and a
                                3
_____ skirt. Her children need shoes. Shoes
        4
_____ on sale. They're $20.00!
        5

# TEST
# UNIT 8 WORK

## A Listening

TRACK 11  Listen and circle.

1. a.    b.

2. a.    b.

3. a.    b.

4. a.    b.

5. a.    b.

## B Vocabulary

Read and match.

1. A server             sells clothes.
2. A custodian          serves food.
3. A mechanic           answers the phone.
4. A salesperson        cleans buildings.
5. A receptionist       fixes cars.

## C Reading

Dear Aunt Kayla,

How are you? We are all well. We have new jobs! Allen is a mechanic. Sandra is a custodian. She doesn't work in the evening. Alba sells clothes at Shop Smart. I paint houses in the morning, and I go to school in the evening. We are busy! Write soon.

Love,
Brenda

Read the sentences. Circle *Yes* or *No*.

| 1. Kayla fixes cars. | Yes | No |
| 2. Sandra works in the evening. | Yes | No |
| 3. Alba is a salesperson. | Yes | No |
| 4. Brenda is a painter. | Yes | No |
| 5. Allen is a student in the evening. | Yes | No |

## D Grammar

Read and circle. Then write.

1.

**A** Does she serve food?

**B** No, she _____.
does  doesn't

2.

**A** Does she answer the phone?

**B** Yes, she _____.
does  doesn't

3.

**A** Does she fix cars?

**B** No, she _____.
does  doesn't

4.

**A** Does he count money?

**B** _____, he doesn't.
Yes  No

5.

**A** Does he clean buildings?

**B** _____, he does.
Yes  No

## E Writing

Complete the story.

| answers | clothes | homemaker | job | serves |

Stephanie cleans her apartment. She takes the

_____ to the laundromat. She goes to
        1

the supermarket. She _____ food to her
                2

family. She _____ the phone. What's her
         3

_____ ? She's a _____ !
     4                      5

Name: _____

Date: _____    Score: _____

## A Listening

TRACK 12 Listen and circle.

1. a.     b.

2. a.     b.

3. a.     b.

4. a.     b.

5. a.     b.

## B Vocabulary

Read and match.

1. making          the mail
2. doing           the grass
3. walking         the laundry
4. getting         the bed
5. cutting         the dog

## C Grammar

Read and circle. Then write.

1. What _____ he doing?
        is    are

2. _____ out the trash.
   Cutting    Taking

3. What _____ they doing?
        is    are

4. _____ lunch.
   Making    Washing

5. What _____ Norma doing?
        is    are

## D Reading

```
●  ●  ●                          New Message
```

TO: Felicia
FROM: Rita
Subject: My family

Felicia,
I have a cold today! My family is helping me. My daughter Kim is making the
bed. My son is washing the dishes. My daughter Lynn is making lunch. My
husband is doing the laundry. I have a wonderful family!

Talk to you soon,
Rita

Read the sentences. Circle *Yes* or *No*.

| | | |
|---|---|---|
| 1. Rita has a cold. | Yes | No |
| 2. Kim is in the bathroom. | Yes | No |
| 3. Her son is in the kitchen. | Yes | No |
| 4. Lynn is in the bedroom. | Yes | No |
| 5. Her husband is in the laundry room. | Yes | No |

## E Writing

Complete the words.

| do homework | take out the trash | water the grass |
|---|---|---|
| make lunch | wash the car | |

1. w a ___ ___    t h e    c ___ ___

2. ___ o ___ o m ___ w o ___ k

3. t ___ k ___    o u ___    t h e    t r ___ s h

4. w ___ ___ er    t h e    ___ r a s ___

5. ___ ___ k e    ___ ___ n c h

Name:

Date:                                          Score:

## UNIT 10 FREE TIME

**A** **Listening**

TRACK 13 Listen and circle.

1. a.     b.         4. a.     b.

2. a.     b.         5. a.     b.

3. a.     b.

**B** **Vocabulary**

Read and match.

1.

He likes to shop.

He likes to work
in the garden.

He likes to go
to the movies.

2.

He likes to exercise.

He likes to visit friends.

3.

4.

5.

## C Grammar

Read and circle. Then write.

1. She _____ to cook.
   <br>like   likes

2. What _____ they like to do?
   <br>do   does

3. Fred _____ to play soccer.
   <br>like   likes

4. What _____ Tina like to do?
   <br>do   does

5. They _____ to volunteer.
   <br>like   likes

## D Reading

**Valley Community Center**

*Morning Classes*

# Dance class
### Learn to dance!

*January 18 to March 20
Tuesday and Thursday
10:00 a.m. to 12:00 p.m.
Room 12*

**$50.00**

Read the sentences. Look at the course description. Circle the answers.

1. This is for _____.
   a. a music class          b. a dance class

2. The class is in Room _____.
   a. 12          b. 120

3. The class is in the _____.
   a. morning          b. evening

4. The class is _____.
   a. $5.00          b. $50.00

5. Students in this class like to _____.
   a. exercise          b. read magazines

**Writing**

Complete the story.

cook    guitar    like    likes    listen

Today is Sunday. My wife is in the kitchen. She likes to

_____. My son is in his bedroom. He likes to
  1
_____ to music. My daughter _____
  2                                                              3
to play the _____. I _____ to work in
  4                                          5
the garden. We like Sunday!

### A Listening

TRACK 14  Listen and circle.

1. a.     b.

2. a.     b.

3. a.     b.

4. a.     b.

5. a.     b.

### B Listening

TRACK 15  Listen and circle the answer.

1. a. At 5:00.              b. It's 12:00.
2. a. Yes, she is.         b. No, she doesn't.
3. a. Getting the mail.    b. Receptionist.
4. a. He's a painter.      b. A red jacket.
5. a. Yes, it is.          b. No, I don't.

### C Vocabulary

Read and match.

1.

2.

3.

shoes

blouse

plumber

bus driver

cashier

4.

5.

## D Grammar

Read and match. Write the letter.

1. What color are the pants? ____          a. Yes, we do.

2. What do you like to do? ____          b. Washing the car.

3. Does he fix cars? ____          c. Blue.

4. What's he doing? ____          d. Yes, he does.

5. Do you like to swim? ____          e. Cook.

## E Reading

### Our Saturday

My family is busy on Saturday. My husband is a salesperson. He sells clothes in the morning. My daughter listens to music. She doesn't like to do her homework. My son takes out the trash. Then he plays basketball. I shop in the afternoon. We watch our favorite TV show at 8:00.

Read the sentences. Circle *Yes* or *No*.

1. She shops in the afternoon.                Yes    No

2. Her husband does chores in the morning.    Yes    No

3. Her daughter listens to music.             Yes    No

4. Her son plays cards.                        Yes    No

5. They watch TV at 7:00.                      Yes    No

## F Reading

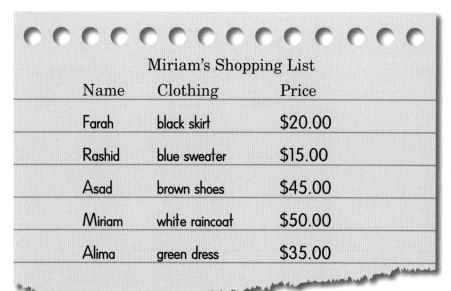

Miriam's Shopping List

| Name | Clothing | Price |
|---|---|---|
| Farah | black skirt | $20.00 |
| Rashid | blue sweater | $15.00 |
| Asad | brown shoes | $45.00 |
| Miriam | white raincoat | $50.00 |
| Alima | green dress | $35.00 |

Read the questions. Look at Miriam's shopping list. Circle the answers.

1. How much is the blue sweater?
   a. $10.00          b. $15.00

2. Who needs a white raincoat?
   a. Rashid          b. Miriam

3. The black skirt is ____.
   a. $20.00          b. $30.00

4. Rashid needs ____.
   a. brown shoes     b. a blue sweater

5. How much is the green dress?
   a. $35.00          b. $25.00

## G Writing

Write the missing letters.

1. o ___ a ___ g e
2. a p ___ o i n ___ m e n t
3. c ___ s t o d ___ a n
4. ___ e c ___ a n i c
5. p u ___ p ___ e

## H Writing

Complete the story.

aide    busy    cashier    money    visit

Dear Grandmother,

Hi! How are you?

We are _____! Alex has a new job! He's a
                    1

teacher's _____. He likes the school and the
                    2

teacher. I'm a _____ at The Clothes Place. I count
                        3

_____. I like my job, too.
            4

We like to _____ friends on Sunday. Sunday is
                        5

our day off!

Love,

Tina

# AUDIO SCRIPT FOR *VENTURES BASIC* TESTS

This audio script contains the listening portions of the *Ventures Basic* unit tests, midterm test, and final test. A customizable copy is available in the *Ventures* Online Teacher's Resources. You can play the audio, or you can read the script aloud.

## Unit 1: Personal information

### Track 2

**A Listening**

1. **A** What's your last name?
   **B** Mendez.
2. **A** What's her phone number?
   **B** 555-5983.
3. **A** What's your area code?
   **B** 415.
4. **A** When's his birthday?
   **B** In July.
5. **A** Where is Asad from?
   **B** He's from Somalia.

## Unit 2: At school

### Track 3

**A Listening**

1. **A** What do you need?
   **B** A pencil.
2. **A** What do you need, Luisa?
   **B** A ruler.
3. **A** Where's my stapler?
   **B** Here. Take this one.
   **A** Thanks.
4. **A** What day is it?
   **B** Tuesday.
5. **A** Where's my pencil.
   **B** On the desk.

## Unit 3: Friends and family

### Track 4

**A Listening**

1. **A** Who's that?
   **B** The father.
2. **A** Who is Luis?
   **B** Rose's brother.
3. **A** Do you have a daughter?
   **B** Yes, I do.
4. **A** Do you have a baby?
   **B** Yes, I do.
   **A** What's her name?
   **B** Marie.
5. **A** Show me the woman.
   **B** Here's the woman.

## Unit 4: Health

### Track 5

**A Listening**

1. **A** What's the matter?
   **B** My head hurts.
2. **A** What hurts?
   **B** My stomach hurts.
3. **A** What hurts?
   **B** My foot.
   **A** Oh, I'm sorry.
4. **A** What's the matter?
   **B** I need some medicine.
5. **A** What's the matter?
   **B** My hand hurts.

## Unit 5: Around town

### Track 6

**A Listening**

1. **A** Where's the bank?
   **B** The bank? It's next to the supermarket.
2. **A** Excuse me. Where's the movie theater?
   **B** The movie theater? Sorry, I don't know.
3. **A** Where's Kim?
   **B** At the hospital.
4. **A** Where are you?
   **B** At the restaurant.
5. **A** How do you get to school?
   **B** By bus.

## Midterm Test Units 1–5

### Track 7

**A Listening**

1. **A** Who's that?
   **B** My son.
2. **A** Where's my notebook?
   **B** I don't know.
3. **A** Do you have a sister?
   **B** Yes, I do.
4. **A** Where's the bank?
   **B** Next to the school.

5. **A** What's the matter?
   **B** My stomach hurts.

### Track 8

**B Listening**

1. What's her name?
2. What hurts?
3. What do you need?
4. Where is he from?
5. Who is Franco?

## Unit 6: Time

### Track 9

**A Listening**

1. **A** What time is it?
   **B** It's two thirty.
2. **A** What time is your meeting?
   **B** At five o'clock on Monday.
3. **A** What time is your class?
   **B** At seven o'clock in the morning.
4. **A** What time is your TV show?
   **B** At eight o'clock on Thursday.
5. **A** Is your concert at noon?
   **B** Yes, it is.

## Unit 7: Shopping

### Track 10

**A Listening**

1. **A** How much are the pants?
   **B** The pants? Twenty-five dollars.
2. **A** How much is the raincoat?
   **B** It's twenty-two dollars.
3. **A** How much is the blue dress?
   **B** The blue dress? It's fifteen dollars.
4. **A** How much is the shirt?
   **B** The shirt? It's eighteen dollars.
5. **A** How much is the orange jacket?
   **B** $89.99.
   **A** $89.99? Thank you.

## Unit 8: Work

### Track 11

**A Listening**

1. A What does she do?
   B She's a cashier.
2. A What's his job?
   B He's a truck driver.
3. A What does she do?
   B She's a homemaker.
4. A What's your job?
   B I'm a salesperson.
5. A What do you do?
   B I'm a plumber.

## Unit 9: Daily living

### Track 12

**A Listening**

1. A What's she doing?
   B She's doing homework.

2. A What are they doing?
   B Making lunch.
3. A What is he doing?
   B Taking out the trash.
4. A What's Mrs. Lee doing?
   B Watering the grass.
5. A What's he doing?
   B He's washing the car.

## Unit 10: Free time

### Track 13

**A Listening**

1. A What does he like to do?
   B He likes to fish.
2. A What does she like to do?
   B She likes to exercise.
3. A What do they like to do?
   B Dance.
4. A What does Paul like to do?
   B He likes to play basketball.
5. A Do you like to read magazines?
   B Yes, I do.

## Final Test Units 6-10

### Track 14

**A Listening**

1. A What color is her skirt?
   B Brown.
2. A What's she doing?
   B Drying the dishes.
3. A How much is this T-shirt?
   B Nine dollars.
4. A What does she like to do?
   B Shop.
5. A What does he do?
   B He's a server.

### Track 15

**B Listening**

**Listen and circle the answer.**

1. A What time is it?
2. A Does she serve food?
3. A What is she doing?
4. A What's his job?
5. A Is your TV show at seven o'clock?

# ANSWER KEY FOR *VENTURES BASIC* TESTS

Each unit test item is 4 points. Unit test sections have five items; therefore, each section is worth 20 points, for a total of 100 points per unit test.

## Unit 1: Personal information

**A Listening**
1. b    2. b    3. a    4. a    5. b

**B Vocabulary**
1. Russia
2. Somalia
3. Mexico
4. the United States
5. Brazil
6. China

**C Grammar**
1. Her    3. His    5. My
2. Your    4. What's

**D Reading**
1. No    3. Yes    5. No
2. No    4. Yes

**E Writing**
1. Samir    4. 555-6978
2. Ahmed    5. February
3. 813

## Unit 2: At school

**A Listening**
1. b    2. a    3. b    4. b    5. a

**B Vocabulary**
1. computer    4. Friday
2. Tuesday    5. desk
3. dictionary

**C Grammar**
1. on    4. in
2. on    5. under
3. under

**D Reading**
1. No    3. No    5. No
2. Yes    4. Yes

**E Writing**
1. chair    4. notebook
2. dictionary    5. floor
3. desk

## Unit 3: Friends and familiy

**A Listening**
1. b    2. a    3. b    4. a    5. a

**B Vocabulary**
1. Ramona is Geraldo's daughter.
2. Pilar is Ramona's mother.
3. Hugo is Geraldo's father.
4. Magdalena is Ramona's grandmother.
5. Geraldo is Pilar's husband.

**C Grammar**
1. do    3. don't    5. don't
2. do    4. do

**D Reading**
1. Yes    3. No    5. No
2. Yes    4. Yes

**E Writing**
1. husband    4. sister
2. son    5. family
3. daughter

## Unit 4: Health

**A Listening**
1. a    2. a    3. b    4. a    5. b

**B Vocabulary**
1. hand    4. arm
2. eye    5. foot
3. leg

**C Grammar**
1. arm    4. foot
2. legs    5. hand
3. eyes

**D Reading**
1. Yes    3. No    5. Yes
2. Yes    4. No

**E Writing**
1. sore throat    4. cold
2. toothache    5. stomachache
3. fever

## Unit 5: Around town

**A Listening**
1. a    2. a    3. b    4. b    5. a

**B Vocabulary**
1. pharmacy
2. by train
3. movie theater
4. hospital
5. by car

**C Grammar**
1. Next to    4. Between
2. Across from    5. restaurant
3. On

**D Reading**
1. Yes    3. No    5. Yes
2. Yes    4. No

**E Writing**
1. by bus    4. by bicycle
2. on foot    5. by train
3. by taxi

## Midterm Test Units 1–5

**A Listening**
(2 points per item)
1. a    2. b    3. a    4. a    5. b

**B Listening**
(3 points per item)
1. a    2. a    3. b    4. b    5. a

**C Vocabulary**
(2 points per item)
1. school    4. car
2. woman    5. headache
3. paper

**D Grammar**
(3 points per item)
1. c    2. d    3. a    4. e    5. b

**E Reading**
(2 points per item)
1. Yes    3. Yes    5. Yes
2. No    4. No

**F Reading**
(3 points per item)
1. a    2. b    3. b    4. a    5. b

**G Writing**
(2 points per item)
1. n r    (January)
2. e s    (Tuesday)
3. i s    (United States)
4. i r    (library)
5. o i    (hospital)

## H Writing

(3 points per item)
1. November    4. eye
2. mother    5. needs
3. office

## Unit 6: Time

### A Listening

1. b    2. a    3. a    4. a    5. b

### B Vocabulary

1. TV show    4. class
2. movie    5. party
3. midnight

### C Grammar

1. No    3. it isn't    5. Yes
2. Yes    4. it is

### D Reading

1. Yes    3. No    5. Yes
2. No    4. Yes

### E Writing

1. appointment    4. birthday
2. afternoon    5. busy
3. at

## Unit 7: Shopping

### A Listening

1. a    2. a    3. b    4. b    5. a

### B Vocabulary

1. blouse    4. sweater
2. tie    5. skirt
3. socks

### C Grammar

1. are    3. is    5. is
2. is    4. are

### D Reading

1. No    3. Yes    5. Yes
2. Yes    4. No

### E Writing

1. children    4. black
2. tie    5. are
3. blouse

## Unit 8: Work

### A Listening

1. b    2. b    3. a    4. b    5. a

### B Vocabulary

1. A server serves food.
2. A custodian cleans buildings.
3. A mechanic fixes cars.
4. A salesperson sells clothes.
5. A receptionist answers
   the phone.

### C Reading

1. No    3. Yes    5. No
2. No    4. Yes

### D Grammar

1. doesn't    4. No
2. does    5. Yes
3. doesn't

### E Writing

1. clothes    4. job
2. serves    5. homemaker
3. answers

## Unit 9: Daily living

### A Listening

1. b    2. a    3. b    4. b    5. a

### B Vocabulary

1. making the bed
2. doing the laundry
3. walking the dog
4. getting the mail
5. cutting the grass

### C Grammar

1. is    4. Making
2. Taking    5. is
3. are

### D Reading

1. Yes    3. Yes    5. Yes
2. No    4. No

### E Writing

1. wash the car
2. do homework
3. take out the trash
4. water the grass
5. make lunch

## Unit 10: Free time

### A Listening

1. a    2. b    3. b    4. b    5. a

### B Vocabulary

1. He likes to go to the movies.
2. He likes to visit friends.
3. He likes to shop.
4. He likes to exercise.
5. He likes to work in the
   garden.

## C Grammar

1. likes    4. does
2. do    5. like
3. likes

## D Reading

1. b    2. a    3. a    4. b    5. a

## E Writing

1. cook    4. guitar
2. listen    5. like
3. likes

## Final Test Units 6–10

### A Listening

(2 points per item)
1. a    2. b    3. b    4. a    5. b

### B Listening

(3 points per item)
1. b    2. b    3. a    4. a    5. a

### C Vocabulary

(2 points per item)
1. bus driver    4. plumber
2. cashier    5. shoes
3. blouse

### D Grammar

(3 points per item)
1. c    2. e    3. d    4. b    5. a

### E Reading

(2 points per item)
1. Yes    4. No
2. No    5. No
3. Yes

### F Reading

(3 points per item)
1. b    2. b    3. a    4. b    5. a

### G Writing

(2 points per item)
1. r n    (orange)
2. p t    (appointment)
3. u i    (custodian)
4. m h    (mechanic)
5. r l    (purple)

### H Writing

(3 points per item)
1. busy    4. money
2. aide    5. visit
3. cashier

# AUTHORS' ACKNOWLEDGMENTS

The authors would like to acknowledge and thank focus-group participants and reviewers for their insightful comments, as well as Cambridge University Press editorial, marketing, and production staffs, whose thorough research and attention to detail have resulted in a quality product.

The publishers would also like to extend their particular thanks to the following reviewers and consultants for their valuable insights and suggestions:

**Barry Bakin,** Instructional Technology, Los Angeles Unified School District, Los Angeles, CA;

**Jim Brice,** San Diego Community College District Continuing Education, San Diego, CA;

**Diana Contreras,** West Valley Occupational Center, Los Angeles, CA;

**Druci J. Diaz,** Hillsborough Country Public Schools, Tampa, FL;

**Linda Foster,** Instructor, Hillsborough County Schools Adult Education Department, Tampa, FL;

**Margaret Geiger,** M.Ed., Dallas, TX;

**Ana L. Herrera,** San Jacinto Adult Learning Center, El Paso, TX;

**Cindi Hartmen,** ESL Instructor, San Diego Continuing Education, San Diego, CA;

**Patrick Jennings,** Tomlinson Adult Learning Center, St. Petersburg, FL;

**Lori Hess-Tolbert,** Frisco, TX;

**AnnMarie Kokash-Wood,** Tomlinson Adult Learning Center, St. Petersburg, FL;

**Linda P. Kozin,** San Diego Continuing Ed, San Diego Community College District, San Diego, CA;

**Caron Lieber,** Palomar College, San Marcos, CA;

**Reyna P. Lopez,** Southwest College, Los Angeles, CA;

**Rosemary Lubarov,** Palo Alto Adult School, Palo Alto, CA;

**Lori K. Markel,** Plant City Adult and Community School, Plant City, FL;

**Mary Spanarke,** Center for Applied Linguistics / Washington English Center, Washington, DC;

**Rosalie Tauscher,** Fort Worth ISD Adult Ed, Fort Worth, TX;

**Timothy Wahl,** Abram Friedman Occupation Center, Los Angeles, CA;

**Delia Watley,** Irving ISD Adult Education and Literacy, Irving, TX;

**Andrea V. White,** Tarrant County College, Arlington, TX;

**Sandra Wilson,** Fort Worth Adult Education, Fort Worth, TX

# ACKNOWLEDGEMENTS

The authors and publishers acknowledge the following sources of copyright material and are grateful for the permissions granted. While every effort has been made, it has not always been possible to identify the sources of all the material used, or to trace all copyright holders. If any omissions are brought to our notice, we will be happy to include the appropriate acknowledgments on reprinting and in the next update to the digital edition, as applicable.

Key: Ex = Exercise, T = Top, B = Below, L = Left, R = Right.

## Photos

All the below images are sourced from GettyImages.

p. 3: John Fedele/Blend Images; p. 4: Monashee Frantz/OJO Images; p. 5: Hero Images; p. 11 (L): Indeed; p. 11 (R): Nick Dolding/Stone; p. 14: David Lees/Iconica; p. 16: Katarina Premfors/arabianEye; p. 19 (1a, 3b): UmbertoPantalone/iStock/Getty Images Plus; p. 19 (2a, 4a): tulcarion/E+; p. 20 (Ex 2.2): Aleks_G/iStock/Getty Images Plus; p. 20 (Ex 2.3): fotodima/iStock/Getty Images Plus; p. 39 (baby): M-image/iStock/Getty Images Plus; p. 39 (girl): Emma Kim/Cultura; p. 39, p. 69 (boy & popcorn): Ljupco/iStock/Getty Images Plus; p. 39 (teenager): LWA/Dann Tardif/Blend Images; p. 39 (woman): davidgoldmanphoto/Image Source; p. 39 (man): Michael Blann/Iconica; p. 45 (Ex 2B.1a): Robert Byron/Hemera/Getty Images Plus; p. 45 (1b, 3a): iodrakon/iStock/Getty Images Plus; p. 45 (2a, 3b): Dan Dalton/Caiaimage; p. 45 (2b, 4b): leungchopan/iStock/Getty Images Plus; p. 45 (4a): Sezeryadigar/iStock/Getty Images Plus; p. 46: 4x6/E+; 47: gawrav/E+; p. 48 (1 eye, 2 eyes), p. 101: PeopleImages/DigitalVision; p. 48 (1 hand, 2 hands): s-cphoto/iStock/Getty Images Plus; p. 48 (1 foot, 2 feet): Valengilda/iStock/Getty Images Plus; p. 51 (cold): BJI/Blue Jean Images; p. 51 (fever): Jupiterimages/liquidlibrary/Getty Images Plus; p. 51 (headache): BSIP/UIG/Universal Images Group; p. 51 (sore throat): pablocalvog/iStock/Getty Images Plus; p. 51 (stomachache): delihayat/E+; p. 51 (toothache): Hemant Mehta/Canopy; p. 59 (1a, 4b): Steve Woods/Hemera/Getty Images Plus; p. 59 (1b, 3a), p. 129 (photo 1): andresr/E+; p. 59 (2a, 4a): Dave and Les Jacobs/Blend Images; p. 59 (2b): Cultura RM Exclusive/yellowdog/Cultura Exclusive; p. 59 (3b): Sam Edwards/OJO Images; p. 61, p. 113 (L): Morsa Images/DigitalVision; p. 63 (man): Nick David/Taxi; p. 63 (woman): Yiu Yu Hoi/The Image Bank; p. 65 (bicycle): GibsonPictures/E+; p. 65 (bus): Geography Photos/Universal Images Group; p. 65 (car): iPandastudio/E+; p. 65 (taxi): Waring Abbott/Michael Ochs Archives; p. 65 (train): Topic Images Inc./Topic Images; p. 65 (on foot): Dougal Waters/DigitalVision; p. 69 (envelope): patpitchaya/iStock/Getty Images Plus; p. 69 (money): H. Armstrong Roberts/ClassicStock/Archive Photos; p. 69 (towels): DonNichols/E+; p. 69 (medicine): fstop123/iStock/Getty Images Plus; p. 69 (popcorn): Ljupco/iStock/Getty Images Plus; p. 69 (bread): Fabio Pagani/EyeEm; p. 71: AlexRaths/iStock/Getty Images Plus; p. 77 (morning): IronHeart/Moment; p. 77 (afternoon): Antons Jevterevs/EyeEm/E+; p. 77 (evening): Iryna Shpulak; p. 77 (noon): Busà Photography/Moment; p. 77 (night): Charles Bowman/Design Pics/Axiom Photographic Agency; p. 77 (midnight): Ivantsov/iStock/Getty Images Plus; p. 85 (shirt, blue dress), p. 95 (pants, dress): rolleiflextlr/iStock/Getty Images Plus; p. 85 (shoes): turk_stock_photographer/iStock/Getty Images Plus; p. 85 (socks): kgfoto/iStock/Getty Images Plus; p. 85 (striped socks), p. 95 (socks): Dave King/Dorling Kindersley; p. 85 (red dress): Tim Ridley/Dorling Kindersley; p. 85 (pants): praethip/iStock/Getty Images Plus; p. 85 (t-shirt): vetas/iStock/Getty Images Plus; p. 85 (studying): shapecharge/E+; p. 86 (tie): NadyaTs/iStock/Getty Images Plus; p. 86 (blouse), p. 87 (raincoat): NAKphotos/iStock/Getty Images Plus; p. 86 (sweater): dendong/iStock/Getty Images Plus; p. 86 (skirt): Hugh Threlfall/Photolibrary; p. 86, p. 87 (jacket): popovaphoto/iStock/Getty Images Plus; p. 86 (raincoat): EdnaM/iStock/Getty Images Plus; p. 87 (tie): Photoevent/E+; p. 87 (skirt): Ratana21/iStock/Getty Images Plus; p. 87 (sweater): ersinkisacik/iStock/Getty Images Plus; p. 87 (blouse), p. 95 (sweater): ARSELA/E+; p. 95 (jacket): SteveCollender/iStock/Getty Images Plus; p. 95 (skirt): peangdao/iStock/Getty Images Plus; p. 95 (raincoat): Photology1971/iStock/Getty Images Plus; p. 95 (shirt): khvost/iStock/Getty Images Plus; p. 95 (blouse): lypnyk2/iStock/Getty Images Plus; p. 95 (shoes): Peter Dazeley/Photographer's Choice; p. 95 (tie): wwing/E+; p. 97 (1a): Jetta Productions/Blend (2a): ImagesBazaar; p. 97 (2b, 4b): kali9/E+; p. 97 (3a): kadmy/iStock/Getty Images Plus; p. 97 (3b): Images; p. 97 (1b): Fancy Yan/DigitalVision; p. 97 AndreyPopov/iStock/Getty Images Plus; p. 97 (4a): sturti/E+; p. 101: Frederic Lucano/The Image Bank; p. 103 (bus driver): tomazl/E+; p. 103 (homemaker): Jose Luis Pelaez Inc/Blend Images; p. 103 (painter): Photo and Co/Photolibrary; p. 103 (plumber): Blend Images - Jose Luis Pelaez Inc/Brand X Pictures; p. 103 (teacher): Caiaimage/Chris Ryan/OJO+; p. 103 (truck driver): ColorBlind Images/Blend Images; p. 107 (truck): mladn61/iStock/

Getty Images Plus; p. 107 (car): Rawpixel/iStock/
Getty Images Plus; p. 107 (cash register): Comstock/
Stockbyte; p. 107 (paints): Bob Elsdale/Stone; p. 107
(books): Moussa81/iStock/Getty Images Plus; p. 107
(telephone): Denis_Dryashkin/iStock/Getty Images
Plus; p. 111 (1a, 3b): Photofusion/Universal Images
Group; p. 111 (1b): CO2/The Image Bank; p. 111 (2a):
Gabrielle Therin-Weise/Photographer's Choice; p. 111
(2b): Maskot; p. 111 (3a, 4b): McIninch/iStock/Getty
Images Plus; p. 111 (4a): Jupiterimages/PHOTOS.
com/Getty Images Plus; p. 113 (R): Caiaimage/
Sam Edwards; p. 123 (1a): monkeybusinessimages/
iStock/Getty Images Plus; p. 123 (1b): JackF/iStock/
Getty Images Plus; p. 123 (2a): i love images/Juice
Images; p. 123 (2b): Tim Hall/Cultura; p. 123 (3a):
Tiina & Geir/Cultura; p. 123 (3b): Johner Images;
p. 123 (4a): Glow Wellness/Glow; p. 123 (4b):
BraunS/E+; p. 124 (Ex 1.1): Gary Latham/Cultura;
p. 124 (Ex 1.2): NanoStockk/iStock/Getty Images
Plus; p. 124 (Ex 1.3): Dave & Les Jacobs/Blend
Images; p. 124 (Ex 1.4): Robert Daly/Caiaimage;
p. 124 (Ex 1.5): Manfred Rutz/The Image Bank;
p. 124 (Ex 1.6): Amy Eckert/Taxi; p. 127 (exercise):
DeanDrobot/iStock/Getty Images Plus; p. 127 (cook):
Portra Images/Taxi; p. 127 (play cards): Jupiterimages/
Stockbyte; p. 127 (garden): Yellow Dog Productions/
DigitalVision; p. 127 (swimming): John Cumming/
Photodisc; p. 127 (play soccer): Westend61; p. 128
(T): Kelvin Murray/Taxi; p. 128 (Ex 3.1): Image Source;
p. 128 (Ex 3.2): crossbrain66/E+; p. 128 (Ex 3.3):
Maxim Pimenov/Hemera/Getty Images Plus; p. 128
(Ex 3.4): Michael Lamotte/Cole Group/Photodisc; p.
128 (Ex 3.5): malerapaso/iStock/Getty Images Plus;
p. 129 (photo 2): Yuri_Arcurs/DigitalVision; p. 129
(photo 3): Paper Boat Creative/DigitalVision; p. 129
(photo 4, photo 6): Hero Images; p. 129 (photo
5): Ariel Skelley/Digital Vision; p. 133 (photo 1):
Donal Husni/EyeEm; p. 133 (photo 2): selensergen/
iStock/Getty Images Plus; p. 133 (photo 3):
Francesco Bittichesu/Photolibrary; p. 133 (photo 4):
chris-mueller/iStock/Getty Images Plus; p. 133 (photo
5): YinYang/E+; p. 133 (photo 6): MicroStockHub/
iStock/Getty Images Plus; p. 133 (photo 7): Cagri
Oner/Hemera/Getty Images Plus; p. 133 (photo 8):
SonerCdem/iStock/Getty Images Plus.

Images sourced from the other libraries.

p. 19 (1b): Julia Ivantsova/Shutterstock; p. 19 (2b):
zirconicusso/Fotolia; p. 19 (3a): Alfonso de Tomas/
Fotolia; p. 19 (4b): Tr1sha/Shutterstock; p. 20
(Ex 2.1): magicoven/Shutterstock; p. 20 (Ex 2.4):
sagir/Shutterstock; p. 20 (Ex 2.5): Michael D Brown/
Shutterstock; p. 20 (Ex 2.6): CrackerClips/Stock
Media/Shutterstock.

**Illustrations**

p. 2, p. 6, p. 8, p. 18, p. 22 (B), p. 23, p. 24, p. 25,
p. 37, p. 40, p. 46, p. 47, p. 60 (Ex 1.6 , Ex 2.4),
p. 61 (3, 6), p. 62 (B), p. 63 (4), p. 64 (T), p. 66,
p. 71, p. 92, p. 100, p. 101, p. 112 (T), p. 113, p. 116
(Ex 3.1, Ex 3.3), p. 126, p. 130, p. 135: QBS Learning;
p. 4, p. 49, p. 55, p. 61 (1, 2, 4, 5), p. 98, p. 124,
p. 125 (B): Travis Foster; p. 7, p. 31, p. 36, p. 86,
p. 88: Monika Roe; p. 9, p. 48, p. 112 (B): Pamela
Hobbs; p. 10, p. 52, p. 109, p. 115: Frank Montagna;
p. 20: Kenneth Batelman; p. 21, p. 34, p. 35, p. 114:
Greg Paprocki; p. 22 (T), p. 26, p. 72, p. 87, p. 90
(B): Jason O'Malley; p. 57: Chuck Gonzales; p. 60
(Ex 1.1–1.5), p. 63 (1, 2, 3, 5, 6): Phil Williams; p. 60
(Ex 2.1, Ex 2.2, Ex 2.3, Ex 2.5, Ex 2.6), p. 99, p. 125
(T): Rod Hunt; p. 89: Greg Paprocki, Monika Roe; p. 13,
p. 91: Victor Kulihin; p. 117, p. 133: Colin Hayes;
p. 12, p. 32, p. 33, p. 44, p. 50, p. 58, p. 70, p. 76,
p. 84, p. 90 (T), p. 96, p. 102, p. 110, p. 116, p. 122:
Ben Kirchner.

Back cover photography by Hero Images; FangXiaNuo/
E+; pressureUA/iStock/Getty Images Plus; Adidet
Chaiwattanakul/EyeEm; pixelfit/E+.

Front cover photography by Jetta Productions/Blend
Images/Getty Images.

Audio produced by CityVox.